Sociology of Religion

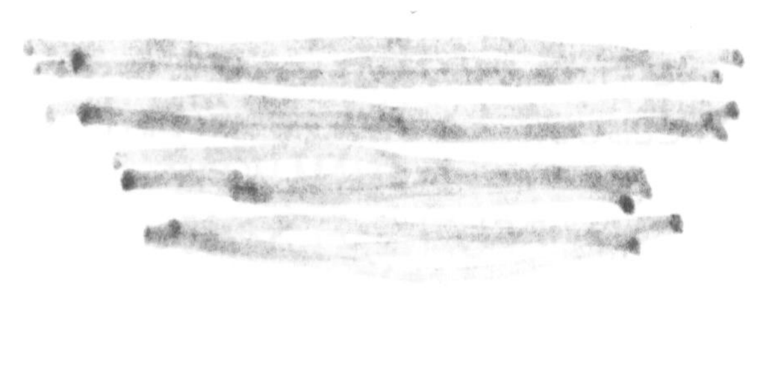

Sociology of Religion

Contemporary Developments

Second Edition

KEVIN J. CHRISTIANO
WILLIAM H. SWATOS, JR.
PETER KIVISTO

ROWMAN & LITTLEFIELD PUBLISHERS, INC.
Lanham • Boulder • New York • Toronto • Plymouth, UK

ROWMAN & LITTLEFIELD PUBLISHERS, INC.

Published in the United States of America
by Rowman & Littlefield Publishers, Inc.
A wholly owned subsidiary of The Rowman & Littlefield Publishing Group, Inc.
4501 Forbes Boulevard, Suite 200, Lanham, Maryland 20706
www.rowmanlittlefield.com

Estover Road
Plymouth PL6 7PY
United Kingdom

British Library Cataloguing in Publication Information Available

Library of Congress Cataloging-in-Publication Data

Christiano, Kevin J.
Sociology of religion : contemporary developments / Kevin J. Christiano, William H. Swatos, Jr., and Peter Kivisto.
p. cm.
Includes index.
ISBN-13: 978-0-7425-6111-3 (pbk. : alk. paper)
ISBN-10: 0-7425-6111-9 (pbk. : alk. paper)
1. Religion and sociology. I. Swatos, William H. II. Kivisto, Peter, 1948– III. Title.
BL60.C465 2008
306.6—dc22 2007048769

Printed in the United States of America

∞™ The paper used in this publication meets the minimum requirements of American National Standard for Information Sciences—Permanence of Paper for Printed Library Materials, ANSI/NISO Z39.48-1992.

Contents

Sociology of Religion

The authors (from left), William H. Swatos, Jr., Kevin J. Christiano, and Peter Kivisto, at the 2007 meeting of the Association for the Sociology of Religion. Photo courtesy of Joanne L. Swatos.

About Ourselves

Kevin J. Christiano is associate professor of sociology and a past chair of the Department of Sociology, at the University of Notre Dame in Indiana—home to the "Fighting Irish." Kevin received his bachelor's degree from the College of William and Mary (alma mater of Thomas Jefferson), where he majored in sociology and minored in French literature. He then earned master's and doctoral degrees in sociology at Princeton University.

Kevin has taught a variety of courses, including the sociology of religion, at Notre Dame since 1983. He has also been a visiting scholar in sociology at Princeton and at Duke University. A past president of both the Association for the Sociology of Religion and the American Council for Québec Studies, he now serves on the editorial boards of six different scholarly journals in sociology, history, and area studies. He is currently the secretary-treasurer of the Section on the Sociology of Religion of the American Sociological Association.

Kevin has always been interested in historical and comparative approaches to the study of religion. During the last two decades he has published research on such subjects as religion and the family, church membership and labor activism, Roman Catholics among immigrants to the United States, and religious denominations at the turn of the last century.

In addition, Kevin studies cross-national contrasts between the United States and Canada. (They are not as alike, in religious as well as other habits, as many in the United States assume.) He closely follows political life in both countries, and has written about the careers of two Canadian prime ministers, Pierre Elliott Trudeau and Jean Chrétien.

William H. Swatos, Jr., is executive officer of the Association for the Sociology of Religion and of the Religious Research Association. He received his undergraduate degree at Transylvania University in Lexington, Kentucky, and stayed in the bluegrass region to complete his doctorate at the University of Kentucky, concentrating in the sociology of religion, family and sexuality, and social theory.

Bill also holds a degree in theology and is a priest in the Anglican Communion. Throughout his career, he has balanced teaching and pastoral work along with professional service within the social scientific study of religion. He currently teaches in the sociology program at Augustana College, a small liberal arts college on the banks of the Mississippi River in Rock Island, Illinois, and serves an historic rural congregation in the Diocese of Quincy.

From the start of his studies in the sociology of religion, the question of the nature of religion and its relationship to the dynamic labeled "secularization" has been an overriding theoretical concern that has never been far from Bill's empirical work. His dissertation focused primarily on church-sect theory, principally in a study of the controversies surrounding the transfer of the Anglican episcopate from the British Isles to the Western Hemisphere in the seventeenth and eighteenth centuries. From that he moved to the study of slave-master relations and religion in the antebellum South. Bill subsequently received a Fulbright lectureship to the Faculty of Theology of the University of Iceland, where he simultaneously developed interests in mediumistic phenomena and in religious pilgrimage. He has continued work in the latter area, most recently in the edited volume *On the Road to Being There: Pilgrimage and Tourism in Late Modernity*, a contribution to the Association for the Sociology of Religion's "Religion and the Social Order" series, which he also edits.

Peter Kivisto is currently the Richard A. Swanson Professor of Social Thought and chair of sociology at Augustana College, where he has taught for twenty-five years.

Peter did his undergraduate work in religious studies and sociology at the University of Michigan during the tumultuous years of the late 1960s. He then completed his master of divinity degree at Yale University. After working as a counselor in San Francisco for a time, he returned to graduate school, this time at the New School for Social Research in New York City, where he received a master's degree in 1977 and a doctorate in 1982.

At Augustana Peter teaches courses in social theory, race and ethnicity, citizenship, and introductory sociology, and has written or edited texts in most of these areas. He has served for the past eighteen years as director of the college's London studies program. Peter is currently completing a term as editor of *The Sociological Quarterly* and will serve as president of the Midwestern Sociological Society in 2010.

About the Book

This book is designed to introduce the reader to the nature and functions of religious institutions and practices in modern societies, with a particular emphasis on conditions in the contemporary United States. Throughout the book, a distinctively sociological perspective is employed to evaluate claims about the viability of religion in what has been called a "post-traditional" world.

If, in this age, God is not dead, how does one account for the notable absence of religious values as animating forces outside the private lives of individuals? If God is long gone, on the other hand, what explains the recent rapid growth in the memberships of conservative religious bodies, or the high levels of interest in non-Western spiritual practices—not to mention a global resurgence of religious particularism? Has the United States shed religion just in time, for belief, some would contend, is a major obstacle to the development of a real understanding of the world's predicaments? Or is this nation only now beginning to realize the dangers of a society bereft of the collective purpose that is symbolized in religious communality?

These and other questions from the sociology of religion will be addressed in a survey of the field and a consideration of different religious traditions. We will examine, among other subjects, individual religious experience; social mechanisms of conversion and commitment; civil religion; the varied processes of secularization; and religious inspirations for, or impediments to, social change. In the process, we attempt to trace the historical background of such topics and to clarify the connections of each to classical theories in sociology.

The second edition of this work responds to comments on the first version that we have received from reviewers in the discipline and from instructors and students alike. As circumstances would have it, the first edition of this book came off the presses almost concurrently with the events of September 11, 2001 (now simply "9/11"). Although incidents of religious violence had already erupted around the world prior to the first edition, the experiences of that day have had a direct effect on the ways Americans and others think about religion—both in general and in their personal lives. But this one event is not all that has changed in the socio-religious landscape across these years.

We have expanded sections that deal with the relationship between ethnicity and religion, especially in the instance of Islam and the population of Middle

Eastern origin. We give greater focus to our treatments of religion's significance in current debates over gender roles and sexual orientation. The chapter on religious change, which uses the Roman Catholic Church as its case, has been augmented to take account of the recent scandals among the clergy and to gauge their impact on institutional life. We observe more fully the interactions of religion and the media, from best-selling books to Hollywood movies, and we devote increased attention to manifestations of faith, both venerable and novel, on the Internet. An original section tracks the growth and spread of Neo-Paganism as a new religious movement. And in every chapter, we have updated information on the demography of religion and sought out the newest statistics on religious behavior; inserted new examples in a series of boxed features; revised and expanded lists of suggested readings; and included photographs, many new to this edition, that depict and dramatize our main themes.

PART ONE

THE BASICS

Copy Negatives Collection (GNEG 6A/33), University of Notre Dame Archives (UNDA). Reproduced with permission of the University of Notre Dame.

CHAPTER 1

By Way of Introduction

"Religion is itself only in practice" might well be taken as a one-sentence motto for the sociology of religion (Vogel 1966: 5). An emphasis on practice somewhat flies in the face of the everyday notion that religions are sets of beliefs. Of course, religious people have beliefs about God or the sacred or some Beyond, but so do nonreligious people. What makes religion *religion*, as distinct from beliefs, is that it is something that people *do*. As soon as we do something, we stand on the brink of social action; that is, virtually any human activity potentially involves interaction with other humans. While it is possible to hold beliefs privately, action puts us into the realm of the social. The *sociology of religion* may be minimally defined as that branch of sociology that is specifically concerned with *how people put their beliefs about the sacred into action as they relate to other people*.

In this book we will be looking at how religion both shapes and is shaped by the sociocultural systems within which it operates across time, place, and circumstance. This book takes as its primary source of examples and illustrations changes in religion in the United States since the 1960s. In and through these we will address the "big questions" in the sociology of religion more generally. We will emphasize particularly the Western traditions as they influence North America, but we also want to note at the outset that we live in a condition of *globalization* that increasingly causes the world to be, in Roland Robertson's felicitous phrase, "a single place" (1992). One of the most important shifts in the last quarter century has been from a basically Eurocentric approach to religion, which characterized our forebears, to a global understanding that includes not only "the Judeo-Christian tradition," as it has often been termed, but also Islam, the religions of Asia, and indigenous traditions of native peoples throughout the world (including Native Americans).

Background

The emphasis of this book is on contemporary developments in the sociology of religion. Yet in order to understand what is going on today in any scientific field, we have to have some grasp of how we got to this point. So we will spend a little time at the beginning of each chapter providing a background against which current developments play themselves out.

Of all of sociology's subfields, the sociology of religion may well have the most distinguished pedigree. Virtually all of the leading lights of early sociology devoted considerable attention to the sociology of religion in one way or another. In fact, the religion questions—what religion is, how it works, how it came into being, why it persists or recedes—were among the most burning that early sociologists confronted. Karl Marx, Émile Durkheim, Max Weber, Georg Simmel, and others each tried to comprehend the role of religion within the larger sociocultural setting that made human existence possible. Each realized that religion was a uniquely human experience, without any analogue in the animal world, which, in the past at least, seemed to have had a controlling effect on the way people lived. Indeed, Auguste Comte, the Frenchman who coined the word *sociology* in the first half of the nineteenth century, saw sociology as virtually a new religion; sociologists would be the "high priests of positivism"—a new scientific system of human action that would replace outmoded theological dogmas and philosophical speculations.

These early sociologists gave us different images of religion, hence raising different kinds of questions. Through these, however, runs a single theme—*religion and social change*. Marx, throughout his work, saw religion as part of a structural system of oppression. Durkheim, in his crucial work *The Elementary Forms of the Religious Life*, published at the culmination of his career, saw religion as maintaining social order or equilibrium. Weber, in a brilliant series of essays known as *The Protestant Ethic and the Spirit of Capitalism*, saw religion as a vehicle for social change. Each of these perspectives—as well as others—has an important contribution to make. None is complete in itself.

Indeed, if all religions worked exactly the same way no matter what the circumstances, religion would hardly be sociologically interesting. Because religion enters into a dynamic interplay with different sociological variables in different times, places, and circumstances, religion is worth studying. The Roman Catholic Church in Chicago in 2008 is different from the Roman Catholic Church in Rheims in 1400; Southern Baptists in an Alabama town of 2,500 are different from Southern Baptists in a midwestern city of 250,000; Jews whose roots are in eastern Europe are different from Jews whose roots are in the Middle East. The early sociologists were all attuned to this, though the specific questions in which they were interested led their work in different directions. Today the big questions for the sociology of religion include, among others, the changing interrelationships between gender and religion, social class and religion, and ethnicity and religion; the secularization debate; new religions; and the changing relationship between religion and popular culture with the growth of mass media.

The Definition Problem

One of the easiest places to get hopelessly bogged down in the sociology of religion is in the matter of definition. We hope to avoid the worst of the mire, but at the same time, it would be irresponsible for us not to introduce the topic. For decades students have been required to memorize Durkheim's second definition of religion (his first did not work, so he tried again):

> A religion is a unified system of beliefs and practices relative to sacred things, that is to say, things set apart and forbidden—beliefs and practices which unite into one single moral community called a Church, all those who adhere to them. (1965: 47)

Durkheim contrasted "sacred things" to those he termed *profane* (though that term is more accurately translated *mundane*—that is, ordinary or everyday—rather than associated with *profanity* as we use this word today). Durkheim developed this definition by studying ethnographic reports on Australian Aborigines, whom he considered to possess the most elemental structures of social life necessary for human existence. His definition became popular because it recognized that the study of religion was "ontologically distinct" from the question of the existence of God or gods, and because he recognized the religious *practice* dynamic as essentially *social* in character. For Durkheim, too, religion was not only normal but also actually socially healthy (or "functional" to society); this stood in contradiction to various psychological theories (for example, those of Sigmund Freud) that saw religious practice as a sign of personal weakness or psychological defect.

Unlike Durkheim, Max Weber demurred from the definition question, claiming that a definition at the outset of an investigation closes the researcher to possible alternatives. Nevertheless, he suggested lines along which such investigations might proceed and identified religion with the category of *meaning*—as in "religion gives 'meaning' to life" (see Weber 1978: 399). William H. Swatos, Jr., and Paul M. Gustafson (1992: 7–12) have systematized Weber's dimensions of religion into a definition-like statement, however, that may be noted for comparative purposes vis-à-vis that of Durkheim: "[R]eligion is a patterning of social relationships around a belief in supernatural powers, creating ethical considerations." For Weber, the belief in supernatural powers was logically primary to the "sacred objects" of Durkheim. "What makes the objects sacred?" Weber would ask. He would answer, "A belief that they are supernaturally endowed." Hence, he would argue for the definitional primacy of belief in the supernatural. Spelled out more specifically, Weber's social relationship dimension involves six components:

> (1) a belief in one or several of a wide-ranging variety of *supernatural powers*, that are (2) evidenced in a variety of *charismatic manifestations*, (3) articulated through *symbolic expressions*, (4) responded to in a *variety of forms*, (5) under the guidance of *various types of leaders*, (6) in a variety of patterns of relationships significantly determined by the *patterned behavior of the lay people* of the community.

The ethical dimension, to which we will turn shortly, involves two additional components: (1) *soteriology* and (2) *theodicy*. These mean, respectively, how people understand themselves to be able to be in a right relationship with the

Marx in Context

Over time, pithy phrases often become quoted outside their original context, giving impressions their authors did not intend. One of the clearest examples of this from the sociology of religion is Karl Marx's phrase that religion is "the opium of the people." Here is the larger context:

> Religious distress is at the same time the expression of real distress and also the protest against real distress. Religion is the sigh of the oppressed creature, the heart of a heartless world, just as it is the spirit of a spiritless condition. It is the opium of the people.
>
> To abolish religion as the illusory happiness of the people is to demand their real happiness. The demand to give up illusions about the existing state of affairs is the demand to give up a state of affairs that needs illusions. The criticism of religion is therefore in embryo the criticism of the vale of tears, the halo of which is religion.
>
> Thus the criticism of heaven turns into the criticism of earth, the *criticism of religion* into the *criticism of law* and the *criticism of theology* into the *criticism of politics*. ("Toward a Critique of Hegel's *Philosophy of Right*: Introduction," 1844; Marx and Engels 1975: 38; emphasis in the original)

Whether or not we agree with Marx's analysis, the content of the phrase "opium of the people," when placed in context, is often overlooked and needs attention in itself. "The opium of the people": To what does this contrast? It contrasts to "the opium of the rich," which was *real opium*; that is, when Marx says religion is "the opium of the people," he means that the masses are not wealthy enough to afford the opium (often in a form called laudanum) that the rich in mid-nineteenth-century England bought to make life's pains go away. When Marx's content is read in context, what he is saying is that religion is the only way that the masses can solace themselves from the pains, both physical and psychological, that life brings them, because they can't afford drugs. Opium use during his day was widespread among the upper classes. Sherlock Holmes buffs will know that his use of opiates is a recurring thread through Arthur Conan Doyle's stories, just as James Bond buffs know that he prefers his martinis "shaken, not stirred." It is impossible to understand the drug problem today, for example, without an awareness of the everyday assumption in our world that pain can usually be relieved by ingesting a substance and without the knowledge that this option began with the rich and has "trickled down" to the rest of us.

Marx's pithy phrase is far more telling about the social conditions of English life in the mid-nineteenth century than he perhaps ever realized; hence it is all the more sociologically valuable.

supernatural powers (how to "get saved" or achieve "harmony with the universe" or "absolute peace"), and how to explain evil—or why bad things seem to happen to those who seem to be good people.

The Durkheimian and Weberian approaches have created the two principal axes around which the definitional debate in the sociology of religion has centered. These are known, respectively, as the *functional* and *substantive* approaches. In the former case (traditionally represented by Durkheim in the sociology of religion), religion is seen preeminently as performing certain functions for society. In the latter case (traditionally associated with Weber), there is an emphasis on the content around which religion centers. An enormous amount of energy has been spent on the definitional debate in the sociology of religion, some of it wasted, some of it not. As we will see when we come to the chapter on the secularization debate, the basis for that debate lies to a large measure in differences in the definition of religion.

One practical way to summarize this debate is to make a distinction between whether we are doing the sociology of *religion* or the sociology of *religions*. In the latter case, it is assumed that there are groups that call themselves religions, and our task is to go study them. We study Methodists or Muslims or Mormons or "Moonies." In the former case, however, we ask questions of a deeper order. These include questions about the origins of religion, how personal belief gets turned into action, why people do or do not choose to share their beliefs, and so on. Historically, this has been a tension within the discipline of the sociology of religion that may be likened in some ways to the distinction between the study of deviance and the field of criminology. The latter starts with an apparently clear-cut definition that crime is a breaking of the law (indeed, as Durkheim rightly observes in this case, if there were no laws there would be no crimes), while deviance is far more nuanced.

Other approaches to the definitional problem in the sociology of religion have been tried. Formal definitions have been relatively unsuccessful thus far, though some newer approaches appear promising (see Blasi 1980). Durkheim's first definitional attempt was, in fact, a formal definition, as was Georg Simmel's definition of religion. Another approach is a neo-Weberian style based on his *Verstehende soziologie*—a method of sociological analysis that stresses the role of the participant actor in definition construction. This approach places a greater definitional burden on the religious person. Swatos (1990) refers to this as a "situational" approach, based on the "definition of the situation" concept of the early U.S. sociologist W. I. Thomas. Religion *is* what the participant says it is. The task of the sociologist of religion is to bring his or her professional training as an *interpreter* of human action to bear on this particular form of action: knowing what a subject *means* by what he or she says and does, and interpreting that meaning through a shared discourse of scientific endeavor.

This approach is practically identical to the "action theory of religion" of Roy Wallis and Steve Bruce (1986) and has some affinities to Robert Bellah's concept of "symbolic realism" (1970b). This approach also has affinities to Clifford Geertz's interpretive perspectives on religious institutions and beliefs (1973: 87–125). Although Geertz may too closely identify religion and culture, he points out that symbols play a double role in simultaneously expressing images of reality and shaping that reality. Religious symbols provide a representation of the way things are (what he calls "models *of*") and serve as guides that direct human activity ("models *for*"). In this view, religions consist of clusters of symbols that compose an ordered whole and provide a program for the ideas, values, and lifestyles of a society. Geertz's work, though originating in a functionalist context, reinvigorated Weberian interpretations of sociology of religion—releasing studies from functionalist "prerequisites" and paving a

Substantive versus Functional Definitions: A Religious Fish Story

Definitions, it is often said, are neither correct nor incorrect. Rather than being evaluated according to accuracy, definitions live or die by virtue of their usefulness, for they are tools of thought. Ideally, definitions help us filter the raw reality that we perceive. They thus shape our thinking and lend it some coherence and facility. Because definitions are best regarded as tools, a good way to appreciate the benefits or drawbacks of any definitional strategy is to compare it to a particular type of implement. To continue the analogy, let's all go fishing!

Welcome aboard our best-equipped deep-sea craft. We have chartered the boat for two consecutive daylong excursions. Each day we will troll the same fertile beds of ocean life in search of the seafood that we most love to devour. On this, our first day, we will use a sturdy net with broad spaces between the twines: Only the largest and heaviest fish will not pass through its openings—but then, what could be wrong with catching only *really big* fish?

We have been out on the water for some time now. Here, help me winch our catch up over the side and position it above the deck. What do you see? Ah, just as I predicted: Our net is half full of fish, whole fish, and nothing but fish. And they are solely (no pun intended) fish of the biggest varieties. Do you imagine that we can outdo this performance tomorrow?

Leap forward to the following day. Our charter captain guides the same boat over the same waters, but we trail a different net. This one boasts a very fine mesh (that is, the openings in it are small and close together). Because little passes through its filters, before long the net is full to the point of bursting. But our most challenging moment occurs when we haul the catch out of the water and down into the boat. Do you see what I see? Sure, we caught some fish (big and small)—but we also have eels, crustaceans, waterlogged driftwood, sodden clumps of seaweed, a pair of rubber boots (both for the left foot), empty cans of beer, and several of those plastic straps that hold together a six-pack.

Which day of fishing was the more successful? How you answer probably depends on what you were looking for. On our first trip from port we caught some fairly big fish, but we did not finish with very many, and they were all of the same types. Don't misunderstand: we *like* those varieties (a preference that we confirmed at dinner that evening), but perhaps we missed something—something out of the ordinary, something more, something *better*!

The second time we bounded over the waves, the result was strikingly different. We not only filled the net with our catch, but we also caught a wide range of fish—as well as some creatures that are not fish, and even a few inanimate (and inedible) objects. The variety was sufficient to please the fussiest fisherman, yet we had to spend most of the time during our return to port sorting through the vast pile of ocean contents that spilled across the deck. And while you may suit yourself, I am not at all sure that I want to dine on a great deal of what we caught. (What *is* that thing with seven legs anyway?)

A *substantive* definition of religion cuts through our reality in a manner similar to the fishing net we employed on the first outing, when our catch consisted of all fish but not all kinds of fish. In other words, we can be confident with a substantive definition that what we have skimmed is what we were searching for in the first place, but we cannot say with certainty that we have exhausted all the possibilities. A *functional* definition is more flexible and more inclusive, and thus better adapted to exploratory studies and comparative work. Like our second net, it takes in quite a bit, and so minimizes the chance of missing something important. But it presents the related danger of including too much, and especially items (like the boots and beer cans) that do not meet our conceptions of, or desires for, the elusive subject.

path away from "secularization"—and encouraged an entire generation of sociologists by expanding what we think of as religion. Geertz's approach involves a two-stage process, the first of which focuses on analyzing the system of meanings embodied within religious symbols (often referred to as *thick description*), and the second of which relates these systems to social structures and psychological processes (see Geertz 2002; Micheelsen 2002).

Implementing the situational approach involves at least three sets of considerations that specify what a situational approach to religion entails and how such an approach may be put into practice in research agendas.

First, religions create *action orientations*—ways people think they ought to act. These may be broadly subdivided into ritual and moral action systems. Note that action orientations do not require total or continuous compliance on the part of actors. One may or may not actually engage in religious action to "know" of it and recognize it as "religious"—for example, prayer, baptism, "Thou shalt not kill." Indeed, some people may never comply with a given action orientation and still recognize it as religious; this is true not only with respect to others but also for themselves. For example, a person may never pray, but that person will still see prayer as a *religious* action. (Indeed, prayer is the most universal religious action.) Negative evidence for this element can also be found, for instance, in the claim of those who oppose the "moment of *silence*" in public schools as an "imposition of *religion*," whereas no dictionary in the world defines *silence* as "religion." Note, too, that action orientations indicate that an action may or may not be religiously meaningful in its performance—for example, circumcision. Similarly, Geoffrey Nelson (1969) and Logie Barrow (1986), in studies of English spiritualism, have each shown that the same phenomena that were accepted as "real" were interpreted religiously by some spiritualist partisans, but areligiously or even antireligiously by others.

Second, religions consist of *systems of discourse*—that is, religions create formal, structured ways of talking about and describing the world, which in turn become part of the lived experience of their participants. All religions have vocabularies that distinguish participants to a greater or lesser degree from nonparticipants. Religious people will talk about going to Mass, being saved, witnessing the Rapture, sitting *shiv'ah*. Young converts to evangelical-charismatic traditions stop saying "No shit!" and start saying "Praise the Lord!" *Most* of these words exist in common discourse and are transvalued (that is, given a new, "higher" meaning). In some cases, however, appeal may be generated by words that are entirely outside the ordinary language system, at least that of the society at hand (for example, foreign languages).

Understanding a religious argot, the special vocabulary of each religious group, is probably the most important bridge over the divide between observer and participant (sometimes called the emic–etic divide), and the same words can develop fine shades of meaning among similar, but still different, traditions. For example, Stephanie Zimmermann and her colleagues (1990), in an article provocatively titled "God's Line Is Never Busy," show how "fundamental differences in church values" between two southern Appalachian denominations, the Southern Baptists and the Church of God (Cleveland, Tennessee), are revealed in "recurrent themes, stories, and metaphors in church leader talk." It is especially important to understand that words change meaning over time and that adherents to the same religious organization may or may not use the same system of discourse. Catholics, for example, now tend to speak of the "Sacrament of Reconciliation," rather than penance or confession. Some Episcopalians refer to their principal Sunday worship as Mass, while others may spend their whole life in the Episcopal Church and never hear this word used in reference to their own services. In general, one could reasonably expect that discourse homogeneity would reflect group size—the smaller the group, the more homogeneous its discourse system.

While we are specifically addressing the matter of discourse, we would like to make an important methodological-ethical point about the role of labeling in the study of religion. Under the rubric of *labeling theory*, social scientists studying deviance have shown the power of words used to label social actions and actors in both the perpetuation and persecution of deviant behavior. When we are studying religion from the situational perspective, it is important to distinguish between labels that religious people apply to themselves, hence forming a part of the discourse system of the religion and legitimately used in social scientific description, and those applied from the outside. Two words often used in religious descriptions will suffice to make our point: The words *fundamentalist* and *cult* are used fast and loose in journalistic treatments of religions, but they are of quite different categories situationally. Although often overextended in a negative way by its critics and the media, the word *fundamentalist* is used by some Christian churches and institutions as a self-description; as such, it forms a legitimate concept for accurate social scientific descriptive analysis. The word *cult*, however, is virtually never used by a contemporary religious group in regard to itself; hence, use of the word *cult* in the contemporary context must be regarded as an ethical breach among social scientists, inasmuch as James T. Richardson (1993) has shown that it constitutes a prejudicial label when applied in ordinary discourse (for example, before a jury).

Third, religion involves a *subjective experience*. This occurs among devotees at various levels, but also among the nonreligious. Such statements as "I'm not religious" or "Religion is bunk" or "Religion is not for me" all imply both a definition of religion and a self-perception as other. The same goes for interreligious comparisons: people who generically list themselves as "Protestant" may actually more than anything else be distinguishing themselves from Roman Catholics, which they know they are not. Although we cannot deny the possibility that there is someone in this world who gives no sense whatever to the term *religion* (or its appropriate translation into another language), we would find such a case the sufficiently aberrant exception to prove the rule. It may well be, for example, that in some premodern societies, *religion* can be translated only as "way of life." This is not a problem at all for a situational approach. Here we can make good use of the terms *extensive* and *intensive*, considering premodern societies to have more extensive religion (that is, religion is coextensive with culture), whereas modern societies have more intensive religion (that is, religion is institutionally differentiated). Both have religions, but the role of religion within the sociocultural system is different. Thus, everyone has a subjective experience (or perception based on experience) of religion, though not everyone is religious. In any society, the voices of those who are "not religious" must be assessed along with the voices of those who do claim to be religious in order to determine with sociological precision the "religious situation" of the society as a whole.

There is also, however, a happy paradox to this subjective element in religion that needs to be grasped early on in the study of religion, lest you otherwise fall into a very misplaced cynicism. The paradox is this: *All religions are true*. What we mean by this is that as long as a person is not lying, whatever a person claims to be his or her religious experience *is* his or her religious experience. This forms the basis on which he or she makes religious claims or claims a religion. This does not mean that all religions are universally valid or that all religions are equally good in their outcomes, but it is not within the purview of the sociology of religion to deny the subjective truth of the religious claims of a person who is putting them forth without guile. Note that there is no basis in the sociology of religion whatever, by contrast, for the alternative assertion that "all religions are false." To make such an assertion denies the validity of human experience and actually flies in the face of the larger sociological project of understanding the human sociocultural condition in its fullness, since we know religions have been and are a part of the experience of many—probably most—human beings.

Perhaps a comparison with another subjective human experience—love—might be helpful. Love may or may not be returned by the person toward whom it is directed, but the person who says she or he is in love with someone is stating a true experience. Love may or may not yield sexual experience, and that sexual experience may or may not be one that someone else might enjoy in the same way that a person describing it passionately does. We may say of someone who says that she or he loves us, "Well, you sure have a funny way of showing it," and so it may be. But to say that "all love is false," because love is subjectively meaningful but difficult to measure objectively, is clearly not a view that is going to get a wide hearing among most people. The subjective elements of these experiences mean that we need to be especially sensitive to the ways in which people tell us the experiences are meaningful to them and then search for correlates of the experiences that follow in interaction patterns. From this we may see how certain forms of love are more or less hurtful to people or are more or less helpful to social relations. The same is true of religions.

It is our view, then, that the Durkheimian definition of religion—though critically important at the time that it was introduced, in that it established beyond all doubt the sociological character of religion—is not, in fact, an accurate portrayal of the nature of religion in our time. Nevertheless, it can still provide important insights into the relationship between social values and societal integration. Because Durkheim largely ignored the role of the participant actor in the social system, he saw only one aspect of a multifaceted social process.

Exploring the Dimensions of Religion

Weber's dimensions of religion provide us with signals or signposts of the kinds of things to which we should be attentive when looking at human activity that we might want to consider religious and also for making comparisons between one religion and another. In this section we want to look at each of these in more detail.

SOCIAL RELATIONSHIPS

Supernatural powers. The word *supernatural* is a clumsy one, but no other seems to do any better. One writer has used "the Beyond" as an alternative. What is meant by the phrase, however, is not hard to state: religious people think that there is a Power beyond themselves that cannot be controlled through means directly accessible to human beings. In an important way, this distinguishes religion from magic as well. The basic premise of magic is that if you know the formula and can put it into practice, the right outcome is bound to occur. Magic is in fact more closely related to science, and some people who have conflicted views of the relation of religion to science may actually have a more magical than religious worldview. Religious people tend to talk about *miracles* rather than magic. A miracle is a miracle because the control of the outcome is outside of human hands. Supernatural powers include God, gods, the Great Spirit, and forces of the universe. One can get in tune with them, but one cannot change them.

Charisma. This is one of the most important concepts that Weber contributed to the study of human social action. It refers to a special "gift of grace" in an individual that causes others to follow that person as a leader. In the context of religion, charisma manifests itself in events that one can observe but cannot explain. Miracles are a charismatic manifestation. Whether it be Jesus walking on water, or the extension of a shortened leg to equal the other, or the speaking in "unknown tongues" (glossolalia), these events "prove" to religious people that supernatural powers exist. Not everyone, of course, accepts this explanation. Some consider miracles to be chance or (possibly hypnotic) suggestion or tricks. Most historically significant religious leaders have evidenced charismatic manifestations, and their leadership has been based at least in part on these. Someone who miraculously heals or makes things appear out of thin air often gains a following. In fact, according to Weber, it is precisely this following (or followership) that validates charisma. What makes a charismatic leader a *leader* rather than a crazy person is that people believe in his or her gifts, which are thus taken as evidence that he or she has a direct relationship to the supernatural powers. He or she manifests divine grace in ways that the rest of us do not.

Symbolic expressions. This dimension is related to the matter of discourse that we mentioned earlier, but it is not only ways of speaking. It can also involve visual signs, like crosses. Because religion deals with the Beyond, it must always speak in metaphors. Because the Beyond is beyond, there is no language in our world that is capable of fully comprehending it. Hence we are either left speechless or we speak in tongues or we use symbols. "The Lord is my shepherd." "Washed in the blood of the Lamb." "I am the door." We put up crosses or stars of David or crescents. We baptize. We receive bread and wine as Christ's body and blood. Much religious conflict is in fact conflict over symbols and the interpretation of symbol systems. Does Christ's blood require wine, or is grape juice okay? Does it matter whether artificial fermentation/defermentation ingredients are added? Should water be substituted? What are the outer limits? May doughnuts and coffee or pizza and beer be substituted for bread and wine? Does baptism require complete immersion in water? Must the water be running? Is any water required? What about how I cut my hair or my beard or what clothes I wear? These kinds of questions about the relationships between forms of symbolic expression and the will of the supernatural powers can take up an enormous amount of energy among religious people.

When we look at the world of religious activity, we also see that there are various ways in which people organize their religious lives. These are the *variety of forms* of religious response. One such important distinction, often missed by modern Westerners, is between congregational and pilgrimage types of religions. The Western traditions—whether Christian, Jewish, or Muslim—tend to formalize religion in terms of a congregation of people. Quite simply, devotees "belong" to a church, synagogue, or mosque. In the Eastern traditions, religion primarily revolves around pilgrimage sites where religious virtuosos—monks, gurus, nuns, shamans—dwell. Devotees make a pilgrimage to a religious center. But even in the West, there is variability among responses. Weber makes a distinction between *church* and *sect*, for example, based on the way one enters a religion: Is the normal mode of becoming a member of a religion being born into it (often symbolized by a rite at infancy, such as baptism or circumcision) or is it through an "adult profession of faith"—becoming a convert? Within Christianity we can also look at the different ways in which people worship, as embodied in church architecture: Does the church focus on an altar, where a sacrificial liturgy is performed? Does it focus on a pulpit, where a message is proclaimed? Or is it more participatory, where people move around during the worship, praying, singing, even dancing?

Perhaps because of the charismatic element, a leaderless religion is virtually unknown. Indeed, some small religions may appear to have more leaders than followers! How leadership is structured, however, is an important element in understanding religious life, hence there are *various types of leaders.*

Weber makes a distinction, for example, between prophets and priests, and then further subdivides the prophetic type into ethical and exemplary prophets. This typology might be applied to Western Christianity by comparing the priesthood to the minister who urges a congregation to social, ethical action and, yet again, to a minister who challenges people to be like him in an evangelistic mode. Jewish and Islamic clergy are primarily teachers, where this role can be fused to one of judge in all disputed matters of religious law. Many religions have leaders who are "set apart from the world" in a monastic vocation. Leadership and form of course interact, but they are not the same thing. Mormonism has a leadership structure, for example, that is not too different from that of the Roman Catholic Church, in that both have male leaders who, in their official capacity, may make statements that "authoritatively" or "infallibly" modify or enlarge church doctrine, which is then passed down through an appointed hierarchy of bishops and priests. But the forms of the religious life between the two are quite different, with Mormonism featuring a message orientation, and Catholicism emphasizing a ceremonial sacrificial rite. An important question in leadership is that of how much authority a leader is presumed to have over his or her flock: Is the leader primarily an adviser-manager or does the leader at least theoretically have control over the lives of those who place themselves under his or her guidance?

Patterned behavior of lay people. This is the final social relationship dimension, and is the unique contribution of Max Weber to this dimensional scheme. Lay people are those whom we in the West would usually term the *congregation*. What Weber realized from his work on charisma was that no leader relationship could exist without followers, and how followers responded to leaders was as important as what leaders themselves said or did. This was crucial to his *Protestant Ethic* essays: how people already in the business world responded to and implemented the Calvinistic teachings of English Puritan pastors—and how those pastors shaped their articulation of their message to fit the conditions of their congregations. Lay people in the same religious tradition may behave quite differently across cultures. For example, in both France and Poland about 80 percent of the population claim to be Catholic, but in France only 12 percent attend Mass monthly, while in Poland about 78 percent of the population do so (McCleary and Barro 2006: 65; Iannaccone 1998: 1487). In traditional Italian Catholic culture, to receive Holy Communion frequently is considered unmanly, while in traditional Irish Catholic culture, just the opposite is the case. When Ashkenazic (eastern European) and Sephardic (Middle Eastern) Jews first returned to Israel after its re-creation as a modern state in 1948, they discovered they had virtually two different religions. Even today in the United States, synagogues are as likely to be known and chosen by Jews in the community on the basis of whether their origins are German, Polish, Russian, or Sephardic than as to whether they are of the Reform, Conservative, or Orthodox denominations. In religiously plural societies like the United States, the role of the laity is especially heightened, as religion is a voluntary activity and the financial support of the laity is essential to keep a religious organization operating.

The International Red Cross and Red Crescent Movement

Entrance to the International Red Cross and Red Crescent Museum in Geneva, Switzerland. Alamy A908A3

The International Committee of the Red Cross (ICRC) was founded in 1863, the consequence of the social movement activism of Henri Dunant, a Swiss humanitarian who provided assistance to the Austrian and French soldiers, both the wounded and the dying, in the 1859 Battle of Solferino—an important event in what became known as the Second Independence War that led to the creation of a unified Italian state. In the immediate aftermath of this bloody conflict, he urged all nations to establish voluntary relief societies. In 1864, the Geneva Convention required that all of the signatory parties offer care for the victims of war regardless of whether they were friends or foes. A worldwide structure emerged over time. The symbol of the ICRC, the red cross, was borrowed from the Swiss flag, which contained a white cross and a red background (like Switzerland, the Scandinavian countries also employ a cross in their flags, as do the English with the use of the St. George cross). The Red Cross simply inverted the colors of the Swiss flag for its symbol. The ICRC defined itself as impartial, neutral, and independent of any government. However, the choice of a distinctly Christian symbol made it difficult for the organization to function in some non-Christian nations. This became evident in the following decade when Russia and Turkey engaged in hostilities. Contending that the Red Cross flag conjured up images of the Crusades, the Red Crescent was introduced. This led to the establishment of the International Red Cross and Red Crescent Movement, which is based in Geneva and today contains 192 member nations. The scope of the movement expanded from a singular focus on war to work aimed at assisting the victims of natural and man-made disasters as well as addressing the suffering of those living in poverty. For over half a century, Israel has lobbied for a third symbol, the Red Star of David. Within Israel, the Magen David Adom Society uses this symbol instead of the cross or crescent. However, it has not been officially recognized by the member states. Rather, in 2005, the International Conference of the Red Cross and Red Crescent added a new emblem, the religiously neutral "red crystal," which is a diamond shape. While no national society is required to use this new symbol, all are permitted to do so, with the understanding that it has the same status as the cross and crescent.

Sources: http://www.redcross.int.EN/fundprincips.html and http://www.news.bbc.co.uk/go/pr/fr/world.europe/4497840.stm.

ETHICAL CONSIDERATIONS

When we discussed the concept of religions as action orientations, we noted that these included both ritual and moral aspects. These two elements unquestionably overlap, but they may also be analytically separated. Going to church is different from not killing one's neighbor; sociologically one may even investigate whether people who go to church are more or less likely to kill their neighbors than people who don't, or whether people who kill neighbors are more or less likely to go to church than people who don't. At a less dramatic level than homicide, we could ask whether religious people treat others better than their nonreligious peers. The short answer is: They do (Ellison 1992; Morgan 1983).

We need to make an important distinction at the outset, however, between religious ethics and moral prudence. Religious ethics are decisions about right and wrong, and corresponding actions, based on some sense of being pleasing to or not offending the Powers, the sacred, the holy. "The will of God," or its appropriate correlate, plays an important role in religious ethics. Moral prudence, by contrast, is a decision based on what is best in the long run for one's own self-interest. For example, if you refrain from sexual activity because you're afraid you'll get pregnant or contract AIDS, that's not religious ethics. That's moral prudence. It's no different from looking both ways before you cross the street or not putting your hand into a fire. While few people would say that "look both ways before you cross the street" is a religious maxim, there do seem to be people who think that abstinence from sex, no matter what the reason, is a religious good. If this were true, none of us would be here, and there would be no religions! People who refrain from sex in the Western tradition on religious grounds, for example, do so for such reasons as a belief that sex should properly be confined to the "holy estate of matrimony" or that refraining from sex frees them from responsibilities and entanglements that draw them away from God.

The first of Weber's ethical considerations is soteriology. The word *soter* is the Latin root for savior, and soteriology may be taken to mean, as we indicated earlier, the things religions tell us to do or to refrain from doing in order to be in a right relationship with the Power(s). These things involve both ritual and moral elements. Thus, in Catholic Christianity, you should be baptized and attend Mass every Sunday, and you should refrain from committing murder, theft, and adultery (as well as a lot of other things). Buddhism has five precepts that are akin to the last five of the Ten Commandments. Most world religions have quite similar sets of activities from which one should refrain, and most teach some ethic of love or respect for fellow humans. Before the era of world religions, however, many religions had insider/outsider ethics: love thy near neighbor, kill the guy in the next tribe. In some respects, Islam continues in its more extreme forms to propagate this dualistic view of the human species through the concept of *jihad*, or holy war. Though more careful Muslim scholars will point out that this is a very limited view of jihad as it occurs in the Islamic faith as a whole—namely as "struggle"—holy war is a part of the concept of jihad and is unique to the Islamic tradition (though the fifth-century Christian theologian Augustine of Hippo did develop a concept of *just war*, which has at times been used in ways that were virtually identical to jihad in their results).

Many religious traditions also include regulations about diet and other biological functions in their soteriological formularies. Eat this. Don't eat that. Orthodox Jews do not eat pork or shellfish, and may not simultaneously consume meat and dairy products. Muslims also do not consume pork. For many years Roman Catholics were generally forbidden to eat meat on Fridays. Mormons may not drink coffee or tea, and, along with many other Christian groups and with Muslims, are to abstain from alcoholic beverages. In general, it seems that the longer a religion is in existence, the more complex its soteriological formulary grows. More and more rules come into existence, so much so that some religious traditions from time to time go through and prune their formularies, as the Roman Catholic Church did in the Second Vatican Council (1962–1965). In addition and over time increasing debate takes place over the interpretation of what is in the formulary. What exactly is murder? What is adultery? What is strong drink? Are bacon bits meat? Where does one cross the threshold of sexual impropriety? For some religious people, these become critically important questions, as they believe that improper actions in this world may exclude them from a life of eternal bliss, or send them to eternal punishment, or return them to this world as a lower life form.

Also on religion's agenda is the problem of explaining evil. We all know that what appear to be bad things happen to people who seem to have done nothing wrong, or nothing so wrong as to experience the suffering they are enduring. These are theodical problems. (The term *theodicy* was coined by the philosopher Leibniz [1646–1716] and adapted by Weber.) The simplest way of resolving theodical problems in themselves is by positing many gods—there are good gods and evil gods, and we are caught in the middle. Most archaic religious forms are polytheistic. In more developed religious systems, however, the theodical problem repeats itself, with a host of different answers. The concept of the devil or Satan is a contemporary variant of the polytheistic good gods/bad gods approach. An alternative approach is found in the doctrine of *karma* in many Asian religions, where suffering misfortune in this world is understood as punishment for misdeeds in a previous existence. Others in modernity suggest that evil is only apparent because we do not see the entirety of God's plan (this was basically Leibniz's position). Some may view suffering as a preparation or testing for heavenly rewards—will one reject God if one has to suffer?—a view that can be traced back at least to the biblical story of Job. According to Weber, every religion eventually has to deal with the problem of evil in some way; it is the reverse of the soteriological coin. If a religion can't explain why bad things happen to us, then why be good?

Taken together, these dimensions begin to suggest the kinds of things we might want to pay attention to as we look at religion sociologically. They certainly do not encompass everything that goes on in religion, but they give us avenues of access to major constellations of activities and problems within religions.

A Definitional Revision

Building on all of this, we wish to offer a neo-Weberian approach to the definitional question, teasing out of Weber the two sets of dynamics that characterize religions: on the one hand, a patterning of social relationships around perceived supramundane power; on the other, ethical considerations. Besides the acknowledgment of ultimacy within a meaning system, we would look for perceived charismatic manifestations, leadership, organization, and patterned intentional action on the part of members of the group, because they consider themselves members of the group, all as social relationship dimensions. Ethically, we would look for some concepts that explain evil and show how to be in right relationship with the ultimate (theodicy and soteriology).

A word about the phrase *perceived supramundane power*: Some idea of a "Beyond" is the sticking point in substantive definitions. Our phrasing differs from that which we first introduced from Swatos and Gustafson's analysis of Weber's work, "a belief in supernatural powers," in two respects. First, we want to eliminate the word *belief* in the definition, because we think it is wrongly identified with intellectualization or propositional theologies that are preeminently Western and did not fully develop even in the West until the Middle Ages. *Perception*, by contrast, emphasizes the proper Weberian order in his initial discussion of how the sociology of religion should proceed in the study of religion, namely, "from the viewpoint of the subjective experiences, ideas, and purposes of the individuals concerned" (Weber 1978: 399). Perception is the subjective experience that is prior to belief(s). People come to believe in something because they have had a prior experience that they are trying to understand or at least accept.

Second, we want to use *supramundane* rather than *supernatural*. Supramundane means extraordinary, beyond what Durkheim would have called the *profane*, a term that has taken on a different meaning. We want to abandon *supernatural* because we are quite willing to admit that "forces" within "nature" may constitute ultimate realities for people. What is important about these forces, however, is that they operate beyond the humdrum, the everyday—most important, the controllable. They call forth something that might be called awe or worship, which leads to ritualization. And this supramundane is accepted as real by the participant in the experience—that is, "really different" from the everyday, the ordinary, life in the "natural attitude."

A final definitional paradox: While we believe it to be the case that all religions are true, we also recognize that religion does not exist. That is, there is no "thing" out there that *is* religion. As Jonathan Z. Smith (1982: xi) has observed, *religion* as we use the term today is "the creation of the scholar's study. It is created for the scholar's analytic purposes by his imaginative acts of comparison and generalization." What we call "religions" are systems of action that humans do that we as students of human behavior see as somehow sufficiently like each other and different from other systems of action to give them a common name. Any attempt at definition, then, is not a claim about what religion "really" is, but simply a conceptual tool. Thus, it is certainly true that at some level "all religions are alike," because if there was not something common among them, they would not be called religions. The dimensions that Weber developed and that we have highlighted, with only slight modifications, give us a way to begin to assess these cognate systems of action. In this respect, we find the formal definition offered by Don Swenson (1999: 69) a convenient summary of our position: Religion, *approached sociologically*, can be considered "the individual and social experience of the sacred that is manifested in mythologies, rituals, and ethos, and integrated into a collective such as a community or an organization."

The Plan of the Book

Chapter 2 is intended to help readers orient themselves to important issues in the sociological study of religion. We open by looking at research methods themselves—the tools of the sociological trade. Assuming we want to know about religion as sociologists, how can we gather valid and reliable information? What research strategies best fit different types of questions we might ask? We also want to look at current theoretical perspectives, ways of explaining and interpreting the data we have gathered. According to R. Stephen Warner (1993; 2005: 105–22), a "new paradigm" or new way of thinking about religious action has been developing during the last several decades, and we think this deserves some attention. We also think it is important to address questions of the larger importance of the sociological study of religion. *Why* is the study of religion worthwhile, both individually and socially? It is our view that religion is not merely amenable to sociological analysis but is also sociologically significant for the understanding of who we are as a culture and as part of a world-system.

The remaining nine chapters of this book look at *some* of the most important areas of contact between religion and society in North America. We have chosen to focus on a limited set of problems that have a relatively strong tradition of research in the sociology of religion and that simultaneously affect our lives today in significant ways. Because religions make all-encompassing claims, however, there is a sense in which religion, through practicing adherents, has some relation to all aspects of society. It is thus possible to explore new topics that extend well beyond the bounds of this text, and we would encourage you to do so.

In chapter 3 we deal with what might be thought to be the great countercurrent to the case for the study of religion—the claim that a process of *secularization* has been advancing with increasing intensity from generation to generation, with the result that religion is dying out among us. We reject this claim, but we take it seriously enough to try to indicate both how and why it arose. Secularization theory is significant because it points to the *changes* that have occurred in our religious life over time. We want to show that while it is neither the case that religion is dying nor that we were all deeply religious, the nature of religious practice in the United States and elsewhere has changed from generation to generation—and will change from generation to generation. Indeed, we want to suggest that one of the great gifts of the sociology of religion to understanding religious history is to show that change is *inherent* in religious belief as long as people are practicing a religion. It is precisely when religion is mistakenly identified as a set of formal beliefs, or dogma, that the claim that religion is "dying" in a society can be offered seriously. Religious beliefs change because people's religious practices change in light of the whole system of social relationships in which they live—and religious practices also influence

Religion is often present and absent in society at the same time, but differently across times. What does this photograph say to you about the interweaving of various times, places, and circumstances in the composition of the sociocultural fabric? Photograph courtesy of William H. Swatos, Jr.

other sectors of the social system. The only religion that doesn't change, in fact, is a dead religion. All living traditions change and must change to live on.

We then turn our survey by looking at the classic American religious pattern of *denominationalism*. While it is true that some Christian denominations that played a significant role in shaping religious life in the United States into the 1960s have lost significant numbers of members, it is *not* true that church membership or church attendance has declined with similar significance. Americans continue to affiliate with "organized religion" and express their religiosity in terms of church membership and/or attendance. When asked about religious life, people in large numbers will still say: "I'm a Methodist." "I was brought up Presbyterian, but now I go to the Baptist Church." "I attend Abundant Life Fellowship." "We go to Temple Beth-Israel for all the holidays." We begin to look at denominationalism through the venerable sociological tool of church-sect theory, but then move on to consider continuities and changes in the U.S. religious landscape. Nevertheless, we still believe that when Andrew Greeley (1972a) described the United States as *The Denominational Society*, he understood perfectly both the underlying principle and actual organization of our religious life, even in what some have described as a "postdenominational" era. This religious *pluralism* that characterizes mainstream American religious culture also permits both older and newer groups to survive at its periphery—the Amish and Hutterites, Orthodox Jews, and perhaps increasingly Sikhs and other world religious minorities, as there is a growing presence of nontraditional religiosity on Main Street America.

Class is a term that has been used in various ways in sociological writing, but regardless of the specifics it has a long association in particular with denominationalism. In traditional Marxist uses, it has been particularly identified with *economic* resources in the narrow sense. More contemporary uses would grant it a larger purview, basically as synonymous with the Weberian notion of *stratification*, but at the same time recognizing that economic power still strongly determines status placement in the high technology, multinational capitalism that characterizes our era. There is a long tradition in the sociology of religion that looks at the interaction of class and religion. Some of this was relatively superficial statistical comparisons of, for example, the average incomes of Episcopalians and Baptists. But there is a stronger analysis of social class that includes not only economic and social factors, but cultural elements as well. Contemporary developments in the sociology of religion have moved away from theories that oversimplified the relationships between religion and social class—toward theories, such as those of Pierre Bourdieu, that integrate issues of cultural and social capital as well (Bourdieu and Wacquant 1992). Such issues as gender and fundamentalism are importantly influenced by class in this larger sense. It may be, for example, that today members of fundamentalist groups are as well educated, as measured by years of formal education, and perhaps even as well paid as more mainline religious practitioners or the nonreligious, but the cultural capital of these groups may be vastly different. James Davidson and his colleagues have shown the continued disproportional predominance of such Protestant church traditions as Presbyterians, Congregationalists, and Episcopalians, accompanied by growth among Reform Jews, in U.S. business, political, and intellectual elites, while Baptists remain dramatically underrepresented (see Davidson 1994; Davidson, Pyle, and Reyes 1995; Pyle 1996). Issues of the material culture of religions and their cultural capital, hence, are not at all unrelated to those of class and status.

One important basis for change in American religious life is the changing ethnic composition of our population; hence we move next to that topic. Because the United States is overwhelmingly "a nation of immigrants" (even "Native Americans" actually seem to have come here from northeast Asia), our religious life reflects the heritages people bring with them. New immigrant groups add to the mix in one way or another. This may result in new "denominations," such as Buddhists, Hindus, and Sikhs, building their own temples and shrines, dressing differently, observing different marriage customs, and so on. However, it may be no less significant as Korean Seventh-day Adventists or Latin American Roman Catholics or Russian émigré Jews arrive in significant numbers within existing congregations that are theoretically of the corresponding denomination, but may in practice be quite different from what these new immigrants bring with them and expect to find here.

This phenomenon is not new. The same thing happened, for example, when Italian, Polish, and eastern European Roman Catholics poured into the United States about a century ago. What is new is that the specific ethnicities that are coming now are different from those that came then. While European immigration has gone from a flood to a trickle, immigration from Latin America and parts of Asia has increased dramatically. Often these new immigrants settle precisely in neighborhoods that were identified with other, earlier immigrant groups. For example, a Czech neighborhood may come to be dominated by Mexican Americans, as in Chicago's Pilsen, or an Irish neighborhood by Filipinos. This has changed and will continue to change American society and, as a result, its religious landscape. But this will not be a one-way process: The existing substratum of denominationalism in the United States will shape how these new groups structure themselves as a part of the new society that we as "Americans all" create. At the same time, the nature of the United States as a denominational society means that new immigration will likely reinvigorate U.S. religiosity. These new religious expressions will simultaneously challenge the old specific religious consensus while enhancing the societal role of religion, hence serving as a desecularizing trend.

In an assessment of the status of the field of the sociology of religion written in 1991, Thomas Robbins and Roland Robertson pointed to *feminism* as one of the most important ideological and social movements to have an impact on the social scientific study of religion during the 1980s. This has not diminished since. "The study of 'women and religion,'" they write, "has become part of the study of religion largely as a result of women demanding 'representation' and then proceeding to attempt a redefinition of the field" (1991: 328–29). In its turn the interests of feminist theory have opened the larger issue of gender not only to sociological investigation but also to wider concern among persons of virtually all religious persuasions. Whether people accept or reject particular arguments for "equal rights" or "male headship" or "reproductive freedom," feminist concerns have set a major agenda for religious discussion. In chapter 7, then, we look at some of the multiple ways in which gender and religion have interacted particularly in the U.S. religious milieu. The study of "women and religion" at some point must logically entail the study of "men and religion," that is, how it is that the principles of sexual differentiation that in various ways are a part of all religious traditions have come into being, why they do or do not persist, and what kinds of changes may occur in other aspects of religious life when gender roles change within society as a whole or in a specific religious tradition. These issues in turn touch on the bodily aspects of religion, as well as religion and material culture. While humans are certainly more than their bodies, they are also human in and through their bodies, and religious life has historically always involved bodily norms—regulations about eating, dress, cosmetology, sexuality, sickness and healing, and the disposal of bodily remains, to name but a few.

From this general discussion of religion's association with the major fault lines of social differentiation in class, race, and gender, we turn to the Roman Catholic Church as a particular case in point of the broader themes of religion and social change that we address in this book—and that of secularization as well. Roman Catholicism is the largest single religious denomination in the United States, both by numbers of adherents and weekly worship practice. Roughly 25 percent of all Americans are Roman Catholic. We can see in the history of Roman Catholicism in the United States:

- the dynamics of the denominational principle
- the struggle from marginal to mainline social status
- the struggle between a culture of origin and a new culture, with conflict and competition as new immigrant groups come to our shores
- changes in institutional structures as some aspects that were historically considered a part of Catholicism (such as schools and hospitals) are secularized
- conflicts over gender roles
- attempts to rekindle a nostalgic past through traditionalist movements
- the power and pitfalls of the media of mass communication, and so on.

The Catholic case provides a way for us to illustrate in this major religious tradition the interactions of the topics that concern contemporary sociologists of religion. Particularly important throughout U.S. history has been the interplay between Catholicism and immigration, and this is only enhanced by new immigration, particularly from Latin America, which forms a cutting edge for change and renewal in North American Catholicism at this time. How North American Catholicism responds to the faith and practice of these new immigrants, and how they in turn react to that response, will have a significant effect on where Catholicism stands in North American society a century from now.

In some ways, noted for example by Martin Riesebrodt in his *Pious Passion* (1993), gender issues epitomize the current contrast within religious life between fundamentalist religion and that of the mainstream. In chapter 9 we do two things. First, we try to clarify and explain the emergence of fundamentalist and evangelical Christian bodies in the United States as apparent powerhouses of conservative political and social activism. Second, we also want to make clear that the fundamentalist impetus is a *global* phenomenon that extends beyond the boundaries of both the United States and Protestant Christianity. In this second section, we attempt to illustrate the usefulness of *globalization theory* for understanding the dynamics of religious change in our time and show simultaneously how sociological theory can provide a groundwork for concerted social action to develop a less hate-filled world. In doing so, we also want to illustrate how it is possible to move from a situational analysis based on participants to a global analysis based on more abstract generalizing concepts. Fundamentalism as a worldview or form of life is bound up with issues of class and power, strongly related to ethnicity, blended into a volatile brew that has within it the seeds for vicious conflict of earthshaking proportions.

There is no question in our minds that if the *changes* that have occurred in American religious life since the 1960s are to be understood, they must be seen in the light of the technological advances of our time, particularly the technologies of mass communication. This is not to say that these technologies *caused* specific changes, but rather that these technologies created an unstable groundwork upon which change was constructed and reconstructed as shifts occurred. The media of modern culture, in a society where free speech is a right guaranteed by the highest law in the land, create the basis for openness of religious (including antireligious) expressions of every variety, increasingly at a global level. At one level, religion may be said to be entirely communication. Although there is certainly a material culture of religion, one does not produce religion the way one produces iron ore or steel ingots or an automobile. One produces religion by communicating ideas. Freedom of religion depends on freedom of communication; hence when communications technologies change, religious expression also will change. This may be as simple as the use of microphones (with attendant possibilities for alterations in church architecture), or as complex as religious television networks, or as radical as Internet religions. But it is inconceivable that communications technology could change and religious life remain static. Through the study of the technologies of religious communications in our time, we may also see the development of new material cultures of religion and the reshaping of older ones.

This book closes with a chapter on issues of church and state and on the appearance of so-called new religions. Precisely because we have a state that simultaneously protects freedom of expression, including religious expression, and protects its citizens from the imposition of religion, there will be conflicts about how these dual dynamics can be integrated, hence numerous "boundary issues." At times of national unity—like the 1950s, with its dynamics of post–World War II unity on the one hand and anticommunism on the other—an apparent consensus may arise that will obscure the extent to which there has been perennial religious ferment in the United States since the earliest years of the republic—indeed, even before. The appearance, particularly in the 1970s, of what came to be called *new religions* struck many people in both academic and lay audiences somewhat by surprise—academicians because of a generalized belief in secularization theory, the larger population because they had entered into a "religion of America" that glossed denominational differences and disparaged religious enthusiasm. In reality, the new religions on the one hand testified to the vitality of the far deeper U.S. tradition of religious innovation, while on the other they heralded the coming of new Americans—immigrants—who had differing faith traditions from the Protestant-Catholic-Jew amalgam described by Will Herberg (1955) and epitomized by the label *Judeo-Christian*. We believe that the propensity for religious innovation in the United States will continue to encourage new religious movements to appear, that most of these will be both uncontroversial and short-lived, that these will take place within both the historic Judeo-Christian context and those non-Christian religions of newer immigrants as well as across the Judeo-Christian/non-Christian divide. We think that this will be a sign of health for the United States as a nation and a fertile field of endeavor for the sociology of religion.

Suggestions for Further Reading

Roberto Cipriani. 2000. *The Sociology of Religion: An Historical Introduction*. Hawthorne, N.Y.: Aldine de Gruyter.

Michele Dillon, ed. 2003. *Handbook of the Sociology of Religion*. New York: Cambridge University Press.

Émile Durkheim. 1994. *Durkheim on Religion*, ed. W. S. F. Pickering. Atlanta, Ga.: Scholars Press.

Richard K. Fenn, ed. 2001. *The Blackwell Companion to Sociology of Religion*. Oxford: Blackwell.

Arthur L. Greil and David G. Bromley, eds. 2003. *Defining Religion: Investigating the Boundaries Between the Sacred and Secular*. Amsterdam: JAI/Elsevier.

Karl Marx and Friedrich Engels. 1982. *On Religion*. Chico, Calif.: Scholars Press.

Georg Simmel. 1997. *Essays on Religion*. New Haven, Conn.: Yale University Press.

Rodney Stark. 2001. *One True God: Historical Consequences of Monotheism*. Princeton, N.J.: Princeton University Press.

Rodney Stark and Roger Finke. 2000. *Acts of Faith: Explaining the Human Side of Religion*. Berkeley: University of California Press.

William H. Swatos, Jr., with Peter Kivisto, Barbara J. Denison, and James McClenon, eds. 1998. *Encyclopedia of Religion and Society*. Walnut Creek, Calif.: AltaMira.

R. Stephen Warner. 2005. *A Church of Our Own: Disestablishment and Diversity in American Religion*. New Brunswick, N.J.: Rutgers University Press.

Max Weber. 1998. *The Protestant Ethic and the Spirit of Capitalism*, 2nd ed. Los Angeles: Roxbury.

Robert Wuthnow. 1992. *Rediscovering the Sacred: Perspectives on Religion in Contemporary Society*. Grand Rapids, Mich.: Eerdmans.

Phil Zuckerman. 2003. *Invitation to the Sociology of Religion*. New York: Routledge.

Photograph courtesy of William H. Swatos, Jr.

CHAPTER 2

Studying Religion

We want to differentiate the sociological approach to religion clearly from important philosophical questions. The existence of God, immortality, good and evil, and so on are vital issues for many people, but they are not central to the sociological enterprise. God may or may not exist. People believe differently about life after death. Ethical debates bring out the best and worst in human thought. Nevertheless, for the sociological study of religion what matters is not whether God exists or whether the soul is immortal or how evil comes to be defined, but the fact that people *act* on beliefs that God does or does not exist, that there is or is not life after death, that evil is or is not a real power operating in the world. This does not mean that sociologists of religion themselves have no personal religious convictions. Many of us do. But our interest in doing the sociology of religion is to see how people's beliefs work themselves out in relation to "lived experience"—that is, how we live our lives in this world.

How Do We Study Religion?

Sociologists use a variety of methods to study social action. Some are more suited to the study of religion than others. For example, it is hard to conceive many formal experiments that could be conducted with respect to religion. Some quasi experiments (partial experiments) are possible, however. Let's say a mass evangelistic crusade is being conducted in an area. It might be possible to pass out leaflets in one community near the crusade site but not in another, and then count attendance from each area; this would test the effectiveness of leafleting. Or a third community could be added where telephone calls were used instead of leaflets. If the communities could be determined to be similar in terms of such characteristics as race, age, education, and socioeconomic status, then this would serve as a possible experimental setting for assessing these different communications techniques. As another example, in a relatively large religious gathering where people were divided into small groups to discuss a controversial topic, some of the groups could be randomly designated to begin with prayer, while others were not. This would indicate whether prayer was an effective means of moderating conflict. Some religious people would be uncomfortable with such experimental structuring of religious life, however, and it is not clear that these kinds of questions are the most important to sociology of religion generally. Sociologists of religion have tended to use either some form of survey or a qualitative technique, such as interviews or participant observation, rather than experimental designs.

This raises, then, a second crucial point: namely, that decisions about what method(s) to use are best made in relation to the kinds of questions we want answered. Every sociological method has both limitations and promises for different kinds of inquiry; some methods are better suited than others to answer particular kinds of questions. Consider something like attendance: If you say you are "interested in studying church attendance," what is it precisely that you mean? Do you mean *how many* people attend a religious congregation across, say, a year? Do you mean what services attract the most people? Do you mean how attendance at worship has differed across time? Probably in all these cases you will want to use some form of *quantitative* data-gathering technique (that is, one that assesses and presents data primarily in numeric form). Or do you really mean you want to know *why* people attend religious worship or meetings? That kind of question is of quite a different character and is almost certain to require a *qualitative* technique (that is, one that presents data primarily in the form of narrative accounts).

Two subpoints here: first, it is essential to recognize that inferring "why?" answers from "how many?" data (or vice versa) is absolutely wrongheaded; second, to get at something approximating the truth, *both* kinds of data are necessary—that is, what we mean when we say "church attendance" probably includes elements of both "how many" and "why." Quantitative and qualitative research styles in themselves should be seen as primarily complementary rather than competitive. In order to determine most appropriately what kinds of methods we want to use, we need to ask ourselves not only "What kinds of data do we want?" but also "Why do we want them?"—that is, "What are we going to do with these data?" This latter question usually has either theoretical or practical aspects to it (and sometimes both), and we will turn to these issues later in the chapter.

Finally, before turning to specific methods, we need to say directly that research *costs*—time or money or both. No research simply happens. Hence, whatever research technique we are going to adopt is going to take time or money to execute. We may do it ourselves, hence it will be our own time, or we may hire someone else to do it, hence it will cost money. If it is our own time, however, there is also what economists formally term an *opportunity cost*, inasmuch as we could at least theoretically be doing something else that might bring direct financial benefit. Even using our own time there may be direct financial costs—for example, the printing of questionnaires for a survey. Thus, whether we are planning our own research or evaluating the work of others, we must ask where the money is going to come from to execute the work and how likely it is to be achieved. Because of the separation of church and state in the United States, in particular, the kinds of public research money that might be available to other sociological subdisciplines are not as likely to be directly available for religious research. Some private foundations, such as the Lilly Endowment, the Pew Charitable Trusts, and the John Templeton Foundation partially offset this loss, and not all projects involving religious research are absolutely excluded from public funding. One big gap in public information about religion in the United States, however, is created by the absence of questions about religion on the U.S. Census; Canada, which does include religion questions in its census, provides a helpful comparison case—although census data themselves must be very carefully interpreted. With this and the prior cautions in mind, we can now turn to principal research strategies in the sociology of religion.

SURVEY RESEARCH

A research strategy that has been used a great deal to study religion, particularly from the 1950s through the 1970s—and is still in use today, though with greater caution—is the survey. People are usually either given written questionnaires or interviewed orally for answers that will fit a fixed set of responses. It is, of course, possible to have more open-ended items using either a written or oral technique, but these are not the dominant mode in survey work.

Early research along this line often settled for simply asking people their religious preference and then relating this to a collection of other items on the interview schedule: presidential voting, socioeconomic status, sexual attitudes, racial attitudes, and so on. As time passed, sociologists became aware that religion is a multidimensional phenomenon, and that self-designated religious affiliation by itself is a relatively poor predictor of anything. Charles Glock and Rodney Stark's *Religion and Society in Tension* (1965), which revised and extended Glock's initial exploration of this approach (1962), was a pioneering effort in this respect. At the very least, one has to ask questions about how frequently the individual participates in the tradition with which she or he indicates affiliation. Yet even here, recent research by Kirk Hadaway, Penny Long Marler, and Mark Chaves (1993; cf. Chaves and Cavendish 1994; Hadaway, Marler, and Chaves 1998; Marler and Hadaway 1999; Marcum 1999; Hadaway and Marler 2005), who have actually counted people in churches over successive weekends, suggests that people *overreport* their religious participation in survey research. Questionnaires additionally may be influenced by class bias, as people who are not well educated may not be able to read and understand clearly the questions they are being asked or have sufficient information to make meaningful choices.

Surveys also often create false dichotomies, as diverse responses over a five- or seven-point scale are collapsed into a simple two-way split when the data are actually analyzed. Consider, for example, two contributions published in a single collection: From the National Opinion Research Center's General Social Survey (GSS) data collected during the 1980s, Phillip Hammond, Mark Shibley, and Peter Solow (1995) and John Simpson (1995) both use the same question relating to homosexual relations: "What about sexual relations between two adults of the same sex—do you think it is always wrong, almost always wrong, wrong

Producing the Sociology of Religion

The primary producers of the sociology of religion are academic researchers based at universities and seminaries. They may be located in the department of sociology or the department of religious studies. There are also independent scholars who have sustained a disciplined program of research and publication in the field through long careers, as well as researchers who work primarily in applied settings. These men and women communicate with each other primarily through a group of professional associations that hold annual meetings and through the journals that these associations produce.

Sociology of Religion: A Quarterly Review is the official journal of the Association for the Sociology of Religion (ASR). It is the only English-language journal devoted exclusively to the sociology of religion. *Sociology of Religion* began its career in 1940 as the *American Catholic Sociological Review* and moved gradually to an exclusive focus on the sociology of religion in the 1960s. From time to time issues of the journal are also published as freestanding volumes for larger circulation. The ASR also sponsors an annual topical series, *Religion and the Social Order*, and provides various forms of financial assistance for the pursuit and publication of research, particularly the Joseph H. Fichter Research Grants. The ASR meets annually in August at the same time and in the same city as the American Sociological Association (ASA). A major feature of the ASR meeting is the Paul Hanly Furfey Lecture, which is subsequently published in the journal. During the 1990s the ASA added a Section on the Sociology of Religion, which is now among the larger divisions of the association.

In the fall of each year, the Society for the Scientific Study of Religion (SSSR) and the Religious Research Association (RRA) meet together. These associations are interdisciplinary, but sociologists of religion predominate among their members. They publish, respectively, the *Journal for the Scientific Study of Religion* (JSSR) and the *Review of Religious Research* (RRR). Historically, the image of the SSSR has been that it is more academic in its focus, while the RRA is more oriented toward application. This can easily be overstated, yet it is true that historically the commitment of the RRA has been to highlight the contribution of research to the various religious communities. Both organizations formally celebrated their fiftieth anniversaries in 1999. They, too, offer support for research projects, and the RRA's H. Paul Douglass Lecture is a biennial feature at their meetings.

Sociologists of religion also publish their work in the major journals of sociology as a whole: the *American Sociological Review*, the official journal of the ASA; the *American Journal of Sociology*; and *Social Forces*. In addition, the American Academy of Religion (AAR) has a number of subgroups whose interests dovetail with those of sociologists of religion, not least the Section on Religion and the Social Sciences, and sociological articles can be found from time to time in the *Journal of the American Academy of Religion* and in such other interdisciplinary journals as *Religion* and the *Journal of Church and State*.

The major association for the sociology of religion outside the United States is the International Society for the Sociology of Religion (whose most usual acronym is SISR, from the French version of the society's name). The SISR has a cooperative relationship with the journal *Social Compass* and meets biennially at locations around the world. Its history in many ways parallels that of the ASR. Sociology of religion also maintains a presence at the quadrennial meetings of the International Sociological Association (ISA) through its Research Committee 22–Sociology of Religion (RC22). RC22 is one of the oldest of the ISA's constituent research committees. Issues of the ISA's principal journals, *International Sociology* and *Current Sociology*, have made major contributions to the sociology of religion on a recurring basis. Especially attractive to English-speaking sociologists of religion is the Sociology of Religion Study Group of the British Sociological Association. This group has a multiday meeting at a British university each spring, with additional single-day study days at other times of the year. It does not produce a journal, but selected presentations from each spring's meetings usually appear as commercially published books. Additional options for collegial meetings and for publication are available to those who are relatively fluent in other languages besides English, especially French, German, Italian, Japanese, and Spanish.

Most academic journals, association meeting programs, and newsletters are also available online as well as in print versions, either under their own auspices or through commercial vendors. Recently the *Interdisciplinary Journal of Research on Religion* has appeared as a journal published solely online (www.religjournal.com). It remains to be seen how much in the future online publication will replace the traditional print journal as a source for the dissemination of research results. Currently, however, the primary virtue of online services seems to be the reduction of libraries' storage space needs for back issues of journals.

Photograph courtesy of William H. Swatos, Jr.

only sometimes, or not wrong at all?" Hammond and colleagues interpret the responses of "always wrong" and "almost always wrong" to indicate "family values." Simpson, on the other hand, treats only the response of "always wrong" to indicate what he terms a "conservative" orientation. Our point here is not to determine which of these two articles is "correct" but instead to show how the data are mobilized and interpreted in the presentation of these authors' results—hence the role of the *researcher*, rather than the participants, in determining an assessment of the meaning of the data. Of course, with a data set like the GSS, it is possible for another trained researcher to reassess these results by recomputing them, either subtracting or adding, respectively, the "almost always wrong" component. Whether or not the general public is capable of performing these operations or grasping their significance is another question.

What is perhaps most important to understand about survey research strategies, however, as Ronald McAllister (1998: 417) points out, is that "[a]t the heart of them all is the asking and answering of questions." Whether a researcher is using a questionnaire she passes out or is doing telephone or face-to-face interviews from a schedule, the frame of likely or possible answers is always structured by the researcher. This methodological assumption presumes that the researcher understands sufficiently the action system under study to ask questions that are consonant with the meaning structures of the participant actors. If there is not a relatively close fit between the understandings of the researcher and the meanings of the participants, data can easily be misinterpreted. Because religions are systems of meaning and discourse, surveys in the sociology of religion must pay extremely close attention to these issues whenever the data being gathered extend beyond those of the simplest sort.

PARTICIPANT OBSERVATION

Increasingly, sociological research in religion is placing greater weight on forms of participant observation or field research, where researchers actually interact directly with subjects in their relevant life-worlds. Traditionally, participant observation has been faulted because there is the temptation on the part of the researcher to *go native*—that is, to identify with his or her subjects to the point at which he or she becomes a partisan on their behalf (occasionally the reverse takes place, but it is the same loss of research objectivity). Participant observation has other ethical considerations both during the research and afterward, since researchers are supposed to operate under the scientific equivalent of the "seal of the confessional": The privacy of those whom they see and hear during their research is inviolate. Field research also generally takes longer to complete while supplying data on a much narrower sample base. Someone who wants a quick answer to a concrete problem is not likely to want to have a researcher spend eighteen months in the field and six months analyzing the data. In addition, ethnographic research often suffers from the "N = 1 problem": Because most ethnographic work is usually limited to one, or at most two, research sites (for example, a single congregation or community), it is impossible in many instances to know whether or how a study's results may be generalized.

The great value of participant observation, on the other hand, is that it allows the participant actors a much larger role in shaping the meaning context of the data (assuming the researcher has the necessary skills to use the data in this way). In particular it has the advantage of letting the researcher see the religious

Researching on the Edge

In 1997, thirty-nine members of a group that called itself Heaven's Gate apparently willingly and calmly ate barbiturate-laced applesauce and pudding, thereby committing the largest mass suicide in U.S. history. The media were largely dumbstruck, but the existence of this group in one guise or another had been documented in academic journals and essay collections, even in *Psychology Today*, for more than a decade by sociologist of religion Robert W. Balch, a professor at the University of Montana. His work suddenly was on journalists' required reading lists.

In an interview with the *Chronicle of Higher Education* writer Scott Heller, Balch talked about how he became involved in this research:

> "[S]tumbling onto this U.F.O. cult pretty much reoriented my entire career." . . . [Balch] was a specialist in criminology when he first heard about the sect led by Marshall Herff Applewhite and Bonnie Lu Nettles, then known as "Bo and Peep" or "The Two." In 1975, Balch and a Montana graduate student traveled with believers from Arizona to California, where members of the group were to watch their leaders depart for the next world.
>
> "I wasn't thinking of sociology. . . . I was just interested in what would happen when they reached California and the prophecy didn't happen."
>
> Because members believed that attachments to mainstream society would keep them from the "transformation," Balch didn't identify himself as a sociologist. Instead, for two months, he posed as a new member, sleeping with the others in isolated campgrounds and depending on churches for money. If anyone asked, members said they were a Bible-study group on retreat.
>
> "The people we observed generally kept to themselves, devoting their energy to overcoming their 'humanness,' so most of the time we had little trouble taking part in the group without committing ourselves." Keeping track of what they saw was another matter. "We had to write our notes in bathroom stalls or get up before dawn when we could write while everyone else was still asleep."
>
> Mostly "spiritual seekers" who had experimented with a number of other alternative faiths, members of the group were not so different from the college students Balch taught. . . . "Under other circumstances I could have seen becoming friends with them. . . . That made it very stressful."
>
> His experience with the U.F.O. cult "was the only time I infiltrated a group," he says. "Even though I learned a lot that couldn't be learned any other way, I wouldn't do it again."

Source: Scott Heller, "Inside Heaven's Gate: A Sociologist Who Went Undercover," *Chronicle of Higher Education*, April 11, 1997, A10.

practice (or action) of participants, which is impossible to do with survey techniques, even if opportunity is given for open-ended response items.

Studies by Melinda Wagner (1990, 1997) and Susan Rose (1988) of independent Christian schools, for example, show that such putatively strict institutions as evangelical-fundamentalist schools and churches actually contain an array of cultural contradictions and patterns of accommodation that hardly conform to what might be a simplistic view of an outsider that all members of these groups believe the groups' official ideologies; studies of some new religious movements have shown the same kinds of results. Hence, a simple survey question such as "Do you send your child to a Christian school?" does not allow us to interpret a positive answer as a sign that the parent necessarily accepts the full theological system offered by that school. In fact, the same is probably true for all religions at all times and places. Anthony Blasi (1990: 151) has wisely noted that religious life has a tentative, fragile, casuistical character that can easily be misinterpreted—particularly by those who do not have any "insider" knowledge of a system they are studying but rather bring meaning prejudices from another system of action.

A series of major studies, for example *Habits of the Heart* by Robert Bellah and colleagues (1985; cf. Yamane 2007), *A Generation of Seekers: The Spiritual Journeys of the Baby Boom Generation* by Wade Clark Roof and colleagues (1993), and *The Next Wave: How Young Adults Are Shaping the Future of American Religion* by Robert Wuthnow (2007) have made an effort to combine survey research with in-depth interviews. While this strategy is not identical to extended participant observation, it is a worthwhile alternative that may be the best strategy for obtaining the most accurate information available. Much like the medical model of both running tests and actually looking at the patient and taking a careful history, this approach overcomes the small-sample limits of participant observation, but at the same time allows sufficient interaction between the researcher and the sample to ensure that the survey results are placed into the proper meaning context and interpreted as closely as possible to the intention of the subjects who responded to the item.

HISTORICAL RESEARCH

Yet another research strategy with a distinguished pedigree in the sociology of religion—certainly reaching back to the discipline's founders—is historical research. Here we mine existing historical records for clues about social life at other times and places in order to learn more about human behavior in a *comparative* perspective; hence we speak of comparative-historical sociology. Historical research is an especially challenging field of research, but it also can be misleading, since we are unable to control the situations under which data are gathered. We have to test our data with special care and recognize the possibility that historians and others who have gathered data for us have worked with diverse ends in mind. In addition, since religion is a system of meaning and discourse, we need to recognize that meanings of words change over time. Hence even a fairly rigid historical approach—such as content analysis, where words are counted rather than simply interpreted—must be treated with care, lest it be assumed that a twenty-first-century meaning of a word or phrase is identical to that of, say, the sixteenth century. Even in a much shorter time frame, for example, a word can be used quite differently across traditions. The label *modernist*, for example, meant one thing for Roman Catholics at the turn of the twentieth century, quite another for U.S. Protestants in the 1910s and 1920s. Nevertheless, absent a comparative-historical approach it is quite difficult to assess the significance of data in our own day. Roger Finke and Rodney Stark's *The Churching of America, 1776–2005* (2005) and Stark's *Cities of God: The Real Story of How Christianity Became an Urban Movement and Conquered Rome* (2006) are particularly significant recent works grounded in the historical approach. These books use primarily quantitative data from the past, interpreted in conjunction with geographical circumstances and such specific events as wars, famines, and technological changes to provide sociological accounts of major historical change. In an essay on the concept of secularization, however, Stark (2000) has also shown how concepts created by historians (for example, a European "Age of Faith") can be too quickly taken at face value with detrimental results. Hence it is important that sociologists of religion revisit the data of history and not simply endorse synthetic concepts from other disciplines.

Theory in the Study of Religion

A theory is an explanation—or at least an attempt at an explanation—of how and why things have come to be as they are (the goal of *understanding*). As Peter Berger has pointed out, "the interest of the sociologist is primarily theoretical" (1963: 17). We don't actually get around to doing sociology until we start explaining whatever data we have found, regardless of how we have obtained them. Gathering statistics or conducting interviews or doing participant observation is not sociology; we start doing social science when we explain why the results we have found are as they are.

Ideally theories also ought to enable us to say, "Well if this is how and why things have come to be as they are, then if certain variables are altered one way or the other, this outcome ought to result" (the goal of *prediction*). Social scientific theories tend to be better in meeting the goal of understanding than they are the goal of prediction, primarily because there are so many confounding variables that impinge across time. Theories, however, also carry interpretive frameworks. That is, in addition to addressing specific means-end questions, they provide a more general perspective on the world or some major sector of it. For example, gene theory not only deals with the relationship of a particular gene to a particular body part, but also makes a more general assertion about the *cause* of why we are as we are. At an extreme this may be phrased as "It's all genetics"—meaning that gene theory can explain the human condition on a broad plane.

FUNCTIONALIST THEORIES

From the 1950s to the 1970s functionalism was the dominant theoretical perspective in the sociology of religion. As a general theoretical approach functionalism "explains the existence of social institutions such as religion in terms of the needs that the institutions would meet" in society (Blasi 1998: 193). Although functionalism had several variants, the main line of approach derived from an attempt by Harvard sociologist Talcott Parsons (1937) to synthesize the work of Durkheim and Weber. Particularly important in this strategy was the use of the Durkheimian definition that we quoted earlier. Society was interpreted primarily through the biological model, or "organismic" analogy of the body, wherein all the parts work together to maintain the equilibrium of the whole. Religion was understood to be the glue that held society together; it provided the basis for social solidarity. At first blush, this view would seem to give religion, hence the sociology of religion, enormous importance, and indeed, within the interests of Parsons himself this was true. More generally, however, this was not the case. Because the Durkheimian definition did not fit modern circumstances, it quickly became apparent to many observers that what was called religion in modern society (that is, the religions that constituted organized religion) was not functioning in this way.

Two reactions occurred: On the one hand there was a "doom-and-gloom" school that saw the supposed declining influence of religion, family instability, and increasing crime rates as evidence that our society was headed into sociomoral chaos. There were cases in which this was taken to mean a larger role for government, or "the state," to replace these institutional functions. For some religious people, furthermore, the doom-and-gloom analysis was also actually appealing, as it seemed consistent with end-of-the-world predictions. A relatively early example of these was probably evangelical popularizer Hal Lindsey's *The Late Great Planet Earth* (1970). A lighter version of the message is provided by the *Left Behind* book series, which we discuss in greater detail in chapter 10.

On the other hand, particularly within the social sciences themselves, there began a search for the "real religion" of society. Since the manifest religions didn't seem to fulfill the Durkheimian definition of religion, then obviously something else must be the "real religion" of society. This effort turned the Durkheimian definition into a Procrustean bed, while at the same time it virtually ignored the persistence of the manifest religions in society.

Functionalist theory spawned directly or indirectly a number of middle-range theories. Deprivation theory, now largely discredited on the basis of empirical research, claimed that religion met needs—economic, social, political, educational—of deprived people; religion, in other words, was a way in which people who didn't have it quite all together adjusted to life. The roots of deprivation theory are in Charles Glock's writing on religious movements (1964; also, Glock and Stark 1965; Glock, Ringer, and Babbie 1967), but he later became convinced that this approach had been tried and found wanting (1985). This was a microfunctionalist theory, relating to the individual, but it also harked back to Marx's "opium of the people" dictum (Beckford 1991). Church-sect theory, which will be discussed in more detail in chapter 4, is a conceptual model for religious organizational change. Rooted in the work of Weber, yet also introduced in this country with Marxian overtones in an adaptation by H. Richard Niebuhr, the predominant use of church-sect theory was to show how radical, or deviant, religious organizations gradually accommodated themselves to the dominant society—that is, restored the social equilibrium and maintained social solidarity. Civil religion was reintroduced into social science through an enormously influential essay by Parsons's student Robert Bellah (1967); this concept and the literature surrounding it, discussed in greater detail in chapter 3, attempted to show that there was a "transcendent religion of the nation" in America that overarched and was separate from the religions of the United States. Ironically, even secularization theory had functionalist roots, as Parsons (1960, 1963) attempted to demonstrate how the Judeo-Christian ethic had so penetrated the United States through its Protestant heritage as to make society itself the bearer of that heritage.

CONFLICT THEORIES

In sociology as a whole, functionalism was dealt a major blow in the Vietnam War era by a Marxist-inspired conflict theory. Because of the Marxist critique of religion, however, this approach never generated a theoretical school of any significance in the sociology of religion. Tangential, but important, aspects of its influence may be seen in studies of liberation theology (or the "preferential option for the poor"), particularly in Latin America, and in feminist theory, which at least in one of its variants sees women as a class oppressed by men as a class, with religious institutions being no less influenced by this tendency than any others. Whereas functionalism used the organismic analogy as its fundamental metaphor, conflict theory takes from physics the dynamic tension created by forces in opposition to each other, much the way the architectural device of the flying buttress is used to support the walls of great cathedrals. While one might think this analogy, too, could produce positive outcomes for the study of religion, the politics of "world Communism" versus capitalism ensured that this was not the case, inasmuch as the theoretical potential of conflict theory became overwhelmed by both real and imagined conflicts of the superpowers.

Another important, less ideological variant of conflict theory, ultimately more relevant to the study of religion, derives from the work of the anthropologist Victor Turner (1974). His work centers on the concept of *social drama*. Social dramas are units of aharmonic processes that arise in conflict situations and represent the time axes of fields—in other words, people act out their disagreements. A field is composed of the individuals, or actors, directly involved in the social processes under examination. Typically these show a regularly recurring processual form or "diachronic profile"—that is, they go back and forth over time—and follow an observable pattern of four phases (see Turner 1974: 37–44). Although not identical, Turner's notion of field can be constructively related to that of Pierre Bourdieu, who writes that any field "presents itself as a structure of probabilities—of rewards, gains, profits, or sanctions—but always implies a measure of indeterminacy. . . . Even in the universe par excellence of rules and regulations, playing with the rule is part and parcel of the rule of the game" (Bourdieu and Wacquant 1992: 18).

Breach is the first of Turner's four phases. A breach occurs in regular norm-governed social relationships between persons or groups within the same social system. People come into conflict on an issue or over a behavior and have what we might call a "falling out." A case can be made that breaches are the inherent dynamic of all sociocultural change that does not result preeminently from external causes—that is, war, earthquake, plague, pestilence, or famine. Hence, Turner's conflict theory is especially well suited to the study of religious change. Most new religious movements throughout history, for example, have resulted from breaches—where different opinions *within* an existing religious pattern have led to breached relationships that have not been accommodated by adjustments within the existing pattern. Unaccommodated breaches can result in the starting of new congregations or even mass movements, such as the Protestant Reformation.

The second step in the drama is that a period of mounting crisis or escalation follows the breach, unless the conflict can be sealed off quickly. Here the effects may extend to the limits of the parties involved. This second stage is always one of those turning points, when a true state of affairs is revealed and hitherto covert and private factional intrigue is exposed—when, in Turner's words, "it is least easy to don masks or pretend that there is nothing rotten in the village" (1974: 39). The involvement of external actors may serve either to slow or to heighten these processes, hence smoothing over or exacerbating the crisis. Turner calls the external system of action the *arena*. It is "the social and cultural space around those who are directly involved with the field participants but are not themselves directly implicated in the processes that define the field" (Swartz 1968: 11; see Turner 1985: 84). The arena is characteristically the group's culture, but also includes territorial and political organization. The ordination of gays and lesbians as ministers of religion, for example, is more readily accepted in those religious groups whose members participate in upper-middle-class liberal sociopolitical and socioeconomic culture of the West than it is among the working class or among African religious elites.

The third stage of the drama takes place as adjustive and redressive action is brought into operation by leading members of the social group. Depending on how this works, a fourth stage will ultimately occur in one of two directions—either the reintegration of the disturbed social group or the social recognition of an irreparable breach or schism. For Turner, this is the moment for an observer to compare relations that preceded the social drama with those following the redressive phase. The scope, range, or structure of the field will have altered. Yet, through all the changes—some crucial, others seemingly less so—certain norms and relations will persist. In Bourdieu's terms, this represents the role of *habitus*—a "strategy generating principle" that permits social actors "to cope with unseen and ever changing situations . . . a system of lasting and transposable dispositions which, integrating past experiences, functions at every moment as a matrix of perceptions, appreciations and actions and makes possible the achievement of infinitely diversified tasks" (Bourdieu and Wacquant 1992: 18). Turner's best-known application of his theory is to the African Ndembu (1967), but in other essays he has applied it to varied cases, both historical and contemporary.

A PARADIGM SHIFT

Although conflict theory presents a valuable alternative to functionalism for modeling actual social relations, it was not conflict theory but secularization theory that began to sound the death knell for functionalism within the sociology of religion. In a seminal article published in 1993, R. Stephen Warner demonstrates that a "new paradigm" (or new theoretical approach) has emerged in the sociology of religion. The core difference within the new paradigm is a movement away from seeing religion as derivative of something else, as it was in functionalism and its many variants, including secularization theory. New paradigm sociology of religion takes religion as real or as an independent variable—that is, as much a part of human behavioral dispositions as any other system of action. By raising serious questions about the relationship between what people called religion and the putative societal "needs" that functionalist theorists claimed religions should be meeting, new paradigm theorists highlighted a crucial disjuncture between practice and theory in the sociology of religion. Yet the mortal blow to macrostructural models was actually dealt by a series of small daggers via the appearance of new religious movements (NRMs) both as separate organizations (for example, the Unification Church, as in the research of Barker [1984]; Bromley and Shupe [1979a]) and within the dominant traditions themselves (such as the charismatic movement in Roman Catholicism, as illustrated in the research accounts of McGuire [1982] and Neitz [1987]). From time to time NRM research is criticized because so much energy has been invested in studying and writing about groups that have attracted only an infinitesimally small proportion of the population into their membership. Two or three books may be available on a group that never had more than a few hundred members or lasted more than a decade, while there is a dearth of information on a century-old denomination of four hundred thousand members. But this misses the point of the theoretical significance of NRM studies to the sociology of religion. The NRMs proved that the religious impulse in American society was strong and vital, ready to bubble up at any stimulation. Stark and colleagues refer to this tendency as the "limits to secularization" (see Stark and Bainbridge 1980b, 1985, 1996). NRMs also proved that the Durkheimian definition simply didn't work in contemporary society. Thus, NRMs forced the breaking of entirely new theoretical ground in the sociology of religion.

RATIONAL CHOICE THEORIES

Although Warner makes clear that new paradigm theory in sociology has several variants (for example, a Geertzian one emphasized in the work of Nancy Ammerman [1997a, 1997b] and Mary Jo Neitz [2000]), it has largely come to be associated with rational choice theory (see Young 1997), though some among the proponents of even this approach reject this specific title. Rational choice theory is preeminently associated with the names of Rodney Stark, Roger Finke, Laurence Iannaccone, and William Sims Bainbridge (see Bainbridge 1997; Bainbridge and Stark 1984; Iannaccone 1992, 1994, 1995, 1997; Stark 1996, 1998). The rational choice approach finds its origins in the classical economic theory of Adam Smith and other figures of the eighteenth-century Scottish Enlightenment (see Iannaccone 1991), and Gordon Marshall (1982) also shows that the work of

Max Weber was as much, if not more, in dialogue with the "ghosts" of these men than with the ghost of Karl Marx, as an earlier generation of commentators said of Weber's work. A major proponent of this broader perspective among sociologists in the United States in the guise of exchange theory was Parsons's Harvard colleague and critic George C. Homans (1958, 1974). Also influential is University of Chicago economist and Nobel laureate Gary Becker (1976).

At the core of rational choice theory is a view of the human being as a "rational" actor, making choices that she or he thinks best, calculating costs and benefits. This model is sometimes referred to by the Latin phrase *homo economicus*. The core proposition of this theoretical orientation is that religious choice making (or religious action) does not differ significantly as a *process* from other forms of choice making—that is, that the decision-making processes that people use in their religious or spiritual lives are not different from the processes that they use to buy a car, contract a marriage, take a vacation, or choose a college or a career. What this means, sociologically speaking, is that religion is not inherently more or less serious than other spheres of human endeavor, except as it is perceived to be by participant actors. Over against the Durkheimian model, rational choice theory insists that collective *action* is always the action of collected *actors*. One simply cannot have collective action without specific individual actors. This is not psychological reductionism but straightforward noncontradiction. As I. M. Lewis (1986: 8) rightly notes, "Whatever Durkheim may have said, the people we study are *not* robots. . . . Excessive preoccupation with the so-called theoretical models," may conceal a "lack of originality and the contrasting richness of the peoples we study." If this becomes the case, "it is *we*, not *they*, who are the puppets." Bainbridge (1985) defends the individualism of this theoretical approach as part of a more general preference for theories that embrace methodological individualism and reject actions among structures (and other "scientific" abstractions).

A couple of caveats about what the rational choice perspective does *not* say may be helpful.

The word *rational* is used in different ways. In philosophy, the rational side of human life is often posited over against the emotional side. This is not the use here. Emotional decision making is also a part of the rational choice model. Let's say that you are shopping for a car and decide to buy the red one because you like the way it looks. The philosophical rationalist would say, "That's not a rational decision." For rational choice theory, it is: You are getting a *reward*, because the red car apparently will make you happier. Of course, later you may realize you made a bad or silly decision. That's not the point. The point is that you did think about the decision and decided to go with color as your ultimate criterion. Someone else may buy a car of a color she admits she does not like, because she got a great price on the car. Her action is also rational. Yet a third person may buy a car that is neither a color he likes nor sold at a particularly good price, because he believes the car will perform with such excellence that these other criteria are mere distractions. This, too, is a rational decision. See how complex this makes the matter of understanding decisions? Rational choice theory says the same kinds of processes occur in religious decision making—one person may join a church, say, for the wonderful music, another for the fellowship of the people involved, another may want to avoid going to hell, another finds the preaching style intellectually challenging, and so on. In rational choice theory, all of these decisions are rational in the sense that they are centered on the satisfaction of wants.

Because it is the case that there are, as Max Weber would put it, "multiple and competing rationales for action," rational choice theory does not detract from those theoretical contributions of people, such as Geertz (1983) and Turner (1974), who wish to emphasize "local knowledge" or "social drama." If it were the case that for any decision there was only one "rational" choice, then of course rational choice theory might succumb to the provocative, but ultimately misplaced, critique that where rational choice theory is right, it is obvious, and where it is not obvious, it is wrong. Because actors are almost always in multiple situations simultaneously, the choice-making process is never simple. There are likely to be both conflicts and circumstantial idiosyncrasies that must be unpacked with the greatest of care. Thus rational choice theory is a general theory of action that in application begs for specificity; indeed, the more one commits to the new paradigm, the greater the need for what Geertz calls "thick description" (1973: 3–30) in order to lay bare the multilayered meaning complexes that intersect in religious decision making.

Rational choice theory is at the same time morally neutral. That is, in themselves there are no good or bad decisions. People may subsequently come to regret decisions they have made, but these subsequent regrets have no influence on the decision. They can't. They come *after* the decision, and basic logic teaches us that temporal priority cannot be laid aside. You may say, "But there are people who make the same dumb decision over and over again." Yes, there are; that may mean they have not learned anything from the experience (that is, it is they who are dumb, not the decisions). But it also may mean that it is simply easier (less costly) for them at the time of decision making to make the same decision even though it will cost them more in the end. For example, someone may take a longer route to school or work even though she knows there's a shorter route, simply because it takes less mental energy to follow the accustomed path than it does to take the new one. The recidivist alcoholic who takes "just one more" drink simply may find that action the least costly way of dealing with a problem situation: It is the most familiar. People may continue to go to an Episcopal church even though they are unhappy with it rather than going through the effort it would take for them to become Roman Catholic or Greek Orthodox. This also explains why, when people do switch denominational affiliations, they routinely elect designations that are not too distant culturally from the ones that they held previously (see Hadaway and Marler 1993; more generally, Greeley 1989; Iannaccone 1990).

No decision *is* a decision. This probably is the most paradoxical truth of "choice" theory, but it is certainly true nonetheless. If you can't decide whether to have a hamburger or pizza for dinner to the point that you have no dinner, then you have had no dinner. That decision will have consequences for you. If you can't decide whether to do a written or oral report in a course that gives you a choice, and you do neither, you will probably earn an F. If you can't decide which girl or guy to date, you may end up sitting in your room alone. The examples run on and on, and they are all true. A decision not to affiliate with any religion means that you are religiously nonaffiliated. We live in a choice-making world where not choosing is choosing.

It would be far too complex here to try to outline how all of this applies to religion. In their primary theoretical manifesto, *A Theory of Religion* (1996), for example, Stark and Bainbridge list seven basic axioms from which hundreds of actual propositions flow for understanding religion, let alone the nuances of those as applied to specific cases (see Stark 1999 for a modification of this theory). We can mention a few possibilities: In "Why Strict Churches Are Strong," for example, Iannaccone (1994) shows that there is a general principle of investment that says that the more people invest in something, the harder they will work to protect their investment. If a person buys a new, fairly expensive car, he or she is likely to be out polishing it when it doesn't even need it (or hiring someone else to do the same); if the same person buys a junker that's already banged up, the only water it's likely to see is the rain. Applied to religion, this says that if people become convinced that a strict church offers them the true path to eternal bliss, and they have to go through a lot (which may mean give up a lot) to get into that church, they are more likely to work a lot harder for that church. In other words, once we become convinced that demands are legitimate, the more demands placed upon us to achieve our goals, the more we'll try to meet. Someone who buys an expensive car usually will spend more in upkeep for that car. Someone who goes to a doctor and doesn't get well goes back to the same doctor. Some students are proud that they are attending a "hard" school or taking a "hard" course.

As another example, it is said that as people get older, they become more religious. Research, however, shows that this needs to be qualified: As *religious* people get older, they become more religious. Nonreligious people seldom convert in old age and may actually become more religiously resistant. Rational choice explains this easily: The more people have invested in something, the more they invest, particularly if they think it pays a good return. Just as older people who have individual retirement accounts (IRAs) are likely simultaneously to draw from them and return money to other instruments available from the IRA provider, so religious people draw more from their religious institution while they also give more to it. Nonreligious people, having made no investment, find altering their life pattern only that much more difficult as they age, while learning a new religious pattern may seem bewildering, hence costly. It is unlikely that people who have not thought religion offered benefits throughout their lives would suddenly adopt an entirely different worldview. An analogue may be found in the movement of people to retirement settings: The people who are happiest when they move to a retirement setting are people who have moved around all their lives; those who are most miserable are those who have lived the bulk of their lives in one place.

At the same time, we should not assume that simply because strict churches are apparently stronger than lax churches, all members of strict churches observe their churches' disciplines strictly. As we mentioned earlier, Melinda Wagner (1990, 1997) and Susan Rose (1988) have each shown that there is an array of cultural contradictions and patterns of accommodation manifested within putatively strict evangelical Christian institutions, such as schools and churches (see also Gallagher and Smith 1999). People may admire a strict religion because they think that's what religion ought to be like, even though they are not entirely prepared to conform to those norms in their own lives. That is, some people consider religion an "institution of oughts," as a result of which they expect a church or denomination to articulate high standards—even if these same people cannot themselves attain them. People in effect pay the religious institution to symbolize an ideal realm of transcendent beliefs and moral practices (see Tamney and Johnson 1998). They may send their children to religious schools not because of particular religious doctrines but because they feel that their children are safer there or that the most crucial aspects of formal education (the "three Rs") are best taught there.

The "strictness" principle does not hold universally, however. Some people are proud of the fact that they attend an "easy" college or have found an "easy" course—and yet become alumni who donate a lot of money to the school. Similarly, some people are drawn to low-demand religions, yet nevertheless are faithful participants and generous contributors. The advantage of the strictness thesis is not that it applies in all cases, because it clearly does not (see Ellison and Sherkat 1995), but rather that it makes actions that seem senseless to outsiders actually reasonable. And this is precisely what good theory is supposed to do: provide an integrated system of propositions that makes understandable (or explains) behaviors that superficially seem to make no sense. Good social scientific theory provides a reasonable, consistent answer to the question: Why would anybody want to do that?

What this means, in part, is that religious motivation comes from diverse sources that lie in individuals' unique biographies. We can certainly talk about types of people, hence creating some abilities at prediction, but we can never assume that two people in the same setting will interpret the actions and claims around them in the same way. Indeed, in terms of Western worship at least, one of the primary values of the sermon is to create a common interpretative context for the congregation; yet even this may fail, as different people get different things out of it.

Rational choice theory has not been without its critics. Principal among these are Roy Wallis (Wallis and Bruce 1984), Steve Bruce (1999), Mark Chaves (1995; Chaves and Gorski 2001), and Jim Spickard (1998). Others aspire to revise and amend rational choice theory to render it more sociologically realistic by insisting that the embeddedness of institutional practice be recognized. They are led by Christopher Ellison, Darren Sherkat, and their colleagues (Ellison 1995; Ellison and Sherkat 1995; Sherkat 1997; Sherkat and Cunningham 1998; Sherkat and Wilson 1995). Cultural, socioeconomic, gender, and other sociological factors play an especially significant role in focusing the lenses through which we perceive religious experience. Nevertheless, in its broad outlines, the rational choice perspective provides a dynamic new theoretical kit for disassembling the parts that make up our religious life.

But that life is more complicated than the theory sometimes admits. Religion is a social institution marked by distinctive features of its social context. These features, in addition, persist beyond the lifetimes of those persons who are alive at the moment of their development. Religion is carried over space and through time by societies. Indeed, the special advantage of societies is that the precipitating conditions for social innovation need not be replicated in every generation. In many locales, religion comes to permeate the cultural atmosphere. In the traditions of these places, one no more chooses religion to play a role in one's life than one chooses to initiate each breath that one takes. As the historian Oscar Handlin described religious membership among European immigrants to the United States, "the Church gave no reason for being; it was. Its communicants were within it not because they had rationally accepted its doctrines; they had faith because they were in it" (1951: 119).

In their own defense, Stark and Bainbridge contend that their propositions "deal with religious commitment in a way that is neither more reductionistic nor less comprehensive than previous treatments" (1996: 52). Perhaps this is so, but theirs is a response based on distinctions of degree and not ones of kind. Religion in *A Theory of Religion* is something whose power arises not from what Peter Berger (1967) would call its "facticity," but rather from the common neediness of those who resort to it. Thus, if rational choice theory is any kinder to religion than was old-time functionalism, it is because the theory harbors a less lofty view of the human being's state in the world, not because it possesses any superior measure of respect for its subject.

In a similar vein, Roy Wallis and Steve Bruce detected in the Stark-Bainbridge theory an "assumption that there is something inherently faulty or unsatisfactory in religion, that it could never be desired except as compensation for something better" (1984: 14). Now, they continue:

> Having a friend in Jesus is a great solace for the lonely, just as the promise of post-millennial power is a welcome hope for those who suffer deprivation and stigma in the pre-millennial world. But to admit that religion may provide compensation for failure to secure [a] present tangible reward is not to advance a theory *of* religion, only a theory *about* what religion is or does for some people. (1984: 18)

Religious faith is not easily comprehended, to be sure, but that is not to say that those who embrace it have accommodated themselves to, or have settled for, an inferior brand of ideology.

All the same, ambivalence once again intervenes. One is under no obligation to conclude, as Bainbridge and Stark accused their first critics of having done, "that a whole theoretical approach is doomed to failure if some of the concepts introduced quickly in early publications seem incomplete." A conscientious reader would agree with them that "the construction of rigorous, deductive-empirical explanatory theory is a big job, requiring the work of many minds over several years. And the final outcome of the war cannot be judged on the basis of whether the first bugle plays exactly in tune" (1984: 146). This is fair enough. Even if one pronounces Stark and Bainbridge's call to arms far off-key, one should wait and keep listening. Certainly more voices (if not bugles) should be heard on these issues. If rational choice theory is reductionist, Stark and his colleagues are making the most of it. They are testing the boundaries of what can be accomplished with a very determined application of a single, explicit approach. Their theory, as Martin E. Marty noted in a review of *The Future of Religion* (Stark and Bainbridge 1985), "can be stretched to suit all purposes. . . . Yet, the 'compensation' theory does plausibly stretch far" (Marty 1986b: 208).

Thus a final caveat: Students of any sociology (sociology of religion or sociology of the railroad) need to be constantly aware of the levels of analysis problem—namely, that sociology works with aggregate or group data. Sociological predictions tell what *types* of people are more or less likely to engage in different *types* of activities successfully or unsuccessfully. This means that sociology can never predict the specific action patterns of specific individuals. Sociologists can say what the probability is that students of one or another social background are more or less likely to succeed in college or to engage in lives of crime or to establish successful marriages or to adopt a particular religious lifestyle. They cannot say this about any specific individual. This is no different from a pharmaceutical company being able to say that a particular drug is successful in treating a set of symptoms 80 percent of the time. A medical doctor will then have to decide whether to use this drug in the treatment of a specific patient. That decision will be based on other aspects of the patient's history, other medications the patient must take, and the probable outcomes of not using the drug or using the drug unsuccessfully—and some room may have to be made, as well, for simple trial and error. Failure to apply the appropriate level of analysis is one of the most frequent sources for misunderstanding sociological data and theories.

Sociologie Religieuse

Although "the interest of the sociologist is primarily theoretical" (P. Berger 1963: 17), we would be remiss if we did not point out that there is also an applied tradition in the sociology of religion, often known by its French title *sociologie religieuse*. (*Sociologie religieuse* literally translates as "religious sociology," but that phrase has come to have different connotations in Anglo-American sociology.) More the practice of geography than sociology, French *sociologie religieuse*, associated with such figures as Gabriel Le Bras (1955, 1956) and Fernand Boulard (1960), was typified by the meticulous tabulation of statistics on ecclesiastical activities such as baptisms and church marriages across decades and even centuries. Painstakingly mapped over parishes, localities, and regions, these figures revealed a historical portrait of striking religious change.

In the United States, applied sociology of religion dates from the very beginnings of sociology in this country, though it took a quantum leap forward with the work of H. Paul Douglass and the Institute of Social and Religious Research that began in the 1920s. This institute came eventually to amass thousands of studies of individual Protestant congregations and regional units, many of which are now available on microform (Brewer and Johnson 1972, 1979; Research Publications

1975). On the Catholic side, a Harvard-educated Jesuit, Joseph H. Fichter (1951, 1954), beginning in the 1950s, extended and improved the French style of research through comprehensive studies of parish life.

Applied sociology of religion continues to be a major professional domain of sociologists of religion. Most of this work is done under the aegis of religious organizations themselves, either directly by in-house staffs or indirectly by paid independent consultants. Much of this work is of a practical nature. Some is entirely atheoretical, but most is simply seeking more immediate kinds of explanations than grand models like functionalism or rational choice theory provide. If a religious denomination wants to know what kinds of individuals assigned as pastors to new churches bring about the greatest numerical growth in congregation size, it can attempt to do research on the already existing congregations that have had this experience (the previous cohort of newly founded churches). The organization really doesn't have to care about more expansive questions of social solidarity or cost-benefit decision making. They can, in effect, assume either of these underlying models and still place the most effective person in the position, if on the one hand they can generate accurate data, and on the other the context of church growth has not significantly altered over the time between the prior new church founding and the present. (Examples of present-day research studies that are most useful to churches in their planning and programs are Bibby [1995]; Chaves and Miller [1999]; Hadaway and Roozen [1995]; Hoge, McNamara, et al. [1997]; Roozen and Hadaway [1993]; Roozen and Nieman [2005].)

A real-world case study may also help illustrate both how *sociologie religieuse* can help in problem definition and how theory can expand upon that foundation: Local Episcopalians with a chaplaincy at a large south-central U.S. state university were disappointed in their program and were seeking a new chaplain to do innovative things. They complained that average attendance at their worship activities was only eight people, whereas the Roman Catholics, who shared a common chapel building, had more than one hundred—enough to stream out of the chapel into the facility's common room. When queried, however, the Episcopalians indicated that thirty-two students on campus had been identified as Episcopalian; when queried further, they indicated that about four thousand students were Roman Catholic. By attendance rate the Episcopalians were doing *ten times better* than the Roman Catholics! They could further have learned that hardly any denomination has a weekly average rate exceeding 50 percent of its membership, and that high school and college students are among the least frequent attendees at services (though those few who do attend are often among the most active). A rational choice approach could complement these *sociologie religieuse* data by indicating the kinds of factors that keep college-student attendance rates down on the one hand, hence, on the other, why those who deviate from the norm tend to be relatively highly committed. This same approach would also indicate that caution should be used in extrapolating data from currently active youth and young adults to future denominational congregants. That is, what young people want in the denomination today may not be what the broad spectrum of potential congregants twenty years from now will be looking for. Denominational planning based on current youths' desires may be inadequately sensitive to the strictness effects of the deviant commitment that is associated with high-level youth activism.

Religious organizations, like all other organizations, need accurate data on which to base their organizational decisions. These decisions, just like decisions made by individuals, will follow rational choice principles; that is, an official or some official body will decide what is best for the group. That decision may or may not prove to be a wise one over time; it may or may not be regretted. We cannot assume that a rational decision made at one point in an organization's development will necessarily seem good at another point. What we should be able to do, however, by understanding the choice-making process, is see how an organization got from one point to another in its development, hence be better equipped intellectually to modify a particular course of action.

Why Study Religion?

You may have had any number of reasons for taking a course in the sociology of religion: personal curiosity, course requirements, professorial popularity, scheduling ease. Rational choice theory would accept the legitimacy of any of these. From a broader perspective, however, other reasons make the study of religion as important today as it has ever been.

Although the social scientific study of religion was somewhat marginalized from the mid-1960s to the mid-1970s, a sea change began in 1979, as sociologist of religion N. J. Demerath III has pointed out (1994). That year recorded:

- the "mass suicides" of more than 900 people in Jonestown, Guyana, that focused attention on the "cult" phenomenon
- the high-gear mobilization of the Reverend Jerry Falwell's Moral Majority as a part of the 1980 presidential campaign of Ronald Reagan, which began the appearance of the Christian Right as a significant force in political discourse in the United States
- the election of Pope John Paul II and his internationalization of the papacy through visits to both Latin America and especially his native Poland—the first real entry of the papacy into then Soviet-controlled territory
- the rise of the Ayatollah Khomeini to power in Iran and the taking of American hostages in the U.S. embassy there

The Iranian situation and all that followed in its wake throughout the Middle East are of signal importance because it so visibly and directly confronted the reigning secular worldview of Western political science.

By 1994, for example, David L. Miller of Syracuse University, at the time of his nomination for the presidency of the American Academy of Religion, could observe that "eighty-percent of organized terror and violence [throughout the world] is being performed in the name of some religious (or putatively religious) ideology or myth, some religiosity or theologism. . . . [R]eligion is now a force in the world, in ways not predicted, and in some cases not welcomed" (1994).

Religion as a Site

In the course of her year as chair of the American Sociological Association Section on the Sociology of Religion, Mary Jo Neitz, professor of sociology at the University of Missouri, Columbia, wrote a column for the section's newsletter in which she described some of the processes that brought her to the study of the sociology of religion. Because they are particularly rooted in the work of Geertz, this seemed to be a good place to share them with you.

> I came to study religion incidentally, because it was a site for looking at something else. In an introductory sociology course I was teaching, I encountered born-again Catholics who claimed that all mental illness was caused by the devil (not a theory present in the discussion in our textbook), and I thought it would be an interesting context for looking at how people come to develop particular worldviews. For myself and many others at that time, religion—often in a new form, one of the new religious movements or charismatic forms within the older denominations—caught our attention: we saw sites for looking at social processes and organizational dynamics in which we had ongoing theoretical interests.
>
> ### THE CULTURAL TURN
>
> For some of us, this was facilitated by the advent of new cultural approaches in sociology. Clifford Geertz's work, for example, not only proposed a frame for seeing religion as a cultural system, but perhaps more important, Geertz revealed how the analysis of popular expressive forms could be as significant and revealing as the study of high culture or official dogmas. New studies appeared examining faith healing and devotional practices, conversion and individuals' search for meaning in a changing society. A later generation pushed this further, identifying religious practices in contexts removed from formal religious institutions—among those grieving after the death of loved ones or among workers in soup kitchens. We learned to look at symbols as models of and also models for behavior. We became interested not only in how cultural forms reflect the social order, but also how culture plays a role in shaping social movements and organizational forms. Even the political clout of the Religious Right can be understood as part of a "culture war."
>
> The cultural turn also helped to make visible religious forms and movements and organizations which had not previously been visible to sociologists. Sociologists began to examine the religious practices of spiritual seekers of all sorts, the efforts of new immigrants to make sense of the religions of their parents in new contexts, the particular ways that women engage and maintain religious cultures in the privacy of their homes, or create new religions in public spaces.
>
> ### THE LOCAL AND PARTICULAR
>
> Another effect of Geertz's work was that it argued for the importance of "local knowledge." . . . Geertz argued for attention to the local and the particular context of whatever we were observing. Interpretivist ethnographers like myself found ourselves exploring ideas of narrative with

comparative historical sociologists, and rethinking what we meant by a case study. . . .

And, of course, looking at the local and the particular also meant taking the religious context seriously. In the late 1980s, I remember being at the Stone Symposium, sponsored by the Society for [the Study of] Symbolic Interactionism, and Carl Couch, who always argued for the importance of generic social processes, was criticizing a paper I had just given. Carl said to me, "but you don't really care about that religion stuff, do you?" Contrary to what I might have answered a decade earlier at the start of my dissertation research, by this point I had to answer that I did care about religion itself. To the extent that religion is the "context" in which I do my work, the context matters.

RELIGION AS A DISTINCTIVE INSTITUTION

Caring about religion itself—as an institution, as cultural systems, as social and cultural movements—led me to explore the work being done in the subfield of the sociology of religion. The conceptual tools developed there had particular usefulness in examining relations between religion and society. For example, while I was still critical of the model of secular change implicit in some theories of church, denomination and sect, I began to see those theories as offering an interesting way of conceptualizing deviance on a cultural level, and the relation between hegemonic denominational cultures and resistant and subversive subcultures.

I believe that my work, and indeed my understanding of American culture, has been much enriched by my movement from seeing religion as a site for studying the theoretical problems which interested me to seeing religious traditions themselves as sources of cultural forms that provide ongoing resources to individuals and institutions in the United States. In talking to other people about shifts in the sociological study of religion, I hear different interpretations of what has changed and how. Not everyone would agree with the emphasis on culture in the account I have presented here. Others, for example, move across bridges between institutional theory and denominational organizations, but they too find the particularities of the religious site to add to the complexity and depth of their analyses.

Source: Mary Jo Neitz, "From the Chair: What Is Distinctive about Studying Religion?" *American Sociological Association Section on Sociology of Religion Newsletter* 5, no. 2 (Winter 1999): 1–3.

And later in the decade, when Martin E. Marty, the preeminent historian of American religion, listed ten reasons for studying religion, his first was: "Religion motivates most killing in the world today" (1997: 20). You may find this to be a sad fact or a fact not likely to be proclaimed from the pulpits of the nation's religious institutions as standard weekend fare, but it is a fact that must be considered by sociologists and can be ignored only at the price of future suffering. More Christians, for example, are probably suffering martyrdom or persecution for their faith today than at any time in history. Of course, this is partly a result of the population explosion—there are more people, hence more Christians, hence more martyrs in real numbers—and partly cultural, as Christianity reaches out of its European domain into Africa. The Holocaust, however, should still be a live recollection of the possibilities for evil that religious prejudice may generate, even in the midst of "culturally advanced" societies—as should more recent atrocities in Bosnia and Kosovo. In short, whether or not we like religion, whether we are or are not ourselves religious, we need to understand what it is about religion that mixes with other human emotional dynamics to produce results that are so at odds with the peaceful teachings that seem to be at the core of all the world's religions. As we will see, globalization theory in sociology is a helpful tool in assessing these contemporary dynamics.

Marty offers nine other reasons for studying religion, too, several of which are particularly important to the sociology of religion. Right after the assertion that "[r]eligion motivates most killing in the world today," he observes that religion also "contributes to most healing in the world today." From pastoral counseling to primitive shamanic rites, to many of the world's great medical centers, religion directly or indirectly is involved in the restoration of relationships and the healing of both mind and body. Increasing research on holistic health and wellness shows the importance of spiritual well-being, not only to mental health but to physical health as well (Levin 1994; see Levin and Koenig 2005).

Religion, Marty points out, is also "globally pervasive; there is a great deal of it." The more our world becomes "a single place," to return to Roland Robertson's phrase (1992), the more important it is to understand the role of religion in cultures. In addition, however, even in the United States, the effect of greater world openness has been that the variety of religions available has increased; the relative sameness of the "Judeo-Christian tradition" that characterized the United States in the 1950s has been broken again and again, not only by NRMs but also by increasing numbers of Muslims, Sikhs, and Buddhists entering the society. "Religion, however defined, helps explain many human activities," and it is "one of the most revealing dimensions of pluralism" (Marty 1997: 48).

Marty notes, as we might expect of a historian, that "[r]eligion has a long past," but adds that "its tentacles are culture wide." Put another way, not only is there a history of religion, but religion has had a historical influence affecting many aspects of all cultures: Modern economics and science, as Max Weber (1998) and Robert K. Merton (1936, 1996), respectively, have pointed out, have been shaped by religious influences; so have education and medicine. But not only the particular ways in which these institutions have risen in the West have been religiously influenced, but also the way in which they failed to develop or actually receded in the East. Thus, to bring us almost full circle around where this chapter began, "Religion gets to be studied because it is practical." Marty at this point deserves to be quoted at length:

> "[G]etting religion" refers to a very practical issue. People in statecraft have to plan strategies in case military action elsewhere might involve their country. Leaders of what we momentarily will call tribes do well to keep an eye on the rites and ceremonies, the myths and symbols and

> stories, of the tribe on the other side of the hill: it might be called upon by its deities or its dancers to attack.
>
> On the domestic political scene, one need hardly elaborate on the practicality of understanding religion in the form of the putative Catholic vote, the various Christian coalitions, ever-changing Jewish interests, or what African American pastors are thinking. Advertisers blunder when they try to sell a project while being insensitive to the religious sensibilities of potential customers. Marketers include religious data when planning where to sell: hog butchers of the world, to take an obvious case, do not target Jewish communities.
>
> In intimate personal relations, such as providing medical care, promoting support groups in struggles against addiction, or making sense of the person to whom one is married, some understanding of religious impulses and religion is practical. Even the widespread religious indifference and ignorance in much of the culture demands study: if people abandon religion or are abandoned by it, academics *get* to study what takes its place. Something will. (1997: 48)

Implicit Religion

The *implicit religion* concept has been working its way into general use in the social scientific study of religion for over a quarter of a century. There are really three streams of development of the concept. Its Anglo-American use, on which we will focus in this section, is certainly to be credited to the British scholar Edward Bailey and, under his aegis, to the Denton Hall Conference on Implicit Religion, held in North Yorkshire, which celebrated its thirtieth anniversary in 2007, and since for more than a decade to the Centre for the Study of Implicit Religion and Contemporary Spirituality, offering degree programs through the University of Wales, Bangor. There is also, however, an Italian approach associated with the work of Arnaldo Nesti of the sociology faculty of the University of Florence (*Il religioso implicito* [1985]; see Nesti, Giannoni, and Dianich [1993]), and a Dutch approach by Meerten ter Borg of the theology faculty of the University of Leiden (*Een Uitgewaairde Enuwigheid* [1991]).

The extent to which the concept of implicit religion has penetrated the study of religion is really quite remarkable, especially in light of the fact that for the most part Bailey has not had a cadre of graduate students to send forth as disciples, nor has he developed an extensive set of major publications. Indeed, his magnum opus, *Implicit Religion in Contemporary Society*, long available only in manuscript, was not published until 1997. He has had a single-minded determination, however, to advance both the use and insight of the concept; yet it must also be said that the concept seems to be one whose time had come. The development of the implicit religion concept was the result of debates in the late 1960s and early 1970s over such concepts as civil religion, invisible religion, civic religion, and European debate and research into popular religion conceived and approached in several different ways. The concept is strongly interdisciplinary in character, and that may be part of its appeal. It is also rooted in the religious studies tradition that asserts that there is an irreducible spiritual or religious dimension within human existence—that everybody has some "ultimate" or set of ultimates, even if it be self (for example, "I believe in putting Number One first" is an implicitly religious credo).

Bailey (1998a) writes that "the concept has at least three (nonexclusive) definitions: *commitment(s)* or *integrating foci* or *intensive concerns with extensive effects.*" This polysemous quality (that is, its simultaneous multiple meanings) may be part of the concept's appeal. Nevertheless, as Bailey also notes, this approach stands at least apart from, if not over against, and "counterbalances the tendency to equate 'religion' with specialized institutions, with articulated beliefs, and with that which is consciously willed (or specifically intended)." Yet this should not be taken to mean that implicit religion is somehow only an inner disposition of individuals. Implicit religions can work at the macro level, and one might see both civil religion in the United States, which will be discussed in greater detail in chapter 3, and civic religion in Britain as macro-manifestations of implicit religion. Macro-manifestations need not be identified with the political, however. There is an implicit religion surrounding Elvis Presley that is generally apolitical and transcends national boundaries. People in England, for example, have "shrine rooms" to Elvis; "pilgrims" come from all over the world to Elvis's Tennessee home, Graceland (a name itself pregnant with religious significance); and various Elvis sightings recur in the tabloids to give this star a hint of immortality that many of his most devoted fans find comforting (Rodman 1996). Sports can have an implicitly religious character, though one should not thereby make the facile jump to a claim that any kind of sports fandom is therefore "making a religion out of sports." As Bailey is fond of saying, there is a significant difference between the assertion that *any*thing *can be* religious and *every*thing *is* religious. The latter is simply neopantheism and, in fact, misses the distinctively religious element within a "religious" experience.

Americans are likely to find echoes of both Paul Tillich's "ultimate concern" (1957) as well as J. Milton Yinger's attempts (1970) to measure ultimate concern as an empirical, functional definition of religion in the implicit religion concept. Certainly both are closely related. Bailey's approach tends to be somewhat less abstract and rationalistic than either of these. He wants to know what issues are important to people, what makes them happy, what gives them joy, what people think is really wrong or disgusting behavior, and so on. He is also willing to accept that people cannot necessarily articulate the reasons for these responses. In his own work (carried out initially in three studies that focused on a boarding high school, a pub, and a parish community), Bailey was most influenced by the English cleric-professor F. B. Welbourn, who spent a great deal of his life in Africa, where he became quite critical of European approaches to the definition, hence study, of religion, as simply being out of touch with the way Africans lived their lives (see Welbourn 1965, 1968). In Welbourn's view the rationalistic, academic, theological biases of European (and American) approaches to the spiritual dimension of human existence brought so many preconceptions with them that they were forcing African data into molds that were totally inappropriate to hold them. Implicit religion became both Bailey's doctoral thesis and his response to reconsidering Western religion in light of Welbourn's critique.

We introduce the concept of implicit religion at the close of this chapter to signal the importance of being sensitive to what might be called, as Thomas Luckmann (1990) has, the "little transcendences" in human life and the need to build conceptual bridges that link these to the "great transcendences" of the world religions. Sociologically it is important to recognize that religion begins somewhere; as the sixteenth-century German mystic Meister Eckhart phrased it, "before man, God was not God." Of course, if there is a Supreme Being, that Being has existed before time and forever, but the naming of that Being and the recognition of the attributes of that Being arise in human experience. To seek how people come to commit, to value, to adore, to hate, to celebrate, to grieve—to do these things and to account for them—is to seek the rough ground out of which religions arise and to which religions are called to speak at all times and in all places.

Suggestions for Further Reading

Edward Bailey. 1998. *Implicit Religion: An Introduction*. London: Middlesex University Press.

Robert N. Bellah, Richard Madsen, William M. Sullivan, Ann Swidler, and Steven M. Tipton. 2007. *Habits of the Heart: Individualism and Commitment in American Life*, 3rd ed. Berkeley: University of California Press.

Kevin J. Christiano. 2007. *Religious Diversity and Social Change: American Cities, 1890–1906*. Cambridge: Cambridge University Press.

Penny Edgell and Nancy L. Eiesland, eds. 1997. *Contemporary American Religion: An Ethnographic Reader*. Walnut Creek, Calif.: AltaMira.

Roger Finke and Rodney Stark. 2005. *The Churching of America, 1776–2005: Winners and Losers in Our Religious Economy*, 2nd ed. New Brunswick, N.J.: Rutgers University Press.

Charles Y. Glock and Rodney Stark. 1965. *Religion and Society in Tension*. Chicago: Rand-McNally.

Mark Juergensmeyer. 2003. *Terror in the Mind of God: The Global Rise of Religious Violence*, 3rd ed. Berkeley: University of California Press.

Wade Clark Roof, with Bruce Greer, Mary Johnson, Andrea Leibson, Karen Loeb, and Elizabeth Souza. 1993. *A Generation of Seekers: The Spiritual Journeys of the Baby Boom Generation*. San Francisco: HarperCollins.

Rodney Stark. 2005. *The Victory of Reason: How Christianity Led to Freedom, Capitalism, and Western Success*. New York: Random House.

William H. Swatos, Jr., ed. 1993. *A Future for Religion? New Paradigms for Social Analysis*. Newbury Park, Calif.: Sage.

R. Stephen Warner. 1988. *New Wine in Old Wineskins: Evangelicals and Liberals in a Small-Town Church*. Berkeley: University of California Press.

Lawrence A. Young, ed. 1997. *Rational Choice Theory and Religion: Summary and Assessment*. New York: Routledge.

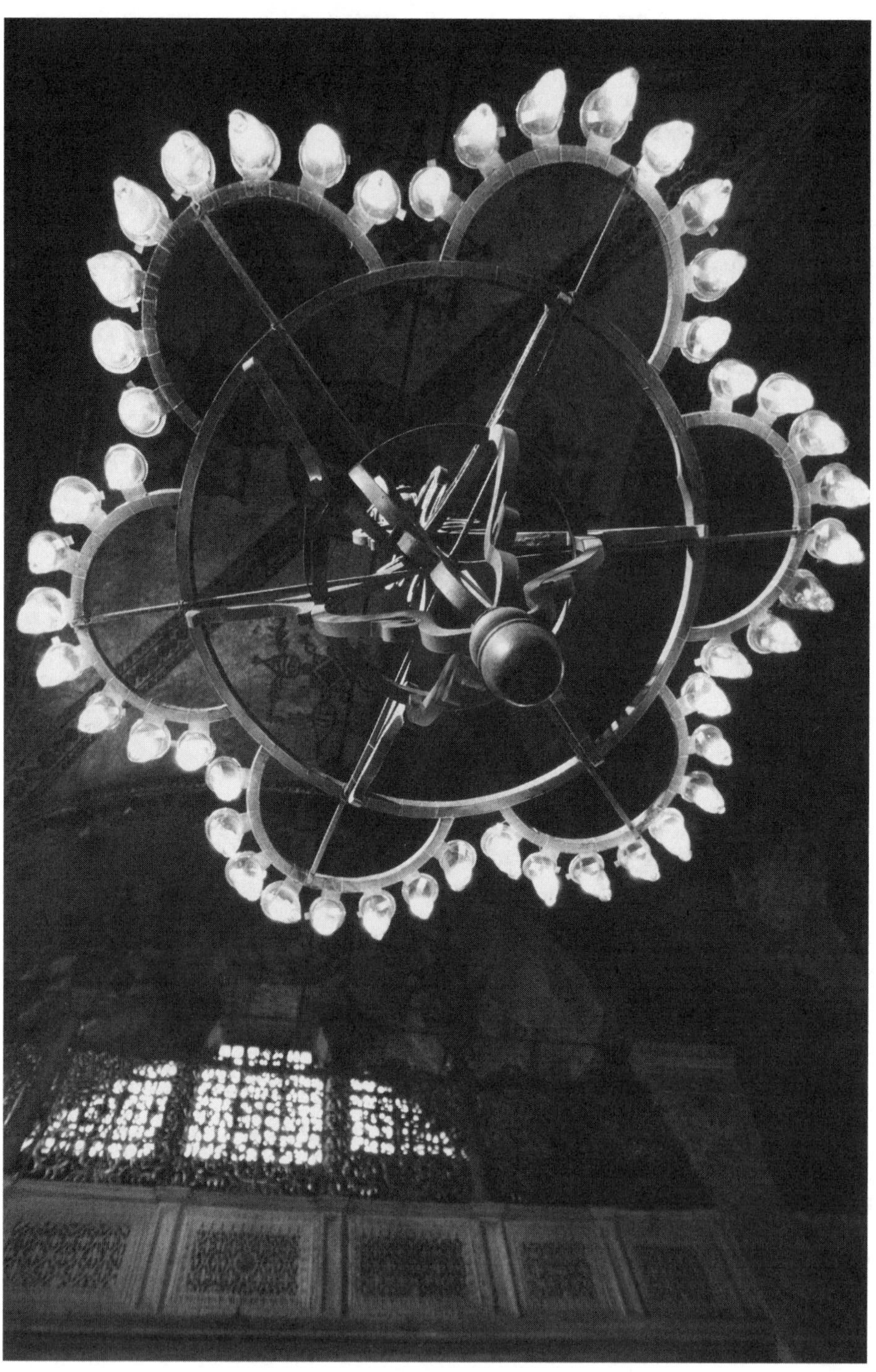

Jupiter Images 22969685

CHAPTER 3

The "Religion" of Secularization and the History of Religions

Like *church-sect* and so many other concepts in the sociology of religion, the term *secularization* was given to us by Max Weber, and was similarly picked up by Ernst Troeltsch, both originally writing in the first decades of the twentieth century. It did not appear significantly in U.S. sociology, however, until the late 1950s. In spite of a cautionary article by Larry Shiner as early as 1967 about the muddled meanings that had come to be attached to the term (hence his suggestion that "we drop the word entirely"), by the early 1970s secularization was the reigning dogma in the field. In this chapter we will review the secularization problematic, the background conditions that led to its use, and the challenges that seem finally to have overtaken it while allowing it to remain an important topic of debate in the sociology of religion.

The "World" of Religion

The word *secularization* comes from the Latin *saeculum*, which could be taken to mean simply an age (or era)—but also, at least by the fourth and fifth centuries, the world, probably as an extension of the idea of a *spirit of an age*. By this date, too, the word had already developed an ambiguous meaning. It could be used to mean something like unending time (the phrases "world without end" or "forever and ever" that often appear still at the end of formal Christian prayers are translations of the Latin *in saecula saeculorum*), or the world "out there" (for example, monastic priests who were "enclosed" and under a formal "rule of life" were distinguished from secular clergy, meaning the parish clergy who served the people out in "the world"). But it was also used to mean a life or lifestyle that is at odds with God (thus people would enter monastic life to flee "the world"). Later the term would come to be used to distinguish between civil and ecclesiastical law, lands, and possessions. In the nineteenth century, the term was adopted formally by the British freethinker G. J. Holyoake, who founded the Secular Society as a group committed to a just world order and a moral program of individual action that would address human problems without the use of supernatural explanations. Thus, the term already had an ambiguous, but increasingly negative, use by the time it was adapted into social science.

To the extent that one may ever speak legitimately of a single integrating focus in a body of work as extensive as Max Weber's, it is *rationalität*—a term that refers to the processes of the rationalization of action, the specific form of social change that enabled the modern world to come into being. Weber was interested in how methods of rational calculation had come to dominate modern life. He referred to this as the "spirit of capitalism." His studies convinced him that from the sixteenth century forward in Western civilization, one sphere of life after another had become subject to the belief that explanations for events could be found within this-worldly experience and the application of human reason; as Shiner puts it, the world was "a self-contained causal nexus" (1967: 216). The consequence of this worldview was that explanations referring to forces outside of this world were constantly being laid aside. The flip side of rationalization Weber termed *Entzauberung*—a word usually translated as "disenchantment," though perhaps more accurately rendered "de-magi-fication" or "de-mysteri-zation." Disenchantment did not simply mean that people did not believe in the old mysteries of religion, but rather that the concept of mystery or the mysterious itself was devalued. Mystery was now seen not as something to be entered into but something to be conquered by human reason, ingenuity, and technological products. Weber gave the name *secularization* to this double-sided rationalization-disenchantment process. Secularization was both the process and the result of the process; however, it is also the case that the term occurs only rarely in Weber's writing.

It is not clear that Weber himself considered secularization to be a specific domain of the sociology of religion. In his essay "Science as a Vocation" (1946: 139), *intellectualization* is used as a virtual synonym. In some respects then, it seems that secularization ought to be more properly considered an aspect of the sociology of knowledge, hence to deal with questions of epistemology, the ways people know or the conditions under which we receive knowledge of "the ways the world works" (Glock 1988). As a student, for example, on what basis do you accept something your professor says as valid knowledge? What criteria do you impose on this textbook as a presentation of knowledge? How do you know we know? How do you judge that something you have learned is worthwhile knowledge? Weber's claim is that appeals to divine authority have lost credibility relative to the past as providing sure knowledge for social action. Practical economic considerations (as contrasted to a heavenly bank account) have come to play an increasing role in measuring the worth of knowledge. At most, the religious point of view will be treated as one among many competing claims to authority. Priests, ministers, rabbis, and mullahs are less sought for solving world problems than economists, physicists, and political scientists, while psychologists, social workers, and medical doctors are the societally recognized experts at the individual or microsocial level. Mark Chaves (1994), for example, explicates secularization along these lines in referring to it as a "declining scope of religious authority."

In the boldest terms, however, as Shiner points out, secularization theory's claims mean the *decline of religion*, that is, religion's "previously accepted symbols, doctrines and institutions lose their prestige and influence. The culmination of secularization would be a religionless society" (1967: 209). Shiner notes five other meanings that also came to be associated with the term:

> - Conformity with "this world." The religious group or the religiously informed society turns its attention from the supernatural and becomes more and more interested in "this world." . . . The culmination of secularization would be a society totally absorbed with the pragmatic tasks of the present and a religious group indistinguishable from the rest of society. . . .
> - Disengagement of society from religion. Society separates itself from the religious understanding which has previously informed it . . . and consequently . . . religion [is limited] to the sphere of private life. The culmination of this kind of secularization would be a religion of a purely inward character, influencing neither institutions nor corporate action, and a society in which religion made no appearance outside the sphere of the religious group. . . .
> - Transposition of religious beliefs and institutions. Knowledge, patterns of behavior, and institutional arrangements which were once understood as grounded in divine power are transformed into phenomena of purely human creation and responsibility. . . . The culmination of this kind of secularization process would be a totally anthropologized religion and a society which had taken over all the functions previously accruing to the religious institutions. . . .
> - Desacralization of the world. The world is gradually deprived of its sacral character as man and nature become the object of rational-causal explanation and manipulation. The culmination of secularization would be a completely "rational" world society in which the phenomenon of the supernatural or even of "mystery" would play no part. . . .
> - Movement from a "sacred" to a "secular" society. Accordingly, the culmination of secularization would be a society in which all decisions are based on rational and utilitarian considerations and there is complete acceptance of change. (1967: 211–16)

More recently, Olivier Tschannen (1991) has provided a graphic summary of the "exemplary infrastructure" or "primitive cognitive apparatus" that may be derived from the efforts of various secularization theorists. This appears in figure 3.1.

All of the propositions advanced by Shiner as well as Tschannen's map share a common presupposition: namely, that there has been an enormously significant *change* in the ways in which society and religion have interacted in the past from the ways they do now. "The modern situation," Robert Bellah writes, "represents a stage of religious development in many ways profoundly different from that of historic religion" (1970a: 39). While different authors peg the historical ground differently, the general view is that by the end of the eighteenth century, the set of dynamics collectively known as the Enlightenment or Great Transformation had laid the groundwork for the demise of traditional religion and that this was measurably enhanced by the work of Charles Darwin on evolution and Sigmund Freud on the unconscious. In this respect, as Frank Lechner,

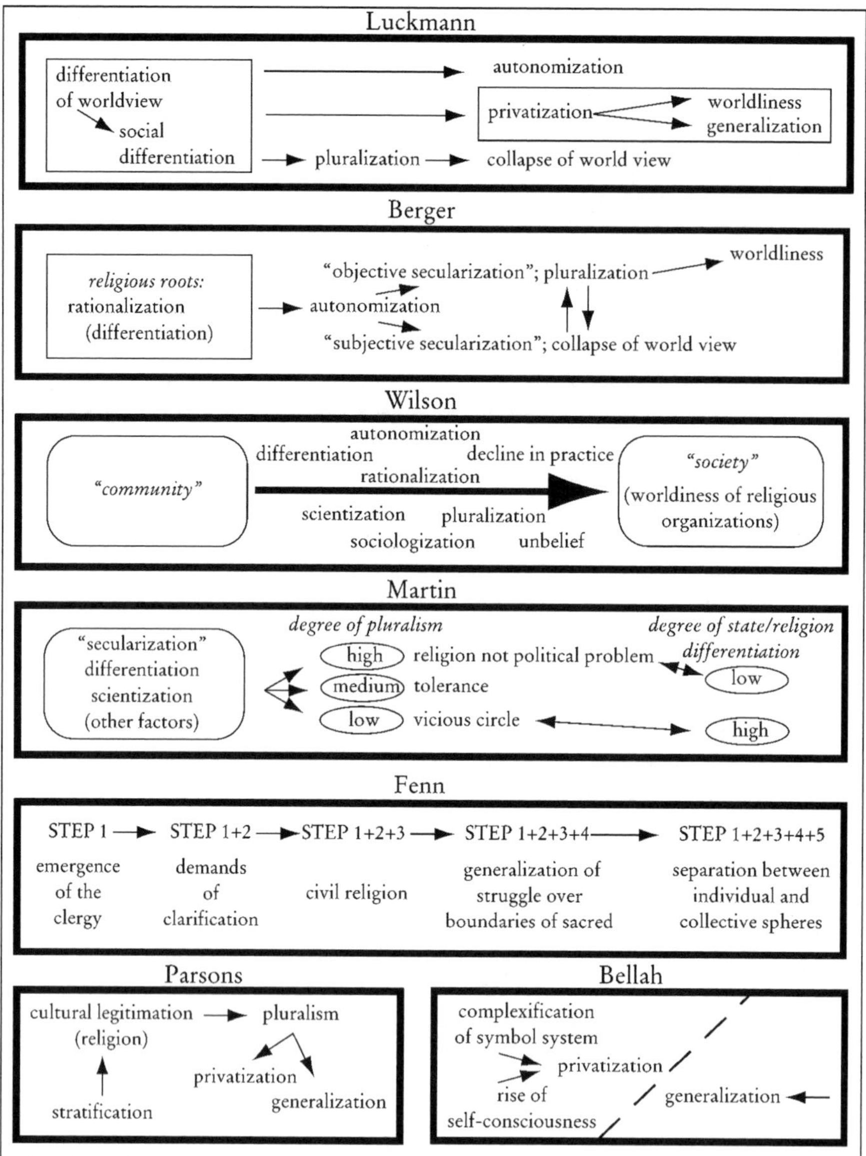

Figure 3.1. The Secularization Paradigm. This diagram illustrates the frameworks through which the major secularization theorists of the 1960s and 1970s explained the transformations of the religion-and-society relationship that they understood to be subsumed under this concept. Source: Olivier Tschannen, "The Secularization Paradigm: A Systematization," Journal for the Scientific Study of Religion *30 (1991): 397.*

in an attempt to defend the secularization thesis, points out, "The sociology of religion only elaborated in more systematic terms what was a common perspective shared by the majority of intellectuals" (1991: 1103).

At the purely descriptive level, secularization may be said to refer to the process of the separation of state and church in Europe, which was much more complex than it was in the United States. Tschannen's application of his map to specific secularization theorists shows that the one element they have in common is that of institutional differentiation. According to Ralf Dahrendorf (1959), for example, the entire European social system was characterized by a state of superimposition, wherein one institutional system overlay another and each had a hand in the other. Church, state, education, health and welfare, the law, and so on were almost inextricably intertwined. Sundering them caused a significant shock to all sectors of the system, a force from which religion was not immune. The United States, by contrast, was characterized by relative pluralism from its earliest years. Church and state were constitutionally separated, and free market, laissez-faire economics circumscribed the role of the state as far as other institutional sectors of the social system were concerned. Nevertheless, even in the United States there grew to be a view that religion was in decline.

Two observations are important to note before we discuss the thesis and the evidence further. The first is that secularization, secularity, or the secular is always relative to some definition of religion or the religious. As Edward Bailey puts it, "*[S]ecular* is really quite easy to define! Its meaning keeps changing yet remains consistent. It always means, simply, the opposite of 'religious'—whatever that means" (1998b: 18). This suggests not only that the "definition of religion question" is not an arcane philosophical debate, but also it shows how premises can influence evidence and outcomes, hence why it is important to examine premises carefully. The second observation is that the "truth" of secularization claims depends on *historical* evidence. If we say, "People are less religious now than they were one hundred years ago," we have not only invoked some presumed definition of religion, but we have also said that we know how religious people were one hundred years ago. Try to *keep these two points at the forefront of your thinking* as you read the rest of this chapter.

The Arguments

There is no question that in most of the Western world there has been sufficient separation of church and state, the primary locus of differentiation, that people are capable of living their lives apart from direct "interference" on the part of organized religion and that people may choose among various religions without suffering civil disabilities. If only this is what is meant by secularization, then there is no debate over "the secularization thesis." But if this is all that secularization means, there would also have been far less excitement about the topic. It would not have been so much something to investigate as simply to state as a factual condition (or as not existing in other parts of the world). Indeed, on this basis we could develop a fairly simple classification system of those societies that had or had not been legally "secularized." (In fact, the term is used in this uncontroversial way to describe institutions that once were controlled by a religious organization and now are not; thus a school or hospital may be said to have been "secularized in 1983," meaning that in that year it went from being under the formal ownership of a religious organization to control by an independent board of trustees or a for-profit corporation.)

There is no doubt that the separation of church and state has consequences for religious organizations and for the lives of individual citizens. At the organizational level, for example, a previously established religion may lose tax support, as happened in colonial Virginia; on the other hand, as also happened in colonial Virginia, other religious organizations gain free access to the religious "market"—that is, other religions may operate on an equal basis. Whether this means the decline of religion, therefore, becomes an empirical question. Individuals no longer may be required to pay taxes to support religion, and they may also be required to conform to certain state norms (like registering the names of children at birth rather than waiting to name a baby in a religious ritual like baptism or circumcision). These may open or close religious options and freedoms, as people can choose to support or reject religious alternatives.

The principal thrust in secularization theory, however, has been stronger than simply church-state issues or the scope of religious authority. It is a claim that in the face of scientific rationality religion's influence on all aspects of life—from personal habits to social institutions—has dramatically declined. Regardless of the sociostructural level of the argument, the underlying assumption is that people have become or are becoming less religious.

Many social theorists doubted that modernity could combine religious traditions with the overpowering impersonal features of our time: scientific research, humanistic education, high technology multinational capitalism, bureaucratic organizational life, and so on. Reacting on the basis of a functional definition of religion, religion appeared to these theorists denuded of almost all the functions it had previously appeared to perform. In this view, religion harked back to some prior level of human evolution uselessly appended to the modern cultural repertoire. People today are awed by human achievements, not divine forces; societies of the future will be constructed around these, not antiquity's notion of the "sacred." Anthony F. C. Wallace, author of an influential text in the anthropology of religion, wrote in the mid-1960s that "the evolutionary future of religion is extinction," and that supernatural beliefs "will erode and become only an interesting historical memory." The global advance of civilization meant that religion will be "doomed to die out all over the world" (1966: 264–65).

This view was evoked in some forms of empirical research as well. In the 1920s, for example, the Institute of Social and Religious Research sent Robert and Helen Lynd to the American Midwest to study the life of a "typical" community. They went to Lynd's home state of Indiana and settled on Muncie, a town sufficiently unexceptional to allow them to attach to it the pseudonym "Middletown." In turn, *Middletown* (1929) became the title of a book that four years later revealed their findings to the general public; it also became a classic among field studies in sociology. Robert Lynd returned to Muncie in 1935 to see how typical "Middle America" was surviving the Depression. *Middletown in Transition* (1937) was the product of this research.

Both of these books included assessments of Muncie's religious organizations, but neither yielded positive outlooks. In the first book, the Lynds concluded that "religious life as represented by the churches is less pervasive than a generation ago" (1929: 407). Yet neither they nor anyone else had done research on the community's religious life a generation previously. In the Depression-era assessment, religious life seemed to them to have declined further: People attending church were older and appeared more passive, as if reflecting the economic downturn. Weekly worship services were not well attended, charitable work did not meet the increasing demand, and young people seemed beyond the churches' pale. Although the religious institutions continued to function as providing "the reassurance so urgently needed" in the face of "the perplexities of a too-perplexing world," these organizations were facing a future of continued displacement (1937: 315).

In the 1970s, however, the National Science Foundation, a federal agency, funded a restudy of Middletown, "Middletown III." If religious organizations were in decline in the 1920s and mid-1930s, what would be their state fifty years from the original study? Their results came as a surprise to the proponents of the "decline of religion" thesis. This project plotted fifteen time series, or sequences, of religion data for Muncie between 1924 and 1978. Among the fifteen trend lines, only two pointed downward (which would indicate a secularization effect). Three more showed no trend, while the remaining ten (67 percent of the total) displayed an upward curve, showing *greater religiosity* in Middletown in the 1970s than the 1920s (Caplow 1982; Caplow, Bahr, and Chadwick 1983).

National survey data from the late 1940s to the present support this finding. In *Religious Change in America* (1989), Andrew M. Greeley reports that in every Gallup poll that has asked whether the respondent believes in God, more than 90 percent say they do. Three-fourths believe in the possibility of life after death and in the messianic divinity of Jesus of Nazareth. About 70 percent, with only the slightest deviation, think that "people who have led good lives" receive some reward in the hereafter, while more than 50 percent also believe in hell. Ninety percent of Americans pray to God, and about two-thirds claim membership in a religious congregation; neither of these percentages has changed significantly in fifty years. About 40 percent of Americans claim to attend religious services each week, and this fraction has altered little over the last thirty years (Greeley 1989: 13–15, 20–43, 58).

Roger Finke and Rodney Stark's *The Churching of America* (2005) has provided a wealth of historical data across two centuries to undergird these observations. They mine early records to estimate, for example, that only 17 percent of Americans claimed religious membership at the time of the Revolution (1776), and that in spite of the revivalism of the Great Awakening of the early nineteenth century, by 1850 only 34 percent claimed membership. While this represents a 100 percent proportional increase over the span, it is also only half the religious organizational membership that we find in the United States today. A study by Laurence Iannaccone (1996) of eighteen nations, most in Europe, shows decreases in church attendance since 1920 only in East Germany, Great Britain, and Slovenia; and Stark (2000: 52) reports "the British trend may already have been reversed, while the declines in Slovenia and East Germany began with the imposition of Communist regimes." Stark and Iannaccone (1994) report that the proportion of British belonging to a "specific religious congregation" is 17 percent—the same number as in 1850, when it had risen from 12 percent in 1800.

The vast majority of Americans, according to survey data, do not appear to have abandoned Wallace's dying religion, or to have fulfilled the Lynds' predictions. "The replacement of religious superstition by enlightened science predicted since the time of Voltaire [1694–1778] may at last be taking place," Greeley noted with tongue in cheek three years after Wallace wrote. "It may well be; though it should be remembered that the prediction has generally been wrong every time it has been made" (1969: 6). Now, forty years after Greeley's generous concession, it seems truer than ever that the predicted demise of religion is probably wrong, certainly premature. What Seymour Martin Lipset wrote as the 1960s dawned seems equally true today:

> The omnipresence and the secularization of religion have been pointed out by those who sought to characterize the main institutional features of American society from the start of the Republic. Certainly, changes have occurred in the nature of religious belief and practice as ours has changed from an essentially rural society to a predominantly urban industrial culture, and as science and intellectual life have touched on religious belief. But by far the most striking aspect of religious life in America is not the changes which have occurred in it—but the basic continuities it retains. (1959: 24)

Virtually no empirical research supports the prediction of a societal slide from a high peak of sacrality into a valley of secularity; indeed, the issues of conceptual confusion raised forty years ago by Shiner now seem all the more urgent for social scientific theory development.

Sigmund Freud referred to religion as *The Future of an Illusion* (1927), but to the contrary, Rodney Stark and William Sims Bainbridge, in *The Future of Religion: Secularization, Revival, and Cult Formation* (1985: 1), claim "the vision of a religionless future is but illusion." Contrary to the unilinear theories of religious decline, Stark and Bainbridge adopt a more cyclical approach reminiscent of the general theory of sociocultural development that Pitirim Sorokin offered in his four volumes on *Social and Cultural Dynamics* (1937–1941), wherein societies move through a progressive dialectic between more idealistic and more sensate cultural forms. As inevitable change takes place in social systems, religions that respond to the needs and conditions in conceptual forms suited to one historical epoch become less effective in addressing core problems of human experience in another. Death is one such example. The problem does not go away. The death rate is the same throughout history: one per person. Hence, the need for a solution remains. Two things happen: On the one hand, movements arise from within existing religious organizations that attempt to restate with even greater certitude the same answers the tradition has always provided; on the other hand, however, new movements also arise from outside the existing traditions, offering new answers to the same questions. Because the existential questions are perennial and their solutions lie beyond rational determination, religious answers will always have a place in human experience. Hence religion as a whole is revived, and secularization is self-limited. In fact, harking back to Sorokin, one might say that secularization is a healthy part of a cycle of religious growth and development.

"The transcendent may no longer be coterminous with all human activity" (if ever it was), as Greeley observes, "but the 'really real' will still persist where the core problems of interpretability are faced" (1969: 169).

The Critique

Twenty years would pass between Shiner's initial expression of reservations about the secularization concept and the next major assault on the thesis. In between, Bryan Wilson (1966), Peter Berger (1967), Thomas Luckmann (1967), and Karel Dobbelaere (1981) would become the principal proponents of secularization theory. Not insignificantly, Wilson, Luckmann, and Dobbelaere are Europeans, and Berger is a European émigré to the United States. All were products of a European Christian intellectual heritage and educational system that, we might now say, romanticized the religious past of their nations.

In his 1986 presidential address to the Southern Sociological Society, sociologist of religion Jeffrey K. Hadden presented a clear, comprehensive, and trenchant analysis of the weaknesses of secularization theory—both in its conception and its predicted outcomes. The core of his argument is that in and from its genesis secularization constituted a "*doctrine* more than a theory" based on "presuppositions that . . . represent a taken-for-granted *ideology*" of

Seeing Is Not Believing

Sociologist of religion Peter Berger embraced secularization theory early in his career but began to have misgivings. One source of these was the Islamic Revolution in Iran along with visits to the Middle East. Here is what he notes about the way academics who had embraced secularism as a belief system ignored evidence of what was happening in their direct observation:

> My only visit to Iran took place about two years before this revolution [in 1979]. Naturally, I spoke mainly to intellectuals, most of whom cordially disliked the regime of the shah and looked forward to its removal. No one expected this to happen under Islamic auspices. Nowhere did I hear the name Khomeini. At about the time of my visit to Iran, Brigitte Berger was on a lecture tour in Turkey, a place she had never visited before and whose language she did not speak. In Istanbul, she noticed many cars with green flags and what looked like storefront mosques, also marked with green flags, which she recognized as Islamic symbols. When she mentioned her observation to her Turkish hosts, they were very much surprised. They either maintained that she was mistaken in her idea that something religious was going on or they discounted the phenomenon as quite unimportant. The people she talked with, mostly social scientists and all secularized intellectuals, literally did not see what was before their eyes—again, because none of this was supposed to be happening. . . . Whether politically on the left or not, they suffer from ideological blinders when it comes to religion, and the tendency is then to explain away what cannot be explained. (1992: 15–16)

social scientists "rather than a systematic set of interrelated propositions"; over time in social scientific circles (which continued to widen in their influence), "*the idea of secularization became sacralized*," that is, a belief system accepted "on faith" (1987: 588; emphasis in the original). Even more than a statement about the present, the ideology of secularization relies on beliefs about the past. (This flank of Hadden's assault, as a matter of fact, was presaged in a series of pieces by Roland Robertson beginning as early as 1971.)

The second thrust of Hadden's attack is a fourfold challenge:

1. Secularization theory is internally weak in its logical structure—"a hodgepodge of loosely employed ideas"—a state that was first revealed by Shiner.
2. Such secularization *theory* as does exist is unsupported by data after more than twenty years of research, a point also made by Peter Glasner (1977) in his critique of secularization theory as a "myth" a decade earlier.
3. New religious movements (NRMs) have appeared and persisted in the most supposedly secularized societies. Indeed, Stark and Bainbridge (1985) have shown that the lower the level of practice or saturation on the part of traditional religion in modern societies, the higher the likelihood of NRM activity.
4. Religion has emerged as a vital force in the political order around the globe.

Hadden concludes this thrust with a series of forecasts of the place of religion in society and in sociology for the next fifty years, concluding that we should "return once more to the past to see the future. Max Weber's search for clues about the place of religion in human society took him deeply into the study of the world's major religions. The future will take us back to where Weber began" (1987: 598, 609, *et passim*).

The "Religions" of Secularization

Max Weber's decision at the outset of his sociology of religion not to define *religion* is well known. So, too, is the definition of Émile Durkheim, preeminently as it was refabricated at the hands of Talcott Parsons and his school of functionalism. Central to the Parsonian thrust was the integrationist or solidarity theme within the Durkheimian formulation: that is, that religion *unites all who adhere to it into a single moral community*. Religion was the glue of society, the source of social solidarity. So strongly believed was this proposition among social scientists that, in cases where it was manifestly clear that what participants in the action system termed *religion* did not integrate the social system, some sociologists nevertheless proceeded undaunted to search out the "real" religion of society—its latent source of solidarity—and proclaim this as sacred rite and ceremony. This approach enjoyed great success in the sociology of religion when applied in monopolistic settings (for example, the Marxist regimes of the Soviet Union or Chairman Mao's China), but encountered problems with pluralism (wherein, for instance, Babe Ruth's bat was proclaimed the "sacred object" of the national "religion" of baseball).

CIVIL RELIGION

The best effort to articulate such a religion for modern society was Robert Bellah's seminal essay "Civil Religion in America," published in the journal *Daedalus* in 1967. Indeed, it may well be that the publication in 1967 of both Bellah's essay and Thomas Luckmann's *The Invisible Religion*, to which we will turn shortly, obscured the impact of Shiner's critique.

Originating in the work of Jean-Jacques Rousseau (1712–1778), with echoes in Alexis de Tocqueville's observations on life in the early years of the republic, *Democracy in America* (published in 1835), the concept of civil religion as articulated by Bellah drew almost unprecedented attention among sociologists and other scholars of religion. The concept refers to a "transcendent universal religion of the nation" and reflects the functional sociology both of Durkheim and of Bellah's mentor, Talcott Parsons. Indeed, it was Parsons who was originally intended to write the *Daedalus* article (Bellah 1989).

Bellah claimed that most people in the United States share common religious characteristics expressed through beliefs, symbols, and rituals that provide a religious dimension to the entirety of American life. Later, he adds that civil religious principles transcend the nation and represent a "higher standard" by which the nation should be judged. Bellah's definition of civil religion in the

God, the Fifty United States of America, and Civil Religion

Although "God" is not mentioned in the Constitution of the United States of America, mention is specifically made of "Nature's God" in the opening sentence of the Declaration of Independence, but that's not all: Virtually every state of the union mentions God or a Supreme Being in its constitution:

40 mention "Almighty God" or "God," 37 of these in their preambles, the other 3 in articles. These range in date from Maryland and Pennsylvania in 1776 to Alaska in 1956.
4 refer instead to "the Supreme Ruler of the Universe"
1 refers to "the Supreme Being" (Iowa, 1857)
1 refers to "the Great Legislator of the Universe" (Massachusetts, 1780)
1 acknowledges "Divine Guidance" ("We the people of Hawaii, Grateful for Divine Guidance, Establish this Constitution." [1959])
1 writes "Through Divine Goodness all men have, by nature the rights of worshipping and serving their Creator . . ." (Delaware, 1897)
1 refers to the "Author of Existence" (Vermont, 1777)
1 refers to "our Creator" and further asserts "that it is the mutual duty of all to practice Christian Forbearance, Love and Charity towards each other" (Virginia, 1776)

Only two of these state constitutions were written after the phrase "under God" was inserted into the Pledge of Allegiance in 1954.

United States is that it is "an institutionalized collection of sacred beliefs about the American nation," which he sees symbolically expressed in its founding documents and presidential inaugural addresses. It includes a belief in the existence of a transcendent being called "God," an idea that the United States is subject to God's laws, and an assurance that God will guide and protect the United States. Bellah sees these beliefs in the values of liberty, justice, charity, and personal virtue, and concretized in, for example, the words "In God We Trust" on both national emblems and the currency used in daily economic transactions. Although civil religion in the United States shares much with the religion of Judeo-Christian denominations, Bellah claims that it is distinct from denominational religion. Crucial to Bellah's Durkheimian emphasis is the claim that civil religion is definitionally an "objective social fact" (1970a: 168; 1974: 255).

Although other U.S. scholars had articulated civil-religion types of ideas (for example, Martin Marty's "religion-in-general" [1959] and Sidney Mead's "religion of the republic" [1963]), the publication of Bellah's essay at the height of national soul-searching during the Vietnam War secured his place as a major interpreter of religion in the United States during the second half of the twentieth century and caused an enormous outpouring of scholarly activity (see Gehrig 1981; Hammond 1976; Marty 1992; Mathisen 1989; Richey and Jones 1974). Such authors as Richard Fenn (1977) and Timothy Luke (1987) specifically related civil religion to the secularization problematic.

A subsequent "civil religion debate" focused on several interrelated issues at the heart of which, however, was a definitional question: in other words, what really qualified as both *civil* and *religion* in the concept? For example, W. Lloyd Warner (1961) had previously delineated a dynamic in the United States that he called "Americanism" and Will Herberg wrote of "the American Way of Life" in his *Protestant-Catholic-Jew* (1955): How did civil religion differ from these? Did people have to know they were civil religious to be civil religious? Was civil religion in the United States more than "an idolatrous worship of the American nation" (Mathisen 1989: 130)? Some general tendencies may be noted here.

First, there was a systematic critique of the concept of civil religion as *religion*, principally from the historian John F. Wilson (for example, 1979). His main criticism was that, contrary to Bellah's insistence, civil religion did not stand alone and did not occupy a position that was clearly differentiated from other institutions such as denominational faith. At most, Wilson thought, we have in the United States expressions of "public religion"—that is, church-based religion drawn out into shared and even secular space. This was partly offset by a shift in Bellah's own work, wherein civil religion became an increasingly evaluative concept, as in his bicentennial volume *The Broken Covenant* (1975). Undoubtedly, the U.S. bicentennial provided a major impetus to civil religion concerns, so much so that James A. Mathisen refers to the period from 1974 to 1977 as the "Golden Age" for discussion of civil religion.

Although the civil religion thesis claims that civil religion exists *symbolically* in American culture, such symbols must be perceived and believed by actual people if the symbols are to be said to have meaning. Several studies by Ronald Wim-

Civil Religion: Faith, Football, and Flags

Civil religion in the United States expresses itself in many ways. This photograph, taken at the University of Notre Dame, is particularly rich with civil religious connotations. Immediately on the surface is the presence of a member of the clergy at the podium, flanked to his rear by a military honor guard and the U.S. flag. But that is not all: On the wall is a picture of legendary Notre Dame football coach Knute Rockne. Rockne converted to Catholicism in 1925, probably from a Norwegian Lutheran background, thus expressing the civil religious value of freedom of choice. Note that Rockne is kneeling, almost as if sainted. History extends the story: In a highly popular motion picture of 1940, *Knute Rockne—All American*, a major role, memorable to his generation, was played by a young actor named Ronald Reagan, later to become president of the United States. Reagan, who had considerable support in his presidential bids from the Christian Right, seldom attended church throughout his presidency, yet regularly espoused a religiously laden rhetoric—reaffirming another civil religious principle, that of voluntarism in religious participation.

Robert Woodward, C.S.C. Collection (GWOO 2/10), UNDA. Reproduced with permission of the University of Notre Dame.

berley (1976, 1979) and others (Wimberley et al. 1976; Wimberley and Christenson 1981) developed statements on civil religious beliefs and obtained responses on them from various public samples. The findings show that people do affirm civil religious beliefs, although most would not know what the term *civil religion* means. Examples of civil religious beliefs are reflected in such statements used in this research as "America is God's chosen nation today," "Holidays like the

Fourth of July are religious as well as patriotic," "A president's authority . . . is from God," "Social justice cannot be based only on laws; it must also come from religion," "God can be known through the experiences of the American people." These large surveys and factor-analytic studies helped give empirical credence to Bellah's conceptual argument that civil religion is a distinctive cultural component within American society that is not captured either by national politics or by denominational religiosity.

Further research sought to determine the locus and incidence of civil religion in the population: "Who is civil religious?" (Christenson and Wimberley 1978). These studies found that, indeed, a wide cross-section of citizens do share such civil religious beliefs. In general, however, college graduates and political or religious liberals appear to be somewhat less civil religious. People identifying with major Protestant denominations and Catholicism show similar levels of civil religiosity. Groups having denominational roots within the United States—Mormons, Adventists, and Pentecostalists—score the highest on an index used to measure civil religiosity, while those with no religious preference, Jews, and Unitarians tend to score the lowest. Despite individual variation on these measures, the great majority share the types of civil religious beliefs Bellah suggested. A correlative body of literature has also developed around how differing religious and quasi-religious movements have contributed to or been influenced by civil religion in the United States. These include studies of Freemasonry (Jolicoeur and Knowles 1978; J. Wilson 1980), Judaism (Woocher 1986), the Quakers (Kent and Spickard 1994), and the Reverend Sun Myung Moon's Unification Church (Robbins et al. 1976).

Subsequently, however, there has not been a consistent, sustained attempt to measure the civil religious dimension in American culture over time or to determine its effects on, say, the nation's politics over time. The reaction that greeted the original publication of Bellah's essay can hardly be detached from concern over the politics of Vietnam and its aftermath. The switching of attention in the study of the religion-and-politics area from civil religion to the "New Christian Right" that has been evident during the last two decades may obscure the role of civil religion in the processes of selective agenda successes and failures on the part of the Christian Right as well as the secular Left (see Williams and Alexander 1994). Not to be ignored either is John Murray Cuddihy's earlier, provocative work *No Offense: Civil Religion and Protestant Taste* (1978), wherein the case is made that civil religion constitutes a set of platitudes that substitutes for either serious religious or political action, or Robert Wuthnow's discussion of "Two Civil Religions" in his *The Restructuring of American Religion* (1988: 244–57).

Although Bellah himself consciously chose to drop the use of the term in his magisterial collaborative assessment of public morality and individualism in the United States, *Habits of the Heart* (Bellah et al. 1985), by the mid-1980s the concept of civil religion had become institutionalized within social scientific and other scholarly work, with a firm consensus that one value component of the complex that makes up "Americanism" is especially religious in nature, hence may be termed *civil religion*.

America's Two Civil Religions

The civil religion of the United States features two equally prominent, if awkwardly integrated, emphases. The first stresses the country's greatness and celebrates its unique role at the head of all the nations of the world. This might be termed the *priestly* pole of American civil religion.

By contrast, another strain in the patriotic creed, while not directly contradicting the first, places more weight on the obligations that attach to extraordinary privilege and power, and the necessity that Americans constantly live up to their loftiest ideals. This is the civil religion's *prophetic* aspect.

Below are excerpts from famous speeches by two noted (and controversial) U.S. politicians of the last half of the twentieth century. In the first, Ronald Reagan, who served as president from 1981 to 1989, gives voice to the priestly kind of civil religion; in the second, Senator George McGovern, the Democratic nominee for president in 1972, illustrates the prophetic brand.

> Some have called it mysticism or romanticism, but I've always thought that a providential hand had something to do with the founding of this country. That God had His reasons for placing this land here between two great oceans to be found by a certain kind of people; that whatever corner of the world they came from, there would be in their hearts a fervent love of freedom and a special kind of courage, the courage to uproot themselves and their families, travel great distances to a foreign shore and build there a new world of peace and freedom. And hope.
>
> We are bound together because, like them, we too dare to hope. We dare to hope for our children; that they will always find here the lady of liberty in a land that is free. We dare to hope, too, that we will understand our work as Americans can never be said to be truly done until every man, woman and child shares in our gift—in our liberty—a light that, tonight, will shortly cast its glow upon her, as it has upon us for two centuries; keeping faith with a dream of long ago and, we dare to hope, guiding millions still to a future of peace and freedom.
>
> —Speech by President Ronald Reagan at the relighting ceremony for the newly renovated Statue of Liberty, Governors Island, New York, July 3, 1986. (Source: "The Speeches: 'We Dare to Hope for Our Children,'" *New York Times*, July 4, 1986, B3)

> In Scripture and in the music of our children we are told: "To everything there is a season, and a time to every purpose under heaven."
>
> And for America, the time has come at last.
>
> This is the time for truth, not falsehood. . . .
>
> [L]et us resolve that never again will we shed the precious young blood of this nation to perpetuate an unrepresentative client abroad.
>
> Let us choose life, not death[;] this is the time.
>
> America must be restored to her proper role in the world. But we can do that only through the recovery of confidence in ourselves. The greatest contribution America can make to our fellow mortals is to heal our own great but deeply troubled land. We must respond to that ancient command: "Physician, heal thyself." . . .
>
> And this is the time. It is the time for this land to become again a witness to the world for what is noble and just in human affairs. It is the time to live more with faith and less with fear—with an abiding confidence that

> can sweep away the strongest barriers between us and teach us that we truly are brothers and sisters.
>
> So join with me in this campaign, lend me your strength and your support, give me your voice—and together, we will call America home to the founding ideals that nourished us in the beginning. . . .
>
> May God grant us the wisdom to cherish this good land [and] to meet the great challenge that beckons us home.
>
> —Speech by Senator George S. McGovern (D–S.D.) on acceptance of the Democratic Party's nomination for president, Miami Beach, Florida, July 13, 1972. (Source: "Democratic Convention: Text of Address by McGovern Accepting the Democratic Presidential Nomination," *New York Times*, July 14, 1972, 11)

Whether or not the civil religion component is the same as the "transcendent *universal* religion of the nation" that late-eighteenth-century French intellectuals envisioned, the response of Americans to the attacks on the World Trade Center and the Pentagon on September 11, 2001, clearly showed the vitality of the concept across mainstream culture in the United States, as Americans rapidly took up two songs: "God Bless America" and "God Bless the USA." The word "God" is obviously religious but at the same time nonsectarian. Both songs also clearly center on the United States as a corporate entity and a nation inherently deserving of God's favor. Each has been suggested as a replacement or alternative national anthem. Members of Congress massed on the steps of the Capitol to sing "God Bless America" two days after the attacks, and the song was added to the 2002 Super Bowl pregame ceremonies, immediately before the national anthem. A video clip of "God Bless the USA" is included in U.S. naturalization ceremonies (see Meizel 2006; Swatos 2006). Virtually nothing at the time of the attacks, by contrast, reflected a hint of national self-criticism. Americans believe in America. And they believe that God believes in America.

INVISIBLE RELIGION

The Invisible Religion was the title given to Thomas Luckmann's *Das Problem der Religion in der Modernen Gesellschaft* (literally: *The Problem of Religion in Modern Society*) when it was published in English in 1967, four years after its German publication. In addition to its own merits, the book gained considerable attention as its publication followed by less than a year that of Berger and Luckmann's *The Social Construction of Reality* (1966), a work of general sociological theory certainly to be considered among the most crucial of the second half of the twentieth century. The connection between invisible religion and secularization is in some ways an ironic one, as is the case for civil religion, since it could be equally argued to be potentially an antisecular argument for the universality of the religious (as in implicit religion). However, by generally casting aside institutionalized organized religion, Luckmann clearly throws his hat into the secularization camp.

The following extract summarizes the style of Luckmann's work:

> The organism—in isolation nothing but a separate pole of "meaningless" subjective processes—becomes a Self by embarking with others upon the construction of an "objective" and moral universe of meaning. Thereby the organization transcends its biological nature.
>
> It is in keeping with an elementary sense of the concept of religion to call the transcendence of biological nature by the human organism a religious phenomenon. As we have tried to show, this phenomenon rests upon the functional relation of Self and society. We may, therefore, regard the social processes that lead to the formation of Self as fundamentally religious. (1967: 48–49)

Religion, in other words, becomes a term for any human thought or action that moves beyond the animal level. To be human is to be religious, but the assertion easily turns around: to be religious is to be human. Religion doesn't refer to anything "out there," but to human social processes. Eating with a fork could be understood as religious. So could using toilet paper. Any time we transcend our biological nature we are engaging in "religious" actions. Although this use of "religion" salvages it from the dustbin of history to which such theorists as Wallace would consign it, it hardly bears any resemblance to what religious or irreligious people in our own day, or any other, think is religion.

What is wrong with this approach to religion? There are, first, a number of problems inherent in Durkheim's work itself. W. G. Runciman has summarized three of these, the most telling of which is that Durkheim's "explanation" of religious beliefs in a this-worldly terminus (society) does not actually "explain" them at all (except to explain them away): "Why, after all," Runciman asks, "is the worship of society any more readily explicable than the worship of gods?" (1970: 98). Intimately connected with this "explanation," however, is Durkheim's search for the source of social solidarity, and behind this is his *presumption* of solidarity. The integrating power in society of religion is *not*, in fact, what Durkheim would call a "social fact," but a largely unsubstantiated social-anthropological *belief* stemming from Durkheimian sources. This belief underlies the "religion" of secularization; that is, contemporary secularization theory is based on the view that religion is defined by religion's "function" of social integration or the maintenance of social solidarity. Not only is the notion of solidarity as definitive of society now suspect (see Beyer 1989), but even if we do accept some concept of solidarity into our theoretical arsenal, there is no reason to presume an integrated wholeness that certainly is now difficult to see, and may well have never existed.

Compounding these problems within Durkheim's theory is the problem of the translation of the title of Durkheim's central text in the sociology of religion into English as *The Elementary Forms of the Religious Life*. As Wilfred Cantwell Smith has noted (1984: 28–29), the difficulty is with the French word *élémentaire*, a word that has a dual connotation in French, but in English must be rendered as either *elementary* or *elemental.* Joseph Ward Swain, the translator, chose the former. In so doing he gave a particularly *evolutionary* twist to Durkheim's work that was in the original, but was also balanced there by *elemental.* This sense was far more the crucial contribution of Durkheim's research—namely, as Smith writes, a study of "what pertains to or is one of the constituent parts or basic components . . . of humanity's religious life." Admittedly, Durkheim "did not wrestle with the fact that modern 'primitives' have just as many years of history behind them as do the rest of us to-day," but the use of "the *elementary* forms of religious life, in the sense of an early stage of development," was not the central thrust of Durkheim's work. The choice of *elementary* over *elemental* reflects "the far from insignificant fact that the translation was made at a phase in Western cultural evolution when sophisticated secular intellectuals tended to hold that chronologically early and in its wake present-day tribal religious life was closer, or more manageably close, to the truth about religion generically than our more developed forms." In short, *elementary* was more consistent with the incipient *doctrine of secularization* than was *elemental* (see W. Smith 1984: 28–29). Rather than a paradigm study of religion, *The Elementary Forms* became a doctrinaire statement about religion.

That this is more than a semantic exercise may be seen quite clearly when we turn to Talcott Parsons's work as the major interpretive treatment on Durkheim in Western sociology for more than a quarter of a century, for Parsons increasingly employed an evolutionary approach in his work over the years. Where did Parsons begin his evolutionary scheme but with Durkheim's (and others') descriptions of the Australian Aborigines—a *contemporary* people? As his work develops, he adds other contemporary accounts of "contemporary peoples, distributed over the earth's surface . . . rearranged to form a general *historical sequence* of societal evolution," while nevertheless admitting that he is "able to say little about the detailed sequence of events in the course of which primitive societies begin their differentiation into more stratified societies" (Vidich and Lyman 1985: 78). The point, however, that is easily lost in such an analysis is that it is for all practical purposes a *completely ahistorical* analysis. The Parsonian evolutionary scheme is not based on a study of religious history but on the more-or-less contemporary religious lives of peoples throughout the world whose evolutionary "stage" has been determined by some a priori definition of development. "Secularization" feeds into this evolutionary sequence as a "requirement" of the universal developmental tendencies that are operating in history to produce the "modern" era—although Parsons himself saw secularization far more positively than many subsequent secularization theorists. (That is, Parsons saw the "end" of religion in modern Western industrial societies not as the death of religion but rather as the infusion of these societies with the fundamental values of the Judeo-Christian tradition—justice, human rights, equality, and so on [see Parsons 1974].)

Hadden also cites profitably the succinct critical summary of Parsons's theory that C. Wright Mills provides in his book *The Sociological Imagination* (1959):

> Once the world was filled with the sacred—in thought, practice, and institutional form. After the Reformation and the Renaissance, the forces of modernization swept across the globe and secularization, a

> corollary historical process, loosened the dominance of the sacred. In due course, the sacred shall disappear altogether except, possibly, in the private realm. (32–33)

Although this statement implies historical description, it is in fact based on *almost no historical evidence*. Rather than systematic studies of the *past*, it draws from commonsense generalizations about history related to systematic studies of the present.

The Myth of the Age of Faith

The underlying religious myth of secularization theory is that in "the past" people were significantly more religious than they are today. That is, that sometime, someplace in the past there was a solidary Age of Faith in which people scrupulously, credulously followed the tenets of one or the other of the world's major contemporary religious traditions. (People who accept this myth usually believe that the Age of Faith gave way to the Age of Reason.) Europeans and Euro-Americans usually point to the medieval era. Yet Dutch historian Peter Raedts maintains that there is a growing consensus that both the Catholic Middle Ages and the Age of Reformation are nineteenth-century creations: "A new era for Christianity in Europe began when after 1800 the churches gradually lost the support of the state and had to organize themselves. And it was not until then that the new mass media and the schooling of all the population made the [C]hristianization of everyone a reality" (Ruyter 1996: 7). In short, the myth of the Age of Faith reflects a particular educational process that did not begin to occur until about two hundred years ago. What happened in that process was that precisely as a serious attempt was made to "Christianize" the entire population, an attempt at resistance also emerged. The Age of Faith, if it ever existed, did so for at most a few decades toward the end of the nineteenth century.

If we think only a little about the medieval period, for example, we run into the contradictions of the putative Age of Faith. In this era, the monastic communities throughout Europe are adduced as evidence for this designation. Leaving aside for a moment the question of how "really religious" the motivations of those who entered these monastic communities actually were (or even whether people entered of their own free will), consider the paradox: Monastic life is understood to be otherworldly asceticism, that is, *withdrawal* from the *world*. If the medieval world was so full of the sacred, why did people want to *withdraw* from it in such numbers? A better history, more attentive to popular religiosity (and the lack thereof), would suggest that this was a "secular" world (as the term itself implies), not particularly any more or less religious than any other "world," and that this world, as it drew toward the Renaissance, more and more came to display what Agnes Heller (1981) has termed "practical atheism," that is, less and less concern about the supernatural in day-to-day affairs. As it did, it slowly penetrated even the monastic foundations until it was hard in many cases to distinguish between the two. At this point the Reformation constituted a renewed demand for sacrality in all relationships—which was then itself undermined in due time, allowing Max Weber to write *The Protestant Ethic and the Spirit of Capitalism* and Peter Berger to say more concisely that through its biblical tradition, "historically speaking, Christianity has been its own gravedigger" (1967: 129).

Not clearly fitting within the secularization account either is the derivation of much scientific, medical, and agricultural history from the monasteries. The great geneticist Gregor Mendel, for example, was a monk, and some of the earliest experiments with electricity were conducted by the abbot and monks of the monastery of Nolet. Whence this interest, if these foundations were so unworldly? Monasteries also preserved not only sacred but secular texts as well. John Paterson writes in his history of St. Brigid's Cathedral foundation at Kildare that "a scriptorium for the production of written books seems to have become active" as early as the seventh century, and "this would suggest that the monastery had become involved in secular affairs" (1982: 26). Prior to the heavy hand of the Christian *reconquista* in Spain, Jews, Muslims, and Christians collaborated in the capital of Toledo, translating important scientific texts from the ancient East. The monasteries were the essential repositories for the texts of Aristotle and other ancient Greek philosopher-scientists—so much so that the historical novelist Dan Brown could frame his best-selling novel *The Da Vinci Code* (2003) convincingly in a series of religious settings.

Pluralism

What can we say of secularization now? We can say that over time our epistemologies have changed, that our ideas of the ways the world works have changed, and that these have entailed corresponding shifts of emphasis in global explanatory structures or bases on which we attribute credibility or truth. The medieval worldview, the Renaissance, the Enlightenment, Romanticism, and the era of modern science represent such alternative epistemologies. When we consider the relatively short history of the scientific worldview, it is not surprising that its epistemology has not fully jelled; furthermore, the phenomenon of globalization creates a contestation among religious epistemologies themselves that, though it has analogues in the past, is unprecedented in its scope today. Perhaps because he is now an American, Peter Berger, one of the leading lights of secularization theory, has come the farthest in repudiating it. In the fall of 1997 he wrote:

> [W]hat I and most other sociologists of religion wrote in the 1960s about secularization was a mistake. Our underlying argument was that secularization and modernity go hand in hand. With more modernization comes more secularization. It wasn't a crazy theory. There was some evidence for it. But I think it's basically wrong. Most of the world today is certainly not secular. It's very religious. (1997: 974)

The theory of secularization as a self-limiting process as proposed by Stark and Bainbridge, however, can help us to understand some of the important social dynamics that lie behind religious developments in our own day. Gordon Melton has noted, for example:

> [D]uring the twentieth century, the West has experienced a phenomenon it has not encountered since the reign of Constantine [c. 325]: the growth of a significant visible presence of a variety of non-Christian and non-orthodox Christian bodies competing for the religious allegiance of the public. This growth of so many alternatives religiously is forcing the West into a new situation in which the still dominant Christian religion must share its centuries-old hegemony in a new pluralistic religious environment. (1998: 594)

In many respects, secularization theory was an attempt to account for how *pluralism* was reshaping the religious map—both geographically and cognitively.

While what Melton writes is a beginning for us to understand our own situation, in fact his observations could be rewritten for much of the world: There is a world religious ferment of contesting epistemologies that is in fact going on without limit around the globe, though it is probably more immediately apparent to the average citizen of the West than to the average person in the Middle East or Asia. Contemporary pluralism means that far more religious worldviews are in immediate competition with each other than has ever been the case in the past. Whereas the United States could once settle on a shared "Judeo-Christian" ethic, its religious map now must accommodate Muslims and Buddhists in increasing numbers. Furthermore, the nature of pluralism is multiplicative. Each new religion (or newly imported religion) spawns more new religions, and as some secularization theorists rightly noted, ever-increasing pluralism does undermine the absolute certainty that has been claimed by at least some religions, though new religions will simultaneously continue to arise making precisely this claim. That is, the more one becomes aware of more and more religions competing in a marketplace-like setting, the harder it becomes to assert that any one religion contains all truth and that the others must be all wrong. While it is certainly possible to make comparisons of "better" and "worse," all-or-nothing rigidity simply doesn't hold up.

In some respects, historically Islamic nations may be more sensitive to this than some of the liberal democracies of the West. As a result, these nations intentionally prohibit the "free commerce" of religion that has become a hallmark of Western democracy. Accounts of the Ayatollah Khomeini's program for Iran, for example, make it quite clear that he saw the Western presence, particularly exemplified by Americans, as a threat to the integrity of Islam. As a matter of fact, Pope Leo XIII attempted to sketch a similar program for Catholics at the end of the nineteenth century when he issued a ruling, the apostolic letter *Testem benevolentiae* (1899), that specifically condemned "Americanism." Because Pope Leo lacked in his day the political-economic resources that were at the disposal of Ayatollah Khomeini, however, Leo's ruling could not have the dramatic impact that

Photograph courtesy of William H. Swatos, Jr.

Sacred or Secular?

People in both the United States and Japan are considered to be very "religious," but their religiosity manifests itself in different ways. In the United States, people have tended to choose a single religious tradition to which they adhere and therein to involve themselves in the life of a particular congregation. Japan, by contrast, has a pilgrimage tradition, wherein people choose among shrine centers to meet particular needs. For example, various blessings for prosperity or good health have often been sought at Shinto shrines, whereas people turn to the Buddhist tradition for funerals. Recently, young Japanese couples have shown a preference for wedding ceremonies that are rooted in the Christian tradition.

In 1997 the *Wall Street Journal* carried a story that detailed how Masatoshi Kurosaki, a Japanese bridal consultant, had purchased the interior and trimmings of an unused Church of England building, St. Mary's, Bristol, and had them shipped to Japan to market "authentic" Christian weddings to enhance his business. However, the Japanese also think a wedding ceremony should take about an hour, while the classical Anglican wedding ceremony seldom takes more than twenty minutes, even with music. In addition, Anglican church law insists that at least one spouse be a baptized Christian, which would apply to only a tiny proportion of the Japanese population.

As a solution, Kurosaki has instead engaged ministers of various evangelical Protestant traditions, whose practice is one in which preaching and conversion are more normative—though not normally at weddings. The result has been a hybrid wedding ceremony in which the couple is not only married but also hears, along with the rest of the guests, a fairly lengthy presentation of the virtues of Christianity. In other words, *more* Christianity is now proclaimed at weddings in the commercial wedding chapel of Kurosaki than would have been the case had St. Mary's remained open in England. Is this secularization? Sacralization? Or simply change?

Sacrality and sexuality have, in fact, often been intertwined. The photograph on the facing page shows a relief by Eric Gill (1882–1940). Do you see this as sacred or secular? Curiously, in an early drawing for the work, Gill gave it the title *Christ and His Church*, a reference to Ephesians 5:25–32 in the New Testament, where Paul says that marriage is a symbol of the mysterious relationship between Christ and his church. Later Gill gave it the title *They,* but then when it was marketed, the title *Ecstasy* was applied. Was this secularization or marketing? Or both? Or neither?

Yet another example may be found in a 1998 *Wall Street Journal* story on Hawaiian Goddess, Inc., a Maui-based company operated by Charles and Caroline Muir that markets workshops on Tantra, a mystical technique rooted in Hinduism that uses sexual intercourse as a means to cosmic union with the "oneness of the universe." The couple was at that time charging $695 for a weekend workshop that they described as "kindergarten Tantra" and that has been endorsed by various celebrities and therapists. Curiously, Tantra was promoted in the United States by Bhagwan Sri Rajneesh—also known as Osho—a self-styled Indian guru, who settled for some time in Oregon and whose disciples became known as Rajneeshees. The Bhagwan, now deceased, was eventually deported from the United States on immigration charges, and his disciples scattered. The question for us as sociologists of religion, however, is: What of Tantra? More people in the United States now know about and practice Tantra than ever before: Is this secularization? Or is it change? What kinds of "beliefs" or "commitments" are required to see a particular practice as "sacred" or "secular"?

Sources: Steve Glain, "In Vogue in Japan," *Wall Street Journal*, July 15, 1997, A1; Asra Q. Nomani, "Naked Ambition," *Wall Street Journal*, December 7, 1998, A1, A6.

the actions of the Ayatollah did. Nevertheless, part of the prejudice that was directed against Roman Catholics in the United States for a considerable number of years must be seen in light of this document. Each case, like Communist ideology in the Soviet regimes, is an attempted monopoly of thought control—or the social condition of monopolism, the antithesis of pluralism.

Religious (or, more broadly, ideological) pluralism clearly creates a marketplace of ideas wherein absolute claims for ultimacy are always at some degree of risk. This gives rise to a model of religious competition or marketplace, and in a double sense. Not only is there competition among religions themselves, but there is also the freedom on the part of buyers (people) to pick and choose among the ideological wares that different religions proffer. This has been referred to as "religion *à la carte*" and the result as *bricolage* (Luckmann 1967; Bibby 1987). The result of increased competition is clearly a shift in market shares. However, Finke and Stark (1988) have shown that the reality of increasing religious competition in U.S. cities was not a decrease, but an increase in religious practice, which they here measure using the construct "mobilization"—a reflection of church membership within a given population. Stark (1992) has also shown that this increase extended to rural areas, but that these changes were often unreported as newer, "marginal" churches were not counted in religious censuses. European religious activity follows this pattern least well, perhaps because the state-church tradition there has created a mind-set to which any and all religion is simply a less desirable "good" than it is elsewhere, due to its having been taken for granted for so long, hence so closely identified with a taken-for-granted culture. With certain notable exceptions, European religious participation has been historically low; yet curiously, for example, European immigrants to the United States generally acted quickly to re-create the churches of their homelands, and along with their immediate descendants were *much more* religious (or at least organizationally active) than was the custom in their countries of origin.

Research on religious pluralism, however, continues to produce mixed results. Mark Chaves and Philip Gorski (2001) have examined much of the empirical evidence on the question of whether diversity in church affiliations leads to declines in religious commitment. They located twenty-six studies that they deemed relevant to this issue, and at first the record appeared to be about evenly split: of the twenty-six, eleven studies supported the claim that pluralism was negatively related to religious participation, ten disagreed, and five found no relationship between the two variables. However, 70 percent of the individual analyses (or 132 out of 193) contained in these studies yielded findings to indicate that religious pluralism and participation were either negatively related or not related at all. Even for the smallest units, such as cities, Chaves and Gorski maintain that the bulk of the results are negative; that is, as the diversity of religions in a local population increases, those people become less likely to engage in religious activity. They argue that, as a result:

> The quest for a general law about the relationship between religious pluralism and religious participation . . . should be abandoned. . . . Rather than an either-or argument about whether religious pluralism

> is, in general, positively or negatively associated with religious participation, the most valuable future work on this subject is likely to include investigations into the social, cultural, and institutional arrangements that determine, in part, religious pluralism's consequences for religious vitality. This will be the route to a more adequate sociology of religion, one that moves toward a political economy of the religious sphere by placing religious markets in larger cultural and institutional contexts. (2001: 278–79)

On the level of the individual social actor, we should also note, similarly, that because people are more likely to want their religion à la carte does not necessarily mean that they are "less religious." The food service metaphor is helpful: first, people who order meals à la carte often actually spend more than they would have if they bought a prix fixe meal. Of course, choosing à la carte does mean that people don't just eat what's dished out to them. However, it should not be assumed that as a result they will eat irresponsibly—three desserts and no veggies. People may just as often choose wisely, passing over rich sauces and heavy starches. Certainly it is true, as Chaves has noted, that the authority of religious officers is reduced in this process; on the other hand, it must be remembered that religious officers are nothing but lay folk who have become supercharged by a religious message. The quality of motivation that leads to becoming a religious officer may change, but in fact this may again result in more rather than less. Consider the surplus of (male and female, married and single, straight and gay) priests in the Episcopal Church, where being a bishop has been likened to shepherding a herd of cats, compared to the shortage of (celibate male) priests in the Roman Catholic Church, where clerical authority is still officially maximized. Episcopal Church membership has shrunk while its number of clergy has grown, whereas Roman Catholic membership has grown while its number of clergy has shrunk.

Picking and choosing is not limited to religious idea sets. Again, contrary to the predictions especially of the earliest secularization claims (extending back to Voltaire and Comte), it is not the case that scientific education leads to a totally scientistic mindset. For example, a study in 1914 by James Leuba, surveying a sample of listees in *American Men of Science*, found that 41.8 percent agreed with the statement "I believe in a God to whom one may pray in the expectation of receiving an answer. *By 'answer,' I mean more than the subjective, psychological effect of prayer*" (emphasis in the original), the strongest of three options. In a recent replication of this study, the percentage was 39.3 percent, not significantly different from that in 1914 (Larson and Witham 1997). In short, more than eighty years of scientific advance has not altered the general religious dispositions of scientists. Additionally, studies find that people in the sciences of mathematics, physics, and chemistry are *more* likely to be religious, whereas it is the human sciences of anthropology, psychology, and sociology where disbelief has become more firmly lodged. These kinds of results have appeared outside Western contexts as well. Studying Muslims in Java, one of the islands of Indonesia, the most populous Islamic nation in the world, Joseph Tamney (1979, 1980) found a *positive* correlation between religious practice and both education

Redefining God

"Do you believe in God?" Some form of that question often appears in surveys of the American population. But what does a "yes" or "no" answer mean? That is, behind the question lies a God concept that people reject or accept. Writer Lisa Miller shares these observations from the spring of 2000:

> With its Tiffany windows, tall organ pipes and stone exterior, century-old West-Park Presbyterian Church in New York seems like a bastion of traditional Protestantism—that is, until the minister starts talking about God.
>
> "O burning mountain, O chosen sun, O perfect moon," intones the Rev. Robert Brashear during his Wednesday night services, invoking earthly images of the deity that sound more like Greek myths than Christian liturgy. "O fathomless well, O unattainable height, O clearness beyond measure . . ."
>
> Across the country, the faithful are redefining God. Dissatisfied with conventional images of an authoritarian or paternalistic deity, people are embracing quirky, individualistic conceptions of God to suit their own spiritual needs. Although a steady 90% of Americans continue to say they believe in God, the number of those who say no standard definition "comes close" to their notion of the deity has more than doubled in the past 20 years, according to market-research firm Roper Search Worldwide Inc. Instead, even many traditionalists increasingly envision a God who is far more amorphous, accessible and above all "down here" than the old bearded man in the sky who has long dominated Western religion.

Table 3.1 shows how some well-known Americans from a variety of lifestyles and religious traditions answer the question "What is God?" Does the fact that some give answers that are less conventional than others do mean that they are less religious? Or merely that religious change has taken place? Is it even possible to conceive that as people present images of God that are less conventional an argument can be made for greater religiosity?

and occupational prestige. People with higher-status occupations and/or people with college-level education were significantly more likely to adhere to orthodox Islamic practices regarding fasting, the giving of alms, and prayer. Studies of similar correlations between higher education and social status and religious conservatism have been found elsewhere in the Islamic world as well as among Christians in the United States (see Stark 2000: 59–60).

The numbers of options among which people may choose (or the degree of pluralism) obviously increases with globalization and with the advance of alternative knowledge paradigms. However, again, it is not the case that pluralism did not exist in the past. One may read, on the one hand, the *Confessions* of St. Augustine, Christian bishop of Hippo in North Africa during the fifth century, and find that he tried several belief systems before settling on Christianity. Indeed, the Roman world into which Christianity came was filled with competing ideological systems, wherein part of the putative uniqueness of Christianity was its claim to exclusivity. Studies by Donald A. Nielsen (1990a, 1990b) of both the early Christian era and of the Inquisition show how much

Table 3.1. When We Talk About God

At the start of the new millennium the *Wall Street Weekend Journal* surveyed religious leaders and professionals in several other fields to find out how they imagine the deity:

Chad Curtis	Former professional baseball player/Christian	"My creator."
Robert Dilenschneider	Founder of the Dilenschneider Group, a public relations firm/Catholic	"Jesus Christ in a white robe with a red cloak around him and a halo on his head."
The Rev. James Forbes	Senior Minister Emeritus, Riverside Church, New York/American Baptist–United Church of Christ	"A force field of positive energy."
Danny Goldberg	CEO of Gold Village Entertainment/Jewish	"Pure love, intense feelings of love."
Anne Rice	Novelist/Catholic	"It may be a sexless being, but it's a being who cares very much about us as fleshly creatures."
Bishop T. D. Jakes	Popular Dallas-based African-American preacher/Christian	"I don't need to see Him to believe Him. I don't see heat, but I know it's hot."
Bill Joy	Cofounder of Sun Microsystems Inc./Protestant	"As scientists we can say God is part of our genes. The desire to believe in God is built into us as a species."
Anne Lamott	Author of *Grace (Eventually): Thoughts on Faith*/ Presbyterian	"In the buds of the apricot tree. Or a baby. Or the California poppies bursting up where there was just dirt before."
The Rev. Pat Robertson	Cohost of the *700 Club*/ Southern Baptist	"I think people who put a face on God are making a big mistake."
Dana Buchman	Fashion designer/ Presbyterian	"I don't believe in God, but I think often of close relatives who've had an effect on my life and values. It's like ancestor worship."

Source: Adapted from Lisa Miller, "Redefining God," *Wall Street Journal* (April 21, 2000), W1, W4 (table).

people were willing to suffer for persisting in holding beliefs that departed from the dominant tradition—first, Christianity versus the imperial cult; later, heterodox Christian beliefs versus the consolidated official church.

Both before and after Christian times, however, alternate belief systems were available, not only in major faiths, but through popular traditions. Disbelief (or atheism) was always an alternative. The book of Psalms in the Hebrew Bible (the Christian Old Testament) is replete with references to "those who say there is no God." In ninth-century Iceland, similarly, at the founding of the country Ingólfur Arnarson laments the death of his half brother Hjörleifur in religious terms: "This I see befall every man who will not sacrifice to the gods." That is, Hjörleifur refused to practice any religion. Icelandic accounts of the settlement period also record by name at least one more atheist: Helgi the Godless. And paganism and Christianity mixed in the country well into the modern period. Keith Thomas, in his comprehensive study *Religion and the Decline of Magic* (1971), records the persistence of non-Christian magical practice in "Christian England" at least into the sixteenth century. Studies of folk religion throughout Europe and the United States confirm this finding and extend it into the nineteenth and twentieth centuries in some places. Similarly, Richard Rankin's study (1993) of religion among the elite of North Carolina in the first half of the nineteenth century records considerable ambivalence toward the practice of religion, especially in the first quarter of the century, and this has been demonstrated to be the case throughout much of the South (see Kuykendall 1982).

With respect to the secularization thesis, then, two aspects of pluralism must be taken into consideration. On the one hand, there is a substantial body of evidence that pluralism of belief—including disbelief—has been an option throughout history that is simply intensified by globalization. On the other hand, pluralism forces us to make a distinction between secularization and what might be called "de-Christianization": that is, new religious movements may emerge or other world traditions may gain dominance over Christianity in the West. Although we do not think this is likely to happen, it is sociologically important to understand that if people cease to believe that Jesus Christ is God and instead believe that Saytha Sai Baba is God, no secularization has occurred. If Muslims in the United States outnumber Episcopalians (or even active members of the Church of England in England!), no secularization has occurred. *Religious change* of course has occurred, and this will certainly have consequences for the societies in which it takes place.

An underlying assumption of secularization that pluralism thus challenges is the idea that "religion" is something fixed. Instead, a sociologist of religion needs to recognize the tentativeness and fragility of religious structures of meaning. Religious concepts easily lend themselves to reification, that is, ideas being treated as if they were objects. As ideational systems, religions are always in interaction with material culture, social structure, other cultural systems, and individual personalities. The theological bias of secularization theory within the sociology of religion has underwritten conceptions of "religion" as essentially fixed, rather than essentially variable. *Sociologically*, however, there is far more reason to conceive religion as variable—indeed, whereas among social institutions religion deals uniquely with a nonempirical, "uncontrollable" referent, religion is *infinitely* variable in a way that other action orientations are not. Only ecclesiological presuppositions and prejudices warrant the notion of religious fixity; thus analyses in the sociology of religion need to be attentive to change as *inherent* in religion, just as change is in other institutional spheres and cultural dimensions.

Suggestions for Further Reading

Robert N. Bellah. 1991. *Beyond Belief: Essays on Religion in a Post-Traditional World*, 2nd ed. Berkeley: University of California Press.

Steve Bruce. 2002. *God Is Dead: Secularization in the West*. Oxford: Blackwell.

Sharon Hanson. 1997. "The Secularisation Thesis: Talking at Cross Purposes." *Journal of Contemporary Religion* 12:159–79.

Michael W. Hughey. 1983. *Civil Religion and Moral Order: Theoretical and Historical Dimensions.* Westport, Conn.: Greenwood Press.

David A. Martin. 2005. *On Secularization: Towards a Revised General Theory*. Aldershot, UK: Ashgate.

Talcott Parsons. 1974. "Religion in Postindustrial America: The Problem of Secularization." *Social Research* 41:193–225.

Rodney Stark. 2004. *Exploring the Religious Life*. Baltimore: Johns Hopkins University Press.

Rodney Stark and Roger Finke. 2000. *Acts of Faith: Explaining the Human Side of Religion.* Berkeley: University of California Press.

William H. Swatos, Jr., and Daniel V. A. Olson, eds. 2000. *The Secularization Debate*. Lanham, Md.: Rowman & Littlefield.

Olivier Tschannen. 1991. "The Secularization Paradigm: A Systematization." *Journal for the Scientific Study of Religion* 30:396–415.

Photograph courtesy of William H. Swatos, Jr.

CHAPTER 4

Religion in the United States

DENOMINATIONALISM AND BEYOND

Americans, it has been said, are the most religious people on the face of the earth. But precisely what this designation means is not abundantly clear. "Organized" religion in the United States appears to be less an institution than a bundle of contradictions. Religion is simultaneously immersed deeply in the sacred and layered lightly over the contours of a secular culture. It is at one moment an unyielding "Rock of Ages" and at the next given to fleeting faddishness. At times it is shunted to the peripheries of life; later, it seems the only reason for life at all. America's faiths are either all furor and ferment, or they are the serene security of tradition. Sometimes they are both. They are less *and* more than what meets the eye.

Perhaps a better approach than asking whether Americans are religious is to inquire about the many ways one can be religious in the United States. In that inquiry, this chapter may be regarded as a preliminary catalog.

The range of terms that have been used to describe religion in the United States since 1960 is as broad as the subject itself. Few of these terms, however, carry a positive connotation. More clearly evident in accounts of the contemporary period in American religion, at least early on, is a language of deterioration, if not doom. To confirm this impression, one need merely scan, for instance, the next-to-last chapter of what was one of the most authoritative sources on U.S. religious history twenty years ago, Winthrop Hudson's *Religion in America* (1987). Words of alarm, in some cases framed in large type at the heads of sections, virtually leap from the page: "disenchantment," "disaffection," "decline," and "disarray" were noted starkly, and their incidence cried out for explanation.

The substance of the most common explanation is probably familiar. In the United States, a national culture that emphasized "dissidence" had, by the 1960s, finally put to flight the forces of faith, leaving religious believers "dispersed" and "dispirited." Seemingly overnight, organized religion in the United States had become an empty shell. A tendency toward "accommodation" of the churches to society, conservatives suspected, had triggered in religious circles a disastrous "crisis" of identity and meaning. "Vacillation" before the secular onslaught of modernity had bred stresses whose only prospect for resolution, according to liberals, resided in "regrouping" and the tentative, if hopeful, search by church leaders for "alternatives" to traditional faith. Believers of whatever rank or opinion would be forced at last to learn, with the psalmist, how to "sing the Lord's song in a strange land" (Psalm 137:4).

Of course, in the social upheaval of the 1960s, none of this was certain and all of it was subject to change—and change it did. Within the space of two decades, in fact, the prevailing message about religion in the United States that could be monitored from the academic heights revealed a decidedly different theme. Yet the vocabulary was equally dramatic. Across the globe was sweeping a strain of "resurgent" religion that, by answering a widespread "hunger for authority," warred against all things modern.

A "new conservatism" soon loomed over the land. With it were allied religious groups (evangelical and fundamentalist Protestants, Pentecostal Christians, Roman Catholic traditionalists, and Orthodox Jews) that threatened for the first time in the twentieth century to capture a foothold in the center of American culture, a no-man's-land that had long before been evacuated of official evidence of piety. Preachers boasted of the votes that they could deliver with the mere mention of a name from their pulpits, and political candidates of both major parties wasted no time in recollecting for curious interviewers, amid the other transitions of adolescence, their long-forgotten memories of having been "born again." Public discourse was thick with expressions of concern over the fate of the moral and spiritual values at the heart of the unique "Judeo-Christian tradition" of the United States. Parents, for their part, began to act to preserve and transmit those values better by enrolling their children in a burgeoning number of religious schools. Confidence in organized religion once again surged, while *Newsweek* declared 1976 to be "The Year of the Evangelicals" after one of them, former governor Jimmy Carter, won the Democratic Party's nomination, and later that year was elected president of the United States.

Churches and Sects

The United States was the first nation founded on Protestant principles. Of course, several European nations had declared for the Protestant cause well before the stable North American colonies of the seventeenth century were founded, but the United States was unique in having its religious roots as a nation virtually entirely in Protestant soil. Although the observation is most often credited to G. K. Chesterton, more than one commentator has remarked that in the United States even the Catholics are Protestants!

Historian of religions Catherine Albanese (1992: 402–30) notes that a pervasive "public Protestantism" succeeded in establishing "the Protestant code, . . . a part of the body of connecting religious characteristics" in the United States. Virtually omnipresent in American society, "the code has expressed itself as clear conditions, institutions, and underlying patterns for behavior within the mainstream." There were both "many religious traditions within the geographical boundaries of the United States" and a "manyness *within* traditions," yet

> even as we immersed ourselves in the religious pluralism, from time to time we could not fail to notice the ways in which different traditions and movements seemed to take on some of the characteristics of the Protestant mainstream. Reform Jews of the late nineteenth century moved their Sabbath services to Sunday morning and imitated the style of Protestant worship. Catholics after Vatican II adopted a leaner and simpler version of the Mass, closer to the demands of the Protestant Reformation. Mormons and Adventists, who affirmed the good life in this world, resembled liberal Protestants in their optimism, while Japanese Buddhists in America spoke of churches, acknowledged bishops, and initiated Sunday services. Meanwhile, blacks who became middle class often gravitated toward congregations that were integrated or that resembled in their style the churches of white mainline Protestantism. In these and other instances, manyness was still thriving, but there were numerous ways in which the boundaries of the separate traditions overlapped the boundaries of Protestantism. (1992: 391)

Protestant principles of social action underlay the United States well before the majority of the country's population was formally affiliated with any Protestant church. Indeed, this is quite the point: From the nation's beginnings religious affiliation was an *option* for its citizens.

Originating in Protestantism, a truly distinctive feature of religion in the United States is its informal system of denominationalism, an institutional pattern that both governs relations among the churches and organizes contact between them and the wider community. In its more theoretical form, denominationalism has been called "the ideology of pluralism" (Ruthven 1988: 306). The system derives its name from the ecclesiological term for the free churches that find themselves at home in a religiously pluralistic society. More formally, a denomination is a voluntary religious association with a specified purpose: "the propagation of its point of view, which it in some sense holds to be true." To achieve this goal, the denomination relies not on compulsion supplied by political enforcement, but on the autonomous energies of "like-hearted and like-minded individuals" (Mead 1954: 291). A sociological understanding of denominationalism is rooted in a larger theoretical-conceptual framework of religious organization known as church-sect theory, and we will turn to this as background to the discussion in this chapter.

In its many permutations and combinations as an explanation of religious organization and religiosity, church-sect theory may be the most important middle-range theory that the sociology of religion has to offer. Although the terms *church* and *sect* have a long heritage in the writings of church historians, the credit for their first attachment to sociological concepts belongs to Max Weber in his essays on the Protestant ethic, written at the turn of the twentieth century (see 1998). Their first popularization among students of religion in the modern sense, however, was through H. Richard Niebuhr's *The Social Sources of Denominationalism*, a 1929 adaptation of the work of Weber's contemporary and sometime associate Ernst Troeltsch (1931). In order to understand some of the confusion and debate in contemporary sociological usage, it is helpful to review how the concepts fit into Weber's sociology of religion and how Troeltsch's work modified them.

WEBER'S SOCIOLOGY AND TROELTSCH'S ETHICS

Weber's sociology is united by the overarching thematic element of the process of the rationalization of action. Weber was attempting to answer the question of why this ultimately global process had come to fruition most completely in the Anglo-American spirit of capitalism. As a part of this project, Weber also had to develop an analytical method that would permit him to resolve the dilemma of his commitment to the principle that sociology was a scientific discipline on the one hand, and on the other, of the difficulty in supplementing empathic interpretive sociology with anything even approximating experimental accuracy. Weber's answer was a comparative methodology using the tool of the *ideal type*—a mental construct based on relevant empirical components, formed and explicitly delineated by the researcher to facilitate precise comparisons on specific points of interest. Like the inch in measurement, the conceptualizations of church and sect serve to enable two or more religious organizations to be compared to each other; church-sect theory in Weber's usage was not a standard *to* which religious organizations were compared but *by* which they were compared (Weber 1949). The critical differentiating variable for Weber was "mode of membership"—that is, whether the normal method of membership recruitment of the organization was by birth (church) or decision (sect).

In the transition from Weber to Troeltsch's *Social Teaching of the Christian Churches* (published in German in 1912), the church-sect typology underwent significant alterations. Troeltsch was not a social scientist, but a theologian attempting to relate types of religious experience to the varieties of social teachings with which they might be correlated. In so doing, he diverged from Weber on two critical points. First, he shifted the emphasis of the type from organization to behavior. Second, he stressed the notion of "accommodation" or "compromise" as distinguishing between the different religious styles. The first departure is most clearly seen in Troeltsch's positing of *three* types of religious behavior: churchly, sectarian, and mystical. The third of these is now generally dropped from consideration by church-sect theorists; in Weber's conceptualization it occurs in a separate bipolar typology, namely, that of asceticism-mysticism, about which we will say more in our closing chapter. Nevertheless, the presence of the mystical type at the outset of Troeltsch's discussion suggests that he was actually using the terms in a conceptually different operation from that to which church-sect is usually put in organizational analysis. The "dichotomy" of church-sect that has been attributed to Troeltsch—whatever its value—must be understood within his three-way scheme and within the instrumental context of the Weberian ideal type as well. Troeltsch and Weber shared primarily method, partially content, and peripherally project. Weber and Troeltsch were working on different, although related, questions; Troeltsch understood Weber's concept of the ideal type, and capitalized on what Weber termed its "transiency," hence making church, sect, and mysticism work for his own purposes.

Subsequent church-sect arguments have largely revolved around an overemphasis on the Weber-Troeltsch association, which assumes that because Troeltsch used Weber's method and to some extent his content, the *intention* of Troeltsch's work was the same as Weber's. However, it was not. *What Troeltsch himself calls a "sociological formulation" of a theological question has been misidentified with Weber's attempt to analyze a sociological problem.* We see the difference between the two projects clearly in the critical distinguishing elements that form the focus for each one's work. While Weber uses mode of membership, Troeltsch adopts accommodation or compromise. Whereas mode of membership can be ascertained relatively directly, accommodation has a more mediated character: What is and is not accommodation is more evaluative, hence dependent on one's perspective. A theological rather than organizational focus comes to frame the theory.

The basis for the shift in usage lies in the way in which the theory was introduced to English-speaking audiences, with the corresponding void created in German scholarship as a result of the two world wars. Thus it was that the first major U.S. publication to use the types was Niebuhr's *Social Sources of Denominationalism*—the work of another sociologically inclined theologian. Though at times possessed by a rather naive evolutionism and a narrow perspective, Niebuhr's work contributed a significant element that was lacking in earlier treatments. He used church and sect as poles of a continuum, rather than simply as discrete categories. Niebuhr did not merely classify groups in relation to their relative sect-likeness or church-likeness, but analyzed the dynamic process of religious history as groups moved along this continuum. An unfortunate result of Niebuhr's work, however, was that taken by itself it tended toward the reification of the types and the hypothetical continuum that he in turn posited. It thus contained further seeds for church-sect theory to develop into an evaluative device, quite outside the sociological frame of reference in which it was conceived. This disjunction was compounded by the fact that Troeltsch's *Social Teaching* was translated in 1931, whereas Weber's methodological work was not available in translation until 1949—that is, Weber's concepts were available to the majority of U.S. readers many years prior to the rules for their intended use. Many of the subsequent difficulties that have attended church-sect theory may be traced to the strange movements of this framework and its methodological base across the Atlantic.

ELABORATION, REACTION, AND REVISION

Subsequent elaborations of church-sect theory have been clearly dependent on the work of Troeltsch and Niebuhr. The original church-sect dichotomy became generally interpreted as a continuum having a multicriteria basis for its analyses. Howard Becker (1932) was the first American trained as a sociologist to use and extend church-sect theory. Attempting to facilitate increased specificity, Becker delineated two types within each of the original two types, resulting in a cult-sect-denomination-ecclesia model. In thus developing the typology, Becker abandoned the ideal-type method for that of "abstract collectivities," ideal realities rather than constructs.

In *Religion and the Struggle for Power* (1946), J. Milton Yinger increased the limitations for specific points along the continuum, extending Becker's four types to six: cult, sect, established sect, class church/denomination, ecclesia, and universal church—the latter most clearly evidencing the increasingly theological focus of the usage. Yinger went further in his specification, however, by subtyping sects in terms of their relationship to the social order: whether they were accepting, avoiding, or aggressive. This development began a wave of interest in the sect type within church-sect theorizing, with numerous writers offering contributions on the best way to treat this possibility, the most lasting of which has been that of Bryan Wilson (1959). The result of this strategy was to shift the focus of church-sect theory from a tool for comparative analysis toward a classificatory system to apply sociological concepts to religious organization.

An exception to this general tendency to focus on religious organizations (first "sects," later "cults") that were increasingly more marginal to mainstream society was the publication of a seminal essay on the *denomination* by David Martin (1962). Although it did little to stem the tide of interest in marginal groups at the time, Martin's article would bear fruit in various ways in new typologies that appeared in the late 1970s. The action sociology models of both Roy Wallis and William Swatos, as well as the rational choice models of Rodney Stark and his colleagues, emphasize the importance of denominational religiosity as the typological alternative to sectarianism (and cultic forms).

On the heels of these developments came criticism of the framework. A number of critics denounced the orientation as meaningless, or at best woefully inadequate to systematic investigation of the empirical world. Church-sect theorizing has been criticized as ambiguous and vague, lacking precise definitions, unsuited to tests for validity and reliability, merely descriptive rather than explanatory, less informative than other possible approaches, historically and geographically restricted, and unrelated to the rest of sociological theory. Despite all these criticisms, however, the theoretical framework into which the original church-sect distinction has evolved allows a tremendous amount of data to be organized and reported.

In response to these criticisms, a number of scholars have also made revisions within the church-sect framework, making it a more viable theoretical orientation for the sociology of religion. One approach adopted by such figures as Paul Gustafson (1967, 1973) and Roland Robertson (1970), as well as Yinger (1970), Wallis (1975), and Swatos (1979), has been to use an explicit visual scheme for modeling and analysis. Alternatively, Stark and Bainbridge (1979) have reached back into earlier work by Glock and Stark (1965) to use pieces of church-sect theorizing in their rational choice modeling.

NEO-WEBERIAN ANALYSES

Particularly significant to this process of rethinking church-sect theory was the work of Benton Johnson. Early in his career, Johnson (1957) critiqued the Troeltschian approach to church-sect. In Johnson's subsequent work (1963, 1971), he returned to Weber and focused on the single universal variable property of a group's relationship to the social environment in which it exists. *Church* is employed as the polar type of acceptance of the social environment, whereas *sect* is the polar type of its rejection. This conceptualization is similar to an earlier one proposed by Peter Berger (1954), in which "nearness of the spirit" was the central focus. In later work, Bryan Wilson (1973) also embraced "response to the world" as the principal basis for classification of sects in an ideal-typical (rather than taxonomic) way. Johnson contends that the sociologist should strive toward the discovery of universal properties at a high level of generality, properties that vary in such ways that typologies might be constructed. He sees "acceptance/rejection of the social environment" as a single variable around which empirical church-sect distinctions may be grouped, asserting that this typological approach is superior to one that simply adds types as historical circumstances change. Johnson's work has significantly affected such differing streams as Swatos's situationalism (for example, 1990) as well as the rational choice modeling of Stark and his colleagues (see Stark and Bainbridge 1979).

Although Johnson's distinction possesses definite advantages in terms of conceptual parsimony, its lack of integration of the historical differences in the basic social structures and cultural systems in which religious organizations function produces potential difficulties in macrosociological analyses. Whereas the microsociologically based rational choice model focuses primarily on the effects of the organizational experience of the decision-maker and only secondarily on the organization-system component, a more culturally oriented analysis would note that different system contexts produce different styles of organizational response that cannot be entirely comprehended by a single, universal variable component. Thus, Swatos bisects Johnson's acceptance/rejection dichotomy with the sociocultural system polarity of monopolism/pluralism (see figure 4.1). Following on the work of both Peter Berger (1967) and David Little (1969), Swatos contends that the nature of the sociocultural system shapes the patterns of acceptance and rejection that are expressed in specific religious organizational forms and rationales. Building on these foundations, Michael York's study of New Age and neopagan movements (1995) demonstrates the continued value of church-sect typologizing as a conceptual tool within a larger analytical framework through which these very recent religious phenomena may also be studied profitably. York introduces the concept of *network*, which has been further elaborated in a constructive church-sect schema as a polar type to *organization* by Hizuru Miki (1999). This advance facilitates both cross-cultural comparisons and the analysis of both new religious movements and quasi-religions, some of which have heretofore been treated under the now ideologically loaded concept of *cult*. Thus, church-sect theorizing continues to be a part of the ongoing scholarship of sociologists of religion, well beyond its initial foundations.

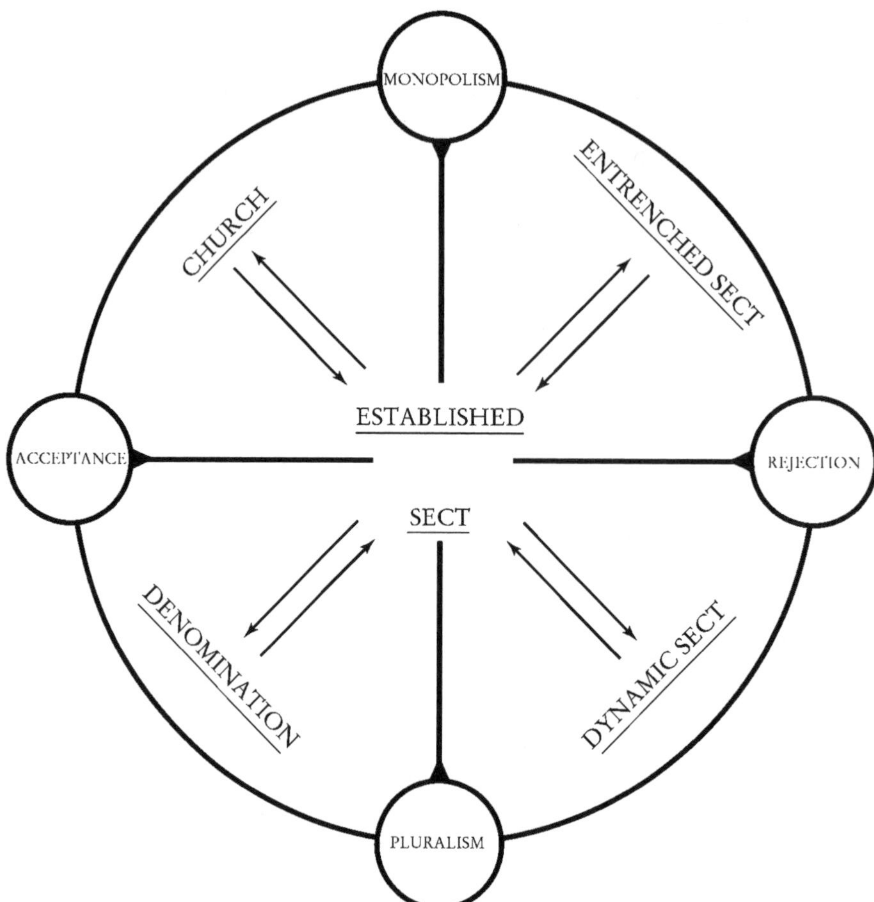

Figure 4.1. Monopolism, Pluralism, Acceptance, Rejection. Swatos's integrated model for church-sect theory illustrates the dynamic relationship that exists between acceptance and rejection of the social environment in which a religious organization operates, on the one hand, and the relative monopolism or pluralism of that environment's social system on the other. This is one example of the kinds of property-space modeling to which church-sect theory increasingly turned by the 1970s. Source: William H. Swatos, Jr., "Monopolism, Pluralism, Acceptance, and Rejection: An Integrated Model for Church-Sect Theory," Review of Religious Research *15 (1975): 177.*

Denominationalism

The term *denomination* was employed first in the late seventeenth century by those groups of Christians in England who dissented from the established Church of England but considered themselves to be entirely loyal to the British state and recognized the monarch as having rights with respect to the Church of England. In 1702, specifically, the Presbyterians, Baptists, and Congregationalists formed "the body of the Dissenting Ministers of the Three Denominations in and about the City of London." The term was introduced to counter the pejorative term *sect*, which in popular use had the sense of deviant or undesirable practices, somewhat as the term *cult* does today. *Denomination* is now used in pluralistic societies for those forms of organized religious expression that generally support the established social order and are tolerant of one another's practices.

TYPOLOGY

The term *denominationalism* was significantly introduced into the subsequent literature of the sociology of religion by Niebuhr's *Social Sources of Denominationalism*. The central thesis of this work was that new religious organizations (sects) begin among the socially "disinherited," but in the United States, as these groups attain higher social status, their religious expressions become more "respectable" or socially accepted; thus there is a movement across generations from sectarian to denominational religious life—or else the sectarian group dies out. Methodism in the United States provides the most classic example of the sect-to-denomination process (Brewer 1952), but other groups also illustrate this type of transition (Bordin 1965).

John Wesley on Wealth and Piety

John Wesley, the eighteenth-century Church of England priest who founded the movement that eventually created the Methodist Church, was particularly sensitive to the peculiar dynamics of wealth and piety, hence the character of the sect-to-denomination/church dynamic. In 1786, close to the end of his life, he wrote:

> I fear, wherever riches have increased (exceeding few are the exceptions) the essence of religion, the mind that was in Christ, has decreased in the same proportion. Therefore do I not see how it is possible, in the nature of things, for any revival of true religion to continue long. For religion must necessarily produce both industry and frugality. And these cannot but produce riches. But as riches increase, so will pride, anger, and love of the world in all its branches.
>
> How then is it possible that Methodism, that is the religion of the heart, though it flourishes now as a green bay-tree, should continue in this state? For the Methodists in every place grow diligent and frugal; consequently they increase in goods. Hence they proportionably increase in pride, in anger, in the desire of the flesh, the desire of the eyes, and the pride of life. So, although the form of religion remains, the spirit is swiftly vanishing away.
>
> Is there no way to prevent this? This continual declension of pure religion? We ought not to forbid people to be diligent and frugal. We *must* exhort all Christians to gain all they can, and to save all they can—that is, in effect to grow rich! What way then (I ask again) can we take that our money may not sink us to the nethermost hell? There is one way, and there is no other under heaven. If those who *gain all they can,* and *save all they can,* will likewise *give all they can,* then the more they gain, the more they will grow in grace, and the more treasure they will lay up in heaven.

Source: *The Works of John Wesley*, vol. 9: *The Methodist Societies: History, Nature, and Design* (Nashville: Abingdon, 1989), 529–30.

This strongly evolutionary view has been considerably modified today. A particularly important contribution to the study of denominationalism was David Martin's article, "The Denomination," mentioned earlier, in which he forced a reconsideration of this organizational form as a historically specific type, rather than as a stage on a quasi-evolutionary continuum. A standard current definition of the denomination would be that of Bryan Wilson, who writes that the denomination is "a voluntary association" that "accepts adherents without imposition of traditional prerequisites of entry" (1959: 4–5), such as belonging to a particular ethnic or national group, or sectarian testimonies of spiritual regeneration. He continues:

> Breadth and tolerance are emphasized. . . . Its self-conception is unclear and its doctrinal position unstressed. . . . One movement among many . . . it accepts the standards and values of the prevailing culture. . . . Individual commitment is not very intense; the denomination accepts the values of the secular society and the state.

Furthermore, and most significantly, individuals in a denomination coalesce around a notably open view of their religious purpose. The elusive goal of a denomination's members is to build and maintain a particular identity as believers without losing sight of all that, at the roots, unites churches and their missions. In the words of Will Herberg's definition in *Protestant-Catholic-Jew*, a denomination is "a stable, settled church, enjoying a legitimate and recognized place in the larger aggregate of churches, each recognizing the proper status of the others" (1955: 99).

The association between denominationalism and pluralism is crucial. In pluralism, one may belong to any denomination—*or none at all*! Religion is pigeonholed and privatized. It is a voluntary activity to be undertaken or dismissed at the discretion of the individual. The denomination is thus marked perhaps most significantly by this voluntarism of support, coupled with mutual respect and forbearance of all other competing religious groups. It is, indeed, this quality of *competition* that is the unique hallmark of the pluralistic religious situation; acceptance of the "free-market" situation in religious ideas is the critical operating principle of denominationalism. Denominations are the organizational forms that dominant religious traditions assume in a pluralistic culture. The distinction between monopolistic and pluralistic societies in typological differentiation between the church and the denomination is drawn particularly in Swatos's church-sect model.

Although denominationalism is now characteristic of virtually all Western societies, it reaches its quintessential expression in the United States; that is, U.S. denominationalism has been the model for religious pluralism throughout the world. Although denominationalism is, strictly speaking, a Protestant dynamic, it has become fully accepted in principle by all major religious groups in the United States. In fact, one could say that the denominationalizing process represents the Americanizing of a religious tradition, which is at the same time and in the same measure a relativizing process. Religious groups that too strongly resist this process will probably face eventual conflict with the legal system. Since the 1940s, social scientists have been particularly interested in the relationship between denomination and both social stratification and sociopolitical variables; the term *class church* was first applied as an equivalent to denomination by Yinger in the 1940s.

Although some religious groups have made specific efforts to eschew the label, *denomination* nevertheless has been the most neutral and general term used to identify religious organizations in the United States. *Organized religion* and *church affiliation* both anticipate the denomination as the dominant religious expression in society. Religious belief and action work together with the sociocultural system to develop a legitimation system as a result of a mutual interdependency. Denominationalism is a structure that allowed Americans to resolve religious differences peacefully. A concomitant result, of course, was to create the context for both a de-emphasis on and eventual discrediting of theology as a source for authoritative knowledge in American society's common life.

To the normatively religious American, denominations are just that—names. They are merely labels or units of measurement, not the thing itself being labeled or measured. Accordingly, denominations are not what, in the end, is important about religion. Lying far beneath the nominal divisions that cut like fences across the religious terrain of the United States are veins of truth and tradition that burrow below the boundaries and enrich the foundations of many churches. It is to these underground lodes of inspiration, and not to "the accumulated corruptions of the Church through the centuries" standing above ground, that contemporary Americans instinctively turn in public discussions of religion. The historical and theological peculiarities of denominations are highlighted only as much as is necessary to shade the groups into unique hues for placement along American religion's intricately calibrated color bar. Thereafter, denominations avoid theological disputation because it may potentially be "divisive" (Mead 1954: 297–300).

In accepting the reality of religious freedom and thereby beginning their transformation into denominations, U.S. churches learned to accentuate that which was general about religion. As church historian Sidney E. Mead read them in the 1950s, the unwritten rules of denominationalism instructed that

> only what all the religious "sects" held and taught in common (the "essentials of every religion") was really relevant for the well being of the society and the state. Obversely this meant that the churches implicitly accepted the view that whatever any religious group held *peculiarly* as a tenet of its faith must be irrelevant for the public welfare. Thus in effect the churches accepted the responsibility to teach that the peculiar views or tenets or doctrines that divided them one from another, and gave each its only reason for separate and independent existence, were either irrelevant for the general welfare or at most possessed only a kind of instrumental value for it. (1954: 301)

DENOMINATIONS TODAY

This is not to say, however, that religion in the United States is amorphous and without structure. To the contrary, factions of faith *do* exist, and a more or less restrained competition has always marked relations among them. What is changing, in the opinion of some observers of church life in the United States, are the lines along which the competing parties are arrayed. Until recently, the perspective on interreligious relations that was framed in the 1950s by Will Herberg held sway among scholars.

Competition within U.S. Christianity, Mead noted in that same decade, was conceived not as "competition between those of rival faiths, but competition between those holding divergent forms of the same faith" (1954: 316). Herberg both concurred in this view and added to it. "The American, when he thinks of religion," he argued, "thinks of it primarily in terms of the three categories we have designated as religious communities"—namely, Protestantism, Catholicism, and Judaism. Fittingly, "particular denominational affiliations and loyalties within each of the communities," Herberg commented, "are not necessarily denied, or even depreciated, but they are held to be distinctly secondary" (1955: 52).

This model operated reasonably well as long as interreligious hostility persisted in the United States and wide social distances separated members of the nation's broadest communities of faith. With time, however, tensions between Protestants and Catholics subsided somewhat, and the attitudes of both toward Jewish believers softened as well. The picture of religious organization has been further clouded in the period since the 1950s with the founding of new religious movements (and coalitions of their opponents), the formation of special interest groups within the churches, the creation of alliances that transcend denominational boundaries, and a wave of consolidations and schisms in the existing churches. Together, these developments have set the stage in the present day for a major realignment of religion in the United States.

Since the 1980s, and particularly with the publication of Robert Wuthnow's *The Restructuring of American Religion* in 1988, there has been considerable debate within the sociology of religion over the current significance of denominationalism in U.S. society. This debate was presaged by a distinction drawn by the church historian Martin Marty in *Righteous Empire* (1970; cf. Marty 1981, 1986a; Jacobsen and Trollinger 1998) between two "parties" in American religion. According to Wuthnow's elaboration of this view, each denomination is now divided between the two parties (roughly, liberals and conservatives) on critical sociopolitical issues—reflecting in turn the relative rise in importance of "the state" as a sociocultural actor since the 1940s. The ecclesiastical party with which people identify is more important to both their spiritual and moral lives than is a particular denominational label, according to this theory.

This realignment involves two related changes in the structure of American religion. First, official denominationalism—even that of the broadest sort analyzed by Herberg—appears to some authors to be waning. Less and less distinctive information is conveyed by denominational labels, they insist, and these organizations more and more have been reaping distrust and alienation from members. Second, in their place have emerged hosts of movements with narrower objectives, ordinarily ones that cluster loosely around items from either conservative or liberal political agendas.

Attention has thus turned away from ecumenical activity, not because the churches themselves deem it to be unimportant, but because there is frankly no need to negotiate peace among noncombatants. The front has moved, and the action, so to speak, is elsewhere. "The primary axis defining religious and cultural pluralism in American life has shifted," writes James Davison Hunter. "The important divisions are no longer ecclesiastical but rather 'cosmological.' They no longer revolve around specific doctrinal issues or styles of religious practice and organization but rather around fundamental assumptions about values, purpose, truth, freedom, and collective identity" (1988: 22). Thus the most heated controversies swirl around such issues as abortion and sexual orientation rather than whether people kneel or stand or sit to receive Holy Communion or have or have not been confirmed by a bishop in apostolic succession. The growth of nondenominational and parachurch organizations is seen as part of this process.

Others argue that this view is historically shortsighted and needs modification. Swatos (1981a, 1994), for example, uses the local-cosmopolitan distinction elaborated specifically in the sociology of religion by Wade Clark Roof (1972, 1978) to argue that denominationalism in the context of U.S. voluntarism is preeminently a *local* dynamic, providing people "place" in a specific setting, and that this dynamic operates as much as it ever did, to the extent that cosmopolitan elaborations (for example, denominational agency structures) can be discounted from analysis. Cosmopolitan denominational bureaucracies are not, according to this thesis, the crucial social dynamic of the typology, but a specific, transitory development. In addition, intradenominational debates have created more internally consistent denominational worldviews: conservatives now dominate the Southern Baptists, while liberals have won the day among Episcopalians and the United Church of Christ. Davidson, Pyle, and Reyes (1995; cf. Davidson and Pyle 2005) have also shown that the liberal denominations continue to remain significantly disproportionately overrepresented among elites in the United States across the twentieth century, with corrections required only to accommodate specific immigration effects. Reform Jews, for example, are now also significantly overrepresented among elites, along with Episcopalians, Unitarians, and Presbyterians; Roman Catholics have achieved approximate parity with their share of the general population. On the other hand, conservative Protestants generally remain significantly underrepresented, which may explain their attempts to achieve greater political visibility.

An often overlooked historical dimension of denominationalism in the United States is the role women played in maintaining the life of the different denominations and in the social-ranking system that these roles may have implied. The uniformly and universally greater interest of women in all phases of religious practice is documented by Leslie Francis (1997) and by Tony Walter and Grace Davie (1998; cf. Stark 2002). The decline of membership in some mainline denominations (for example, Methodists, Presbyterians, Episcopalians, and Congregationalists [United Church of Christ]) is at least partly due to the increased presence of women in the workforce, which has resulted in a corresponding absence of women to undertake volunteer activities. Women in these denominations are also more likely to be in the professional classes and thus to have job responsibilities that do not end with the workday. Denominations that have declined in membership directly correspond to those that have most endorsed gender equality, while those that have gained membership are more gender differentiated. These also tend to attract membership from the working stratum, where even women working outside the home are, relatively speaking, more likely to have more "free" time to devote to church activities, and are less likely to experience role redefinition in the home.

Regardless of which side of the current debate on the significance of denominationalism is ultimately vindicated, both perspectives emphasize the crucial role of the *congregation* as the place where religious ideology and the lived experience of the people who do or do not choose to wear a particular denominational label meet. The greater significance in the study of religion in the United States that has been accorded recently to congregations is evidenced in the works of, among others, Nancy Ammerman (1994, 2005; cf. Ammerman 1997a); Randall Balmer (1996); Penny Edgell Becker (1999); Mark Chaves (2004); Gary Dorsey (1995); Carl Dudley, Jackson Carroll, and James Wind (1991); Wade Clark Roof (1996); R. Stephen Warner (1988, 1994); James Wind and James Lewis (1994); and Phil Zuckerman (1999). This points to a second important dialectic in U.S. religiosity: that between denomination and congregation. *American denominationalism is not now, nor has it ever been, realized except through the life of specific local units or congregations.*

Congregationalism

Used in three interrelated ways, the term *congregationalism* emphasizes the role of the laity within the church (as contrasted to the ordained, set-apart clergy). As you will recall from our introductory chapter, this focus was of unique significance to Max Weber's analysis of religious organization. Congregationalism is especially important to understanding religion in the United States, though it is characteristic of Western religious traditions in general. "Over 350,000 Christian congregations gather each Sunday in the United States," in addition to Jewish, Muslim, and other bodies, "forming the largest and most important community grouping in the fabric of American society" (TAD 1999a: 54).

One use of *congregationalism* is to refer to the U.S. denomination once called the Congregational Church, now formally titled (since a 1950s merger with the Evangelical and Reformed Church) the United Church of Christ (UCC). This body is the inheritor of the established church of New England formed through a Puritan-Pilgrim alliance in the early seventeenth century, shortly after immigration from England. (In England today, historically Congregational churches are now part of the United Reformed Church; in Canada, most Congregational churches merged into the United Church of Canada in the 1920s; one group of Congregational churches in the United States that did not join the UCC merger is now known as Congregational Christian Churches.) New England Congregationalism spawned a number of offshoots, including Unitarianism.

Point/Counterpoint: The Denominational Debate

Denominational allegiances have different significations for different people, and members may think quite differently from leadership elites. Two *Wall Street Journal* writers reflect these different perspectives.

Lisa Miller has looked at the ways in which individuals conceptualize their allegiances. She writes:

> "I'm an Episcopalian, and I think of myself as a practicing non-Jew," says Katherine Powell Cohen, a 36-year-old English teacher in San Francisco. "I'm a Mennonite hyphen Unitarian Universalist who practices Zen meditation," says Ralph Imhoff, 57, a retired educator. . . .
>
> If America has always been a melting pot, these days its religious practices have become a spiritual hash. Blending or braiding the beliefs of different spiritual traditions has become so rampant in America that the Dalai Lama has called the country "the spiritual supermarket." Jews flirt with Hinduism, Catholics study Taoism, and Methodists discuss whether to make the Passover seder an official part of worship. . . .
>
> For the traditional denominations, this cross-pollination presents an excruciating dilemma. If denominational headquarters bend the rules to accommodate the hybrids, they risk watering down their identities. But if they stick to the straight and narrow, they may define themselves out of existence. . . .
>
> Meanwhile, membership is growing in organized religions that take a broad view of God—for example, where pastors use Eastern and Western scriptures in their Sunday sermons and will marry people of all religious backgrounds. Unitarian Universalists have increased their numbers by 25% over the past 15 years.
>
> Even the clergy of mainstream religions are starting to broaden their view of God. At St. Gregory of Nyssa, an Episcopal church in San Francisco, two senior ministers have created a service that includes the worship of Jesus Christ, dancing and the ringing of Buddhist cymbals. . . . There are many references to the divinity of Jesus in the liturgy of St. Gregory's, but the priests and congregation agree that many divinities are being invoked there—and that in the end they are all the same. "It's one God talking to everyone."
>
> Many traditionalists remain just that, saying the spiritual hybrids are inauthentic. . . .
>
> The Rev. Glaucia Vasconcelos-Wilkey, who works in the office for worship at the Presbyterian Church (USA), dislikes what she calls the "me-oriented, consumerist, market-oriented style of worship" that she sees developing in many of the country's churches. She prefers a more ritualized "Christo-centric" version of Presbyterianism. . . . She sums up: "We are embarking on this because it is successful. But even 'success' is a marketing word."

Writer Barbara Carton, by contrast, examines how some of the major denominations in the United States are attempting to reassert their distinctive roots, "[f]earful that years of ecumenism and church switching among baby boomers have chewed away at what makes them unique":

> Some congregations are casting off generic texts and hymns. Others are requiring denominational training for children for the first time in years. Adult-education classes such as "How to Spell 'Presbyterian'" are sprouting up to explain dogma—and those who don't agree are sometimes advised to worship elsewhere.
>
> The United Methodist Church, the faith's main U.S. bloc, plans to launch a $20 million media campaign, its largest such effort ever . . . to

> raise denominational awareness. . . . The Evangelical Lutheran Church in America, the largest Lutheran branch with 5.2 million members, last year began "Project Identity," a $5.2 million, two-year public-relations campaign, including TV and radio ads.
>
> The reassertion of sectarian beliefs began in the early 1990s, many ministers say, but has lately grown much stronger. Some clerics say that years of smorgasbord services have left their members feeling disconnected. "There's a limit to how far you can go with the ecumenical approach and not end up feeling scattered," says the Rev. Brian C. Taylor, an Episcopal priest. . . .
>
> Project Identity was started after a 1996 poll revealed that only 3% of Americans could say anything about Lutheranism other than it was a religion. Lutheran leaders ruefully recall a Pennsylvania newspaper that several years ago published a photo of Martin Luther King, Jr., instead of Martin Luther, alongside an ad for Lutheran services.
>
> University Baptist church in Seattle is typical of the changing tides. About 60% of the congregation did not grow up Baptist. . . . [I]n recent years University Baptist began reasserting its sectarian identity. Classes in the Baptist faith were started. Traditional hymns . . . were revived, and there was "more talk about Baptist denomination, talk about Baptist bylaws and how Baptists make decisions."

How these two perspectives—the eclectic individual and the formal organizational—do or do not come together may well determine the future of denominationalism in the United States.

Sources: Lisa Miller, "The Age of Divine Disunity: Faith Now Springs from a Hodgepodge of Beliefs," *Wall Street Journal*, February 10, 1999, B1–B2; Barbara Carton, "Protestants Look to Their Roots: After Decades of Ecumenism, Denominations Emphasize Sectarian 'Brand Identity,'" *Wall Street Journal*, October 19, 2000, B1, B4.

The name *Congregational Church* is taken from the fact that this denomination theoretically vests authority in the local congregation; that is, it has a congregational polity. (Other forms of polity [organization] are presbyterian and episcopal, though neither of these polities has had the same impact on religious life in the United States as congregationalism, and in practice both are modified by congregationalism in the United States.) In strict usage, the local congregation *is* the church. It calls (hires) its own minister (and can fire him or her as well). It also decides acceptable forms of doctrinal profession, liturgy, and so on, and decides on what forms of "fellowship" it will accept with other churches—for example, whether it will allow members of a different congregation to receive various sacramental ministrations, particularly Holy Communion, and the terms on which it will allow members of other congregations to join its congregation. The congregation also normally owns the property on which any facilities it uses are located (for example, the worship building, education facilities, and offices).

As a form of polity, congregationalism descends from the Jewish synagogue tradition (*synagogue* is a Greek word for "a gathering together"), where in Or-

The congregational tradition of weekly worship finds its roots in ancient Judaism. This new American synagogue continues that tradition by using a former residence as the core of its building. Photograph courtesy of William H. Swatos, Jr.

thodox practice a synagogue is created whenever ten men gather together for prayer. In its modern usage, however, which is quintessentially American, congregationalism has come to symbolize a greater principle—namely, the religious voluntarism of denominationalism. The upshot of U.S. religious-political ideology is that religion is an entirely voluntary activity: Not only may we go to whatever church we choose, but we also may go or stay home whenever we choose, and we do not have to go to or join any church at all. Furthermore, the church is largely seen as serving the needs of its congregation, rather than the reverse. By establishing a voluntary basis of financial support for the church in the United States, the role of the congregation is considerably more magnified than it is even in other countries where freedom of religion is the norm. In this sense, all U.S. churches are congregationalist in a radical way: Unless a church has been extremely well endowed financially by prior generations, if the congregation leaves, the church must be closed. (This is very different, for example, from Scandinavian churches, where state support ensures that a regular program of activities will go on, even though only a tiny percentage of the population attends church. By the same token, some Scandinavians [and others] find offensive the religious practice of passing an offering [collection] plate or basket during worship—perhaps *the* worship experience that cuts across virtually all religious traditions in the United States.)

Steeped deeply in the Pilgrim myth, the voluntaristic principle that is inherent in congregationalism colors all religion in the United States, not simply the Congregational Church or even Protestantism or Judeo-Christianity. Buddhist, Islamic, Roman Catholic, and national Orthodox groups in the United States all must adjust to aspects of this organizational worldview in order to survive. There was, historically, a Catholic version of congregationalism in the United States (called *trusteeism*) that was discontinued in the nineteenth century (see Carey 1987; Dolan 1992), but several recent works have emphasized continued popular attachment to a local parish, especially in the Roman Catholic case. "Whatever their opinions about the issues dividing the church," observes historian R. Scott Appleby, for example, "the vast majority of American Catholics tend to think of themselves as members of a parish rather than of a movement" (1997: 17; cf. Gamm 1999; McGreevy 1996; McMahon 1995). Americans can and do worship as well as vote with their feet and their pocketbooks. A degree of accommodation to this aspect of the "American way of life" is inherent in all religious practice. Similarly, Americans are more likely to conceive *religion*, whether they see it positively or negatively, as a congregational activity (often phrased as "belonging to a church" or "organized religion"). In recent usage this may be distinguished from personal religiosity by referring to the latter as *spirituality*.

American Religious Renewal

The renewal of religious activity that began in the mid-1970s was not limited solely to the cultural mainstream. Indeed, this may be the most important contrast between it and the "revival" of religion that occurred in the 1950s. After only a brief period of gestation, religious roots that had been transplanted from Asia and elsewhere took hold in the soil of a New World that had always provided fertile ground for cultural hybrids. Harvey Cox, the Harvard divinity professor whose best-selling book *The Secular City* (1965) celebrated the post-Christian geography of the urban landscape, marked this movement away from tradition but nonetheless back to the sacred a scant four years later with the publication of a new overview of the religious terrain, *The Feast of Fools* (1969), and yet later with another, *Turning East* (1977b).

By the mid-1970s, it appeared that all of the United States was caught up in broad-based religious enthusiasm. Commentators "saw religiousness everywhere," remembers Martin Marty—"religion was 'in'" (1987: 18–19). What explains so radical a transformation as this? How, over twenty years, did the country move readily from the throes of a "religious revival" in the 1950s, to rank secularity in the 1960s, and back to pious devotion in the 1970s? The answer, some scholars believe, lies in a dual quality that they attribute to religious life in the United States.

On the one hand, Americans are remarkably susceptible to taking in whole worldviews, secular as well as religious, in a single breath from the ideological breezes that waft unimpeded from coast to coast. Moreover, such constantly shifting winds are inevitable in an environment where, both by strictly enforced law and fiercely defended custom, the people hold, in accord with Thomas Jefferson's 1786 "Statute of Religious Liberty" for Virginia (reprinted in Commager 1935: 125), that "Almighty God hath created the mind free." The First Amendment to the U.S. Constitution explicitly guarantees the free exercise of religion, and expressly forbids Congress from establishing any creed as the favorite of the state. Citizens do not hesitate to press to the limit the ample liberties that they are thereby afforded. As one pundit once remarked, the problem with Americans is not that they refuse to believe in anything, but that they believe in far too many things—and would believe in everything if they could.

In the middle of this continuing enterprise of cultural innovation there exists, on the other hand, a solid bedrock of religious belief and practice in the United States. This foundation has remained relatively undisturbed, even during the most turbulent eras in the rearrangement of the national consciousness. For example, most Americans believe in the existence of a Supreme Being, and demand a similar belief of fellow citizens who aspire to social respectability. For example, according to a Gallup survey, 81 percent of Americans believe in heaven; 70 percent believe in hell (Religion News Service 2004). Curiously, the

"Life" after Life?

Taken together, one feature the principal historical religions share most in common is that they try in one way or another (which may be quite different) to provide an answer to the question, "What will happen to me when I die?" In 2007 *AARP The Magazine*, an official periodical of the American Association of Retired Persons, presented the results of a professional survey it commissioned about what people age fifty and over today actually think about the afterlife, regardless of their religious affiliation. Admitting at the start that people over fifty are probably more likely to think about the afterlife than people in their thirties, their findings give an interesting look into the American view of the afterlife in our own day.

Specifically, almost 75 percent agreed with the statement "I believe in life after death," though when separated by gender, women were almost 30 percent more likely to say this than men. Eighty-six percent say there is a heaven, while 70 percent also believe in hell. In both cases, however, the respondents are about evenly divided over whether heaven and hell are real places or whether they are "states of being." Ten percent think everyone goes to heaven, 29 percent associate entrance into heaven with belief in Jesus Christ, while 25 percent think it's connected to being "good." But when hell comes up, 40 percent associate it with being bad, while the proportion who associate it with not believing in Jesus Christ drops to only 17 percent. Wealthier and better educated persons are slightly less inclined to believe in heaven than their poorer, less educated counterparts. When asked about reincarnation, 23 percent answered affirmatively, but somewhat contrary to popular opinion, the highest percentage by region was in the Northeast, not on the West Coast. Boomers tend to believe in reincarnation and in ghosts more than people over sixty, and especially so in contrast to people over seventy. Unfortunately, the study left relatively underexplored the 25 percent who agreed with the statement "I believe that when I die, that's the end." In either case, the most positive interpretation of the results as a whole is that 77 percent of the sample, regardless of their particular perspective on life after death, are not frightened by thoughts of what happens after death. Again, this makes the 23 percent who *are* frightened the most interesting, least explored population.

Source: Bill Newcott, "Life After Death," *AARP The Magazine* (September/October 2007): 68–73.

Baylor Religion Survey (Bader et al. 2006) reports that 72 percent of Americans believe in "life after death," yet 82 percent "probably" or "absolutely" believe in heaven, while 71 percent "probably" or "absolutely" believe in hell. Americans disagree, however, in their conceptions of God's nature and in their notions about what aspects of life in the here-and-now might interest the deity.

Convictions as skeletal as these have from time to time been condemned as superficial and shallow. Yet, by the standards of Benjamin Franklin, who is revered as one of the country's founders (though he was no orthodox Christian), Americans may be considered a highly religious people. Franklin's notion of a proper faith contained seven "essential" articles, a minimum prescription that, not incidentally, also approached his personal maximum. Although Franklin was reared as a Presbyterian, he was quick to abandon attendance at church services. Nevertheless, "I never was without some religious principles," he pleads in his *Autobiography*. What were these principles, exactly?

> I never doubted, for instance, the existence of the Deity; that he made the world, and govern'd it by his Providence; that the most acceptable service of God was the doing [of] good to man; that our souls are immortal; and that all crime will be punished, and virtue rewarded, either here or hereafter. (Reprinted in Goodman 1945: 117–18)

Few contemporary Americans would dissent in any comprehensive way from Franklin's creed. For "good" people in this society, the creed functions as it did for Franklin: as an eternal ethical baseline against which past and future actions would be judged. Indeed, the promise of divine judgment is one element of religion in the United States that inclines it toward cyclical motion, for whenever the faithful become too comfortable in the assurance of their election in the eyes of the Almighty, there emerges within the church a faction of dissidents who stand ready to call all believers back to the primitive faith of yesteryear. This process results over the long run in an ongoing tug-of-war between the defenders of religious propriety and the critics of any church that would sell its spiritual birthright for a mess of secular pottage.

One sociologist who has studied this struggle at close range, R. Stephen Warner, insists that "the United States is particularly susceptible to such spiritual discontents," in part because its people are so routinely churched and so highly moralistic about religion. Stated more simply, Americans take religion seriously. Hence, "the impulse to sectarian protest," according to Warner, "is built into the very structure of our religious institutions" (1988: 28).

Throughout the American experience, spasms of religious fervor thus have alternated with states of, at best, lethargy among believers. Furthermore, there is little in the nation's traditions, legal or other, that would legitimately regulate these oscillations or, for that matter, the barely more stable pluralism that reigns in between. Martin Marty has a good grasp on this cultural dynamic when he observes:

> The nation is as pluralist as ever, and in the operative aspects of its national life—in the university, the marketplace, or the legislature—

> America remains secular, with no single transcendent symbol to live by. Unless theorists and theologians reckon with *both* all-pervasive religiousness *and* persistent secularity, they will again be left stranded with each cultural shift, in search of theories to match their perceptions. The double paradigm will no doubt diminish the audaciousness of certain prophecies and projections: bold predictions of the purely secular city or a thoroughly sacral culture are obviously highly dramatic. But these predictions are as likely to be wrong as right, as the human record in general, and the recent American generational shift in particular, show. (1987: 22)

Because writing on religion in the United States is thus prone to move back and forth between competing poles of interpretation, generalizing on the subject, as Marty notes, is often more precarious than it is simply difficult. Out of respect for this danger, discussion in this chapter adheres closely to the single task of describing accurately what *is* known about selected aspects of denominational religion in the contemporary United States. To summarize the facts on something as multifaceted as religious behavior, one is best advised to cling to empirical specificity, even at the sacrifice of an overarching theme for the narrative. If there is a common thread to these observations, it is that modern American religion, though composed of some rather stable elements of belief and historical habits of practice, is nonetheless extremely changeable. The American experience itself testifies to the malleability of ideas in a climate of freedom, where tradition does not run deeply beneath conceptions of social order.

Mainlines and Sidelines in Religion in the United States

Figure 4.2 and tables 4.1, 4.2, and 4.3 summarize the differences among religious involvement, beliefs, and practices by principal denominational groups and interdenominational "family" groupings.

Several things are immediately apparent: On the one hand, the Roman Catholic Church, a single religious body, is the largest religious organization in the United States. About one-fourth of the U.S. population claims Roman Catholic allegiance; in Canada this figure rises to almost half. Catholicism is also a growing religion, gaining 16.2 percent in its membership from 1990 to 2000, although its growth is not occurring at an equal rate among all its constituencies. Hispanic and other immigrant Catholics account for virtually all net growth in U.S. Roman Catholicism. At the same time, however, Protestant groups, particularly those with a Pentecostal orientation, are making significant inroads with the American Hispanic community (see Christiano 1991, 1993; Greeley 1988, 1997; Perl, Greely, and Gray 2006). This will be a continuously unfolding story well into the present century.

Protestants belong to many different specific organizations. The largest Protestant denomination in the United States is the Southern Baptist Convention

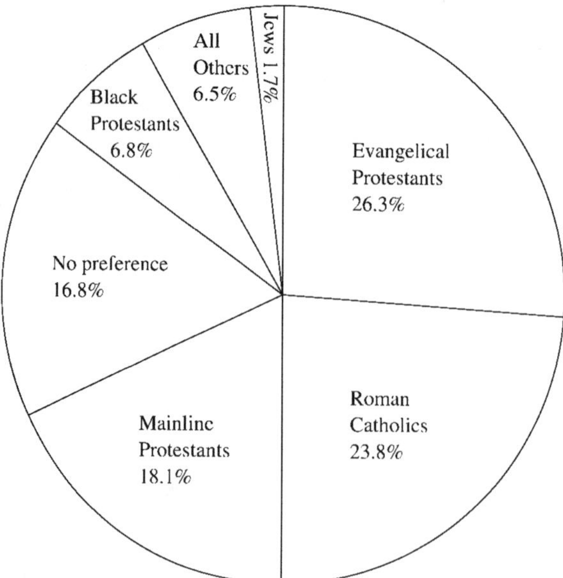

Figure 4.2. The Families of American Religion. Source: The Pew Forum on Religion and Public Life, U.S. Religious Landscape Survey: 2008 *(Washington, D.C.: The Pew Research Center, pp. 5, 10, 12.*

(SBC), not surprisingly a church of congregational polity. The SBC gained its distinction as the largest Protestant denomination only in the late 1960s, when it surpassed the formerly dominant United Methodist Church (UMC), compared to which it is now almost twice as large. The shift from the UMC to the SBC is significant because the UMC is generally considered a moderate Protestant church, while the SBC is firmly in the conservative camp (see Ammerman 1990). Commentators such as Roger Finke and Rodney Stark in *The Churching of America* (2005) have used the UMC-to-SBC shift in an attempt to demonstrate that religions that set clear boundaries between what they expect of their members and how the culture around them behaves (the strictness thesis) are more likely to grow than are religions that accommodate the culture (cf. Iannaccone 1994). They insist that it is this *cultural* dynamic more than specific individual defections from liberal to conservative churches that accounts for differences in growth patterns. However, the SBC did post its "first membership decline in 73 years" in the late 1990s, when it became "embroiled with a boycott of Walt Disney enterprises" and passed resolutions requiring of its constituent congregations more conservative stances on wifely submission to husbands and on women's ordination (TAD 1999c: 55). Hence, there may be a limit to the extent to which denominations can simultaneously experience large-scale growth and articulate strict positions that appear to conflict with dominant cultural trends.

Nevertheless, the biggest losses continue to be in the liberal Protestant churches—the United Church of Christ, for example, lost 15 percent of its membership from 1990 to 2000. Large gains were registered by the Salvation Army, Mormons, and Assemblies of God.

Table 4.1. Membership of American Religious Bodies at the Turn of the Twenty-first Century*

Roman Catholic Church	62.00
Southern Baptist Convention	19.90
National Baptist Conventions	13.50
United Methodist Church	10.40
Jewish	6.14
Church of God in Christ	5.50
Evangelical Lutheran Church	5.11
African/Colored Methodist	4.55
Latter-day Saints (Mormon)	4.22
Presbyterian Church (U.S.A.)	3.14
Assemblies of God	2.60
Lutheran Church, Missouri Synod	2.52
Episcopal Church	2.31
Buddhist	2.00
American Baptist Churches	1.77
United Church of Christ	1.70
Muslim	1.60
Churches of Christ	1.56
Pentecostal Assemblies	1.50
Disciples of Christ	1.44
Baptist Bible Fellowship	1.20
Hindu	1.10
Jehovah's Witnesses	1.04

*In millions. Data derived from both actual denominational records and estimating sources; kindred groups combined in some cases. See Finke and Scheitle 2005, Jones et al. 2002, Linder 2003.

Table 4.2. Growth, Decline, and Participation among American Christian Religious Bodies

Church Growth 1990–2000 (percent)	
Salvation Army	225.0
Latter-day Saints (Mormon)	19.3
Assemblies of God	18.5
Roman Catholic Church	16.2
Church Decline 1990–2000 (percent)	
United Church of Christ	–15
Presbyterian Church (U.S.A.)	–12
United Methodist Church	–7
Weekly Church Attendance (percent "weekly or almost every week" 2002, 2005 [Gallup])	
Churches of Christ	68
Latter-day Saints (Mormon)	67
Southern Baptists	60
Methodists	44
Presbyterians	44
Lutherans	43
Episcopalians	32

Sources: Jones et al., 2002; Religion News Service, 2006.

Table 4.3. Religious Beliefs and Practices by Western Religious Tradition

Religious Affiliation	Black Protestant	Evangelical Protestant	Mainline Protestant	Catholic	Jewish	Unaffiliated
Belief about God						
No doubts that God exists	100.0%	86.5%	63.6%	74.8%	42.9%	11.6%
Don't believe in anything beyond the physical world	0.0%	0.4%	0.7%	1.1%	7.2%	37.1%
Beliefs about Jesus						
Jesus is the son of God	95.1%	94.4%	72.2%	84.9%	9.6%	1.0%
Jesus is a fictional character	0.0%	0.0%	0.9%	0.2%	2.3%	13.7%
Belief about Bible						
Literally true	40.6%	47.8%	11.2%	11.8%	8.9%	1.0%
Ancient book of history and legends	1.5%	6.5%	22.0%	19.8%	52.6%	82.3%
Prayer						
Once a day or more	74.1%	67.1%	44.1%	46.1%	32.8%	10.1%
Never	3.7%	3.6%	11.6%	6.9%	16.6%	68.4%
Read Scripture						
Weekly or more	54.4%	42.1%	16.0%	7.1%	1.4%	1.5%
Never	3.7%	9.3%	21.9%	33.1%	27.0%	67.3%
Attend Religious Services						
Weekly or more	43.1%	45.2%	24.3%	32.8%	7.3%	0.0%
Never	10.6%	11.8%	13.5%	9.3%	28.9%	89.3%

Note: Differences in percentages for all beliefs and practices are significant across religious traditions. Sample interpretation: Three-fourths of Catholics (74.8%) have no doubts that God exists.

Source: Baylor Institute for Studies of Religion. *American Piety in the 21st Century.* Waco, Texas. September 2006.

The decline of the 1960s was the result of several interacting variables, the most important of which is clearly the decline in the birth rate. Whether out of economic necessity or concern for zero population growth or the desire for a freer lifestyle as a result of more dependable birth-control technology, Americans dramatically reduced the number of children they were having. Fewer children meant slower church growth, both directly and indirectly, since previously parents not only brought their children to church but were also themselves drawn back into a church life that they may have partially abandoned in their teenage and young adult years. This was particularly true among nonimmigrant whites of higher socioeconomic status; hence it most severely affected the moderate and liberal Protestant churches and the Conservative and Reform Jewish traditions. As one illustration of how this works out in practice, for example, at the end of the twentieth century, Gallup data showed that "69% of Americans are aged 45 or younger. 69% of Episcopalians are aged 45 or older" (TAD 1999b: 47). Stated briefly, couples in conservative Protestant churches marry at an age that is earlier than average, stay married longer, have larger-than-average families, and keep their offspring in the church longer than their counterparts in the more liberal churches. These latter organizations, by contrast, host older couples with fewer children—and even these "leak away" (but not necessarily to religious conservatism) at a higher-than-average rate. They are "graying" quickly, and have a higher rate of attrition by death. Although belief-and-value issues should not be discounted, in many respects the driving forces behind the expansion of memberships in conservative churches and "the decline of the mainline" are largely demographic (see Hout et al. 2001, 2005).

If we combine the Protestant groups as a whole, however, we see that the United States remains a strongly Protestant country, and in recent years the growth shift has been from the liberal or moderate churches to those in the conservative camp. All of the doomsaying that has been directed toward liberal Protestantism notwithstanding, what this actually means is that the country is becoming *more* Protestant, not less. The African-American Protestant churches represent a distinct position in U.S. religious history that has been only slightly altered by greater racial integration during the last fifty years. On the whole this tradition continues to be numerically strong: Only 12 percent of the U.S. population is African American, but more than three-fourths of all African Americans identify with this tradition. Its weakest link is among young adults in urban settings. African-American Protestants are generally theologically conservative but socioeconomically liberal.

The "no religious preference" category, which remained relatively stable from the 1950s to the 1980s, has begun to grow at an accelerating rate. Michael Hout and Claude S. Fischer (2002) report, for example, that the proportion of Americans with no preference doubled from 7 to 14 percent during the 1990s, and those reared with no religion increased from 2 to 6 percent of the adult population. They also report, however, that most of the increase came in the form of "unchurched believers," rather than from a growth in skepticism toward religion. Even with these increases taken into account, the proportion of persons in this category still remains small when compared to this fraction in other modern industrialized nations.

More interesting is the "other" category and the Jews. While we will spend a significant amount of attention on both of these categories in the chapter on religion and ethnicity, it may be worth noting here that the "other" category is also growing, while the Jewish category remains alternatively stable and declining. (The Jewish category was seriously declining until recent immigrations from the former Soviet Union and other Eastern Bloc nations.) On the one hand, Jews have been semi-integrated into the U.S. mainstream as a kind of variant on the dominant Protestant theme (see Silk 1988). They were seen as the people of the Old Testament, hence related to "the Judeo-Christian ethic," a public religious morality akin to Franklin's creed that combined Old and New Testament moral themes into a single fabric—first so phrased only in the 1930s during a period of rising anti-Semitism before World War II. The increasing number of "others" threatens the integrity of this moral canopy and of the special place that has been accorded to Jews as a not-quite-other religious group in U.S. society. Except for reasons of marriage, furthermore, Judaism offers relatively little inducement for the conversion of outsiders, while Islam, Buddhism, and some Hindu sects are happy to receive converts both from the "nones" and from those who become disenchanted with the Christian message.

Although there are some differences in attendance patterns between religious groups (and survey reports of attendance data have been called into question, as we have mentioned previously), in general about half the U.S. population claims to attend religious services more frequently than monthly. About 20 percent attend sporadically, while about a third rarely attend. Similarly about half of the population that is religious consider themselves "strong" in their religion—that is, they are strong Presbyterians, Methodists, Catholics, and so on. This does not mean, however, that denominational switching does not take place. Switching does tend, however, to be more religiously intrafamilial than extreme. Liberal Protestants move from one liberal denomination to another, or perhaps to a moderate denomination. Conservatives stay in the conservative stream, and so on. Not surprisingly, liberals are more likely to switch than conservatives. Catholics switch less often than Protestants. Jewish/Christian marriages are more likely to lead to religious dropping out or marginalization than are marriages across Christian traditions, but when conversion does occur in Jewish/Christian marriages, Jews convert to Christianity at about the same rate as Christians embrace Judaism. We do not yet have adequate data to give a picture of marriage-and-family patterns for those cross-religious marriages outside the Judeo-Christian groupings.

The 1960s also brought value changes—partly in sexual-familial values (greater premarital permissiveness, later marriage and childbearing, easier divorce, higher incidence of women in higher education and in the workplace), partly in political-economic values—that affected traditional religious worldviews. Some of these values were moderated in a more conservative direction in the 1970s and 1980s, as it seemed that some 1960s remedies failed to work and new threats appeared (for example, AIDS). Those religious groups that compromised least with the dominant culture in the 1960s stood most ready to reap the harvest of this return to religion. The gains were by no means uniform, however. Religious forms that addressed a more expressive spirituality, such as Pentecostalism, or that were able to reformat their worship experience to mesh better with the technology of popular media—such as the Willow Creek "megachurch" style that produces its Sunday services more like variety-show entertainment than a traditional Protestant worship experience—attracted far greater numbers than did those expressions, albeit theologically conservative, that used more staid delivery styles, traditional hymnody, and limited lay participation. Even within the liturgical traditions of Roman Catholicism and the Episcopal and Lutheran churches, charismatic worship and contemporary liturgical styles attracted greater numbers. Historical traditions struggled to become more warm and "user friendly," recognizing the churchgoer (or potential churchgoer) as more of a consumer and less of an adherent.

Indeed, there has been a more general trend in American religiosity to speak of *spirituality* rather than religion; that is, people will use the adjective *spiritual* ("a very spiritual person") to describe someone about whom a generation or more ago the word *religious* might instead have been used. Religion (or religiousness) tends to be restricted more to the sphere of organized religion; hence some newer religious organizations, rather than calling themselves churches, will use words like *fellowship*, *community*, or *center*. These subtle shifts of language serve to emphasize the more individualistic, consumerist quality of religious life on the part of the baby-boomer generation, which is now between forty and sixty years of age and is entering an era of influence on religious trends in North America. As a result of the shifts that took place in the 1960s and 1970s, this group is more institutionally wary and more concerned to find a religious lifestyle that "fits," rather than conforming to a set of customary religious norms. This affects both traditionally conservative and religiously liberal churches. A Baptist pastor in California, explaining why the word *Baptist* was been dropped from the church's name, states, "People just don't like the denominational tags anymore. All they want to know is, 'What's in it for me?'" And a person who attended and joined a church called "Community Church of Joy" later admitted that "[w]e probably came here for a year before we knew it was Lutheran" (quoted in Sargeant 2000: 5–6). Although the numbers are small overall, the Faith Communities Today (FACT) survey of American congregations nevertheless shows that almost twice as many congregations changed their names in the years 2000–2005 as did in the five preceding years. Nor is this restricted to single congregations. For example, as the new millennium dawned, the Reorganized Church of Jesus Christ of Latter-Day Saints—a group of Mormon descent that separated in the 1860s from the main body and is closer to evangelical Christianity than to Mormonism today—changed its name to the Community of Christ. (Note particularly that the word *Church* has been omitted.)

Thus while it is true, for example, that conservative Christian congregations are growing, certainly in comparison to those of the liberal-moderate mainline, the conservatism of these congregations is often quite selective. In particular, both their worship styles and modes of education have been more attentive to technological developments in terms of the use of audiovisual advances and to a style of presentation that is more consistent with that of entertainment media generally than with a particular faith tradition. In fact, one of the most telling changes in the temper of American religious life has been the shift among more conservative Christian groups toward an appropriation of the media of mass consumption, while the liberal denominations have been increasingly inclined to critique consumerism as a debasement of Christian virtues within the larger society. During much of the twentieth century, conservative Christian groups eschewed the mass media of motion pictures and pop music; in the current era the most likely church on any weekend to feature upbeat music and the use of video technology is also evangelical in its theological infrastructure. This is one of the most significant changes in American religious expression in the last quarter century.

Evangelicals and Fundamentalists: Alike and Different

Taken together, the moderate and liberal Protestant bodies of the American religious "mainline" are as close as the United States has come in its modern history to an officially established church. In the period before World War II, these denominations held fast to their domination of organized religion. When a religious voice spoke to the larger national culture in those days, it was usually a Christian voice. On top of that, chances were good that the voice was a Protestant one, and probably one emanating from within the broad borders of the mainline of Protestantism rather than its sectarian margins.

Through the 1950s, the twentieth century had been good to the fortunes of mainline Protestant churches, but by the end of the 1960s, circumstances at large were poised to change. In 1965, some of American Protestantism's flagship denominations were enjoying record highs in membership. Fifteen years later, in 1980, practically all of them reported sharp declines. "Though not one of the most dramatic developments of those years," in the opinion of a well-placed observer, "it may prove to be one of the most significant, especially for students of social behavior" (Kelley 1972: 1).

Several examples, can illustrate the changes. Members of the mighty United Methodist Church, planted securely within the U.S. middle class and distributed geographically across the country's wide midsection, numbered more than 11 million in 1965; by 1980, the Methodists could claim only about 9.5 million members, a number that had declined to 8.4 million twenty years later. The United Presbyterian Church, a bastion of respectability in the Reformed tradition, boasted 3.3 million members in 1965. In 1980, 2.4 million or so Presbyterians of this affiliation could be counted—a net loss of almost a million members, more than a quarter of the original total. And today there are probably more Muslims in the United States than Episcopalians.

During this same time period, membership in Protestant churches located off the mainline, in the long-neglected fundamentalist and evangelical branches of the faith, veritably soared. The largest body of outsiders, the Southern Baptist Convention, moved from approximately 10.8 million members in 1965 to 13.6 million in 1980, and to almost 16 million by 2000. More explosive still was growth in the Assemblies of God, a Pentecostal group. They nearly doubled their membership, from 570,000 in 1965 to almost 1.1 million in 1980, and more than doubled it again to 2.6 million at the turn of the new century. Equally notable gains in size during this time were registered by other small, conservative bodies—for example, the Churches of God, the Jehovah's Witnesses, the Church of the Nazarene, and the Seventh-day Adventists. Precise measurements of group size are always difficult to formulate, however, because different sources use different modes of estimation, and they adjust their figures at different intervals and by using different methods. The Association of Statisticians of American Religious Bodies, whose membership consists of persons with the responsibility for obtaining and reporting these data, continues to work toward creating greater uniformity of reporting across religious traditions. For the most current data on those bodies participating in this organization, see www.asarb.org/statistics.html.

Who are the fundamentalists and the evangelicals, the members of these churches that have proved to be so successful in the membership numbers game? There are no settled definitions of the two designations, but students of the movements have come to a loose agreement about the meanings of both terms and their proper usage. Evangelical soteriology, or theory of salvation, is what is important for the task of definition.

An evangelical is often defined as a Protestant whose faith in Jesus Christ compels an acceptance of Him, in the words of the most oft-repeated formula, "as personal Lord and Savior." This act of acceptance customarily follows a confession of one's sinfulness; an acknowledgment of the need to repudiate sin and surrender the totality of one's life to Jesus; and an invitation to Christ to deliver the believer into redemption and holiness through an experience that is likened, for its feeling of revitalization, to a second birth. Believers who have thus been *born again* are expected to exercise reserve and circumspection in their personal lives, yet they are to reach out at the same time by "witnessing" about their faith to those who are still "unsaved."

Fundamentalists share much of this background of belief, but they typically go further in theology and lifestyle (see the overviews of the literature surrounding the evangelical/fundamentalist distinction in Chapman 1999; Woodberry and Smith 1998). With respect to theology, fundamentalists are ardent proponents of the *literal* truth of the Bible. (Although evangelicals likewise display great respect for the Bible and endeavor to make it central to their faith, often holding it to be "inerrant in matters of faith and practice," most among them would stop short of the fundamentalist doctrine of literalism.) Fundamentalism is basically a materialist view of sacred texts, in that the fundamentalist regards the words of the text as being authoritative in themselves.

Not surprisingly then, fundamentalists regard quite gravely the biblical call to "come out from among them, and be ye separate" (2 Cor. 6:17). The fundamentalist lifestyle strives to avoid undue entanglement with the things of this world. Fundamentalists routinely shun the mass media and other institutions of secular society, and labor to establish their own periodicals, publishers, and schools. Even their churches zealously guard their independence. For fear of weakening their message, congregations of fundamentalists spurn offers of denominational attachments and opportunities for interreligious cooperation. "*Compromise* and *accommodation* are among the most dreaded words in the fundamentalist vocabulary," notes Nancy Tatom Ammerman (1987: 4).

Estimates of the sizes of these two groups vary inversely with the rigor of the criteria that are employed to define them. These differences can be examined by reference to tables 4.4 and 4.5. Table 4.6 shows how different approaches to conceptualizing the term *evangelical* can result in far different assessments of how strong evangelicalism is in the United States. For example, if agreement with the statement that "salvation occurs only through Jesus Christ" is used to measure evangelicalism, then 46 percent of the population might be considered evangelical. Others suggest the use of the "born-again" experience. This cuts the percentage to thirty-one. If people are asked directly, by contrast, whether they are affiliated with one of the movements of evangelicalism, the total is only 17 percent, yet 26 percent belong to religious denominations that are generally classified as evangelical. Table 4.6 shows how these different dynamics operate in the practical arena of support for pro-life measures with respect to abortion. (Pro-life attitudes on abortion in this study include respondents who oppose abortion in all circumstances or would permit abortion only in extreme circumstances, for example, when the life of the mother was at stake.) Clearly, people who accept all four of the principal doctrines and are in an evangelical Protestant denomination and define themselves as part of the evangelical movement are overwhelmingly pro-life. Note, however, that people who accept only one or two of the doctrines, even though they are both affiliated with a denomination of the evangelical tradition and consciously define themselves as part of the evangelical movement, are actually *below* the national average in their pro-life support.

In any event, however, a combination of public-opinion and voting data suggests that the mass of conservative Christians in the United States is large and that evangelicals have found a place among American elites, especially in the political arena (see Lindsay 2007). A 1980 Gallup survey discovered that almost 40 percent of U.S. adults who were interviewed agreed with the assertion that the Bible is the "actual word of God, and is to be taken literally, word for word." In that same year, 38 percent of Gallup's nationwide sample claimed to have been "born again," and fully 44 percent indicated that they had "tried to encourage someone to believe in Jesus Christ or accept Him as his or her Savior" (Warner 1988: 53). Also in 1980, polls performed for the *New York Times* and the *Washington Post* put the proportion of the U.S. public that had been "born again" at 42 and 44 percent, respectively (Johnston 1982: 186).

How might the diverging trajectories of mainline and conservative Christian church bodies in the contemporary United States be explained? A hotly debated solution has been to correlate the doctrinal and behavioral demands of a church with its growth rate in order to formulate an answer. What most crucially distinguishes members of conservative churches, according to at least one controversial analysis, is that they are not comfortably reconciled to much in the prevailing social and moral climate. Their churches "are not 'reasonable,' they are not 'tolerant,' they are not ecumenical, they are not 'relevant.' Quite the con-

Table 4.4. Various Operational Measures of Evangelicalism

A	*B*	*C*
Doctrinal Distinctives	*Movement Criteria*	*Religious Traditions*
Bible "True," 44%	Fundamentalist, 5%	Evangelical Protestant, 33%
Jesus Only, 46%	Charismatic or Pentecostal, 8%	Roman Catholic, 23%
Witness, 37%	Evangelical, 4%	Mainline Protestant, 17%
Born Again, 31%		Secular, 20%
All Four, 14%		Black Protestant, 8%
		All Others, 7%

Table 4.5. Pro-Life Attitudes on Abortion for Groups Based on Combinations of Doctrinal Distinctives, Religious Movements, and Traditions

Combinations	*Percentage of Population*	*Percentage Pro-Life*
4 Doctrines, Evangelical Tradition, + Movement	5.1	81
3 Doctrines, Evangelical Tradition, + Movement	3.8	70
4 Doctrines, Evangelical Tradition, No Movement	3.2	65
3 or 4 Doctrines, Catholic	4.0	56
3 or 4 Doctrines, Black, + Movement	1.9	56
3 or 4 Doctrines, Mainline, + Movement	1.5	55
3 Doctrines, Evangelical Tradition, No Movement	4.0	50
3 or 4 Doctrines, Mainline, No Movement	5.1	46
1 or 2 Doctrines, Evangelical Tradition, + Movement	3.2	36
0 to 2 Doctrines, Evangelical Tradition, No Movement	8.3	28
National Average	100.0	38

Source: Lyman Kellstedt, John Green, James Guth, and Corwin Smidt, "Evangelicalism," *Encyclopedia of Religion and Society* (Walnut Creek, Calif.: AltaMira, 1998), 176–77.

trary!" (Kelley 1972: 25). And it is exactly those qualities of strictness and separatism, this argument continues, that endow conservative churches with their present vitality. Hence Christian Smith and colleagues can write of *American Evangelicalism: Embattled and Thriving* (1998). Another, more classically sociological way of saying this is that they tend toward the ideal-typical sectarian mode of religious expression and organization.

Because members of conservative churches must work and struggle and sacrifice to remain members in good standing; because they must suffer ridicule and rejection at the hands of cultural elites; because, in short, their churches require tangible evidence of commitment from them, they take church membership to heart and find meaning in its experience. The existential challenge of membership in a mainline denomination pales, so the sectarian strictness thesis goes, in comparison to the daily drama of the Bible believer set against a fallen world. It fails to supply the meaning for which the believer craves and on which religious faith thrives.

The whole question of the implications of doctrinal and behavioral "strictness" has received considerable attention in the sociology of religion since the

Originating in Southern California, the Vineyard movement has been among the fastest-growing evangelical groups to emerge in the last quarter of the twentieth century. This center directly faces the west entrance of England's Winchester Cathedral. Photograph courtesy of William H. Swatos, Jr.

early 1970s. Dean M. Kelley's book *Why Conservative Churches Are Growing* (1972) got the ball rolling, and it was followed quickly by both criticisms and defenses of its main thesis (see Bibby 1978; Kelley 1978). Gary D. Bouma (1979) challenged Kelley's explanation for conservative church growth with statistics on fertility from the relatively conservative Christian Reformed Church, a church in the United States that descends from the Dutch Reformed Church but has a more liberal counterpart in the Reformed Church in America. Tangentially, Rodney Stark and William Sims Bainbridge (1980a; Bainbridge and Stark 1981) isolated the importance of personal social ties in religious recruitment. The argument that conservative success inheres more in inculcation than in outreach or evangelization is a mainstay of pieces by Reginald W. Bibby and Merlin B. Brinkerhoff on "the circulation of the saints" (1973, 1983, 1994; cf. Brinkerhoff and Bibby 1985). The strongest challenge to this view comes from Robin D. Perrin and Armand L. Mauss (1991, 1993), particularly from their studies of one conservative group, the Vineyard Christian Fellowship. Later, Stark and his collaborators popularized the idea that to opt for membership in a "strict" church was not a perversion of decision making, but a "rational choice" (see Iannaccone 1994, 1996; Iannaccone, Olson, and Stark 1995; Stark and Iannaccone 1997).

We have already seen how rational choice theory uses the demands of conservative Christianity to explain its success. It would therefore be simple, in keeping with this interpretation, to imagine that the staggering rates of growth recorded by fundamentalist and evangelical churches since the 1960s could be attributed to the superior attraction of their common worldview to former members of practically undemanding and spiritually moribund liberal churches. But studies that have been carried out in the interim demonstrate that the decline of the Protestant mainline and the increase in adherents to conservative Christianity have occurred without much direct defection and in the relative absence of explicit references to doctrine. In other words, conservative Christians in the United States have made the most of the natural level of appeal that their doctrines possess. Their churches readily assimilate new adherents, but not ordinarily through the regular and usually quite strenuous efforts that they sponsor to convert the secular minded. Rather, the spread of fundamentalist and evangelical religious allegiances is a more subtle process, one having more to do with the internal organization of such groups than with their externally directed recruitment campaigns.

Fundamentalists and evangelicals first of all cultivate a close-knit family life, partly as an alternative to the many potentially competing elements of the wider world that they explicitly reject. The emotional intensity of family relations in turn lends extra power to the religious messages that are diffused through the home. Conservative Christians who have married outside the fold, or who have converted without the cooperation of their spouses, are often successful in guiding their husbands or wives to eventual church membership. Within marriage, childbearing is an honored pursuit, and there are numerous informal inducements for couples to create large families. The status of women in these congregations is especially elevated as they become mothers as well as wives. In addition, fundamentalists and evangelicals place great emphasis on rearing children in "the nurture and admonition of the Lord," a practice of thorough religious socialization that obviously contributes to the retention of members later in life (Christiano 2000: 64–68). Outside the immediate household, relatives, friends, neighbors, coworkers, business partners, and others who figure somehow in the daily lives of religious conservatives are frequently persuaded, through the strength of personal ties to an evangelical Christian, to make a commitment to Christ.

Conservative churches also do an efficient job of tracking and recovering their committed clientele when it becomes geographically mobile. In a statistical study of twenty evangelical congregations, fully 72 percent of the new members who were added to church rolls in the five years between 1966 and 1970 already identified with evangelical Christianity; that is, they were newcomers to the area or transfers from affiliated bodies. Eighteen percent of the additions were children of evangelical parents. Only about 10 percent were actual strangers to the evangelical tradition; their presence was the consequence of interreligious marriages and drifts away from other churches, not vigorous proselytizing of the "unchurched" in the community (Bibby and Brinkerhoff 1973).

Follow-up research on the identical congregations a decade later concluded that "recruitment patterns have remained largely the same." Most new arrivals in the pews of these churches were "young people, recruited through friendship and family ties," not the previously unaffiliated (Bibby and Brinkerhoff 1983: 253). Hence, the coauthors of these studies express confidence that growth in the memberships of conservative churches represents more a "circulation of the saints" than an authentic incursion by the churches into the ranks of the secularized.

Sometimes even more mundane processes are at work behind the increase in memberships of conservative denominations. Bouma's analysis (1979) of statistics from the Christian Reformed Church suggests that its postwar expansion is due primarily to the addition of immigrants to the United States from the Netherlands who were trained in the Dutch Calvinist tradition and to the relatively high fertility rate of the members as a group. Because population growth rates are geometrical rather than arithmetical, even a one-child difference in average family size over a few generations can result in a significant real increase in church membership without any reference to outside recruitment at all. Similarly, a one-child decrease in family size over generations can result in significant decline—the effects of the death of older generations being powerfully compounded by the absence of rising generations, as the elderly often may lose potential connections to their religious base when family members are not nearby. Residential migration also plays a role in the changing religious profile of the United States. As more of the national population moves south and west to the Sun Belt states, old religious connections are broken, and people without current identities as church members may more likely conform to the dominant religious culture of the region, which is Protestant and conservative (see Newman and Halvorson 1980: 55–58). In some respects at least, "demography is destiny" for U.S. churches.

Suggestions for Further Reading

Nancy Tatom Ammerman. 2005. *Pillars of Faith: American Congregations and Their Partners.* Berkeley: University of California Press.

Margaret Lamberts Bendroth. 2002. *Growing Up Protestant: Parents, Children, and Mainline Churches.* New Brunswick, N.J.: Rutgers University Press.

Stephen Ellingson. 2007. *The Megachurch and the Mainline: Remaking Religious Tradition in the Twenty-First Century.* Chicago: University of Chicago Press.

Phillip E. Hammond. 1992. *Religion and Personal Autonomy: The Third Disestablishment in America.* Columbia: University of South Carolina Press.

Benton Johnson. 1993. "The Denominations: The Changing Map of Religious America." *Public Perspective* 4 (March–April): 3–9.

Bernard M. Lazerwitz. 1998. *Jewish Choices: American Jewish Denominationalism.* Albany: State University of New York Press.

Evangelicals and a Different Mainline

For well over half a century, religious freedom was severely repressed in what was the USSR. With the overthrow of Soviet Communism in the late 1980s, a considerable measure of religious freedom quickly emerged in the new Russia. The following table presents recent data on how Russians rate various religions. Some of these ratings are not too different from what we would find in contemporary North America. Others, however, are quite shocking. For example, if we combine the "bad" and "very bad" categories, Baptists are rated much less desirable than are Hare Krishna devotees. Pentecostals carry a slightly more negative rating (and a less positive rating) than Krishnaists. In fact, only Jehovah's Witnesses rank lower than Baptists in Russians' eyes—and by only 2 percentage points, a statistically insignificant difference. (But note that the "no opinion" category is dropped from these data, which apparently affects Jehovah's Witnesses to reduce their positive ratings, while Baptists have more positive ratings than do those in these other groups. Other groups, like Methodists and the Unification Church ["Moonies"], show that a majority of the population has no opinion of [hence probably does not know about] these groups.)

Table 4.6 Russian Attitudes Toward Different Religions

	Attitudes Toward:			
	Very Good	*Good*	*Bad*	*Very Bad*
Orthodoxy	44	50	1	0
Islam	8	51	16	5
Catholicism	5	53	9	3
ROC Abroad	4	39	13	6
Buddhism	3	35	15	7
Old Believers	4	33	21	7
Judaism	2	28	19	8
Lutherans	2	27	12	6
Baptists	2	23	33	12
Krishnaism	1	20	20	13
Methodists	1	16	15	7
Pentecostals	1	15	24	12
Adventists	1	14	17	10
Jehovah's Witnesses	1	13	26	21
Munism [Moonies]	1	10	18	15

Source: Kimmo Kaarianen and Dmitrii Furman, "Orthodoxy as a Component of Russian Identity," *East-West Ministry and Church Report* 10, no. 1 (Winter 2002). "Russian" refers to all citizens of the Russian Federation, and not exclusively to ethnic Russians.

Wade Clark Roof. 1999. *Spiritual Marketplace: Baby Boomers and the Remaking of American Religion*. Princeton, N.J.: Princeton University Press.

David A. Roozen and James R. Nieman, eds. 2005. *Church, Identity, and Change: Theology and Denominational Structures in Unsettled Times*. Grand Rapids, MI: Eerdmans.

Kimon Howland Sargeant. 2000. *Seeker Churches: Promoting Traditional Religion in a Nontraditional Way*. New Brunswick, N.J.: Rutgers University Press.

Max Weber. 1985 [1906]. "'Churches' and 'Sects' in North America: An Ecclesiastical Socio-Political Sketch." *Sociological Theory* 3:1–13.

PART TWO

RELIGION AND SOCIAL DIFFERENTIATION

University Photographer Collection (GPHR 1427), UNDA. Reproduced with permission of the University of Notre Dame.

CHAPTER 5

Social Class, Religion, and Power

A CLASSIC FIELD OF INQUIRY

Few would dispute the assertion that people's social class locations have a bearing on their religious beliefs and practices. Similarly, most are prepared to agree that religious allegiances and commitments are capable of shaping the ways people act in the economic and political realms. However, as sociologists of religion are only too well aware, the relationship between class and religion is complex, ambiguous, and subject to change. For earlier generations of scholars, building on the work of classical sociology, the reciprocal relationship between religion and social class was a topic of major interest. In recent decades, however, among sociology's "holy trinity" of social divisions, the class factor has increasingly yielded the front stage to research devoted to race and ethnicity on the one hand and gender and sexual orientation on the other. Yet as we shall see in this chapter, the relative neglect of class and power does not mean that the topic has been ignored entirely. Moreover, it does not suggest that class divisions are less relevant today than they were in the past. Thus, while class and power are a neglected field of inquiry in comparison to the attention paid to the other elements among major social divisions, they nevertheless remain important topics for the study of religion (cf. McCloud 2007).

Sociological Classics

In the formative period of sociology, two figures stand out among the discipline's founding members due to the particular emphasis they place in their work on the relationship between class and religion: Karl Marx and Max Weber. It is at some level curious indeed that these two had such an impact. Perhaps two of the most oft-quoted phrases emanating from the classic period of sociology are attributed respectively to these two authors: Marx's assertion that religion was the "opium of the people" and Weber's description of himself as "religiously unmusical." In Marx's case, this statement would appear to point to a person whose antipathy to things religious was such that he was inclined to an account that essentially wrote off religion. In Weber's case, his self-description would appear to suggest that at a very personal or existential level he was not able to comprehend or to develop an empathetic understanding of religious belief.

Nevertheless, both managed in profound ways to influence the subsequent development of class analysis in the sociology of religion. Thus, before turning to an analysis of class and religion in U.S. society, we turn first to an exploration of the legacy bequeathed by Marx and Weber.

MARX: THE PERMANENT EXILE AND PROPHET

Commentators on Marx have often alluded to the impact of his Jewish heritage on his thought—despite the fact that his father had actually converted to Lutheranism in an effort to promote his own upward mobility and despite the fact that Marx himself became both a self-proclaimed atheist and an anti-Semite (see, for example, Mazlish 1984: 37–38). In particular, they have pointed to the parallel between the proletariat and the Jewish people: both are depicted not only as the victims of oppression, and thus in terms of their suffering, but also as a chosen or elect with a historical mission to accomplish. The exploitation and the degradation that the proletariat experiences in a capitalist economic system are viewed as an uncanny parallel to the life of the exiled Jews in Egypt. Likewise, the socialist world of the future that Marx devoted his life to realizing can be seen as the counterpart to the Promised Land of Israel. To make the parallel complete, Marx, as the critic of capitalism, assumed a prophetic role, the voice of one crying in the urban industrial wilderness of nineteenth-century Paris and London. Moreover, like Moses, he died before setting foot in the Promised Land.

The parallels can take us only so far in appreciating the significance of Marx's thought. The distinctiveness of his work is due to the singular way he wove the disparate strands of a philosophy inspired principally by G. W. F. Hegel, a political theory rooted in nineteenth-century socialist currents, and economic thought into a distinctive—if somewhat uneven and easily frayed—analytic framework for understanding the dynamics of capitalism. Marx viewed his efforts as ultimately constituting a scientific—and not an ethical or ideological—account of this historically specific economic system. As an indication of his aspiration to contribute to science, he attempted to dedicate the second volume of *Capital* (1867) to Charles Darwin, who politely declined the offer (Padover 1978: 363–64). However, Marx did not believe in science for science's sake. Instead, he believed that he was also advancing a theory that would prove to be a useful tool for those intent on effecting a revolutionary upheaval of the capitalist system in favor of socialism. In other words, he wanted to translate theory into action, or *praxis*, as it is often termed by Marxist scholars.

Marx was the product of the Enlightenment, embracing its call to replace faith by reason and religion by science. He was convinced that social relations should be guided by reason, rather than by the blind force of tradition. Moreover, he thought that one of the virtues of capitalism was that it stripped away the halo of the past and permitted people to free themselves from the burdens of tradition-bound parochialism. It is within this general context that Marx's understandings of two interconnected themes—the future of religion and the relationship between religion and social class—need to be located. Put another way,

Marx's quest to identify the sources of religion was intimately tied to his quest to overcome religion.

Two foundational concepts shaped Marxist theory: *alienation* and *exploitation*. The former figures prominently in the writings of the young Marx, particularly in works such as the *Economic and Philosophical Manuscripts*, while the latter is the central theme in his mature works, including the multivolume *Theories of Surplus Value* and the three volumes of what is probably his best-known work, *Capital*. Marxist interpreters are divided over whether the mature Marx broke with his earlier writings, as, for example, the French Marxist Louis Althusser (1970) claimed, or whether they ought to be seen as cut from the whole cloth, as commentators such as Shlomo Avineri (1968) argue. While we think the latter position is more compelling, it is clearly the case that the emphases in Marx's work shifted over time. For our purposes, the significance of each of these concepts for religion needs to be identified.

Alienation is a condition characterized by a lack of attachment, purpose, and meaning—and, above all, freedom. While alienation has presumably characterized the human condition in precapitalist epochs, Marx focuses primarily on the historically specific manifestations of contemporary alienation brought about by the triumph of capitalist industrialization. Marx considers alienation to be one of the inherent contradictions of capitalism, contradictions that are manifested in the class divisions that have emerged in this economic system—most evident in the dialectical tension between private property and its capitalist owners against wage labor and the industrial working class, or proletariat.

For Marx, according to Avineri (1968: 106), "The most obvious phenomenal expression of alienation is the worker's inability in capitalist society to own the product of his work." By selling their labor for wages, workers simultaneously lose connection with the object of labor and become objects themselves. Workers are devalued to the level of a commodity—a *thing*—through the process Marx described as "universal salability." They become alienated from the objects created by their labor as their employers, the capitalist owners of industrial enterprises, expropriate those products. Marx articulated this philosophically in his essay "Alienated Labor":

> The fact simply implied that the object produced by labor, its product, now stands opposed to it as an alien being, as a power independent of the producer. The product of labor is labor which has been embodied in an object and turned into a physical thing; this product is an objectification of labor. . . . The performance of work appears in the sphere of physical economy as a vitiation of the worker, objectification as a loss and a servitude to the object, and appropriation as alienation. (1964: 122)

In other words, far from realizing themselves through their labor, from fulfilling essential human needs through productive activity, workers experience labor as forced, rather than as a voluntary activity. As a result of the institution of wage labor, workers' activities are no longer the result of their own autonomous decisions. Work becomes an alien activity, one that no longer serves the needs of *homo faber* (that is, the human "maker" or self-creator), but can only be a means for satisfying other needs. Marx concluded:

> We arrive at the result that [the worker] feels himself to be freely active only in his animal functions—eating, drinking, and procreating, or at most also in his dwelling and personal adornment—while in his human functions he is reduced to an animal. The animal becomes human and the human becomes animal. (1964: 125)

Marx contends that in capitalism workers are alienated from the products of their labor and the act of work itself, from others, from nature, and ultimately from themselves.

At the same time that Marx was composing this philosophic critique of capitalism, his future collaborator, Friedrich Engels, was writing what would become a classic sociological documentary, *The Condition of the Working Class in England* (1844). Engels vividly described the negative impact of rapid industrialization on cities such as Manchester, portraying the foul pollutants emanating from factories, the squalor of overcrowding, and the social problems generated by impoverishment. In the bleak industrial landscape he described, human relations were seen as distorted and pathological. People increasingly became self-seeking, isolated, and brutally indifferent to the suffering of others. In short, this empirical account reinforces the philosophical critique proffered by Marx.

What are the implications of this conception of alienation for Marx's assessment of religion? Norman Birnbaum, a sociologist sympathetic to both the Marx of the early years and the religious dimension of social life, summarizes the connection nicely when he writes that for the youthful, humanistic Marx, "religion is a spiritual response to a condition of alienation" (1973: 12). In other words, Marx's view suggests that alienated people turn to religion to find consolation from their suffering, hence the idea of religion as an opiate. In this sense, religion performs an important *function* for people. Contrary to the crude antireligious perspective of latter-day Marxists such as V. I. Lenin, Marx never suggested that religion ought to be prohibited. That would be akin to forcing opium addicts to kick their habit cold turkey.

But Marx did look forward to a day in which religion's attractions would disappear, because he considered religious beliefs to consist of myths or illusions—distortions of reality that prevented people from seeing clearly both the root causes of the problems they confronted and the potential solutions to those problems. In this respect, the imprint of figures such as Ludwig Feuerbach and those generally associated with the left-Hegelian movement is evident; likewise, there is a similarity between his views and those of, for example, Sigmund Freud, who was referring to religion when he titled a 1927 book *The Future of an Illusion*. The comparison with Freud is instructive. Freud saw religion as the response to psychic distress on the part of people with weak egos, and thought that only those with strong egos could confront the world directly, along with all the pain it was capable of inflicting. Freud promoted a stoic worldview as the appropriate response of a mature humanity to the inevitability of suffering and death.

In contrast, Marx thought that the conditions that produced alienation could be overcome if class-conscious workers overthrew capitalism and established a classless socialist society. Though he offered little by way of advice regarding how workers might go about achieving this goal and even less about what such a society might actually look like, he was nonetheless convinced—he had an abiding faith, one might say—that socialism would spell the end of alienation. The end of alienation, in turn, would undermine the need for religion, thereby causing its demise.

The mature Marx's attention turned to exploitation. While the intricacies of his economic theories are beyond the scope of our interests here, Marx the economist was convinced that the exchange relationship between capitalists and workers was an unequal one wherein the former ended up with far more in the bargain than the latter. Marx saw in this difference the source of what would become the linchpin of a distinctly Marxist economics: surplus value. Surplus value is the ultimate source of profit, and thus its expropriation is crucial for capitalism to survive. The rate of surplus value is also a measure of the rate of exploitation of workers by capitalists. Suffice it to say that the following image summarizes Marx's view of the inherent relationship between the capitalist and the worker: "Vampire-like, [the capitalist] only lives by sucking living labor, and lives the more, the more labor it sucks" (1967: 257).

Marx was aware that for capitalism to survive, it needed to achieve legitimacy. To the extent that it did, it meant that workers harbored false consciousness. Marx and later Marxists such as Georg Lukács (1971) and Antonio Gramsci (1971) saw the importance of ideologies as systems of cultural beliefs and values that served the ruling class insofar as they served to justify and legitimate the status quo. In this regard, religion was seen as a valuable component of ideologies of domination. Religion thus was conceived to be a powerful conservative force that served to perpetuate the domination of one social class at the expense of others.

A concrete example of this Marxian perspective on religion in an applied setting can be seen in the case of the Industrial Workers of the World (IWW), or Wobblies (Winters 1985; Christiano 1988; Stark and Christiano 1992). They were a radical union that for a time early in the twentieth century sought to represent the anger, hopes, and interests of the most socially dispossessed sector of the U.S. working class. One of their archenemies was the Salvation Army, which reached out to these same workers. In what amounted to a jurisdictional dispute among two competitors for the souls of the working class, the Wobblies entertained an ongoing assault on what they referred to as the "Starvation Army," accusing it of encouraging "pie in the sky" rather than demanding "roast beef and apple pie" now.

Filtered into academic sociology in a manner that likely would not have pleased Marx, who more than once uttered the dictum "If this is Marxism, then I am not a Marxist," two interconnected but analytically separable research agendas developed out of the dual themes of alienation and exploitation. The first, influenced by the alienation theme, suggests that religiosity is a product of deprivation. The assumption of this position is that members of the lower classes are more religious than members of the middle or upper classes. A second tradition, connected to the exploitation theme, yielded a research agenda in which sociologists were encouraged to explore the social sources, the content, and the societal effects of the varied uses of religious beliefs and ideas in class-based ideologies. Derived from the image of religion as an opiate, this research tradition has plumbed the varied ways that religion has served to legitimate, maintain, and perpetuate existing class structures and social inequality.

WEBER: THEODICY, RELIGIOUS ETHICS, AND SOCIAL CLASS

A scholar of prodigious range and penetrating insight, Max Weber had a profound impact on the sociology of religion in general and on the study of the relationship between religion and social class in particular. The "religiously unmusical" Weber has been portrayed as offering a sociology written "with the ghost of Marx hovering over his shoulder" (Salomon 1945: 596). In part this is true. Weber sought to combat the materialist thrust of Marx and his subsequent often self-appointed disciples by urging an appreciation of the relative autonomy of ideas. However, while clearly influenced by Marx, the notion of the reactive Weber can be overdrawn. His thinking was also shaped by Friedrich Nietzsche, to whom Weber was temperamentally closer insofar as both evidenced an angst-ridden response to their sense of the death of God and the disenchantment of the world (Jaspers 1964).

Relevant to our concerns in this chapter, J. Milton Yinger (1970: 288) has identified a point of departure from Nietzsche. For the German philosopher, religious belief had at its core a class basis. This was because he contended that religion—he was specifically speaking about Christianity—was grounded in *resentment*, the resentment that the poor and the powerless felt and could do little about. Weber, Yinger argues, countered Nietzsche by concluding that this type of religious belief is ultimately grounded in suffering, not resentment.

This shift led Weber to an important point about the significance of theodicies: explanations for the existence of suffering. Weber's discussion of theodicy is brief, serving as a bridge to his discussion of salvation. *Theodicy* is defined as "the problem of how the extraordinary power of . . . god may be reconciled with the imperfection of the world that he has created and rules over." This problem is particularly acute for those who understand their god as "a transcendental unitary god who is universal," but it is not found only there (1978: 519). Weber finds it in the religions of ancient Egypt, in the nontheistic religions of Hinduism and Buddhism, as well as where it would be expected in the monotheistic world religions: Judaism, Christianity, and Islam. Distilling the characteristic features of the theodicies of the world religions, Weber identified five varieties or forms that the answers to this problem take—answers that, in his view, speak to the varieties of forms that religion itself takes: a messiah who initiates the end of the world as we know it, the transmigration of souls, a universal day of judgment, predestination, or dual divinities of good and evil.

The second manifestation of the ethical dimension to which Weber turned was the problem of *soteriology*, by which he meant the matter of what constitutes salvation and how to achieve it. This problem occupies considerably more space than theodicy in his work. Nowhere does he specifically define salvation, but in speaking of such things as wealth and long life, he notes that "the crassest utilitarian expectations frequently replace anything we are accustomed to term 'salvation.'" By implication, then, salvation is perceived broadly; in any case, as social scientists, he writes, "our concern is essentially with the quest for salvation, whatever its form, insofar as it produced certain consequences for practical behavior in the world" (1978: 526, 528). This was the major preoccupation of his research into the ethical dimensions of the major world religions.

However, for the topic of social class, we return to the matter of theodicy. Weber actually makes a case for the class-specific nature of different theodicies. Thus, he distinguishes between theodicies of misfortune and good-fortune theodicies. The former are what Weber had in mind when thinking about Nietzsche's resentment. Theodicies of misfortune tend to the belief that wealth and other manifestations of privilege are indications or signs of evil. The accompanying soteriology points to rewards that will be obtained in the world to come. Weber thought that this transvaluational orientation was a characteristic feature of lower-class religious beliefs. In contrast, theodicies of fortune emphasize the notion that privileges are a blessing and are deserved. Thus, Weber wrote:

> Other things being equal, strata with high social and economic privilege will scarcely be prone to evolve the idea of salvation. Rather, they assign to religion the primary function of *legitimizing* their own life pattern and situation in the world. This universal phenomenon is rooted in certain basic psychological patterns. When a man who is happy compares his position with that of one who is unhappy, he is not content with the fact of his happiness, but desires something more, namely the right to this happiness, the consciousness that he has earned his good fortune, in contrast to the unfortunate one who must equally have earned his misfortune. Our everyday experience proves that there exists just such a need for psychic comfort about the legitimacy or deservedness of one's happiness, whether this involves political success, superior economic status . . . or anything else. What the privileged classes require of religion, if anything at all, is this legitimation. (1978: 491)

Weber concerned himself with class matters in another way in his studies of world religions. One of his preoccupations in them was with identifying the classes, subclasses, or strata that were the main carriers—or promoters—of a particular religious belief system. Of special concern were the economic ethics connected to those beliefs. Thus, in his studies of the religions of China and India, he contends that Confucianism manifested a status ethic related to its main advocates, the cultured elite with literary educations, while Buddhism at the hands of monks yielded an ethic that prompted contemplative world rejection.

In his parallel examinations of the religions of the Occident, he contended that Judaism was the religion of an outcast or "pariah" people, Christianity at the beginning found its key source of support among itinerant artisans, while Islam was "a religion of world-conquering warriors" (Weber 1946: 268–69).

At the same time, Weber was at pains to argue that religion was not merely an expression of the worldview of or legitimation for the social location of a particular class or stratum of society. Thus, he wrote, "It is not our thesis that the specific nature of religion is a simple 'function' of the social situation of the stratum which appears as its characteristic bearer, or that it represents the stratum's 'ideology,' or that it is a reflection of the stratum's material or ideal interest-situation" (1946: 269–70). He tried to avoid the crude materialism that he associated with Marxism. (He appears to have been more familiar with Marxist contemporaries than with Marx himself, particularly the early Marx.) At the same time, he saw ideas as grounded in the social world, and thus he did not want to replace materialism with an equally crude idealism. Ideas for Weber, including religious ideas, have a relative autonomy but are also fashioned and refashioned by class and status groups to meet their particular needs. Rather than viewing these matters in terms of simple cause and effect, Weber argued for the search for what he called *elective affinities*, which implies a more dialectical relationship between ideas and actors. In what would have been a commonplace railroad analogy in his day, Weber wrote:

> Not ideas, but material and ideal interests, directly govern men's conduct. Yet very frequently the "world images" that have been created by "ideas" have, like switchmen, determined the tracks along which action has been pushed by the dynamic of interest. "From what" and "for what" one wished to be redeemed and, let us not forget, "could be" redeemed, depended upon one's image of the world. (1946: 280)

Nowhere was this more evident than in Weber's "Protestant ethic" thesis. In this brief series of essays, first published during 1904 and 1905 specifically as a riposte to Werner Sombart's *Modern Capitalism* (1902), all of Weber's concerns and fears are on display. It has also been one of the most important and controversial topics in the sociology of religion.

Near the end of *The Protestant Ethic and the Spirit of Capitalism*, which is an excursion into the formative period of capitalism, Weber turned his attention to the future rather than the past, writing:

> This order is now bound to the technical and economic conditions of machine production which today determines the lives of all the individuals who are born into this mechanism, not only those directly concerned with economic acquisition, with irresistible force. Perhaps it will so determine them until the last ton of fossilized coal is burnt. . . . But fate has decreed that [the future will become] an iron cage. (1998: 181)

The metaphor of the iron cage is a reflection of Weber's deep concern that the rationalization promoted by the modern industrial world posed a threat to individualism and freedom. To the extent that he could not see a way out from this disenchantment of the world, he expressed himself in profoundly pessimistic terms.

While this particular theme is crucial to debates about secularization, already discussed in chapter 3 of this book, the Protestant ethic thesis also raises questions about social class. The crux of *The Protestant Ethic and the Spirit of Capitalism* is an attempt to identify those factors that made possible the rise of capitalism in various locales in western Europe, and not elsewhere, for inherent in this issue he thought was a key to understanding why the iron cage was such a real prospect. Weber argues that Protestantism was part of the causal chain that led to the development of the modern world-system dominated by Anglo-American capitalism.

Central to Weber's answer is his understanding of the "spirit" of capitalism. The capitalist mentality encouraged, in his view, a unique orientation toward economic activity. It contrasted sharply, for example, with that of economic traditionalists, who were content to work merely to get by, as well as with persons motivated solely by greed or by a desire for ostentatious displays of wealth. Weber found in deist Benjamin Franklin's "Poor Richard" writings a perfect instance of what he meant by the capitalist spirit. To claim, as Poor Richard did, that "time is money" and that "a penny saved is a penny earned" is to define accumulation as the goal of economic activity, with self-discipline and rational calculation as valued behaviors. The capitalist should be seen as a rational miser—a person devoted to the task of creating wealth, not to enjoy its fruits, but to reinvest it to generate even more wealth.

Why would someone act this way? Like a monk who gives up the pleasures of the world to devote himself to an otherworldly life of prayer and contemplation, the capitalist is an ascetic. Unlike the monk, however, the capitalist remains in the world and amasses wealth. Weber called this unique economic ethic "*inner-worldly asceticism*" to distinguish it from the world-rejecting variant found in monastic life. He argued that such a mentality could not be understood without linking it to the religious transformation brought about by the Protestant Reformation. Indeed, he contended that it was not by chance that capitalism arose in certain places in western Europe where and when the Protestant Reformation took root.

Specifically, Weber attempted to illustrate how the emergence of inner-worldly asceticism revolved around two figures associated with the two stages of the Reformation, Martin Luther and John Calvin. Luther's importance for the Protestant ethic thesis involved his rejection of the idea that the highest form of religious vocation (*beruf*), or "calling," demanded a retreat from the world to the monastery. Luther's theology is based on a radical alteration of the idea of vocation, wherein all worldly occupations could be seen as religiously inspired callings. Mundane work acquired religious significance. This was an important step toward activity in the world, but according to Weber it was not sufficient to explain the ultimate impact of Protestantism on the emergence of capitalism.

Rather, Calvin's contribution proved to be decisive. According to his doctrine of predestination, an omnipotent and omniscient God had determined, even before people were born, whether they were among the saved or the damned, chosen for eternal life in paradise or an eternity in hell. This created the social-psychological condition of salvation anxiety, producing considerable inner turmoil for believers who wanted to know something about the state of their eternal souls. It is useful to locate this anxiety in the world of the sixteenth and seventeenth centuries, when death was considerably less predictable than it is today and plagues ran rampant. According to Weber, the Protestant ethic emerged as a consequence of a dynamic interaction between Luther's understanding of vocation, on the one hand, and salvation anxiety, on the other. Simply put, the faithful searched for a sign that would give them some sense of their relationship to God, and they found it in economic success. In other words, believers viewed the acquisition of wealth to be an indication of God's grace and good favor. The result was that people were motivated to acquire wealth through disciplined work because by so doing they gained some assurance of their status as one of the elect.

Weber argued that among the English Puritans, epitomized by Richard Baxter, the tension of Calvin's austere doctrine of predestination was resolved by a belief (based principally on the biblical book of Proverbs) that God would reward in this life those whom he had elected to eternal glory, who lived according to his laws. Thus, the "rising parvenus" of the English middle classes were told that if they strictly followed biblical teachings for the conduct of life, as interpreted by the Puritans, and they succeeded in their businesses, this would be a sign of their election to eternal salvation. But they also learned that heaven's reward would occur only if they also used the fruits of their labors properly. Specifically, they were to invest all of their income beyond the necessities of a frugal lifestyle, in so doing making even more money, to invest similarly all the days of their lives. This is the connection between the Protestant "work ethic" and capitalism, not merely as an economic philosophy but as a social ethic that establishes a distinctive lifestyle.

It is not that Protestantism as a specific set of Christian dogmas was either necessary or sufficient to "cause" modern rational capitalism to appear, but that Protestantism, especially at the hands of the late sixteenth- and early seventeenth-century English Puritans, succeeded in creating a system of meaningful action that functioned historically as the "last intensification" (Collins 1986: 93) in a causal chain that led to modern capitalism, which Weber called "the most fateful force in our modern life" (Weber 1998: 17).

Contrary to a common misunderstanding of Weber's thesis, Protestantism was not to be seen, in a simplistic, monocausal way, as the cause and the capitalist spirit as the effect, otherwise detached from their historical context. Rather, the connection was one of an elective affinity. In other words, it was not by chance that capitalism emerged in precisely those lands where Protestantism had become the dominant form of Christianity. Weber did not mean that this was the whole story in understanding the rise of capitalism. In his view, however, it was an important piece of the puzzle—one overlooked, for example, by those inspired by Marx's materialist theory of social change. In the studies of the major world religions noted above, Weber attempted to identify the elements of their respective economic ethics that seemed to work against the development of the capitalist spirit.

Weber's influence on subsequent analyses of class and religion cannot be overstated (see Swatos and Kaelber 2005; Swatos and Kivisto 2007). In part, his work provides for a more supple and complex approach to the topic than Marx's work. While at times serving as a corrective to tendencies in Marx and Marxism in general, Weber's work has also acted to complement and enrich this tradition. In the discussion that follows, we examine some of the ways Weber shaped the research agenda of sociologists seeking to understand the complexities of the U.S. religious landscape.

Religion and the U.S. Class Structure

The complexities of American society make the task of comprehending the reciprocal relationship between religion and class particularly perplexing. In the first place, the United States has not historically been as class-conscious as nations such as Great Britain. This is in no small part because race and ethnicity have played such a prominent role in establishing social divisions and conflicts in the United States. The ways that class and race or ethnicity are related make for heightened complexity. Likewise, the religious diversity of the United States is a complicating factor. With no established religion, but with a Protestant majority, the country has been characterized by considerable organizational diversity, witnessed in the large number of denominations that attract different clienteles. The roots of religious stratification can be traced to the colonial period in American history (Pyle and Davidson 2003).

To make the situation even more complicated, sociologists do not all agree about what they mean by social class. Some, following Marx, define class as a set of relationships to the economy. Others, more influenced by Weber, who suggested that it was important to consider not only economic class location, but also status and power considerations, look at social class as a cluster of shared characteristics of income, wealth, occupation, and education. Some sociologists prefer to speak about stratification rather than class and prefer to focus on occupations. They view some jobs as being more prestigious than others, and thus carrying greater "status honor." Class schemes that classify persons by reputation, occupation, or some other set of related characteristics are more closely aligned to a Weberian perspective. While both ways of looking at class have proved to be useful, at times in reviewing the literature one can come away feeling that clear definitional distinctions either are not made or work at cross-purposes.

In addition, there is no shared agreement about the number of social classes in U.S. society or about what they should be called. For Marxists, the main classes in a society are the ruling bourgeoisie and the oppressed proletariat, with a variety of other classes also being present, such as the petite bourgeoisie, peasants, landowners, and lumpenproletariat. More common in sociology today are the more mundane categorizations of upper, middle, and lower classes. But are

John D. Rockefeller and the Protestant Ethic

In the early industrial era, John D. Rockefeller became the wealthiest man in the world. This passage suggests his personal view of religion and business:

> In his needy youth, John Rockefeller had saved dimes and collected the dimes of others to aid his church; he had continued most faithfully to do glory to God in many ways, with touching and humble gifts: five cents for the Sabbath school, twelve cents for a mission, ten cents for a religious paper—all noted in his diary since the age of sixteen. Then as he prospered he gave himself over more and more to a pious evangelism: in the Bible classes he taught at the age of twenty-eight in Cleveland he urged his pupils . . . to arm themselves with the Puritan virtues. He took as his text: "Seest thou a man diligent in his business? He shall stand before kings." He warned his hearers, further, to be "moderate," not to be "good fellows," to take no drink nor to gamble. Through the years, the faith of the evangelists, with its deep emphasis upon the liberty of the individual conscience, grew stronger in Rockefeller. . . . Hence when upon one occasion of a princely gift to the Church the bitter cry of "tainted money" was set up against Rockefeller, he said simply and feelingly: *"God gave me my money."*

Source: Matthew Josephson, *The Robber Barons: The Great American Capitalists, 1861–1901* (1934; reprint, San Diego: Harcourt Brace Jovanovich, 1962), 318.

there three classes, as this would imply, or are there more? Some scholars have suggested that there are six classes: upper upper, lower upper, upper middle, lower middle, upper lower, and lower lower. Yet others expand the number to nine by adding a "middle" category, as in middle-upper class, which would rank second in this typology, in contrast to the upper-middle class, which would rank fourth. And the list goes on.

Finally, in identifying social classes, some researchers are interested in developing objective criteria and applying them, while others argue that it is important to consider the subjective views of class operative among members of the public at large. This being said, we proceed to examine some of the most consequential ways that the sociology of religion has enhanced our understanding of religion and class.

U.S. CLASSES AND RELIGION IN THE INDUSTRIAL AGE: 1870–1970

One of the most influential analyses of classes in the United States during the first half of the twentieth century emerged from social anthropologist W. Lloyd Warner's community studies conducted in New England, the Midwest, and the South (Warner 1942a, 1942b, 1973; Warner and Lunt 1941). By linking measures of income and wealth to prestige or status, Warner argued that there were three major class categories in the United States. However, he also thought it useful to divide each of those categories into two sectors. At the top were the two sectors of the upper class. The first was composed of old money. Below them, even if they had more wealth, were the nouveaux riches, people with plenty of money but lacking the prestige and the finer graces of the old-money elites. Collectively, they represented only 3 percent of the total population. The middle class was likewise divided between the business and professional members of the upper-middle class, and the small shop owners, teachers, ministers, social workers, and so forth who could be seen as modestly successful in economic terms. The composite size of the middle class was slightly less than 40 percent. Thus, the majority of the population was found in the two groupings of the lower class, where more than 30 percent were located in the ranks of the solid blue-collar working class and about a quarter of the total representing the underemployed and unemployed (Warner and Lunt 1941: 88). The U.S. class structure could thus be viewed as a pyramid shape, with a small upper class at the top, followed by a substantial middle class, with an even larger lower class at the base. A view of U.S. class structure during the first half of the twentieth century that was similar to this framework—even though not identical in all particulars—informed most sociological work on the relationship between religion and class.

Religious affiliations are related to people's social class locations, though not in a simple way given the fact that other variables—particularly race and ethnicity—also play important roles. This was a central thesis of H. Richard Niebuhr's influential book *The Social Sources of Denominationalism* (1929). Niebuhr attempted to answer the question of why it was that the denominational divisions characterizing the American religious marketplace could be readily defined in class terms. Although most denominations could claim membership from the upper classes, middle classes, and lower classes, it was also true that certain classes were overrepresented in various denominations.

As a theologian, Niebuhr found these divisions troubling in light of the Christian ideal of unity. His polemic against denominationalism need not concern us here. What is relevant is his proposed explanation for the underlying sources of the divisions within Christianity in the United States, which is based on his interpretation of the church-sect distinction, as indicated in chapter 4. Niebuhr argued that churches by definition are inclusive, and because members are born into them, churches do not place excessive behavioral demands on their members. Moreover, churches seek to accommodate to the larger society, and, as such, accept the status quo. For this reason, these institutions fail to meet the needs of the lower classes, and particularly those who suffer from the most extreme forms of economic deprivation. Simply put, the lower classes' view of the society they inhabit is at odds with that of the churches. In Weberian terminology, churches are incapable of providing a theodicy adequate to meet the religious needs of this sector of society.

As a consequence, the lower classes are inclined to create and join sects, which are far more exclusive and more demanding in terms of behavioral expectations, and exhibit an adversarial relationship to secular society. Niebuhr thought that members of the lower class were especially attracted to organizations characterized by doctrinal purity, a democratic or populist emphasis on the priesthood of all believers, ethical austerity, and considerable tension with society at large. A dynamic quality was added to this analysis inasmuch as when a sect proved to be successful and grew, it became more churchlike. When this occurred, its original theodicy of misfortune was refashioned, transforming it into a good-fortune theodicy, and in so doing replacing the original sect's adversarial stance with a more accommodating one. This then set in motion the creation of new sects, since the preconditions for their formation remained as long as the economic conditions that ensured the existence of a sizable lower class persisted.

Liston Pope's *Millhands and Preachers* (1942) is a classic community study making use of Niebuhr's general framework to analyze the implications of the class character of denominations. The book reports on a famous episode in U.S. labor history that took place in the textile town of Gastonia, North Carolina, in 1929. The conflict pitted on one side the white workers in Gastonia's mills, including former farmers who, having lost their land, had been forced to seek employment in the textile industry, and the mill owners on the other side. The conflict was intense and at times violent, attracting national attention in the form of outside union organizers and other supporters of the workers converging on the town. Supporters of the factory owners fought a spirited propaganda campaign in opposition to the demands of the workers for union recognition and for improvements in matters such as wages, benefits, and safety in notoriously dangerous factories.

In this context, the churches of Gastonia were polarized between those that supported the owners and those siding with the workers. Pope discovered that the mainline churches in the town, particularly the large Methodist and Baptist congregations, had benefited from the capitalist paternalism of the mill owners. The owners had, for example, given land to congregations and assisted them financially in building and maintaining their churches. Ministers had seen their salaries supplemented by the benevolence of the owners and had become accustomed to their involvement in myriad aspects of congregational life. In return, the ministers of these churches, who were associated with the upper and middle classes in Gastonia, exhibited an unwillingness to criticize the owners for the ways they ran their factories or treated their workers. Rather, from the pulpit and in other public pronouncements, they depicted the owners as benevolent altruists. At the same time, these ministers were critical of union organizers and political radicals, and were quick to condemn them for presumed Communist influences, their aggressive tactics, and their outsider status.

In contrast to the mainline churches, the newer Holiness and Pentecostal churches—sects in Niebuhr's typology—came to the defense of the workers. They had not been the beneficiaries of the benevolence of the factory owners, whom they were quite prepared to criticize for exploiting their workers. Though not prepared to embrace left-wing political ideology, they shared with Socialists and Communists an antipathy toward the hegemonic classes in Gastonia and a desire to side with the workers, whom they saw as disinherited and oppressed.

Thus, part of the Christian community promoted order, stability, and conservatism, and in so doing proved to be a powerful source of legitimation of the status quo and of existing disparities in the distribution of wealth and power. Another part advocated change intended to advance the cause of justice and fairness, and as such served as a guide to those who were intent on challenging the established social order. Pope's main point was that this cleavage was chiefly along class lines, with the upper- and middle-class churches serving as voices of order, while the lower-class-dominated sects were sympathetic to the calls for change (see also Pope 1957; Earle et al. 1976).

Pope's conclusions appeared to offer confirmation of Niebuhr's "social sources of denominationalism" thesis. However, the uniqueness of a one-industry town dominated by paternalistic capitalism in a Southern state made it difficult to extrapolate to the society at large. How typical, for example, were the positions on economic issues taken by the mainline churches in Gastonia, which were heavily dependent on economic elites in the community? Subsequent evidence suggests that mainline churches are typically more liberal than lower-class sects on such matters (Yinger 1970: 301). Nevertheless, it does suggest that class differences factor into denominational differences regarding economic ethics.

Up to the middle of the twentieth century, the class character of different denominations was one of the characteristic features of their distinctive identities. During the 1940s, two important studies, one by Hadley Cantril (1943) and another by Liston Pope (1948), provided a rank ordering of denominations along socioeconomic lines. Among Protestant denominations, three dating to the colonial era stand out as being the characteristic affiliations of the upper class: Episcopalians, Presbyterians, and the United Church of Christ. In addition, Jews and Unitarians were overrepresented in the upper class. Of course each of them also had sizable middle-class constituencies and smaller but non-negligible membership levels from the lower class.

The denominations with the highest percentage of middle-class membership were the Lutherans and Methodists, though they also had sizable lower-class memberships and were decently represented in the upper class. Baptists, Roman Catholics, and the Eastern Orthodox were divided between middle- and lower-class members, with perhaps a slightly larger percentage from the lower class than from the middle. Though represented in the upper class, they were a decided minority. The smaller fundamentalist and Holiness churches were chiefly religious affiliations of the lower class, though they had some middle-class membership as well.

To round out the picture, if one factors race into the class division, African-American churches during the era of Jim Crow racial segregation would be seen as largely populated by members of the lower class. However, the relatively small black middle class was also represented, and indeed played important leadership roles in these church bodies.

Within these general divisions, the prominence of Protestant elites in the upper echelons of American society has been pronounced. More specifically, the confluence of race, ancestry, and religion in defining the upper class led to the invention of the term *WASP*, which refers to white Anglo-Saxon Protestant. At the local level, upper classes took several variants, such as the dominance of Puritans in Boston's history from colonial times into the twentieth century and the similar

Symbols of Sacred Status

The photographs on these pages depict the symbolic sides of the socioeconomic divides that cut across religious expression. The great pipe organ bespeaks not only the power and wealth that built it, but also a lifestyle that is associated with the musical tradition it embodies. The simple, hand-drawn sign says something quite different: Note especially the word *deliverance*.

Photograph courtesy of William H. Swatos, Jr.

Photograph courtesy of William H. Swatos, Jr.

dominance of Quakers in Philadelphia. At the national level, among economic and political elites, a unity was achieved that transcended these local differences. According to sociologist E. Digby Baltzell (1966), himself a scion of the Philadelphia upper class, a Protestant establishment had been forged and nurtured throughout American history. He spoke of it as an *aristocracy*, a term that flew in the face of the idea of the United States as a society with an open class system predicated chiefly on meritocratic notions by conjuring up the image of a caste-like elite. In his view, the WASP establishment could be defined as those whose names appear both in the *Social Register*, which is an indicator of inherited privilege, and in *Who's Who*, a listing of achievers.

How, in a class society characterized by upward (and downward) mobility, can a small stratum defined by similar background perpetuate its privileged position in society? This is a question that scholars such as C. Wright Mills (1956) and G. William Domhoff (1967) answered in part by pointing to unique patterns of socialization and the significance of particular organizational affiliations. For example, children were expected to attend a select number of elite prep schools, such as St. Paul's, Hotchkiss, Choate, Exeter, and Chapin. From here they headed to the Ivy League, where, even if they had not been particularly distinguished students, they could avail themselves of legacies, the upper classes' version of affirmative action. These were seen as something akin to birthrights for the offspring of old money and as crucial rites of passage for the children of the recently rich. The social function of these educational institutions was to prepare these children of privilege for assuming the reins of power. They also helped to integrate this class stratum, uniting old and new wealth as well as those from different regions of the country (Karabel 2005).

The organizational affiliations of adults perform a similar socializing function. Thus, in major cities, membership in private men's clubs, such as New York City's Knickerbocker Club, San Francisco's Pacific Union, and Philadelphia's Philadelphia Club, is an important marker of insider status. This is likewise the case with clubs that are national rather than local in their membership, such as the Bohemian Club, founded in 1872 and based in San Francisco, which continues to hold a summer retreat at Bohemian Grove, its estate outside the city. Many of the most powerful people in American society who are not officially members of the club are invited to attend this retreat.

In this regard, religious membership served as yet another boundary-defining device to distinguish who was inside and who outside. The Protestant denominations most typical of WASPs helped to define genuine acceptance into the caste-like world of the elite. Among the new rich, provided they were Protestant to start with, switching denominational affiliations from, say, Lutheranism to the Episcopal Church was a way of enhancing social status—in the process severing ties with one's past in an effort to fit into the world of the Protestant establishment.

Religion proved to be one of the critical barriers constructed to exclude Catholics and Jews from entry into the U.S. aristocracy. Anti-Catholic bigotry and the genteel (and not-so-genteel) anti-Semitism of the era were part of the ideological worldview of the Protestant establishment. These prejudices served to justify efforts to prevent the upwardly mobile members of these groups from ascending to political and economic leadership positions (Bensman and Vidich 1971: 72–73). Thus, religious affiliation led to the implementation of quotas at Ivy League schools in order to ensure that the number of Jews admitted was limited, thereby preventing meritocratic considerations from threatening the status quo (Synnott 1979). Likewise, restrictive covenants in deeds to property ensured that Jews and Catholics could not buy residences in many upper-class neighborhoods. Moreover, wealthy Jews and Catholics—even if they were wealthier than established elites—could not hope to become members of the private clubs and other social institutions so important in forging upper-class alliances.

Thus, upper-class Jews and Catholics created their own class-specific worlds similar to, but distinct from, those of the Protestant elites. Baltzell contended that if the elite in American society was virtually entirely WASP in 1900, Catholics and Jews had entered the elite world by 1950. Rather than becoming integrated with the older Protestant elites, however, they constituted the second and third segments of a triple melting pot. He predicted that the "pinch of prejudice will increasingly be felt as more and more non-Anglo-Saxon Protestants rise to this level of society." Despite their gains, he also argued that "the nation's leadership is still dominated by members of the WASP upper class" (1966: 66).

This dominance can be seen in the world of philanthropy. Baltzell contrasts philanthropy to charity. The latter refers to the Catholic view that requires, as a proper Christian response to the poor and their suffering, spontaneous and stopgap measures intended to provide immediate relief but not to end the underlying problems of poverty. In contrast, philanthropy "was an infinitely Puritan and rational response to social conditions that . . . were dysfunctional to the best use of talent in promoting an efficient division of labor, or hierarchy of callings" (1996: 77). The inheritors of this tradition included figures such as John D. Rockefeller and Andrew Carnegie, who served as models for the philanthropic efforts of the Protestant establishment. Arthur Vidich and Stanford Lyman depict the approach to Christian stewardship of such figures as these in the following way:

> Whereas both Christian Socialists and secular radicals emphasized *redistribution* of wealth, Rockefeller, Carnegie, and other industrial giants, guided by the plutocratic version of the Social Gospel, considered its *rational management* to be appropriate expression of their special calling to holy stewardship. "The problem of our age," wrote Carnegie, "is the proper administration of wealth, so that the ties of brotherhood may still bind together with the sick and poor in harmonious relationship." Rockefeller used this theme to reorganize his own philanthropy to meet the new standards of "scientific giving." . . . The rationalization of philanthropy was to follow the same path as that taken by capitalist institutions, . . . [where] foundations, boards, institutes, and universities would superintend the scientific administration of major aspects of education, health, human welfare, and social uplift in America. Even when it was to be centralized and bureaucratized, the plutocratic pattern of giving was to retain the Protestant desire to uplift unregenerate souls and encourage their committed participation in and for the benefit of society. (1985: 132)

If religion at the top of the class structure served as a powerful tool of legitimation, what about its role in shaping the economic life chances of members of other classes? A considerable amount of attention was directed to this topic by sociologists of religion during the 1950s and 1960s. One line of investigation attempted to assess the relationship between religion and economic success by employing Weber's Protestant ethic thesis. The general logic of such work was to determine if the Protestant ethic that Weber thought had played such a distinctive role in the emergence of industrial capitalism continued in any significant way to contribute to the economic success of Protestants. Actually, as some people involved in this research clearly understood, Weber thought that the intimate link between this ethic and the spirit of capitalism was no longer necessary, because once capitalism was fully functional, it operated without need of its religious basis. As Weber himself put it, "Today the spirit of religious asceticism—whether finally who knows?—has escaped the cage. But victorious capitalism, since it rests on mechanical foundations, needs its support no longer" (1998: 181–82).

Thus, whether or not this was fully appreciated, what the research on the Protestant ethic—or, as it was sometimes called, *work ethic*—actually attempted to ascertain was whether Protestant and Catholic worldviews were sufficiently different to contribute to differing socioeconomic outcomes (Mack, Murphy, and Yellin 1956; Mayer and Sharp 1962). The most influential body of data that was used to explore the differential mobility patterns of Catholics and Protestants derived from the University of Michigan's Detroit Area Study, and out of this project, the most influential single work was Gerhard Lenski's *The Religious Factor* (1961). Lenski made clear that the sense of vocation so crucial to the Weber thesis no longer was apparent among Detroit's Protestants. Similarly, they no longer exhibited the inner-worldly asceticism of their forebears.

On the other hand, Protestants were found to have higher educational attainment levels and were more economically upwardly mobile than their Catholic counterparts. In attempting to account for these differences, Lenski focused on such factors as attitudes regarding economic activity, educational attainment, traditionalism, rationalism, and views on the family. What he concluded was that on various indicators—not of the Protestant ethic, but of a more generalized achievement orientation—Protestantism produced more achievement-oriented individuals than Catholicism did (see, for example, McClelland 1961). Compared to Catholics, Protestants were less bound to tradition or to kin, were more willing to be geographically mobile in the pursuit of economic advantage, and placed a greater value on education as a tool for economic advancement. These factors—and Lenski singled out differences regarding kinship ties as being of singular importance—shaped the achievement orientation among Protestants and accounted for the fact that they were more likely than Catholics to rise in the class system.

Unwilling to heed Andrew Greeley's (1964) call for a moratorium on this line of inquiry, sociologists generated a veritable cottage industry of research on the twentieth-century relevance of this modified version of the Protestant ethic thesis. It also produced a considerable amount of criticism. Not in dispute was whether Protestants ranked higher in the class structure than Catholics: They did. Likewise, Protestants were more upwardly mobile than Catholics. The dispute revolved around accounting for these differences (Anderson 1970: 151–58). Greeley, for example, thought that what was being offered up was a distorted version of the Weber thesis that oversimplified history, failed to appreciate the diverse ethnic composition and styles of Catholicism, and drew unwarranted conclusions from the data. Subsequently, Gary Bouma (1973) reviewed research reports that had been stimulated by Lenski's study and concluded that most of them were not adequate to the task of the causal inferences they drew and tended to be theoretically overly simplistic. Finally, Howard Schuman (1971) attempted to replicate Lenski's own study, concluding that there was little evidence to support the claim for a continuing presence of the Protestant ethic in the United States.

Related to this general debate was the matter of the role played by the theodicies of misfortune that defined lower-class religious sects. The most commonly held view was that the otherworldly character of Holiness and Pentecostal groups worked against upward mobility. Taking exception to this viewpoint, Benton Johnson (1961) studied Holiness sects to determine whether it was in fact the case that these institutions functioned primarily as a mode of emotional release and compensation for and escape from the harsh realities that beset their members. Contrary to this view, he argued that an economic ethic similar to, if not precisely the same as, the Protestant ethic was operative. By promoting the values of sobriety, hard work, and self-reliance, these religious bodies functioned as agents in the socialization of the lower classes into the dominant values of American society.

The problem with this argument is that the values Johnson identified as most relevant are those that serve to promote an otherworldly asceticism. Holiness sects are not described as promoting the inner-worldly asceticism wherein secular vocations become central. Nor do they promulgate the virtues that are instrumental for an achievement orientation. Thus, while Holiness sects might be seen as promoting working-class values, the evidence Johnson offers does not lead one to conclude that they articulate an economic ethic that will facilitate economic upward mobility (Keister 2003; Beyerlein 2004). Sect members might work hard in order to avoid unemployment, but they are unlikely to find in their core religious values a stimulus for economic behaviors consonant with the bureaucratic ethic of corporations or the entrepreneurial ethic of business owners.

THE CLASS/RELIGION NEXUS IN A POSTINDUSTRIAL SOCIETY

The past several decades have witnessed two interconnected changes that have far-ranging implications for the relationship between social class and religion. On the one hand, changes in the U.S. economy have reshaped the class structure. On the other hand, we are in the midst of a restructuring of the institutional character of religion in the United States. Because these changes are relatively recent in origin and the changes are still under way, there is considerable uncertainty and ambiguity about what their full implications will ultimately be. However, in this section we attempt to examine some of the most salient shifts that have occurred, revisiting in the process some of the issues that had earlier preoccupied sociologists of religion.

By the middle of the twentieth century, it became clear that the earlier portrait of a class system that could be described as a pyramid needed to be revised. This was because the middle class had grown dramatically, replacing the working class as the largest class in the nation. Moreover, those on the upper end of the working class were now receiving incomes that allowed them to pursue essentially middle-class lifestyles. For example, they were increasingly inclined to move out of traditionally urban working-class neighborhoods to the suburbs, and they aspired to send their children to college. Thus, the middle of the class structure expanded, leading to a diamond-shaped form. As we shall see below, the most dramatic changes have occurred in that expanded middle. But before turning to this class, we shall first revisit the upper and lower classes.

Despite changes in the economy, the established upper classes have managed to preserve their privileged positions, using their wealth along with their social and cultural capital to their advantage. At the same time, especially in the high-tech world of computers and communications technologies, the number of nouveaux

The arrest of serpent handler Charles Prince. Reprinted with permission of the Knoxville News-Sentinel Company.

Holiness Religion's Other Side

Among the most intriguing of the Pentecostal-Holiness churches are the serpent-handling groups in Appalachia, who believe in the literal interpretation of Mark 16:18, which proclaims that the faithful "shall take up serpents," and if believers "drink any deadly thing, it shall not hurt them." In this passage, the fate of one prominent figure in this movement, Charles Prince, is described:

> Then, at the apex of his ministry in the churches of the hollows, where rattlesnakes and strychnine and the scriptures mingle in a deadly serious game of faith on Saturday nights and all day Sundays, he died. His death came as a shock and a surprise to the Holiness world. Prince had just pulled a very large yellow rattlesnake from a box when the rattler sank two fangs into the muscular section between the thumb and the forefinger of his left hand. Two small wounds were underneath the thumb where the animal had slammed in two stubby, sawed-off teeth to assure that its victim would not free itself soon. Prince rarely ever acknowledged when he had been bitten, and similarly on this night, he disregarded the bites and laid the snake on the pulpit. Despite the effects of the venom, he continued his service, pausing from time to time to drink strychnine from a clear mason jar. As time elapsed, he became less and less active until he became limp. In the end, Prince was a man of the Word, and he died by his interpretation of the Word as church members gathered to pray at his side.

Despite, on the one hand, occasional deaths caused by snakebites or poison, and on the other hand criminal prosecution, the snake-handling community persists, attracting young and old, male and female alike.

Source: Thomas Burton, *Serpent Handling Believers* (Knoxville: University of Tennessee Press, 1993), 103.

riches in start-up companies in such locales as Silicon Valley and similar centers of the new economy rose dramatically. Emblematic of this new cadre of superrich is Bill Gates, founder and principal stockholder of Microsoft and the richest person in the world according to *Forbes* magazine (March 2007). At the same time, anti-Catholic prejudice and anti-Semitism have become less pronounced, opening up the prospect of greater inclusiveness in the upper class. These two changes—one economic and the other cultural—raise questions about whether the Protestant establishment has managed to preserve its caste-like character or whether the winds of change have undermined it.

Baltzell (1976) thought that aristocrats—or elites—in a democracy were necessary, but he also appreciated the need to bring new talent into that elite. He was concerned that limiting access at the top to WASPs was not beneficial to society at large—or, for that matter, to the upper class itself. Moreover, he understood that in a society that valued pluralism and openness, such a world was unlikely to sustain itself over the long term. In fact, Nelson Aldrich contends that Baltzell "was writing an epitaph to the WASP." Howard Schneiderman, once a student of Baltzell, concurs. "We do have an elite," he states, "but it doesn't form a consanguine class of interconnected families who intermarry and pass power along from generation to generation" (quoted in Grimes 1996: E3).

The Most Important Baptism of the Twentieth Century?

In an almost happenstance occurrence during his 1904 visit to the United States, Max Weber went to visit some immigrant kinsfolk just outside of Mt. Airy, North Carolina. While there, he had opportunity to witness a "living water" baptism—that is, an adult Christian baptism conducted in an outdoor stream. Whether or not he accurately understood the circumstances of the persons involved in the event he witnessed, Weber nevertheless interpreted it as objective legitimation of his thesis that Protestant religion was connected to credit-worthiness, a principle on which his thesis of the origins of capitalism hung. "Living water" baptisms still occur among evangelical Christian sects, especially in the South, as public sign and seal that a person has accepted "the Christian lifestyle." This photo taken in the upland South in 1987 displays a mode and setting virtually unchanged from the time of Weber's visit (see Weber 2002: 128–31).

Photograph courtesy of Warren Brunner.

This view has been called into question by a series of studies conducted by James Davidson (1991, 1994; see also Davidson, Pyle, and Reyes 1995) and Ralph Pyle (1996). Collectively, this body of research contends that claims about the demise of the Protestant establishment have been premature. Making use of data derived mainly from *Who's Who*, these researchers have concluded that the Protestant establishment persists in a form quite similar to that of the past, while at the same time changing to what they refer to as a "modified 'fair shares' approach," wherein other religious groups have found their way into the elite world of the upper class. What remains the same is that members of the mainline denominations rooted in the colonial era—Episcopal, Presbyterian, and United Church of Christ—are still disproportionately represented in the ranks of the elite. This is the case even though these three denominations have experienced declining overall memberships. Members from the more middle-class denominations, such as Methodists and Lutherans, have made only marginal gains, while Baptists and sectarians remain underrepresented among the ranks of the nation's economic and political elites. Thus, within the Protestant community as a whole, there appears to have been relatively little change between 1930 and 1990. In contrast, Catholics and Jews made substantial gains during this period.

On the basis of these findings, Pyle concluded:

> Religion still serves as a social identifier that places individuals within particular status communities and creates bonds between those with similar religious backgrounds. Far from being dissociated from class and status concerns, religious denominations themselves serve as social groupings ranked along a clearly ordered status hierarchy. . . . A fair shares perspective stresses that upper-group advantages persist in spite of what appears to be a trend toward meritocratic allocation processes. The movement of a limited number of newcomers to high positions does not represent the end of an older order. (1996: 280)

A decade later Pyle revisited his earlier research and concluded: "Despite some narrowing of differences among the religious categories on socioeconomic indicators, religious groups continue to be distinguished on the basis of their socioeconomic positioning, and the overall religious group status ranking remains largely unchanged from the rankings of fifty years ago" (2006: 76). There are limitations to this persistence of the Protestant establishment thesis, based in no small part on the sources of the data that have been used. Pyle notes that the process of selection for *Who's Who* may bias results. However, he doesn't speak to the matter of whether the Protestant establishment continues to draw a line around itself and the Jewish and Catholic members of the upper class. We need to know considerably more about such factors as the extent to which religious and ethnic discrimination persists in terms of gaining entrée to private clubs and the other important social institutions of the Protestant establishment (Korman 1988). We need to know just how significant a role legacies play in gaining admission to Ivy League schools (Massey et al. 2003; Karabel 2005). We need to know whether the business interests of elites remain separate or are increasingly interconnected. We need to know whether historic patterns of marrying within the group (endogamy) have persisted among the upper classes or whether the triple melting pot is becoming a single pot.

Moving to the opposite end of the class hierarchy, the religions of the poor appear to be relatively unchanged. The general consensus remains that for the most marginalized members of society, religion continues to perform a compensatory function. In a comparative study of two Southern Baptist congregations, one middle class and the other largely lower class, Bart Dredge (1986) found evidence to support this contention. His analysis of sermon contents at the two congregations found that in the former they offered justification for the parishioners' social status, while in the latter the emphasis was on consolation. In other ways, the lower classes do religion differently from those who are higher in the class structure. For example, those in the lower classes are more likely to engage in private prayer, accept without question the fundamental doctrines of their faith, and have deeply felt religious experiences. At the same time, they are less likely than those higher in the class structure to join churches or, when they do, to become involved in the congregation's associational life. These findings have persisted for at least forty years (Demerath 1965; Davidson 1977; Coreno 2002).

The most significant changes have occurred in the middle class, for it has felt the full impact of economic change. During the past three decades, sociologists have increasingly explored the transformations of contemporary industrial societies with a conviction that we have entered a new epoch in the history of capitalism. A number of commentators have attempted to describe this new society. For example, Peter Drucker (1993) has referred to the new world as a "knowledge society," Ralf Dahrendorf (1959) as the "service class society," and Zbigniew Brzezinski (1970) as the "technetronic era." However, the phrase that has become most influential is "postindustrial society," coined by sociologists Daniel Bell (1973) and Alain Touraine (1971) at approximately the same time.

The central thesis of Bell's version of postindustrial society is that we have increasingly moved from a goods-producing society to a society organized around the production of knowledge and information. Think of the economic impact of an innovation like the Internet and you immediately get the idea. In such a society, the class structure changes because there is a heightened demand for highly educated professionals who possess the scientific, technical, managerial, and administrative training needed to ensure that the economy functions well. This means that a postindustrial society is one in which the professional middle class grows significantly. Two decades earlier, C. Wright Mills (1951) had referred to this as the white-collar middle class, distinguishing it from the old middle class composed mainly of small businesspersons, farmers, and independent professionals. The new white-collar sector of the middle class consisted of salaried professionals working chiefly in corporate and governmental bureaucracies. Though better paid and with higher social status than blue-collar workers, white-collar workers shared one thing with the blue-collar workers that made them different from the old middle class: They were employees. The difference between blue collar and white collar was chiefly the difference between manual versus mental labor.

In attempting to locate those in this stratum, Alvin Gouldner, dubbing them the "New Class," argued that it would be a mistake to see these individuals through any of a number of perspectives that other social scientists had advanced: benign technocrats, a new ruling class, allies of the old middle class, or servants of the ruling class. His alternative to these interpretations of the significance of this New Class is to see it as a "flawed universal class." Gouldner wrote that, "The New Class is elitist and self-seeking and uses its special knowledge to advance its own interests and power, and to control its own work situation" (1979: 6–7). At the same time, he saw it as a potent force in shaping the future, though it is not clear whether that will be beneficial to society at large because the class is "morally ambiguous."

What are the implications of the rise of the New Class for religious institutions? What are the religious proclivities of members of this New Class? At the moment, these and related questions can be answered only provisionally due to the fluidity and complexity of current trends. However, one way of attempting to explore the potential significance of the New Class on religion in the United States is by locating its presence in terms of a long-standing tension within Protestantism that Martin Marty (1970) has called the *two-party system*. By this term, he referred to a split that occurred in Protestantism about a century ago that pitted fundamentalists against modernists. Fundamentalists were the conservative and evangelical faction, with sectarian tendencies and an emphasis on private or individual religion. In contrast, the modernists, aligned early on with the Social Gospel movement, were politically liberal, culturally progressive, and oriented toward public religion. Though rooted more deeply in the nation's history, the conflict came to fruition during the industrial age. While clearly an oversimplification of a far more complex situation, Marty's thesis nonetheless proved to be attractive insofar as it did succeed in capturing something of the essence of what today have been referred to as "culture wars" (Hunter 1991, 1994).

Within this divide, and coincidental with the rise of the New Class, the religious marketplace has changed as conservative evangelical denominations have grown (Kelley 1972; Hout, Greeley, and Wilde 2001). At the same time, mainline Protestant denominations have witnessed significant membership losses of a third or more, and their share of the religious market has accordingly declined (Roozen and Hadaway 1993). Is it possible to speak about an elective affinity between this denominational realignment and the growth of the New Class? If so, what is the nature of the relationship?

Peter Berger (1981), who contends that a class struggle among competing elites vying for power and status is currently under way, has offered one answer to these questions. The conflict, as he defines it, is between the old elites, made up of the business and financial class, and a new elite, made up of intellectuals, educators, and administrators. In his view, the old elite is attracted to the conservative "party," while the new elite is attaching itself to the liberal "party." The assumption he makes is that the worldview of the New Class is consonant with liberal theology, while members of the old guard are drawn to evangelical Christianity, in part as a reaction to the efforts of the New Class to grab power. Demographically, this thesis falls on its face insofar as the growth class is seen as joining precisely those denominations that have lost members, while the essentially fixed sizes of the old elites are somehow seen as contributing to the growth of conservative churches. The argument is problematic in another way as well. In depicting New Class members as elites, Berger inaccurately locates them in the upper class, rather than treating them as a sector of the affluent upper-middle class, as class theorists such as Mills and Gouldner intended.

Members of the New Class are highly educated and cosmopolitan. They work in the new post-Fordist assembly-line capitalism, which emphasizes flexibility and individualism while devaluing institutional loyalty and long-term commitments to people or places. In Richard Sennett's (1998) portrait of the "corrosion of character" that the new capitalism has effected, the New Class is depicted as affluent but anxious, with little ability to forge or sustain community ties. Whether unduly pessimistic or not, Sennett's portrait does capture important elements that contribute to the distinctive character of New Class members. Unknown at the moment is what this means in terms of their religious behaviors. Will it mean that they will tend to avoid church memberships, knowing that they don't acquire social status by such memberships, and that, like their relationship to work, they feel the need to treat all social engagements as temporary? Or will they turn to religion as a site for stability and certainty in an otherwise unstable and uncertain world? Is it possible to speak about the New Class in the singular, or might we not find that those educated in the sciences develop a different orientation toward religion from those educated in the humanities (Hargrove 1986: 185–86)? In attempting to understand better the dynamic and changing way in which social class and religion influence each other, this particular topic will be of major concern to the sociology of religion in the years to come.

Suggestions for Further Reading

E. Digby Baltzell. 1966. *The Protestant Establishment: Aristocracy and Caste in America.* New York: Vintage Books.

Michael Hout, Andrew Greeley, and Melissa J. Wilde. 2001. "The Demographic Imperative in Religious Change in the United States." *American Journal of Sociology* 107:468–500.

Sean McCloud. 2007. *Divine Hierarchies: Class in American Religion and Religious Studies.* Chapel Hill: University of North Carolina Press.

H. Richard Niebuhr. 1929. *The Social Sources of Denominationalism.* New York: Holt.

Jerry Z. Park and Samuel H. Reimer. 2002. "Revisiting the Social Sources of American Christianity, 1972–1998." *Journal for the Scientific Study of Religion* 41:733–46.

Ralph E. Pyle. 1996. *Persistence and Change in the Protestant Establishment.* Westport, Conn.: Praeger.

Mark A. Shibley. 1996. *Resurgent Evangelicalism in the United States: Mapping Cultural Change since 1970.* Columbia: University of South Carolina Press.

William H. Swatos, Jr., and Lutz Kaelber, eds. 2005. *The Protestant Ethic Turns 100: Essays on the Centenary of the Weber Thesis.* Boulder, Colo.: Paradigm.

Robert Wuthnow. 1988. *The Restructuring of American Religion: Society and Faith since World War II.* Princeton, N.J.: Princeton University Press.

John A. O'Brien Papers (GOBR 1/39), UNDA. Reproduced with permission of the University of Notre Dame.

CHAPTER 6

Religion and Ethnicity

A COMPLEX RELATIONSHIP

Diversity—religious and ethnic—is one of the most pronounced features of U.S. social history; it has shaped and continues to shape our ongoing reinterpretation of what it means to be an American. Diversity raises questions about the role of and the extent to which we can speak about having shared values and identities in such a pluralistic environment. It requires us to ponder the social, economic, and political forces that contribute to the incorporation or assimilation of newcomers in our midst, while simultaneously thinking about those forces that work against incorporation.

As an immigrant-settler nation, the United States has wrestled throughout its entire history with issues related to its capacity to absorb newcomers. At the same time, those newcomers and their offspring have had to struggle with the pressures and problems involved in adjusting or adapting to their new homeland while at the same time sorting out how much of their ancestral cultures and behavioral patterns could and should be retained. Ethnic and religious groups have had to assess the advantages and disadvantages of remaining insular, living their lives within the confines of the ethnic enclave, or being open to new patterns of engagement with others.

This chapter is devoted to exploring these issues; it does so by focusing on the interstices between religious and ethnic identities and attachments. It is clear at the outset that religious identities are often intimately connected to ethnic (or racial or national) identities, and indeed in many instances these identities can be seen as mutually reinforcing (Kivisto 2007). Like language, traditions, and cultural values, religion is frequently one of the significant, boundary-defining markers as well as a key building block shaping the content of ethnic identity. For example, while not all Scandinavian immigrants to the United States were Lutheran, the vast majority were, and the emergence of various ethnic forms of Lutheranism played a singularly powerful role in the development of the distinctive cultures of Swedish America, Norwegian America, Danish America, Finnish America, and Icelandic America. Likewise, among the Eastern Orthodox, the link between national origin and religious affiliation is made explicit in the very names of such church bodies as the Russian Orthodox, Greek Orthodox, Serbian Orthodox, and so forth.

The reverse can also be true, as ethnic cultures serve to demarcate religious boundaries and have an impact on the content of religious beliefs and practices. Thus, the African-American experience has profoundly shaped various religious expressions—largely Christian, but also including Islam—within that community. It can be seen in the prophetic call for social justice characteristic of progressive Christian denominations, in the expressive spirituality of black Pentecostalism, and in the angry denunciations of a white racist society emanating from the mosques of the Nation of Islam. Similarly, among Roman Catholics, one can detect differences in attendance patterns, levels of spirituality, and modes of religious expression predicated on whether the congregation is primarily Italian, Irish, Polish, or Mexican.

In some cases, the link between ethnicity and religion is more powerful than in other cases. Over time, the specifically ethnic character of some religious groups has declined. This has tended to be the case, for example, among most mainline Protestant denominations. However, there are groups for which the bond seems inseparable, such as the Amish and the Hutterites.

Before proceeding to an analysis of the contemporary interrelationships between ethnicity and religion, it is first necessary to clarify some of the debates that have shaped discussions of concepts and theories in the sociology of race and ethnic relations.

Clarifying Terms: Ethnic, Nationality, and Racial Groups

Max Weber, in an oft-referenced passage from *Economy and Society* (1978: 385–98), set the stage for contemporary social scientific attempts to study ethnic groups in their varied guises and forms. As an early challenge to biological or related views asserting the immutability and ahistorical character of ethnic categories, Weber proposed to historicize them, and in so doing he pointed to their fluidity and their socially constructed character. He suggested that scholars pay attention to the varied ways that such markers of identity are employed, at both the individual and the collective levels. But more than that, Weber managed to capture something of the ineffable quality of ethnic groups when he pointed to the inherent difficulty of attempting to offer a precise definition of the term, writing that, "The concept of the 'ethnic' group dissolves if we define our terms exactly."

DEFINING ETHNIC GROUPS

With or without this cautionary message in mind, subsequent scholars have offered a variety of related definitions of ethnic groups. In one of the more influential efforts to specify what is unique about ethnic groups, E. K. Francis (1947) treated them as a subtype of what sociologists call *Gemeinschaft* groups, whose self-identity is based on emotional rather than functional ties, bearing a resemblance to kinship groups. Ethnic groups are characterized by their involuntary nature (that is, people are simply born into them) and by the emotional bond that links individuals to other groups, whether or not they know them personally.

For our purposes, ethnic groups are composed of people who are presumed, by members of the group itself and by outsiders, to have a shared collective origin and history, and a common set of cultural attributes that serves to establish boundaries between the group and the larger society. This definition combines both an objective and a subjective component. Adding to this definition, it is possible to elaborate further by suggesting a number of variables that in differing combinations are characteristic of the spectrum of what constitutes ethnic groups. For example, in identifying criteria to be used in determining which groups would be selected for inclusion in *The Harvard Encyclopedia of American Ethnic Groups* (Thernstrom et al. 1980: vi), the editors drew up the following laundry list: common geographic origin; migratory status; race; language or dialect; religious faith or faiths; ties that transcend kinship, neighborhood, and community boundaries; shared traditions, values, and symbols; literature, folklore, and music; food preferences; settlement and employment patterns; special interests in regard to politics; institutions that specifically serve and maintain the group; an internal sense of distinctiveness; and an external perception of distinctiveness.

NATIONALITY GROUPS AND TERRITORIALITY

How do nationality groups differ from ethnic groups? A century ago, when immigration to the United States was at its peak, these two terms were frequently used as synonyms, essentially shorthand for a description of the new arrivals' nations of origin. However, this use tends to mask an important distinction. Craig Calhoun (1997: 40) has hence suggested that ethnicity should be seen as constituting "an intermediary position between kinship and nationality." What this makes clear is that nationality groups, like ethnic groups, appeal to similar loyalties in some regards, referring as they do to shared histories and traditions and emotional bonds among members. However, what is distinctive about nationality groups is that their sense of peoplehood is shaped by a political agenda that calls for the creation, reconstitution, or preservation of a nation-state. An integral part of the identity of nationality groups concerns territorial claims, with much of the ideological discourse of nationalism offering a justification for such entitlements and an account of the implications of such claims for other groups.

In some instances, ethnicity and nationalism are intimately connected. Such is the case with German nationalism, where the two have been fused in a blood-and-soil version of citizenship. Or, as historian George M. Fredrickson describes it, "German identity and citizenship have traditionally been rooted in a relatively pure form of ethnic nationalism" (1999: 38). Thus, in Germany today people of German ancestry who have resided in Russia for two centuries are seen as eligible for immediate citizenship, while Turkish guest workers, even when they have lived in Germany for decades, are perceived as outsiders. By contrast, France since the Revolution has professed a "civic" rather than ethnic form of citizenship. What this means, at least ideally, is that anyone who is willing to embrace French political and cultural values is capable of becoming a citizen. What we see is nationalistic particularism in one case, and a more universalistic version of citizenship in the other.

The United States has historically advanced a version of nationalism much like that of the French, and, as with that case, the ability to absorb immigrants from different ethnic groups has been predicated on the presumed capacity of those newcomers to assimilate, or be incorporated into the mainstream of the dominant society. As such, while there has been and continues to be an ethnocentric cast to U.S. nationalistic discourse, nonetheless, in its fundamental contours it is an instance of civic nationalism.

In comparative perspective, nationality groups have not played as significant a role in the United States compared to many other liberal democracies. In no small part, this is because the population is chiefly made up of voluntary immigrants and their descendants. Immigrants were not in a position to advance group-based territorial claims. As such, the key ingredient of nationalism was lacking. Contrast this situation to that in Canada, where descendants of the nation's two colonial groups—the French and the English—have continued a conflict over territory that dates back to the seventeenth century. The struggle to keep Canada united in the face of Québécois separatism is a conflict absent in the United States. Also missing in this country is anything paralleling the attempts by political authorities in Canada to find a way to juggle individual rights with collective rights. Rather, in the United States, we have clearly tended to opt for the primacy of individual rights.

This is not to say that there are not national minorities in this country. There are. The most important group to advance territorial claims is Native Americans or "First Nations," the indigenous peoples who inhabited the continent long before the arrival of Europeans. Forced from their ancestral lands, Native Americans today continue to seek redress for their losses, including, in numerous cases, the retrieval of lands taken illegally by Europeans. The only other instance of nationalism among ethnic groups in the United States can be found at various historical periods in rather small segments of the black community. It could be seen in the call of Marcus Garvey for a return to Africa, the Communist plan during the 1930s for the creation of a southern Black Belt, or the Nation of Islam's vague notions of community control. Significantly, Native Americans and African Americans are the only two groups in the nation who are not voluntary immigrants—although some Hispanic Americans may also be considered to be in this position.

THE SPECTER OF RACE

These two cases also raise, in the U.S. context, the contested issue of the relationship between race and ethnicity. Within the social sciences, three competing positions have been articulated concerning this relationship. One position contends that race and ethnicity are fundamentally different concepts. In stark contrast, another views them as basically synonymous. The third position, which we find most persuasive, views race as a subset of ethnicity (recall the definition from *The Harvard Encyclopedia of American Ethnic Groups*).

Race is a highly controversial concept. During the nineteenth and early twentieth centuries, a variety of presumably scientific conceptions of race were articulated. Significantly, no consensus emerged about the actual number of races in the world. Thus, among early ethnologists, Johann Friedrich Blumenbach and the Comte de Buffon contended there were five, while Carolus Linnaeus identified four, and Baron Cuvier three. Racial groups were demarcated and depicted based on perceived physical differences, which in turn were treated as indicators of differences regarding intellectual abilities, personality traits, cultural values, and even moral character. Inevitably such conceptualizations consistently revealed an ethnocentric bias in which whites from northwestern Europe were seen as possessing superior traits, while all others were, to various degrees, deficient and thus inferior. In other words, race categories had explicitly racist ideology built into them.

Such racialist thinking proved to be bad science, but despite this it has had a profound impact on public policy: for example, it underpinned the eugenics movement, a late-nineteenth-century effort to use rudimentary genetics to discourage procreation of "undesirables" and encourage desirable "types" within the population, which was used as a rationale for putting an end to mass immigration. The passage of the Immigration and Naturalization Act of 1924 was the culmination of the role of racialist thought by nativists.

However, also beginning in the 1920s, racial classifications that were rooted in biology came increasingly into disrepute, and many anthropologists called for the outright abandonment of race as a meaningful concept. Particularly influential here was the work of Franz Boas (1931) and his famous student, Ruth Benedict (1940, 1943), who did much to discredit notions of racial or ethnic distinctions rooted in biology. For example, Frank Livingstone noted the lack of clearly demarcated differences among population groups, and concluded that "if races have to be discrete entities, then there are no races" (1962: 42). Moreover, the general consensus among social scientists was that biology had failed as an explanatory tool in analyzing social and cultural differences among groups. As geneticist N. P. Dubinin wrote in a U.N. Educational, Scientific, and Cultural Organization (UNESCO) publication, "Theories of the alleged inequality of human races have no scientific basis" (1956: 69).

The social sciences since the 1920s have largely abandoned biological explanations in favor of cultural and social-historical ones. As a result, the few attempts to revive biological notions of race have been overwhelmingly rejected on scientific and political grounds. Such was the fate of Richard Herrnstein and Charles Murray's *The Bell Curve* (1994), which sought to reintroduce a genetic explanation for group differences in IQ scores (see the critique by Fischer et al. 1996). Only sociobiologists have attempted to effect a rapprochement between biology and the social sciences, but, as their critics claim, they tend to do so by offering what is in effect a modified form of biological reductionism (see, for example, Lopreato and Crippin 1999).

The interplay of intersections among culture, religion, power, and ethnicity is displayed in the seal of the Tribal Council of the Seminole Tribe of Florida. Though the tribe has been persecuted by the U.S. government in the past and continues to have ambiguous relationships with both state and federal governments, its tribal council's seal nevertheless incorporates the uniquely American civil-religious phrase "In God we trust." Reproduced with permission of the Seminole Tribe of Florida.

If racial categories can actually be accounted for in cultural and social-structural terms, then the distinction between racial groups and ethnic groups evaporates, as the former can be subsumed in the latter. Such a claim has been made by various sociologists, including the Jamaican-born Harvard sociologist Orlando Patterson, who thinks that we cannot speak about race in any meaningful way, and thus he opts to "use the term *ethnic* instead of *racial* and refer to *ethnic group* instead of a *race*" (1997: xi; emphasis in the original).

Critics of this position contend that failing to distinguish between ethnic (read: European-origin) and racial groups results in a tendency to gloss the differences in levels of prejudice, discrimination, and oppression suffered by some groups compared to others—differences, these critics go on to note, that are based on public (and not scientific) definitions of racial groups. While this concern is understandable, those making such a claim fail, in our estimation, to articulate a persuasive argument for maintaining a conceptual distinction between race and ethnicity. Stephen Cornell and Douglas Hartmann (1998: 25–35), in seeking to preserve the distinction, advance a novel view that treats ethnicity and race as being potentially overlapping, thereby allowing for the possibility that some groups are both racial and ethnic. However, the factors they identify as key to keeping race a separate category, which include the emphasis on physical differences and a comparative lack of power, do not provide a particularly convincing alternative to the "race as subset of ethnicity" perspective. For this reason, we prefer to borrow from Ewa Morawska (1999: 30) and speak of "racialized ethnicity" when addressing groups such as African Americans, for whom issues related to race loom large in the articulation of ethnic identity.

Relational Patterns between Religion and Ethnicity

According to our definition of ethnicity, religion can be one of the factors shaping it. However, from the perspective of religion, ethnicity can be a variable shaping both its institutional and ideational form and content. Harold Abramson (1980: 869–70) distinguished four variations in the possible relationship between religion and ethnicity. Phillip Hammond and Kee Warner (1993) have amplified the discussion of the first three, and both of these works have been reconsidered recently by Peter Kivisto (2007).

The first, which Hammond and Warner refer to as *ethnic fusion*, involves cases where ethnicity is the major foundation of a religion. Two examples that rather closely approximate the ideal type are the Amish and Hutterites, two groups tracing their ancestry to Germanic origins. As sectarian dissident groups, they have long sought to remain aloof from the larger society and have been rather successful in these attempts. To the extent that they have been successful, they have managed to preserve the fundamentals of a tradition-directed culture that is at odds with the dominant culture. While certainly not immune to the impact of the larger society, as evident in the arrest a few years ago of several young Amish men in Pennsylvania for selling cocaine, what is remarkable about these two groups is the fact that they have managed so long to navigate a self-chosen segregation from the larger society. Of course, what makes these groups unique is precisely their desire to live "in, but not of" the larger society. Non-Christian examples of ethnic fusion include Hasidic Jews and the members of the Nation of Islam.

Hammond and Warner term the second variant *ethnic religion*. In this case, the link between religion and ethnicity is pronounced, though it does not amount to the fusion of the first type. When religion is linked to language and to national identity, a unique blend of ethnic religion occurs. The examples cited by Harold J. Abramson include "the Dutch Reformed, the Greek Orthodox, the Church of England, the Serbian Orthodox, and the Scottish Presbyterians"

(1980: 870). As Hammond and Warner point out, "Ethnicity in this pattern extends beyond religion in the sense that ethnic identification can be claimed without claiming the religious identification, but the reverse is rare" (1993: 59).

The third type is *religious ethnicity*, which is the most common pattern in the United States. In this case, more than one ethnic group may share the same religion. Two of the examples cited at the beginning of this chapter provide good illustrations of this type: the five Scandinavian countries—and, one should add, Germany—that are the main historic components of Lutheranism; and the Irish, Polish, Italian, Mexican, and other nationalities that are the major components of Catholicism. Outside of Christianity, one could also add the Spanish, German, eastern European, and, more recently, Israeli origins of American Jews. Likewise, Islamic believers in the United States come from numerous national backgrounds, including Syria, Iran, and Iraq. Buddhists may be from Japan, India, or one of several southeast Asian nations. The difference between this type and the previous one is, according to Hammond and Warner, that "[r]eligion in this pattern extends beyond ethnicity, reversing the previous pattern, and religious identification can be claimed without claiming ethnic identification" (1993: 59).

Abramson (1980: 870) mentions a fourth type, *ethnic autonomy*, which is seen as the one least frequently found. In this case, religion plays a very minimal or marginal role in defining ethnic identity. One example he cites offers an indication of just how uncommon this relationship is: the Gypsies or Roma. The other example he cites, Native Americans, is problematic. Indeed, the anthropological literature would not simply challenge placing Native Americans in this pattern, but would suggest that they are better located at the opposite end of the spectrum, in the religious fusion classification. Before the arrival of Europeans, North America's indigenous peoples practiced a wide variety of religions. Religious practice was closely bound up with the ethos of distinctive tribal communities. Certainly, the religious fusion type would seem an appropriate characterization of the era prior to Christian missionary conversion efforts. Where such conversion occurred—and it was widespread—it is likely that such tribal communities looked like ethnic variants of a religious body, similar to the way African Americans are related to Southern Baptists; that is, after the Civil War, African Americans established the National Baptist Convention that was similarly modeled on, yet different from, the dominant tradition—a U.S. tradition that they as well as whites had a hand in originally forming (Wax 1971: 42–50).

With this conceptual framework, we can proceed to examine the contours of the role that ethnicity has played in shaping religion in the United States. Given the fluidity of the relationship between the two over time, an appreciation of the main contours of historical change is necessary if we are to make sense of contemporary patterns. As the remainder of the chapter will reveal, the prominence of Christianity has persisted, though what this means has changed based on internal changes within Christianity and on the presence of various non-Christian groups. In all of this, the migration of different ethnic groups factors prominently in defining religious group boundaries and intergroup relations.

Ethnicity in the "Righteous Empire"

During the formative period of the nation's history, the vast majority of the population was Protestant. It was also composed of immigrants who overwhelmingly came from the nations of northwestern Europe. In racial terms, they identified themselves as white.

Historically, British settlers played a hegemonic role in constructing a white Anglo-Saxon Protestant culture and polity—that is, they set the stage on which political-cultural action would take place. However, the early colonists from the British Isles were, within the Protestant framework, quite heterogeneous. Four distinctive groups had a significant impact on the formative period of nation building:

1. The Puritans were the first wave of immigrants, originating from eastern England. These religious dissenters departed England in a quest for religious freedom from the existing state church, and in their "errand into the wilderness" sought to fuse religion and politics into a theocracy. Given this goal, they were inclined to be unreceptive to religious dissent.
2. Another wave of immigrants, not so much true cavaliers as adventurers of merchant capitalism, originated in southern England. Elitist and traditionalist, this group became a central force among the slaveholding class in Virginia and served to give the Church of England a toehold in the colonies.
3. The third group was the Society of Friends, or Quakers, who came from the English Midlands and Wales. This dissenting body of religious pacifists settled in what is today Pennsylvania and western New Jersey, where—in stark contrast to the Virginia establishment—they promoted egalitarian and democratic ideals. Their religious convictions led them to found the first antislavery society in the Western world.
4. Finally, the Scots-Irish arrived and settled on the Appalachian frontier. Among the ranks of these latter arrivals was found considerable antipathy toward English domination of Scotland. This group provided the basis for the growth of Presbyterianism in the United States.

Despite the considerable diversity contained in British America, these immigrants were melded into what Charles Anderson described as "the larger Anglo-Saxon Protestant core society" (1970: 41). Furthermore, British Americans, due to this cultural hegemony as well as their political and economic power, were in a position to dictate the terms of entrance for other ethnic groups, who in turn had to find ways to respond to this situation. As Thomas Archdeacon suggested, "The pattern of combining cultural accommodation with resistance was common to all non-British European immigrant groups" (1983: 94).

The diverse elements of British America served to promote openness to religious pluralism under the Protestant umbrella. Thus, the other major western and northern European immigrant groups founded a variety of Protestant denominations. The religiously heterogeneous Germans, the second-largest immigrant group, included Lutherans, the German Reformed, Mennonites, Dunkers, and Moravians. In addition, pietists founded small utopian communities such as New Harmony, Indiana, and the Amana Society in Iowa. Emigrants from Holland forged a Dutch Reformed presence, while Scandinavians established ethnically based Lutheran denominations, the first and largest of which was the Swedish Augustana Synod.

Within Protestant America during the nineteenth century and the first half of the twentieth, these groups managed to retain distinctive ethnic identities, whether their particular pattern linking religion and ethnicity constituted ethnic fusion (for example, Dunkers), ethnic religion (for example, Dutch Reformed), or religious ethnicity (for example, Swedish Lutherans). In all cases, religious institutions played an important role in transmitting elements of the homeland culture to the U.S.-born generations, including the preservation of language. Indeed, up until World War I, many of these religious bodies held services either entirely or partially in the homeland language.

Viewed as more desirable immigrants because of their religious heritages, these groups confronted far less prejudice and discrimination than was the case with Roman Catholic or Eastern Orthodox Christians. One of the unintended consequences of this fact was that as the second and third generations—familiar with American society and fluent in English—came of age, they were in a position to take advantage of an open religious marketplace. Thus, the upwardly mobile might opt to switch from their immigrant churches to higher-status denominations, thereby accelerating the process of assimilation.

The Ethnic Factor in the Formative Period of U.S. Catholicism

The situation was quite different for Catholics until after the middle of the twentieth century. What is clear in the Catholic case is that ethnic animosity became intimately intertwined with anti-Catholicism with the arrival of Irish immigrants in the first half of the nineteenth century. The first Catholics in the United States were of English origin. They accommodated to a religiously hostile environment by settling in Maryland, but their English ethnicity served to take some of the edge off the Protestant-Catholic tension. Exemplified by the Carroll family of Maryland, the earliest Catholics in the British colonies (and later the new nation) were small in number, relatively affluent, and rather subdued in their exertion of religious particularity. As such, they attracted little negative attention.

However, with the mass migration of desperately poor Irish Catholics, all this changed. Especially after the disastrous potato blight, which was a principal cause of the Great Famine, nativist hostility toward Catholics intensified. The Irish entered the Protestant empire and quickly dominated the development of U.S. Catholicism. They were the chief contributors to the leadership of the Church, and large numbers of priests and nuns emigrated from Ireland to establish and maintain parishes and related religious institutions. Soon the Irish constituted an absolute majority of the Catholic population, and due to their presence the size of the Catholic community rose fourfold in the three decades before the Civil War. Though other groups, most notably the German Catholics, played a role in the expansion of a Catholic institutional presence, none was as powerful as the Irish proved to be. Theirs was a grassroots movement. The Irish entered the American church at the bottom, but by the latter part of the nineteenth century they led its hierarchy. This hegemonic position meant that Catholics arriving from southern and eastern Europe from 1880 to 1924, during the period of the Great Migration, were forced to confront an Irish-dominated institution.

The Irish hierarchy found themselves struggling on two fronts: internally with other ethnic Catholics, and externally with a hegemonic Protestantism. Regarding relations within the Catholic Church, they sought to position themselves vis-à-vis new arrivals—with the largest groups of immigrants from Italy and Poland being most significant—as the arbiters of competing efforts to shape the character of Catholicism in the United States.

The comparative responses of the Italians and Poles, both of whom arrived in large numbers after 1880, are instructive. The Italians proved to be less of an obstacle to Irish domination, due to what historians have seen as a less intense level of religiosity on the part of Italians. They were less pietistic than the Irish: The role of magic in the everyday life of poor immigrants from southern Italy challenged the impact of religion, and a tradition of anticlericalism meant that Italians were somewhat less intent on participating in Catholic institutions. This does not mean that the Church was irrelevant, for they used it to mark the major events of life (birth, marriage, and death) and as the focus of religious festivals, which were generally highly localized communal celebrations.

Two facts conspired to weaken further the role of the Church in the immigrant community. First, Italian priests and nuns did not migrate in large numbers, and, related to this, Italians were suspicious about the impact that the Church's Irish leadership would have on their children. Italians did not send their children to parochial schools in the same proportion as the Irish. While the latter were suspicious that public schools would result in the Anglicization of their children, Italians harbored concerns that parochial schools might lead to the "Hibernization" of their offspring (Femminella 1985), leading them to lose their Italian heritage, while assimilating Irish cultural folkways and mores.

In marked contrast, the Poles exhibited a level of religiosity similar to the Irish. A majority of Polish immigrants aligned themselves with the Church, which in the homeland had been intimately connected to nationalism, Catholicism serving as a key ideological resource for the resistance to external domination. Though a poor immigrant group, they invested heavily in establishing a Catholic presence in the Polonias that emerged in major cities. The number of ethnic parishes grew from fewer than twenty in 1870 to about eight hundred by 1930 (Greene 1975; Parot 1981; Wrobel 1979).

Conflict between Poles and the Irish-controlled church was endemic during this formative period. One of the most obvious examples occurred when the Reverend Francis Hodur led a group of dissidents in a challenge to authority that resulted in excommunications and the subsequent creation in 1904 of an independent church body, the Polish National Catholic Church. Though only a minority of Poles joined this breakaway church, its creation reflected the attitudes of many Poles toward the Irish hierarchy. As a result, efforts to accommodate the Poles were undertaken, including supplying their parishes with Polish-speaking priests and elevating Poles to leadership positions.

At the same time, the Irish had to contend with the forces of Protestantism's "righteous empire." Overlaying this situation was a history of political and economic conflict pitting the English against the Irish. In order to prevent their offspring from losing their attachment to their heritage, Irish immigrants created parochial schools at great financial cost as necessary alternatives to public schools. Public schools were viewed as potent forces promoting Americanization, which in the eyes of Irish Catholics meant a view of national identity determined by English Protestant elites. The Irish feared that the future of their religion and culture was at stake, and parochial schools could provide them with a bulwark against a forced assimilation into the Protestant empire. Catholics likewise founded numerous colleges and universities, including flagship institutions such as the Catholic University of America (1887), Georgetown University (1789), and the University of Notre Dame (1872), as their way of, in the words of historian Philip Gleason (1995), "contending with modernity." The Third Plenary Council of Baltimore in 1884 not only created the *Baltimore Catechism*, which all young Catholics were expected to memorize, and the Catholic University of America, but also set as an ideal that all Catholic children be educated in Catholic schools.

Nativist hostility to Catholic immigrants wove negative stereotypes of the particular ethnic groups making up the church with critiques of the Catholic Church as an antidemocratic and authoritarian institution antithetical to key national values. This hostility took organizational form in such groups as the American Patriotic League, the American Protective Association, the Ku Klux Klan, the Native American Party, and the Order of United Americans. Anti-immigration sentiment ultimately resulted in gaining the upper hand politically insofar as it was translated into the Immigration and Naturalization Act mentioned earlier, which effectively ended mass immigration for the next four decades. During this time, ethnic Catholics fought a defensive battle for acceptance, while simultaneously seeking to carve out social space for the maintenance of a distinctive Catholic milieu.

The Jewish Diaspora

In *The Transformation of the Jews* (1984), Calvin Goldscheider and Alan S. Zuckerman observed that in less than a century, the center of world Jewry shifted from Europe to the United States. Indeed, there are today more Jews in the United States than there are not only in Europe, but also in Israel. Throughout their history, Jews have been a diasporic people. In the case of Jews in the United States, three waves of immigration occurred prior to 1965. The first involved a relatively small number of Sephardic Jews who trace their origins to Spain and Portugal. Because of the Spanish Inquisition, these Jews were forced into exile, settling in Holland and England, and it is from these two locations that they migrated to North America. In the second wave were Ashkenazic Jews emigrating from Germany. The third wave, also Ashkenazic, was by far the largest and came from various countries in central and eastern Europe, with Poland and Russia contributing the greatest numbers.

The Jewish community was divided between religious adherents and secularized Jews (many of whom were attracted to various forms of political radicalism). In turn, religious Jews were divided into three major divisions, and they created an institutional presence that reflected these theological differences. Many German Jews opted for an assimilationist strategy, seeking acceptance and even incorporation into the host society, while simultaneously attempting to invent a modern Judaism. The Reform movement was a reflection of this effort to find an alternative to the inherited Orthodox position, which emphasized traditionalism and was suspicious of rationalism, liberalism, and various currents of modernist thought. Reform Judaism, though it has roots in Germany, especially among higher-status Jews, proved to be far more successful in the United States, where it did not have to confront a powerfully entrenched traditional community.

Many of the religiously devout from central and eastern Europe refused to embrace the German-dominated Reform movement. As their numbers grew in the late nineteenth and early twentieth centuries, the Orthodox community likewise grew. Orthodox Judaism was the vehicle for an antiaccommodationist stance toward the hegemonic culture. It served as the institutional home for traditionalists intent on limiting social relations with Gentiles, while demanding the strict observance of Jewish law (*halacha*). For the same reason as their Catholic counterparts, the Orthodox founded religious schools (*yeshivot*) to educate their children. Orthodox Jews also established such institutions of higher education as Yeshiva University (founded in 1886 and taking its current form in 1927). Within Orthodoxy one could detect a continuum ranging from the ultratraditionalist to the moderately traditionalist (Heilman and Cohen 1989; Glazer 1957).

Reform Judaism, though representing a minority of religious Jews, was influential because of the comparatively higher socioeconomic status of its adherents. Modeling themselves in many ways after Protestant Christians, Reform Jews established a system of Sunday schools for religious instruction and founded a seminary for rabbinical training. They were inclined, however, to send their children to public schools and universities, seeking accommodation with the outside world rather than self-imposed segregation from it.

The Conservative movement, which was a distinctly American phenomenon, created a middle position between Orthodox and Reform Judaism. The Jewish Theological Seminary (1886) became the center of theological life for moderate accommodationists who wanted to preserve more of the tradition than they thought was the case with Reform Jews. Conservative Judaism proved to be the choice of middle-class or lower-middle-class non-German Jews. Because central and eastern European Jews ended up outnumbering German Jews, this became the largest branch of Judaism (Woocher 1986; Sklare 1972).

As the largest non-Christian religious minority in the United States, Jews have confronted higher levels of prejudice and discrimination than other

European-origin groups (Higham 1970). Anti-Semitism existed in the raw form of far-right groups such as the Ku Klux Klan and in more genteel circles. The old stereotypes of Jews as Christ-killers coexisted with images of the Jew as Shylock, an unsparing character in Shakespeare's *Merchant of Venice*, the conspiratorial notions of the "international Jew" intent on dominating the world politically and economically, and the radical Jew responsible for fomenting Communist movements (Ribuffo 1986). The impact of anti-Semitism was such that Jews were denied full incorporation into civic and social life long after the barriers for incorporation of other European groups had crumbled.

Herberg's Thesis and the Triple Melting Pot

As our discussion thus far indicates, the ethnic character of U.S. religious institutions was a prominent feature during their formative periods and after these groups had gained a foothold in U.S. social life. However, after World War II, ethnic communities began to erode. Ethnic institutions experienced declining memberships as the U.S.-born generations opted for inclusion in the institutions of the larger society. Ethnic enclaves saw younger members departing for the suburbs. Language loyalty declined precipitously. Mass culture progressively replaced ethnic culture (Greene 1990). Public schools proved to be a powerful Americanizing force, providing students with a multiethnic environment where new friendship and dating patterns developed that transcended ethnic boundaries (Fass 1989). In short, a multiplicity of indicators revealed that the salience of ethnic identity was declining for the third generation and beyond.

This occurred at differing rates for different groups, depending on the particular institutional framework of differing ethnic communities. For example, parochial schools managed to preserve ethnic affiliations better than the public ones—thus the major ethnic groups that were Catholic or Orthodox Jews were comparatively more successful in shoring up ethnic communal life. However, while the pace varied, the direction was the same. All of the major European-origin groups began to experience what Richard Alba (1985) has referred to as the "twilight of ethnicity."

Sociologists have long assumed that the key indicator of whether the social distance between ethnic groups and the larger society had been overcome was the rate of intermarriage (Bogardus 1959; Park 1950). Changes in marital patterns became evident a few decades into the twentieth century, leading sociologists to speculate about the extent to which ethnic barriers were breaking down and assimilation was occurring. Ruby Jo Reeves Kennedy (1944), using the results of research conducted in New Haven, Connecticut, advanced a novel argument in which she suggested that the salience of ethnicity was declining, and as it did, religion became the more important boundary dictating marital choices. She referred to her thesis as the "triple melting pot." It received popular expression in Will Herberg's 1955 book, *Protestant-Catholic-Jew*, which expanded the argument to suggest that in a more general sense religion was replacing ethnicity as the social compass by which people located

Many American Jews Are Reasserting Their Faith

Eli Almo, a 47-year-old real-estate developer in Seattle who owns a chain of retirement communities, grew up in a secular Jewish home with little formal Jewish education. As a teenager, he visited Israel and became intrigued with knowing more and began studying Hebrew. As a student and young adult in Seattle, he was befriended by a modern Orthodox couple who invited him to spend the Sabbath with them but also took him to movies and clubs during the week. "I thought, 'Boy, this is wonderful if Judaism is like this—you can be observant and do things like other people do,"' Mr. Almo says.

Today Mr. Almo considers himself an observant Jew and holds a weekly Torah study class in his office that attracts high-tech executives and lawyers. "Especially here in Seattle, you see people who have become successful in business yet realize they need something to grab onto in life," says Mr. Almo.

The resurgence of Jewish life extends beyond Orthodox Jews, who account for about 10% of American Jews, to Reform and Conservative Jews, who together make up about 70% of the Jewish population (the remaining 20% identify with small Jewish groups or with none at all).

[In 1999], reversing decades in which Reform Jews pared back the use of Hebrew in religious services and minimalized Jewish traditions such as wearing skullcaps, the Reform Jewish movement called for greater use of Hebrew and inclusion of new prayers and music. "We sense that our Judaism has been a bit too cold and domesticated." . . .

Enrollment in Jewish day schools run by all Jewish organizations has increased 65% in the past 20 years to 200,000. This summer, more than 11,000 Jewish children are attending Jewish summer camps run by Reform Jewish groups—twice as many as six years ago.

Source: Jonathan Kaufman, "Finding Center: Many of America's Jews Are Reasserting Their Faith," *Wall Street Journal*, August 20, 2000, A1, A10.

themselves in the social structure. Kennedy claimed to have discovered a regrouping of intermarriage in New Haven defined by these three major religious divisions. A later reexamination of Kennedy's data by Ceri Peach (1980) questioned her findings. Agreeing with the claim that ethnic intermarriage rates were rising, Peach was not convinced that ethnic divisions in shaping marriage pools had been replaced by religious divisions.

Whatever the case was for New Haven in the 1940s, subsequent research on intermarriage rates since the mid-twentieth century clearly reveals that intermarriage is a widespread phenomenon, especially with Catholic and Protestant ethnics. Due to the persistent legacy of anti-Semitism, the rate of Jewish intermarriage lagged behind that of the two Christian groups, but in recent decades, Jewish intermarriage rates have also risen dramatically. Alba summarized these findings when he wrote, "The increase in ethnic intermarriage is responsible for what may be the most profound ethnic change among whites: the widespread dispersion of ethnically mixed ancestry" (1990: 15). As a result, he suggests that by the last decades of the twentieth century, we were witnessing the emergence of a new ethnic group composed of the constituent elements of ethnic groups from all parts of Europe, a group he calls the European Americans. Mary Waters (1990: 104), in her discussion of "ethnic options," concurs to large extent with Alba, though she believes the ability of people to make voluntary choices in shaping personal identities means that a thin symbolic ethnicity might persist for some time into the future. However, ethnic identity implies fewer and fewer behavioral consequences. According to Waters, race, rather than religion, serves as the most salient boundary, not only in terms of intermarriage, but also in shaping all other facets of social relations. In other words, the parallel is obvious: European Americans are white Americans.

The implications of race for religion will become more evident in the remainder of this chapter. At the conclusion of this section the major implication of the twilight of ethnicity for distinctive European groups on religion is that for most groups, the cables connecting ethnicity to religion have either been severed or have become seriously frayed. Two examples from the Evangelical Lutheran Church in America (ELCA) afford paradigmatic insight into where we are at the beginning of the twenty-first century. As an indication of the lingering, though waning, impact of ethnicity, a debate in the ELCA over whether to establish "full communion" with the Episcopal Church met with resistance sufficient to prevent it from receiving the two-thirds majority required when it was first put to a vote. A theological dispute over the matter of the "historic episcopate" was at the core of the dispute. Underlying this dispute, *New York Times* religion reporter Gustav Niebuhr noted, is the belief that "many Lutherans in the upper Midwest, the faith's historic heartland, retain a suspicion of bishops, a legacy of their Scandinavian ancestors who came to the United States determined not to allow bishops the power they had in their native lands" (1999: A10). If this resistance is a product of ethnicity, it is also the position of a minority in the ELCA, and an aging minority at that. Second, the ELCA has in a variety of ways sought to reach out to ethnic groups that have not historically been part of its membership core. Thus, in a program of urban ministry called "In the City for Good," congregations around the country are being funded to support outreach programs. Among the groups specifically identified in currently funded plans as outreach objectives are African Americans, Central Americans, Ethiopians, Haitians, Mexicans, Puerto Ricans, and Sudanese. Such is the situation when historical patterns connecting religion to ethnicity are rearticulated.

The African-American Religious Experience

As the largest racialized ethnic minority in the United States from colonial times to the late twentieth century (a situation that will soon change as the Hispanic population continues to grow), African Americans are the most significant group of involuntary immigrants in the nation. Imported for their use as cheap labor, they confronted and were forced to find ways to respond to what Orlando Patterson has called the "human parasitism" at the core of the institution of slavery (1982: 334–42). Their history and U.S. history have been shaped profoundly by this situation, and by the fact that they entered the

Americas with far fewer of the cultural or institutional supports available to voluntary immigrants (Kivisto and Ng 2006: 86–92). Out of a debate between sociologist E. Franklin Frazier and anthropologist Melville J. Herskovits over the extent to which Africans managed to hang on to traditional cultural resources, there is a general consensus that Africans lost far more than other groups. Coming as they did from numerous tribes with different religions—native religions and Islam—it is impossible to speak about a shared history. This heterogeneity made cultural preservation even more difficult than it otherwise might have been. In his important work on slave religion, Albert Raboteau concluded that in North America, "the gods of Africa died" (1978: 86), and especially as a result of the Great Awakenings that produced American evangelicalism, Christianity became the dominant religion among Africans in the United States, both slave and free.

This is not to say that a continuity of African perspectives failed to survive the Middle Passage. Ecstatic experiences and the persistence of folk beliefs served from an early date to imprint a distinctive character onto African-American Christianity. Scholars continue to debate the relative importance of Protestant Christianity and African religions in this syncretistic religious expression (Blassingame 1972; L. Levine 1977).

One of the ongoing debates about African American Christianity concerns the function it played in defining the pre-Emancipation community. On one side are those, such as E. Franklin Frazier (1964), who depicted Christianity as an "invisible institution" that promoted an essentially otherworldly religion serving a compensatory function for a powerless slave community. As such, Christianity during the antebellum period was an example of a religion of the oppressed. This view had received earlier expression by the early black American sociologist W. E. B. Du Bois in 1903, when he wrote that the slave, "losing the joy of this world, eagerly seized upon the offered conceptions of the next" (1961: 147).

Subsequent scholarship has called this position into question. Perhaps no one has more forcefully done so than the historian Eugene Genovese, especially in *Roll, Jordan, Roll: The World the Slaves Made* (1972). Applying an orientation toward cultural hegemony and the ways the oppressed respond creatively to that hegemony rooted in the writings of Antonio Gramsci, Genovese makes a compelling case for viewing African-American religion as an important cultural resource in challenging injustice and oppression. Indeed, he contends that it was the singular most important resource slaves had in articulating a rhetoric of resistance to servitude. Though slave owners had attempted to inculcate a version of Christianity designed to encourage the acceptance of their fate on earth—encouraging slaves to be docile, obedient, and respectful toward their masters—slaves found instead a message of freedom in this religion. Christianity proclaimed a message of salvation that provided a rationale for activist involvement in political struggles for liberation. Moreover, out of this religious worldview, slaves managed to create an autonomous community, one that entailed a rejection of the cultural paternalism of their masters.

In their assessment of these contrasting positions, C. Eric Lincoln and Lawrence H. Mamiya (1990) suggest a more dialectical approach that views

African-American religion as being both compensatory or otherworldly and, to borrow from the language of Hart M. Nelsen and Ann K. Nelsen (1975), "community-prophetic." In other words, the African-American religious experience has from its earliest "invisible" articulation to the present contained a tension between various dialectical poles: otherworldly versus this-worldly, communal versus privatistic, and resistance versus accommodation. As such, they contend, it is a manifestation of Du Bois's notion of the double consciousness of the African American (Lincoln and Mamiya 1990: 10–16): On one hand you're not an American, but the reality is you're not an African either, so you struggle between two poles, both of which have been denied.

After the Civil War, a wide variety of black religious bodies emerged as key institutions in the African-American community. Some congregations were unaffiliated, local ventures. Others became segregated affiliates of white-controlled denominations, sometimes with a white pastor, other times with a black one. A third variant included churches affiliated with other African-American congregations, either as regional associations or as national denominations (Baer and Singer 1992: 15).

The three major denominational streams that have attracted by far the most African Americans are Baptist, Methodist, and Pentecostal. Among the most important Baptist denominations at present are the National Baptist Convention, USA (with 7.5 million members, this group includes almost a quarter of all African Americans), the National Baptist Convention of America, and the Progressive National Baptist Convention. The latter two groups are the result of internal denominational conflicts that led to schisms. Of the eight Methodist denominations, the largest are the African Methodist Episcopal Church (the oldest and largest, with 3.5 million members), the African Methodist Episcopal Zion Church, and the Christian Methodist Episcopal Church. Of the eight Pentecostal denominations, the Church of God in Christ, with 5.5 million members, is by far the largest (Lincoln and Mamiya 1990: 20–91). Collectively, these seven church bodies attract approximately 80 percent of the African-American population, with an additional 8 percent belonging to the Roman Catholic Church (Baer and Singer 1992: 55).

At the beginning of the twentieth century, more than 90 percent of African Americans lived in the rural South. This would change, beginning with World War I, as a mass internal migration northward, toward the "Promised Land" (Lemann 1991), led African Americans into an urbanized industrial world. Here they confronted racist hostility, including a series of race riots in major and minor cities across the country. De facto segregation also led to the rise of the urban ghetto, which contained a complex institutional structure composed of churches, businesses, voluntary associations, and civic organizations. In this milieu, the internal stratification of the community led to a class structure that paralleled that of the larger society.

This class structure influenced religious affiliations. Mainstream churches catered to status-conscious professionals and business people. These churches typically had social ministries concerned with the economic betterment of the community as well as its political empowerment. Some of these churches were quite conservative, while others found allies among liberal white Protestants. At the other end of the socioeconomic spectrum, many poor blacks were attracted to a variety of sects. The phenomenon of the storefront church is an enduring feature of inner-city neighborhoods. Typically headed by a charismatic leader, these small congregations tend to be Holiness or Pentecostal in orientation.

In addition to these groups, a number of unconventional sects and cults also took root in the urban milieu, including those founded by colorful and controversial figures such as Father Divine's Peace Mission Movement and Daddy Grace's United House of Prayer for All People. Father Divine's Peace Mission blended a message of social reform with both a call to racial integration (whites played a role in the organization's leadership) and a simultaneous appeal to a nonmilitant form of black nationalism, drawing for the latter on some of the ideals of Marcus Garvey. Most important, the movement stressed the need for personal transformation as a prerequisite for social change (Erickson 1997; Watts 1992). Daddy Grace's United House of Prayer differed from the Peace Mission in two main ways. First, it did not promote social reform. Second, Daddy Grace was a flamboyant, charismatic figure who was viewed as a messiah by his followers. When he died, he had amassed a fortune, and despite an internal struggle for control of the organization after his death, the sect has managed to survive (see Baer and Singer 1992).

Islam took root among urbanized northern blacks with the mysterious arrival of Wallace D. Fard who, despite his ambiguous racial identity, began in Detroit to preach a message of messianic black nationalism that, it was claimed, was rooted in Islam. Fard contended that the black race had been oppressed by whites, which he referred to as "blue-eyed devils," and that Christianity was part of that oppression. Blacks were portrayed as the first race. The white interlopers, it was claimed, had stolen their culture, and it was time to reclaim their identity and their rightful place in world history.

Fard disappeared, and the mantle of leadership shifted to Elijah Poole who, abandoning his "slave name," became known as Elijah Muhammad. He became the head of the Nation of Islam, attracting a following among poor blacks in major cities. The Nation of Islam emphasized economic independence and black separatism, and so constituted a major rejection of the integrationist goals of mainstream African-American institutions. Temples and mosques opened in cities across the country, along with businesses run by the Nation. Young, clean-shaven, neatly attired men appeared on street corners selling newspapers, working with prisoners, or engaging in a practice known as fishing, whereby Nation of Islam members would stand outside black churches and urge parishioners leaving services to abandon their slave religion for Islam. The prominence of Malcolm X and the conversion of the boxer Cassius Clay, who became known as Muhammad Ali, served to make the Nation of Islam visible to the larger society (Gates 1996; Lincoln 1973).

Ideological conflicts within the Nation focused on its relationship to more traditional forms of Islam. Leader Elijah Muhammad, contending that Fard was Allah incarnate, promoted a perspective diverging considerably from orthodox Islam (akin to the relationship of Mormonism to Christianity). Opponents within the group sought to move closer to other Islamic organizations. In so doing, the particularistic racialist rhetoric of the Nation would be called into question by the universalistic beliefs of mainstream Islam. The episode that brought these competing views to a head occurred when Malcolm X, after a pilgrimage to Mecca, renounced his earlier embrace of Elijah Muhammad's views in favor of mainstream Islam and was shortly thereafter assassinated.

After the death of Elijah Muhammad, the organization split. His son, Wallace D. Muhammad, broke with his father's views and established the American Muslim Mission, which is estimated to have one hundred thousand members. This group moved adherents in the direction of mainstream Sunni Islam. Louis Farrakhan (born Louis Eugene Walcott into the Episcopal Church) carried on the more heterodox tradition of his predecessor, adding to it a penchant for vocal anti-Semitism (Lee 1988). While the approximately twenty thousand members of the Nation of Islam constitute a very small minority within African America, Farrakhan's influence extends beyond the confines of the organization. Perhaps the impact of the Million Man March, which he organized in 1995, is the best indication of his influence among non-Islamic blacks. Beyond that singular event, Edward Curtis (2005) has argued that since the 1920s black Muslims have continued to promote—with some success—the idea that the black historical experience can be best understood through a Muslim lens.

During the civil rights movement, the mainline Christian churches played an important role. Contrary to those such as Gary Marx (1967), who contend that religiosity served as an impediment to political activism, Nelsen and Nelsen (1975) show that black churches were an important component of the civil rights coalition, while members of black sects tended to be averse to becoming activists. The largest denominations of the African-American church were a significant constituent of the civil rights movement of the 1950s and 1960s, along with both established civil rights organizations such as the National Association for the Advancement of Colored People (NAACP) and the Brotherhood of Sleeping Car Porters, and newer organizations such as the Congress of Racial Equality (CORE) (Haines 1988; Morris 1984). One of the key organizations to emerge during this era was the Southern Christian Leadership Conference (SCLC), which became the institutional base for Martin Luther King, Jr., and served, as Aldon Morris aptly argued, as "the decentralized political arm of the black church" (1984: 77), a theme further explored and extended in Andrew Billingsley's *Mighty Like a River: The Black Church and Social Reform* (1998). During the earliest phase of the civil rights movement, the role of organized religious groups was instrumental in the push to end Jim Crow ordinances and practices, to challenge de facto segregation, and to promote reformist social change (see McAdam 1988). However, it lost some of its earlier influence during the later period of black-power militancy. Nevertheless, it is out of the black church that figures such as the onetime presidential candidate Jesse Jackson arose. King and Jackson were not alone in this respect. To them could be added the names of Andrew Young, Joseph Lowery, Adam Clayton Powell, Leon Sullivan, and even Al Sharpton, who began leading public meetings in Brooklyn as a "boy evangelist."

During the post–civil rights era, African-American religious bodies have been forced to respond to changes both within and outside of their community. The growth of the black middle class and its exit from the inner city has resulted in an increasingly bifurcated community, dividing those who are entering the U.S. mainstream from those who have been left behind in impoverished ghettos (W. Wilson 1996). The legal barriers to integration, economic improvement, and political power have been dismantled, but racism has not been eradicated and serious problems plague the most disadvantaged.

In this context, Cheryl Townsend Gilkes (1998) has summarized the ways organized religion among African Americans has responded. In the first place, unlike mainline white churches, black churches have not experienced declines in membership. Middle-class blacks have been more likely than whites to maintain the location of congregations in poorer neighborhoods, their weekly attendance at church services serving to reconnect them to the less affluent remaining in the inner city. Many in the middle class still have family and friends in these neighborhoods, as well, but the church provides an institutional base for them to maintain community bonds and to offer tangible support for the poor. In short, according to Gilkes, "the church became the site for personal, social, and cultural integration and reintegration as class configurations changed" (1998: 109). The church has proved itself to be a central institution in the African-American community, but this assessment needs to be tempered somewhat, for not all black churches are actively engaged in their neighborhoods. Omar McRoberts (2003) discovered that in many of the twenty-nine storefront churches he studied in Boston's Four Corners section, church members neither lived in the neighborhood nor took an active interest in improving the surrounding social conditions. Theological differences and class differences play a role in determining levels of civic engagement. R. Khari Brown and Ronald E. Brown (2003) argue that some black churches serve as training grounds for citizenship, while others simply do not, with middle-class and higher-educated blacks being far more likely to participate in the civic culture than their poorer and less educated counterparts. With this qualification, we can still agree with Gilkes's bottom-line assessment. In part, the continuing importance of the black church is reinforced by the fact that American religious institutions remain extremely segregated, with the number of interracial congregations remaining persistently low (Christerson et al. 2005; Emerson and Smith 2000).

From Different Shores: The New Immigrants

With the passage in 1965 of the Hart-Cellar amendments to the Immigration and Nationality Act of 1952, the United States resumed mass immigration after a four-decade period during which, as a result of the legislation passed in 1924, relatively small numbers of newcomers were permitted to settle in the country. While the period between 1880 and 1924 witnessed the largest number of immigrants entering the country in its history, the post-1965 levels are also very high. In fact, the last decade of the twentieth century may have reached an immigration level exceeding that of the century's first decade, which had up to that point been the decade of peak immigration (Min 1999; Portes and Rumbaut 2006; Ueda 1994). Unlike the earlier period of migration, when the vast majority of immigrants were European, the overwhelming majority of newcomers since 1965 have originated in Latin America, the Caribbean, and Asia. The new immigrants are split between the educated and professional classes, who are often poised to enter the economic mainstream, and the uneducated and unskilled, who end up either in the bottom tiers of the economy or on the margins in the underground economy. The difference between the two groups is sufficiently pronounced that as the second generation comes of age, some scholars, taking the lead from Alejandro Portes and Min Zhou (1993), speak about the "segmented assimilation" of this immigrant wave.

New racial fault lines have begun to emerge. In the first place, as non-Europeans, the new immigrants have changed the racial character of the nation, especially in states where they are most highly concentrated, including California, New York, New Jersey, Florida, and Illinois. One change noted earlier that will occur early in the twenty-first century, if it has not already occurred, is that Hispanic Americans will outnumber African Americans. With the growth of racial minorities, the Euro-American population will comprise a significantly smaller percentage of the overall population. And, despite appeals for the creation of a multiracial Rainbow Coalition on the part of progressive politicians such as Jesse Jackson, there is evidence of tension among various races. This was particularly evident in the 1992 Los Angeles riot, which has been described as the nation's first multiracial riot. Evidence suggests, for example, that Korean merchants were specifically targeted by African-American rioters, and stores owned by Koreans suffered a disproportionate amount of damage (Min 1996).

It should be noted that scholars have only recently turned their attention from the immigration process to the adaptation process (Min 1999). In beginning this shift of focus, attention has recently turned to the role ethnic institutions play in the adaptation process. Part of this emerging body of scholarship is turning its sights to religious institutions. In a review of the literature in the early 1990s, Kivisto (1993) found that the study of religion and the new immigrants was in general rather underdeveloped, and moreover the literature exhibited an uneven treatment. Thus, for example, while Korean Americans have received a fair amount of attention, Filipinos—the largest of the new Asian groups—have not. Religion has not received sustained attention among any of the major Hispanic groups. Likewise, for the practitioners of non-Judeo-Christian religions, a relative paucity of research had been completed at that date.

A major effort to respond to this underdevelopment has emerged under the leadership of R. Stephen Warner and Judith Wittner. The project received conceptual shape with Warner's "new paradigm" (1993) for the study of religion. Warner and Wittner (1998) and Helen Rose Ebaugh and Janet Saltzman Chafetz (2000) have directed a number of ethnographic studies of new immigrant religious communities over a wide range that includes Hindus and Christians from India, Korean and Chinese Christians, Iranian Jews, Zoroastrians, evangelical Hispanics, Haitian Catholics, and Rastafarians (see also Leonard et al. 2005).

THE NEW ETHNICS AS PROTESTANTS, CATHOLICS, AND JEWS

According to the findings of the New Immigrant Survey Pilot (NIS-P), two-thirds of new immigrants are Christian. While this means that a sizable majority fall within the nation's traditional patterns, this figure also indicates that the new immigrants are less likely to be Christian than the population at large, where 82 percent report being Christian. In addition, the percent of immigrant Christians who are Catholic is considerably higher than the general population—42 percent versus 22 percent (Jasso et al. 2003: 218). Hence, one of the consequences of the new immigration is that the Roman Catholic community has grown rapidly, and at present constitutes a larger portion of the U.S. Christian community than at any earlier point in history. Moreover, the groups that make up Catholicism in the United States are changing. At present, Hispanics constitute almost a third of the Roman Catholic membership. This is chiefly because the largest immigrant group, the Mexicans, and all other Hispanic groups, in addition to many Filipinos and some Southeast Asians, are Catholic. At the same time, Protestantism, especially its evangelical variety, has made inroads into these communities (see Christiano 1993; Vidal 1991).

Catholic parishes have often been transformed, due to changing residential locations, into congregations that are composed predominantly of new immigrants. However, the priests are rarely from those particular ethnic communities, and parishioners have at times had a strained relationship with the Catholic hierarchy, not unlike tensions evident in the early twentieth century with such groups as Italians and Poles. This tension is especially likely when a local congregation resists what it perceives to be the assimilationist strategies of Church leaders. One of the attractions of Protestantism for some new immigrants is that congregations have far more control over their local affairs than do Roman Catholic parishes. For example, in an ethnographic study of a Filipino church in Chicago affiliated with the United Church of Christ, Orlando Tizon (1999) discovered that the members placed a high value on their ability to create an institution that served as an important vehicle for preserving their ethnic heritage. The ability to hire their own Filipino clergy, and to make up their own minds about when to hold on to Filipino traditions and when to embrace facets of the culture of the host society, made this church particularly attractive to its members. At the same time, Tizon noted that tensions between the first and second generations have already arisen over the pros and cons of preserving a distinctive ethnic heritage versus encouraging rapid Americanization.

Many of these issues resonate with the experiences of the old immigrants. However, the impact of racial categorizations sets these new arrivals apart from those who arrived before 1930. Min (1999) suggests that race will prevent assimilation from occurring as rapidly as it did in earlier periods, and because of the transnational connections new immigrants have forged (due to improvements in international travel and in communications technology), the new immigrants can be expected to remain bicultural and rooted in both their homeland and their receiving nation for some time into the future (Foley and Hoge 2007; Kivisto 2001, 2003). Religious and cultural boundaries become increasingly disconnected from the political boundaries of nation-states. As Peggy Levitt (2007) put it in her comparative study of contemporary religious immigrants, "God needs no passport." Suffice it to say, given how recent these developments have been and the relative paucity of research to date, it is premature to draw many conclusions about outcomes. A good example of enduring immigrant biculturalism, however, resides among Puerto Ricans, who are formally citizens of the United States, but who maintain a historical and linguistic distinctiveness. Frequent communication and travel between the island and the mainland make for a new combination (more than for a clash) of cultures (see Díaz-Stevens 1993; Fitzpatrick 1987; Fitzpatrick and Parker 1981).

Cecilia Menjívar's insightful comparison of Catholic and evangelical Protestant Salvadorans illustrates both the potential for and the limitations of religious transnationalism, which in this case suggested that transnational religion was a greater presence among Protestants than Catholics (2000; see also Menjívar 2006). Manuel Vásquez and Marie Friedmann Marquardt's work (2003: 119–44) has examined the back-and-forth character of Pentecostal churches in El Salvador. Yet another example of this line of inquiry is Levitt's study (2001: 159–79) of the transnational religious practices of Dominicans from the village of Miraflores residing in the Jamaica Plain section of Boston. In this case, the Dominicans have had to confront a U.S. religious establishment intent on promoting a pan-Latino Catholicism at the expense of a distinctly Dominican version, resulting over time in changing beliefs and practices. This in turn has had an impact on religion in Miraflores, where remittances have helped to revitalize religious life in the community. Not all of the new immigrants are defined as nonwhite. The largest such group among the new immigrants is Jews, who have entered a new homeland where earlier Jewish immigrants established a distinctive presence, leading to the Jewish-Christian rapprochement that occurred after World War II and culminating in the notion of a civil religion described by Herberg. The two primary nations of origin of the new immigrants, who entered the United States after a dramatic reduction in anti-Semitism, are the former Soviet Union and Israel. Many of the new arrivals were secular in their homelands. The efforts of Reform and Conservative Jews to reach out to them have met with limited success, in no small part because both offer versions of Judaism that are largely unknown outside of the United States. Thus, when recent immigrants have opted to affiliate with religious institutions—and a sizable number have done so—they have tended to choose the Orthodox Hasidic movement, including the ultra-Orthodox Chabad (Gold 1999: 133–35).

BEYOND PROTESTANT, CATHOLIC, JEW

A major transformation in the religious landscape is under way, as more and more of the new immigrants are neither Christian nor Jewish. The three other major world religions have grown in the post-1965 era, along with numerous smaller groups ranging from the Bahá'i to Rastafarians (see McMullen 2000; Murrell, Spencer, and McFarlane 1998). While becoming proportionally larger,

Religion and the New Immigrants: Roman Catholicism and the Vietnamese

New Orleans also reflects the church's new ethnic diversity. While the city has long been home to a large African American Catholic population, in recent years it has also been absorbing many immigrants from the Caribbean, Central America, and Southeast Asia.

In a former marshland that has become a suburban neighborhood sits the Mary, Queen of Vietnam parish, founded in 1983. During a midmorning Sunday mass, the white-walled sanctuary was packed with worshipers, its pews, built to seat 1,000, so full that ushers had to search for spots for latecomers. "It's typically this crowded," said Anh Cao, 31, a law student at Loyola.

Social issues seem to elicit a generally conservative response from young parish members, as when the question of whether women would be ordained is raised with members of a youth choir.

"I have never thought of that," said Kim Phan, 24, a graduate student at the University of New Orleans. "I've never imagined a woman could be a priest."

Hieu Hoang, 22, a junior at Louisiana State University and a member of a parish women's group, the Daughters of Mary, offered a similar response.

Mr. Cao said Vietnamese Catholics strongly opposed abortion, in keeping with church teaching.

Such attitudes reflect the continuity of traditional Vietnamese Catholic values, said Joseph Trung, 32, a choir director and composer. "It comes from the family, it comes from the community," he said. . . .

Monsignor Dominic M. T. Luong, pastor of Mary, Queen of Vietnam, said the parish had about 3,000 members when it began in 1983. But . . . he said [by 1999 there were] 17,000 Vietnamese Catholics in the New Orleans archdiocese. . . .

The local Vietnamese population, he said, had produced 31 priests and 47 of its young men and women are studying to become priests or nuns, at a time when a growing shortage of priests has meant that an ever-larger number of tasks . . . is falling to lay people.

Source: Gustav Niebuhr, "Pope's Visit to U.S. to Focus on Future of Church Growth," *New York Times*, January 25, 1999, A20.

these groups began with very small numbers and so, despite substantial growth, they remain a very small percentage of the overall population. Thus, although there were three to four times more members of nontraditional faiths in the U.S. at the end of the last century compared to 1970, they constitute less than 3 percent of the total population (Smith 2002a: 582).

Among the major religions, the most dramatic growth has occurred with adherents to the Islamic faith. There are between 2 and 3 million Muslims in the United States at present. Some demographic forecasts suggest that Muslims either already have or will soon replace Jews as the second largest religious group after Christians. Whether or not this projection proves to be true, at present Muslims probably constitute no more than 1 percent of the population (Smith 2002b: 414). While there has been a Muslim presence in the United States since the beginning of the century, their numbers prior to the 1970s were quite small.

The earliest immigrants tended to come from the Middle East, particularly Lebanon and Syria, and the Balkans, especially Bosnia and Albania. Many were merchants or traveling salespeople. The first mosque in the United States was constructed in Cedar Rapids, Iowa, in 1934, and after that time a number of relatively small religious centers sprang up (Naff 1985). Today there are more than twelve hundred mosques across the country, with most major urban centers revealing an Islamic presence. However, the heaviest concentration of Muslims continues to be in the Midwest (Haddad and Lummis 1987: 11).

The new Islamic immigrants reflect the fact that Islam is a global religion. According to Haddad and Lummis (1987: 3), they come from more than sixty countries. Many come from the Middle East, including Syrians, Iraqis, Lebanese, Turks, and Iranians. Some have established ethnic enclaves predicated on these varied national origins. Thus, for example, Syrians have created a substantial ethnic community in Detroit, while Iranians have done the same in Los Angeles. Muslims from eastern Europe have increased in numbers, especially after the fall of Communism. In particular, the conflict in the former Yugoslavia has led since the early 1990s to an influx of Muslim refugees from Bosnia and Kosovo. However, unlike in the past, Muslims from other parts of the world have also settled in the United States. This includes sizable numbers of Muslims from Pakistan, India, and Afghanistan, as well as smaller numbers from countries such as the Philippines.

Given the diversity of the Islamic community in the United States, the extent to which mosques and other Islamic organizations are based on the specific ethnic origins of members varies. In larger cities, where numbers make it possible, one can find ethnically specific mosques, while in other areas Islamic institutions are panethnic. While differences within Islam itself (for example, the differences between Sunni and Shi'ite) contribute to divisions, and potential conflict, within the immigrant community, these are sometimes reinforced by ethnic differences. However, at times religious and ethnic differences are crosscutting rather than mutually reinforcing, making possible various forms of panethnic cooperation.

Beyond cooperation among new immigrants, the future relationship between Muslim immigrants and indigenous Muslims in the African-American community is uncertain. It is likely, given the theological and ethnic differences between immigrants and members of the Nation of Islam, that these two expressions of Islam will remain distant from each other. More orthodox indigenous Muslims, such as members of the American Muslim Mission, and immigrants have much in common, however, and it is probable that the future will include explorations about how best to develop common ground.

Though smaller than the Islamic population, Hinduism and Buddhism have also grown during the past three decades. Hindus are the smaller of the two, with most adherents coming from India. Raymond Brady Williams (1998: 182–83) has noted that home shrines are more important than temples to a majority of Hindus. Given the relatively small size of the Hindu population, this has been beneficial because it has made possible the continuity of religious practice in the new environment even in situations when the social and/or

Muslims and Christians and Arab Americans

Although the Arab and the Muslim populations of the United States overlap to an important degree, the tendency in uninformed popular and political discussion is to refer to the two groups as if they were one and the same. This mistake, however, can lead to significant confusion. To offer just a pair of examples: contrary to frequent assumptions, most Arab residents of the United States *are not* Muslims, and most Muslims in America *are not* Arabs.

ARAB AMERICANS

The Census Bureau first reported separately on the Arab segment of the U.S. population after its 2000 nationwide canvass. Its tabulations yielded a figure of 1.2 million persons—out of more than 281 million people in America—who claimed some Arabic background as their primary or secondary ethnic identity. Despite the fact that this total had doubled since the initial measurement of the size of the Arab-American population in 1980, analysts of the Arab community have contended that this number is a considerable undercount. The true size of their group is closer to 3 million, they would insist (see Read 2003: 209).

The single largest subset of Arab Americans in 2000 (37 percent) were Lebanese, followed equally by Syrians and Egyptians at 12 percent each (Brittingham and de la Cruz 2005: 1, 3; de la Cruz and Brittingham 2003: 1–2). The Census Bureau further documented that Arab Americans were younger on the whole, more affluent, and more highly educated than the national average. Indeed, more than one third of American adults with Arab ancestry in 2000 held a college degree (Brittingham and de la Cruz 2005: 11, 14–15; Read 2003: 208–10, 218).

Arab Americans as a group are geographically concentrated and highly urbanized. Almost one half of their number in the 2000 census made their homes in regions of just five of the United States: California (San Diego and Los Angeles—especially the suburbs around Glendale and Burbank), New York (New York City), Michigan (Detroit and its environs), Florida (Jacksonville), and New Jersey (Jersey City and Paterson). Their highest density was in Michigan, where they constituted 1.2 percent of the state's population in 2000, and 30 percent in the city of Dearborn, famous as home to the Ford Motor Company (de la Cruz and Brittingham 2003: 4–5, 7–8).

CHRISTIANS AND MUSLIMS

Among Arab Americans, Christians of various rites are thought to outnumber Muslims more than two-to-one. Christians, it is clear, predominate among longer-standing Arab residents of the United States, while Muslims are a majority within the newer, first-generation immigrant groups from Arab lands. As for the followers of Islam at large, the latest estimates are that one third of the Muslim population of the United States derives from the countries of South Asia (with Pakistanis making up the largest contingent), another one quarter are Arabs, and 20 to 30 percent are African Americans, who mostly are converts to the faith (Bukhari 2003: 9–11; Peek 2005: 216, n. 2; see also Bagby, Perl, and Froehle 2001: 3, 16–17, 22). Like the Arab-American community, the Muslims of the United States are both younger and better educated than other groups (Bagby, Perl, and Froehle 2001: 15, 23; Bukhari 2003: 12).

Precisely how many Muslims there are, in raw numbers, across the broader American population is a matter of great dispute among religious activists and social demographers alike. The former are given to declaring that there are currently at least 6 million Muslims in the United States. In fact, use of the 6 million count by scholars (Peek 2005: 216), journalists (Van Biema et al. 2001; but see Broadway 2001; G. Niebuhr 2001), and religious leaders themselves (Taylor 2001) is commonplace. But this statistic is, at best, a guess, for there is no authoritative source of data on the size of the Muslim community. Muslim congregations, for their part, maintain no centralized system of membership records. On the secular side, the federal government, as we have seen above, now routinely gathers information on the ethnic backgrounds of individuals, but it does not collect any information on their religious affiliations. Thus, sociologists of religion who have attempted to confirm a count of American Muslims have encountered sizable obstacles.

Part of the problem in arriving at an agreed-upon figure is that, until recently, Muslims in America did not establish a relation of religious membership that is strictly comparable to a Christian's idea of "belonging" to a church. A pioneering study of mosques in the United States (Bagby, Perl, and Froehle 2001: 2–3, 12), for example, counted more than twelve hundred such places of Muslim worship, with a reported 2 million people "who associate themselves" with these institutions through participation in communal prayers and other regularly scheduled activities. Yet such a measure would not embrace everyone in the United States who identifies himself or herself as a Muslim.

An alternative approach would be to try to extrapolate a count of Muslims from their representation in national probability samples. But such a strategy is notoriously difficult to pursue when the researcher is dealing with small (and therefore unstable) fractions in the first place—and surveys of the United States usually indicate that Muslims are somewhere between 0.2 and 0.6 percent of the total population (Pew Research Center 2007: 9–10; T. Smith 2001: 6, 2002b: 411). Still, after an extensive review of polling results and official statistics, public opinion researcher Tom Smith has concluded that "it is hard to accept estimates that Muslims are greater than 1 percent of the population"—a proportion that translates into approximately 2.1 million adults or 2.8 million people of any age (2001: 5–6, 2002b: 414).

DISAPPEARING CHRISTIANS

Ironically, given that Christian Arabs in the United States outnumber Muslim Arabs two-to-one, the reason Americans outside of the major geographic pockets of Arab-American concentration in the U.S. today tend to equate "Arab" with "Muslim" may be that there are so few Christians left in the Middle East, with their numbers declining extremely rapidly. For example, in the 1970s about a third of Palestinians were affiliated with Christian congregations. Less than 1 percent of the Palestinian population is Christian today. Baghdad had more than 1 million Christians less than a decade ago. By 2007 the number had declined by 60 percent, with thirty thousand leaving each month. The various Christian congregations in Iran have lost at least half their congregants over the past decade and a half—some as much as 90 percent. A similar situation exists in Lebanon. Hence, Americans who see television news photos of the Middle East today are unlikely to see distinctly Christian imagery or activity.

Where have they gone? In greatest numbers Iraqi Chaldean Christians have come to the United States or gone to Australia. Iranians seem to prefer France, some aided by Ha'aretz, an organization originally founded in the early years of the nineteenth century to help Jews move to the Holy Land. There are also refugee camps in Muslim countries immediately adjacent to the centers of greatest conflict. In many areas of the Middle East, Christians are aggressively stigmatized as "Crusaders" and accused of being American agents. Targeting minority Christians is one method Islamic extremists employ to deflect attention away from the pressing socioeconomic difficulties caused by their own aggression, which has as its primary result the destabilization of the lives of the Islamic majority. Persons who have escaped from these conditions are not likely to make an immediate effort to draw attention to themselves in their new homelands, especially inasmuch as they may have left behind relatives who remain in danger.

financial capital needed to create temples has been lacking. In major metropolitan regions, where the number of Hindu immigrants makes possible such ventures, temples have been built, including the large and ornate Rama Temple in suburban Chicago and the Meenakshi Temple outside Houston. In these areas of high Hindu concentrations, some temples have been founded along regional lines or on the basis of devotion to particular gurus. In addition, Jains and Sikhs, two religious groups distinct from but with an affinity to Hinduism, have begun to create their own religious institutions. Another interesting development in Western Hindu practice has been the transformation of the International Society for Krishna Consciousness (ISKCON) from a highly controversial "new religion" of the 1970s into a Westernized neo-Hindu movement that is reaching out to and attracting immigrant Hindus in the United States and Canada (see Rochford 2007).

The recent growth of Buddhism relies primarily on immigrants from several Asian nations, including China, Korea (though a majority of Korean immigrants are Christian), and the smaller nations of Southeast Asia (see Numrich 2008). Buddhism first arrived in the United States in the late nineteenth and early twentieth centuries among Chinese and Japanese immigrants. However, in both cases religious conversions served to limit the impact of the religion. The Chinese were inclined to practice the religion at home, and thus few temples were constructed. In the case of the Japanese, a more tangible institutional presence arose, but a major generational shift took place that eroded allegiance to Buddhism. Although a majority of the *Issei* generation, who immigrated from Japan, were Buddhist, many converted to Protestant Christianity, and a substantial majority of the *Nisei*, or second generation who were born in the U.S., did likewise (Daniels 1990: 257). There is, however, also an American Buddhism that stretches back into the nineteenth century, and received renewals—first after World War II and again beginning in the mid-1960s (see Coleman 2001; Tamney 1992; Tweed 1992). Buddhism in this variant has primarily attracted a slice of the intelligentsia in the United States, and it remains to be seen how it will relate to the Buddhism of the new immigrants (Cadge 2004).

These photos show two efforts of new immigrants to establish worship spaces on their own: the purpose-built Hindu Rama Temple in suburban Chicago and the Albanian Islamic Cultural Center in Clearwater, Florida, which was converted from a former commercial structure, basically by adding a minaret. Photographs courtesy of Nirmala Salgado (top) and William H. Swatos, Jr. (bottom).

Thus, the growth of Buddhism has emerged on a very small historic base. It has done so in a manner that closely resembles that of Hinduism. The role that ethnic and national divisions will play over time is not entirely clear. The possibility of a pan-Asian Buddhism might arise if the various Asian groups find it in their interest to work collectively in the political and economic realms. To do so will require overcoming ethnic hostilities, such as that between the Chinese and Vietnamese, which are rooted in homeland politics (Chen 1992; Hurh 1998; Min and Kim 2002).

What over time will be the place of Islam, Hinduism, and Buddhism in the pantheon of U.S. civil religion? What are the implications of their presence for the notion of the United States as a "Judeo-Christian" nation? Will these religious differences serve to reinforce ethnic differences? Will the second, third, and later generations of these newcomers maintain their ancestral religious allegiances, or will they convert, as many in the earlier waves of non-European immigrants did, to Christianity? What will be the response of the various Christian denominations? (Since Jews have avoided proselytizing, they are not included here.) Will they engage in missionary work or will they promote pluralistic tolerance of religious differences? While these are questions that we can answer only with the passage of time, the new immigrants raise the more fundamental and enduring question about how we make sense of the relationship between religion and ethnicity in a pluralist liberal democracy.

Suggestions for Further Reading

Antonio M. Stevens Arroyo. 1995. *Discovering Latino Religion: A Comprehensive Social Science Bibliography*. New York: Bildner Center for Western Hemisphere Studies.

Andrew Billingsley. 1998. *Mighty Like a River: The Black Church and Social Reform*. New York: Oxford University Press.

Helen Rose Fuchs Ebaugh and Janet Saltzman Chafetz. 2000. *Religion and the New Immigrants: Continuities and Adaptations in Immigrant Congregations*. Walnut Creek, CA: AltaMira.

Frederick C. Harris. 1999. *Something Within: Religion in African-American Political Activism*. New York: Oxford University Press.

Wsevolod W. Isajiw. 1999. *Understanding Diversity: Ethnicity and Race in the Canadian Context*. Toronto: Thomson.

Peter Kivisto and Wendy Ng. 2006. *Americans All: Race and Ethnic Relations in Historical, Structural, and Comparative Perspectives*, 2nd ed. New York: Oxford University Press.

Omar McRoberts. 2003. *Streets of Glory: Church and Community in a Black Urban Neighborhood*. Chicago: University of Chicago Press.

Joane Nagel. 1996. *American Indian Ethnic Renewal: Red Power and the Resurgence of Identity and Culture*. New York: Oxford University Press.

Manuel A. Vásquez and Marie Friedmann Marquardt. 2003. *Globalizing the Sacred: Religion across the Americas*. New Brunswick, N.J.: Rutgers University Press.

R. Stephen Warner. 1998. "Approaching Religious Diversity: Barriers, Byways, and Beginnings." *Sociology of Religion* 59:193–215.

Fenggang Yang. 1999. *Chinese Christians in America: Conversion, Assimilation, and Adhesive Identities*. University Park: Pennsylvania State University Press.

Alamy APX094

CHAPTER 7

Gender, Sexuality, and Religion

SPIRITUALITY IN DIFFERENT VOICES?

In chapter 1 we noted the importance of feminism in its impact on the social scientific study of religion since the 1980s. The feminist call for factoring gender into discussions of religious topics has served to question notions of a universal human condition and a singular human vantage point on the religious dimension. Operating with a domain assumption that contends that universality tends to equate to a masculinist perspective, a central thematic focus of a feminist perspective involves ascertaining the extent to which it is appropriate to speak about the gendered character of religious experience. As Janet Jacobs puts it: "The inclusion of gender as a category of analysis challenges this [masculinist universalist] bias by recognizing women as legitimate subjects of research and gender as an important lens through which to interpret the meaning and symbol systems of religious cultures" (1998: 206). By focusing on the significance of women and women's experience, the study of gender transforms the androcentric paradigms of traditional research.

During the last twenty years, then, a significant body of scholarship has been produced to advance the study of the reciprocal relationship between religion and gender. That body of scholarship is rich and varied, concentrating on a number of particular topics. At the same time, as we shall indicate, there are areas that have been relatively neglected and require more research.

As Mary Jo Neitz (1998) reminds us, religion has at once been a major institutional means of controlling women, while at the same time women have frequently found in those very institutions a possibility for carving out autonomous spaces that have facilitated the discovery of distinctive gendered voices for expressing their spirituality. The gendered character of religious expression has taken on added salience in recent decades, due to the transformations in the larger society brought about by the women's movement and the impact of these changes on traditional gender roles within religious institutions. In short, as traditional gender roles have been called into question, women have demanded greater equity and power, hence religious organizations have been forced to respond to the demands of change (even if the response has been to say "no").

Perhaps one of the clearest manifestations of such a change involves the demand that women be permitted to enter the ranks of the ordained clergy. Significant increases in the proportion of women in the seminary classes of mainline

Protestant denominations have led to a professional feminization, the implications of which are now beginning to be felt. At the same time, opposition to the ordination of women remains strong in official Roman Catholic circles and among many fundamentalist Protestants. The resistance of the current pope to any considerations of ordaining female priests, compounded by the shortage of priests for many Roman Catholic parishes, has simultaneously led to conflict and opened channels through which women perform duties traditionally assigned to male priests, but not actually requiring the charism of the priesthood. In the case of Southern Baptists, the leadership of the denomination has in recent years shifted from its earlier position, taking a more hard-line stance against women in the pastoral, preaching ministry.

Women's ordination, as important as it is, is by no means the only issue that reflects the rise of gender concerns in American society since the 1960s. Liberal denominations have responded affirmatively to the many demands for inclusiveness and gender equality emanating from the women's movement. This has often meant undertaking internal policies of affirmative action, including such policies as ensuring that church councils contain adequate representation of women and that representative numbers of male and female delegates are sent to synodical conventions and similar denominational meetings. However, movements among religious conservatives—Christian, Jewish, and Islamic—have been formed in part to rebut the feminist agenda, even though they acknowledge thereby the importance of that agenda in secular society. Conservative movements uniformly claim to be "pro-family" and attack the feminist agenda as antifamily. In so doing, they stress the importance of the father as head of the family and the role of the mother as nurturer. These movements attempt to link many social problems to the breakdown of family life as they conceive it to have been in the past (which, as Stephanie Coontz [1992] insightfully points out, often means an idealized version of a 1950s family that never really existed).

Not unrelated to feminist issues, finally, is the rise of concern for the accommodation and incorporation of gays and lesbians within religious institutions. Concerns of gay/lesbian spirituality largely grow out of gender issues raised by feminism, with gender equality being seen as extending to equality of sexual preference and expression. This particular topic has become something of a flashpoint in recent years. Within mainline denominations, major conflicts have emerged over the matter of inclusion and acceptance of gays and lesbians (see Wellman 1999). At the same time, within fundamentalism one discovers a considerable amount of demonization of individuals with same-sex preferences and of their associated lifestyles.

Yet another aspect of gendered spirituality has been the rise of explicitly women-centered religious groups. Many of these are neopagan in character, often using the style of Wicca. Some women-centered groups also occur within mainline traditions, however, such as the Roman Catholic WomanChurch movement. These groups, whether formally or loosely organized, usually develop their own ritual expressions that emphasize a more powerful feminine spirituality than their adherents find in the dominant expressions of faith. Such feminist expressions even extend beyond the Western traditions into American Buddhism.

Martin Riesebrodt (1993) contends that gender issues epitomize the current contrast within religious life between fundamentalist religion and that of the mainstream. The main topics explored in this chapter illustrate the validity of this assessment. In terms of institutional practices, the ordination debate and, related to this, the changing religious roles—both clerical and lay—performed by women reveal the conflict between modernizers and traditionalists. This conflict is visible again in our examination of the culture wars that have arisen in the United States since the 1960s. The convulsive debates over the legalization of abortion, the appropriate form and content of the contemporary family, and the struggle for gay and lesbian rights parallel the discussion of institutional practices with a consideration of the tension between fundamentalists and modernizers at the level of cultural values. The theme is reinforced in the concluding section on the ways different segments of society have reacted to received images of God. Each of these topics will be explored in this chapter.

The Ordination Debate

At the moment, about half the Christian denominations in the United States ordain women. Those that do include the mainline branches of the Presbyterian, Methodist, Baptist, and Lutheran churches, and the Episcopalians, United Church of Christ, and Unitarian Universalists. In addition to those more liberal denominations, other church bodies supporting the ordination of women include the Assemblies of God, the Church of the Nazarene, and the Salvation Army. While these latter groups have ordained women for a considerable period of time, many of the mainline churches have commenced such policies and practices more recently. The result: The number of ordained women has risen significantly in recent decades, reaching more than fifty thousand, which represents almost nine percent of the nation's clergy (Nesbitt 1997; Lehman 1985).

The three largest denominations on record opposing the ordination of women are the Roman Catholic Church (the largest religious body in the United States), the Southern Baptist Convention (the largest Protestant denomination in the nation), and the Lutheran Church, Missouri Synod (Chaves 1997: 1). The question we shall explore in this section is how to account for this divide within the Christian churches.

By way of a thumbnail historical sketch, prior to the sixteenth century the Christian church throughout Europe—Catholic and Orthodox—operated with the belief that priests should be male. In the Catholic Church an added stipulation a few centuries earlier required that all priests should be celibate. Among Reformation churches, celibacy was abandoned in favor of a position that held that it was not only appropriate, but also helpful, to have married men assume clerical roles in order for the clergy better to "minister to the needs of families" (Zikmund, Lummis, and Chang 1998: 93).

The patriarchal character of Christian institutions in the ancient and medieval worlds was unmistakable. Women were to a large extent excluded from power in the religious hierarchy. Despite this, religious women sometimes found

Does Your Barbie Have a Prayer Mat?

Getty 55845873

Barbie dolls are disappearing from the stock of many Middle Eastern toy stores. She has been superceded by Fulla, a dark-eyed doll whose creator claims she displays "Muslim values." The doll is sold wearing either a black abaya or a long coat and white head scarf, but under these coverings, the dolls wear attractive dresses. The doll also has a pink prayer rug. In addition, the manufacturer, ironically named New-Boy Design Studio, markets sets of clothes (including the prayer rug) for girls to dress like their dolls, as well as Fulla backpacks, Frisbees, and pool toys. Fulla will also be marketed clothed as a medical doctor and as a teacher, both acceptable occupations for women in Muslim societies.

opportunities within the religious establishment that were lacking entirely in the secular world. For example, Teresa of Avila (1515–1582), the Spanish mystic, proved to be a formidable figure in reforming the Carmelite religious order, a task that revealed her keen administrative abilities and her qualities as a leader (Medwick 1999). However, within both Catholicism and the Reformation church bodies, women were decidedly second-class members.

The exclusion of women from clerical roles began to change by the latter part of the eighteenth century. Rebecca Larson (1999) found that Quaker women in colonial America began gradually and without significant dissent to assume ministerial roles. During this period, the Society of Friends was the third-largest religious body in the colonies, and thus changes in this denomination reflected something about the main currents of colonial society. Larson reports that by the late 1700s, there were more than one thousand female Quaker ministers, explaining how this change developed in the following way:

> The theological basis for Quaker women's ministerial activity was the power of God to use any "instrument," however weak, for his purposes. But the effects of women's participation in this role were more complicated than this religious justification. As the Protestant Reformation had destroyed old cultural patterns and reshaped social behavior, Quaker belief in universal access to the Inward Light dramatically altered traditional gender roles and spheres of activity. Virtuous women, traditionally silent in public and confined to the domestic sphere, gave public testimonies and traveled to spread the message of "Truth." The repercussions of these changes became obvious in the nineteenth century, as Quaker women, habituated to public speaking and influence, were prominent in social reform movements such as abolition, temperance, prison reform, and women's rights. (1999: 302–3)

The Society of Friends did not officially ordain Quaker women. Mark Chaves (1997: 16) dates the beginning of the ordination of women in the United States to the mid-nineteenth century, as Congregationalists—the precursors to today's United Church of Christ—led the way in 1853. The last of the denominations to date to permit female ordination was the Episcopal Church, which made the change amid considerable controversy in 1976. Two time periods stand out as peak decades for the shift to permitting female ordination: the 1890s and the 1970s. Chaves attempts to explain this transformation by making use of the "new institutionalism" associated with sociologists such as Walter Powell and Paul DiMaggio (1991), who use the term *institutional isomorphism* to describe how interacting organizations tend, over time, to become more alike. In so doing, these organizations maintain their legitimacy with each other. Chaves writes: "When an organizational practice or structure becomes commonly understood as a defining feature of a 'legitimate' organization of a certain type, organizational elites feel pressure to institute that practice or structure. If there is a cultural norm that says, 'In order for an organization to be a *good* organization, it must have characteristic X,' organizations feel pressure to institute characteristic X" (1997: 32–33).

Of particular importance in Chaves's account is the relationship between specific institutions and the state. Those with closer ties to the state discover that governmental actions have a profound impact on the culture and the policies of the institution. Religion in this regard is perceived to be no different from other institutions. In fact, at the same time that some denominations began to accept women into the ranks of the clergy, educational institutions also began to accept women into training for some heretofore male-only professions such as law and medicine.

The ordination of women began when it did because larger societal changes propelled certain denominations to change in order to remain connected to external organizations. For example, during the last several decades, women began to assume new work roles outside the home, and at the same time there was a dramatic increase in the number of middle-class women pursuing higher education. In a period of heightened expectations in the secular world, these expectations impinged on the religious realm (Greenspan 1994). Of singular importance is the role played by the women's movement, because, as Chaves and Cavendish observe, "part of what it means to have an active social movement is that movement activists and adherents promote change in a variety of societal institutions, including religions institutions" (1997: 576).

This accounts for why ordination did not become a real issue until the 1950s. Prior to that time, women—such as the Quakers described above—wanted to be permitted to preach and prophesy. They did not, however, seek to mobilize to challenge gender inequality within the religious realm. This changed with the birth of the first wave of the women's movement, a movement that advocated equal rights for women. Activists targeted institutions throughout society that served as barriers to equality, and religious institutions were not exempt. The struggle for woman suffrage challenged political institutions, the right to own property challenged the patriarchal family, and ordination was a demand for entrée into the clerical realm.

Movement activists such as Elizabeth Cady Stanton saw equal access to clerical positions as crucial to overcoming gender inequality in denominational life (Chaves 1997: 37). In the case of Anna Howard Shaw, the president of the National American Woman Suffrage Association, this request took a personal form as she sought and was accepted into the Methodist clergy. Pentecostal and Holiness churches were in the vanguard of denominations promoting gender equality. Rebecca Harris (1995: 11) has suggested that the reason that these sectlike organizations were in the forefront of the move to ordain women was that they were more experimental in nature and therefore the most open to accepting the idea of equal rights for women. At the same time, two more entrepreneurial women were instrumental in founding new denominations: Mary Baker Eddy in the case of Christian Science and Ellen G. White with the Seventh-day Adventists.

While a number of denominations formally granted ordination to women by the early years of the twentieth century, relatively few women were actually ordained. The number would not increase appreciably until the second half of the century. Between 1950 and 1980 the number of denominations ordaining women rose. This, of course, coincides with the rise of the contemporary women's movement, which, as Chaves notes, "left untouched virtually no organizational field, including religion" (1997: 46). Women began to enter seminaries in significant numbers, seeking to break down the barriers of a "male-stereotyped" occupation (Zikmund, Lummis, and Chang 1998: 97). In fact, in anticipation of changes that had not yet occurred, women began to enter seminaries for training in denominations that had not yet accepted female ordination. These seminaries, not surprisingly, often became centers for activists demanding institutional change (Chaves and Cavendish 1997; Swatos 1992: 295–98). This situation is a prime example of the "loose coupling" between actual practices and formal policies: These denominations, while still formally prohibiting women from becoming ministers, permitted them to enter educational institutions specifically designed to train future clergy. A variant of loose coupling continues in the seminaries of the Roman

Catholic Church today, where enrollments are buoyed by female students, who have taken the places of the once-substantial numbers of men preparing for ordination. Some women are being trained explicitly for functions in the church that have devolved to lay persons, but more than a few harbor an expectation that at some point they will be able to use their professional degrees as priests—or that it would be an injustice if they were not so allowed.

As a consequence of this progressive expansion of ordination opportunities for women, their numbers in the ministry rose steadily during the second half of the twentieth century. During the 1950s, only 2.1 percent of the clergy were women. That figure doubled to 4.2 percent by 1980, while fifteen years later it had reached almost 9 percent (Neitz 1998; Nesbitt 1997: 25). In many of the mainline seminaries today, more than half the students preparing for the ministry are women.

But what about those denominations that have refused to change their ordination policies? They were certainly not immune to the pressures of the women's movement and to other external pressures to change. It is not a coincidence that many of the denominations that resisted change actually adopted formal policies prohibiting female ordination during the peak periods of change. As such, these denominations became party to a traditionalist countermovement intent on resisting the winds of change.

Besides the women's movement, there were other external forces influencing whether denominations were prepared to change their ordination policies and practices. Part of the institutional isomorphism noted above can come about as a result of interorganizational contacts. For example, if some denominations have granted full clergy rights to women, other denominations involved in ecumenical relations with them will feel increased pressure to do the same if they are to continue to be perceived by outsiders as legitimate and successful organizations (Chaves 1997).

Part of the explanation for the resistance to change by various denominations rests with their particular theological perspectives, which Chaves seeks to locate in terms of their resistance to modernism—seen as a desire to avoid assimilation into modern culture. In so doing, he invokes a version of the two-party thesis. One camp of resisters is composed of biblical inerrantists or fundamentalists, seen, for example, in the case of the Southern Baptists. He defines the other camp as the liturgically sacramental denominations, which would include Roman Catholics and the Lutheran Church, Missouri Synod (two church bodies, it should be noted, that also do not permit intercommunion with other denominations). Denominations endorsing biblical inerrancy argue against female clergy on the basis of what they take to be a literal interpretation of a select number of biblical passages, particularly those that suggest that women should not have authority over men or share authority with men. Sacramental denominations believe that males must perform sacraments if they are to be valid. The clergy represent Jesus Christ, and for the bread and wine to become the Eucharistic body and blood of Christ, it is essential for the presiding cleric to share the same sex as Jesus. In Roman Catholicism, for example, the representational aspect of the clerical role is referred to by its Latin formulation: *in persona*

Christi. That is, the priest is thought to function "in the person of Christ" as he presides at the sacrifice of the Mass (Jewett 1980: 79–80; Chaves 1997: 86).

In more general terms, opposition to the ordination of women is a factor among those denominations whose image of God is a masculine one and whose view of how "He" works in the world conflicts with the changing views of appropriate gender roles in the larger society. Ordaining women is part of a larger challenge to established patterns of authority, and it threatens to undermine an otherworldly orientation. Such bodies are intent on resisting accommodation to the secular world, for to do so is perceived to imperil the eternal salvation of believers.

However, as Nancy Nason-Clark (1987a) has pointed out, theology is not the whole story. Religious beliefs alone are insufficient to explain a refusal to grant women the opportunity accorded to men in entering the ranks of the clergy. In a study of the very divisive debate within Britain's Anglican community that took place when the issue of ordination was before it, Nason-Clark interviewed a cross-section of the clergy. She discovered that those most resistant to female ordination harbored the most traditionalist views of appropriate gender roles. These clergy were far more likely than those on the other side of the debate to believe that the domestic sphere was the proper arena for women, whose primary role ought to be that of nurturer. They were less sympathetic to women who tried both to pursue careers and to rear families, and they were similarly less inclined to support demands for gender equality in the workforce.

Parenthetically, it should be noted that there might well be significant differences of opinion between the clergy and laity over this issue. In this regard, evidence exists to support the claim that the laity have become over time increasingly supportive of the idea of female ordination, even in some church bodies that continue to oppose ordination (Hoge 1987). This is especially evident in the Roman Catholic Church, where attitudes have changed appreciably since Vatican II. A Gallup poll conducted in the early 1990s found that more than 60 percent of U.S. Catholics think that the ordination of women "would be a good thing" (Gallup 1993).

In all of this, denominations that have approved the ordination of women differ in important ways from these conservative churches. On the one hand, they argue against biblical literalism, adopting a more metaphorical interpretive stance in reading sacred texts. On the other hand, they do not place the same value on the liturgy as do the sacramental denominations. In this regard, it is not surprising that Lutherans and Episcopalians were among the last of the denominations to accept female ordination—and only among some Lutheran bodies and only with continuing controversy in the Episcopal Church—given the fact that they are considerably more sacramental than, for example, Methodists or Presbyterians.

Women in Clerical and Lay Roles

How have female clergy fared and what kind of impact have they had on churches? These interrelated questions have begun to be addressed only relatively recently, as the numbers of women who have entered the clerical ranks reached a critical mass and the effects of their presence have been felt (see for example, the early study of Carroll, Hargrove, and Lummis 1983). One thing is clear: Women face substantial barriers to inclusion. Nason-Clark (1987b, 1998) observes that the difficulties women encounter in finding a church often begin before they have completed their seminary educations. When searching for jobs, they frequently are required to respond to questions posed by church officials or by congregations that their male counterparts do not have to address. For instance, if they are married, they are queried about whether they are geographically mobile. In other words, a woman is expected to show how her career can fit into her spouse's career—something men are not asked to explain. They are asked to explain how they plan to handle pregnancy and the job, and how the congregation ought to deal with the possibility of pregnancy leaves. Younger female clergy and those who are not married face unique challenges insofar as questions about whether congregations will accept them are often raised.

Once in the ministry, women continue to find that they have not yet achieved parity with men. They tend to find placements more difficult to obtain, receive lower pay, and are generally employed in less privileged congregations. Paula Nesbitt (1997), in a representative sample of 1,227 clergy in the Episcopal and Unitarian Universalist denominations, found that male and female clergy have appreciably different career trajectories. The career path for the successful male is from a smaller to a larger and wealthier congregation, and from a supervised to solo to supervisory position. In contrast, women more typically start and remain in supervised positions. They often get tracked into such positions as assistant minister for children's education or pastoral care, since it is implicitly assumed that their strengths rest with their presumed nurturing abilities. This tracking phenomenon is also visible with respect to chaplaincies in such institutions as schools and hospitals. Very few of the most prestigious senior-pastor positions in the largest and wealthiest congregations are held by women. In short, female clergy at the moment appear to confront a "stained-glass ceiling" (Purvis 1995; Sullins 2000).

Whether this will persist over time is difficult to assess. Given the fact that many women who entered the clergy did so within the last twenty years, it might be reasonable to assume that if their careers are to begin to resemble those of men, they should begin to obtain higher-status solo positions and supervisory roles beginning in the next decade or so. One of the complicating factors in tracking career trajectories in the ministry is that increasingly—for both men and women—this is a second career, and thus what were in the past normative career paths beginning in an individual's twenties are generally not normative today.

At the moment there is some evidence to suggest that status discrimination is diminishing. Younger male clergy often share with their female counterparts beliefs about gender equality, and thus in some respects the issue of inclusion becomes a generational one. Moreover, sometimes as a result of formal plans and other times through informal decision making, the mainline denominations can point to women in high-ranking positions in the church hierarchy. It is nevertheless still difficult to assess whether these changes represent widespread acceptance of women in positions of clerical authority across a denomination or defection from the denomination by those who disagree with its decisions. The Episcopal Church is a case in point. Having been the last among the American denominations usually perceived as "liberal" to accept the ordination of women, it has now gone the farthest among them by electing a woman to serve in its highest office, Presiding Bishop. On the other hand, the Episcopal Church's membership is in decline, as is its current financial support, and its membership is aging dramatically. Formal efforts are now underway to provide for a dual executive structure, with those who cannot accept her leadership—complicated further by her support for gay ordination—having a separate leadership and seeking international recognition as the "true" representative of the worldwide Anglican communion. Absent significant increases in the number of younger-aged members, it may well be the case that the Episcopal Church will enact in the United States the future predicted for British Methodism by Steve Bruce at the start of the new millennium, that is, that the Episcopal Church will be absorbed into some form of pandenominational liturgical Protestantism.

A question that has only begun to be addressed by research is the impact of female clergy on the profession itself and on the congregations they serve (Royle 1987). Influenced by the work of feminist theorist Carol Gilligan, particularly the conclusions she arrived at in her groundbreaking book, *In a Different Voice* (1982), some of this research suggests that women are changing the shape and character of ministry as a result of a different way of making moral judgments compared to men. Central to Gilligan's work is the claim that men and women employ different logics in making ethical decisions. For men, the typical logic revolves around the application of abstract moral principles to concrete situations, whereas for women it entails placing a premium on assessing the relational or interpersonal implications of any decision. A number of studies have discovered that female pastors tend to avoid making authoritative pronouncements based on their clerical status, instead opting for dialogue. They tend to downplay hierarchy in favor of democracy, and in so doing they place a premium on achieving consensus and emphasizing the relational character of decision making. Thus, their congregations tend to be more democratic, and the laity often feels that it has been empowered (Nason-Clark 1987b; Ice 1987; Lehman 1993; Lummis 1994).

How have women fared in denominations that have resisted calls for female ordination? In the case of Roman Catholicism, the Church hierarchy faces a dilemma insofar as a serious shortage of priests exists, and in efforts to replenish the supply they are not permitted to attempt to attract women into the priesthood (Hoge 1987). As post–Vatican II Catholics in the United States are less inclined to encourage their sons to enter the priesthood, the Church has been forced to confront this as an enduring rather than a temporary problem. It has led to an awareness of the need to use nuns and the laity in functions that in the past were the sole preserve of priests. Changes in canon law have made possible a new role for women in public ministry. Given these circumstances, women (and nonordained men) have begun to perform such duties as lectors, altar servers, and Eucharistic ministers. This has generated a certain amount of controversy within the Roman Catholic community. Ruth Wallace (1992, 1993) has studied this phenomenon and discovered that the laity is increasingly comfortable with women serving in a pastoral role. Nevertheless, the hierarchy remains intractably opposed to innovating either with respect to women priests or a relaxation of the celibacy requirement for men who enter the priesthood. This was reaffirmed explicitly in the exhortation *Sacramentum caritatis* of Pope Benedict XVI in February 2007.

Southern Baptists, a denomination in which laity and local churches have a much stronger voice, have also moved to tighten their ministerial definitions. As part of a larger internal power struggle in which the conservative wing has succeeded in gaining control of the Southern Baptist Convention, this denomination has taken a more oppositional position to female ordination in recent years. The result is that tensions within this large body have intensified, and the appropriate role of women in the ministry is one of the most divisive issues in this conflict. In short, a reaffirmation of patriarchal leadership has meant that women have had a difficult time combating entrenched male hegemony in the denomination (Ammerman 1990). Some commentators have also suggested that this aggressive campaign against ordination on the part of conservatives may well signal an impending schism in which moderates decide to leave a denomination no longer responsive to their opinions—something that may already have happened in everything but name.

Turning to lay congregational roles, there is a long history in all denominations of women performing a variety of key jobs, including those associated with church school classes, altar guilds, and the preparation of meals for functions ranging from weddings to funerals. In short, women performed the duties associated with the domestic sphere within the life of the congregational "family." Many of these tasks were linked to an institutional substructure within congregations composed of women's guilds and circles. Within these groups women were in a position to exert varied levels of influence on the larger life of the congregation. It is unfortunate that this "women's work" has been largely an understudied phenomenon.

Research on churches in the United States needs to be directed toward the life-worlds of the "church women" of Methodist, Lutheran, Baptist, UCC, Episcopal, and other mainline denominations. What is far too often overlooked is the extent to which these groups were a crucial mainstay of Protestant church life. Yet to date, relatively little such research has been undertaken. Why is this the case? A major part of the answer rests with the fact that until the 1970s men largely taught "official" religion to men in the seminaries. Since men held the key official positions in the churches, this meant that the glue that held congregations together and made them function was presumed to originate from the men in power. In other words, the unofficial component of religious life—precisely the arena where women operated—was largely ignored. Ironically, feminist research has not yet remedied this situation. This is due in no small part to the fact that feminists have tended to focus either on exploitation or on innovation rather than on routine practice. As a result, we tend to lack as clear an understanding as we might of the role of women in creating and maintaining the Protestant presence in the United States.

What is fairly clear is that historically men have dominated the most powerful lay positions in congregations, such as membership on church councils and on important congregational committees. In some instances this was because of de jure denominational policies, but in most cases it was a de facto instance of gender segregation. This situation has changed in significant ways in mainline Protestant denominations and in the Roman Catholic Church as women have begun to assume lay leadership roles to an extent hitherto unknown (see R. Wallace 1992). In some instances, the church hierarchy has encouraged this change, sometimes by formulating explicit policies aimed at promoting gender equity. In other instances, the impetus has come from the congregational grassroots.

At the same time, if one wishes to assess the differences in mainline Protestantism from the 1950s to the present, the differences in the composition and activities of women's groups in the local churches become immediately apparent when one looks at congregational life as lived experience. The 1950s-style daytime women's group populated mainly by homemakers whose children were in school is virtually unknown today. Although there have undoubtedly always been women's groups of older women, these have now come to predominate. The character of such younger women's groups as remain has also changed; programs have shifted from church rummage sales and suppers to more substantive issues—though what these issues are and how they are treated varies across the liberal/conservative spectrum.

The picture in fundamentalist denominations differs from these changes as they attempt to find ways of reaffirming what they perceive to be a God-ordained gendered division of labor. These churches have not been as immune from societal changes as this might suggest, however, and there is impressionistic evidence to suggest that even here, moves have been made to permit women to assume at least some leadership roles in areas that were once all-male preserves. Pentecostal and Holiness churches, which, unlike the larger fundamentalist bodies, have long ordained women, also afford women influential lay leadership roles, and indeed have done so for a longer time than mainline Protestant denominations (Poloma 1989). Similarly, Hans Baer (1993) has shown that in the African-American Spiritualist churches the female laity has a considerable amount of power and influence.

Culture Wars: Gender, Religion, and Family Values

Contemporary cultural conflicts have proved to be extraordinarily divisive, leading sociologist James Davison Hunter (1991) to characterize them as "culture wars." Given the fact that proponents on either side of the most contested cultural issues tend to defend their stances in absolutist terms, the concern of some observers is that there is little if any room for dialogue. This has led to intransigence and to an escalation of conflict that Hunter finds disturbing because he fears it poses a threat to democracy. He explains his concern in the following passage:

> Can democratic practice today mediate differences as deep as these in a manner that is in keeping with the ideals set forth in the founding documents of the American republic? Or will one side, through the tactics of power politics, simply impose its vision on all others? The question is not an idle one—for the simple reason that cultural conflict is inherently antidemocratic. It is antidemocratic first because the weapons of such warfare are reality definitions that presuppose from the outset the illegitimacy of the opposition and its claims. Sometimes this antidemocratic impulse is conscious and deliberate. This is seen when claims are posited as fundamental rights that *transcend* democratic process. The right to have an abortion and the right to life, for example, are both put forward as rights that transcend deliberation. Similarly, opposing claims are made on behalf of gay rights, women's rights, the rights of the terminally ill, and so on. (1994: 3)

Contrary to Hunter, it is not true that cultural conflict is itself antithetical to democracy. In fact, democratic regimes assume a plurality of interests. The reality is more complicated than the stark bipolar portrait of warring sides suggests, inasmuch as an underlying commitment to tolerance is crucial to democratic practice (Walzer 1997). For one thing, only a minority of the population aligns itself with either polar position. That being said, the abortion issue is perhaps the most contested one in the current culture wars.

ABORTION AND THE POLITICS OF THE BODY

Abortions in the United States were generally outlawed until the landmark 1973 *Roe v. Wade* Supreme Court decision, which granted a woman the right to decide whether she would have an abortion, but limited that right to the first two trimesters of a pregnancy. The assumption was that abortions were inappropriate once the pregnancy had moved to a stage where it was possible that the fetus might be viable outside the womb. This decision was hailed as a major triumph by the women's movement, which had articulated as one of its centerpieces the idea that women have a right to control their own bodies, and this includes making decisions about reproduction. In the same instance, abortion opponents decried the decision. This was a defining moment for them insofar as it marked the beginning of their mobilization to reverse the Supreme Court's decision and to rally public sentiment to their cause. Abortion opponents understand a human life to exist from the "moment of conception," when egg and sperm join, hence fertilization occurs. For conservative Christians in particular, this concern is also bound up with doctrine of the conception of Jesus Christ in the womb of Mary by divine intervention.

In her participant-observation study of women activists in pro-choice and pro-life groups, Kristin Luker (1984) discovered that in key respects their backgrounds and their life-worlds differed appreciably. Moreover, those differences contributed to a situation in which they viewed and talked about abortion in dramatically different ways. Pro-choice activists tended to have higher socioeconomic backgrounds and higher levels of educational attainment than their anti-abortion counterparts. They had the educational credentials to pursue professional careers and had the desire to do so. Thus, from their distinctive social location, it was important to be able to maintain reproductive control in order both to work outside the home and to rear a family. Abortion, like readily available modes of contraception, was seen as essential in making this control possible.

Pro-life activists, Luker found, were less prepared economically and educationally to pursue professional jobs and instead defined themselves primarily in terms of their roles as mothers. They were heavily invested in the idea that self-fulfillment and meaning in their lives were linked to motherhood. Not only were they opposed to abortion, but also many were opposed to, or had serious reservations about, birth control. Luker argued that these two groups lived in such different moral communities that it was hard to imagine how they could engage in real dialogue.

This was reflected in different discursive practices. Thus, those who defined themselves as pro-choice tended to define their opponents not as pro-life, but as anti-abortion, and those who defined themselves as pro-life were not averse to accusing their opponents of being murderers. Even when speaking about pregnancies, the two language communities differed. Pro-choice advocates would speak about "unwanted" pregnancies, a phrase that Luker did not hear among the members of the pro-life group, who instead called such pregnancies "unplanned." Her conclusion lends credence to Hunter's concern that the conflict between camps is such that dialogue appears extremely difficult, if not impossible. What is clear is that differences in class, status, and lifestyles have a profound impact on one's views about abortion.

What makes Hunter's pessimism less convincing is the fact that a substantial majority of people see themselves somewhere between these two camps. Relatively few Americans are prepared to suggest that we ought to prohibit abortions in any and all circumstances, something that would appear warranted if abortion amounts to murder. At the same time, they exhibit discomfort with the idea of abortion on demand and with abortion being used as a form of birth control. Nevertheless, a majority of Americans support abortion rights, though with varying degrees of enthusiasm and with varied kinds of provisos being added. In other words, while activists seek to polarize the debate, those in the middle view abortion as a far more complex and ambiguous issue.

The responses of the Christian denominations to this debate to large extent parallel the ordination debate. Fundamentalist churches have found an ally in the battle against abortion in Roman Catholicism—and given fundamentalists' legacy of anti-Catholicism, this is a fascinating irony! These denominations are on record in opposition to abortion, and in fact the rank-and-file activists in the antiabortion movement tend to be firmly rooted in one of these religious traditions. Thus, in a long and protracted battle over whether a midwestern city of three hundred thousand that did not offer any abortion services at its hospitals would become home to a Planned Parenthood clinic, the community-based coalition opposed to this plan was rooted in a number of local fundamentalist churches and Catholic parishes. It should be noted that while not all members of these denominations oppose abortion rights, higher levels do than one finds among mainline Protestants and the nonreligious (Gallup and Castelli 1989).

For their part, mainline Protestants have generally been supportive of abortion rights, but their denominational statements have stressed that whether a woman opts to have an abortion involves a grave ethical decision. Considering it a good thing to reduce those situations where people feel compelled to seek out abortions (for example, in cases of unmarried teenagers, the very poor, and those living in psychologically stressful circumstances), they have at the same time affirmed the right to do so if it is warranted. What distinguishes the mainline stance is that it reflects a willingness to view this decision as one that needs to be made by the individual involved. Since an individual's conscience is the final arbiter, this means that within these churches one can expect to find considerable diversity about the issue. In other words, official denominational statements are designed to promote tolerance and a diversity of opinions. This general way of framing the debate—which is also, it should be noted, a position embraced by a majority of the U.S. public—is a reflection of the modernist character of these denominations, in contrast to the traditionalism of fundamentalists and Catholics. Often overlooked from this social history of religions standpoint is the extent to which this coalescence of Roman Catholics and conservative Protestants represents a dramatic reversal of relatively antagonistic relationships between these two bodies that persisted into the 1950s, with each excluding the other from any possibility of being genuinely Christian. The "family values" alliance that today unites these two groups represents one of the most remarkable changes in American religious behavior in the nation's history.

FAMILY MATTERS

A different issue of contention in American society during the past three decades concerns the changing American family and, related to this, the changing role of women in society. Anthony Giddens captures this situation well when he writes:

> The family is a site for the struggles between tradition and modernity, but is also a metaphor for them. There is perhaps more nostalgia surrounding the lost haven of the family than for any other institution with its roots in the past. Politicians and activists routinely diagnose the breakdown of family life and call for a return to the traditional family. (1999: 53)

He goes on to point out that the traditional family was first and foremost an economic unit in which the inequality between men and women was an intrinsic part. Not only were women lacking fundamental social rights, but so were

Historically the separation of the sexes for worship, reflected here in a recent Hindu ceremony in the United States, has been the norm among religions. Changes began primarily among liberal Protestant groups in the United States in the mid-1800s. In much of the world outside the West, however, the practice of separation remains the norm, even among Christian groups. Photographs courtesy of Nirmala Salgado.

children. Finally, he notes that except for courtly elites, sexuality in the traditional family was intrinsically linked to reproduction.

In particular, the rising divorce rate and the rapid entry of women into the workforce signaled significant changes to the nuclear family, or, more appropriately, to an idealized version of the nuclear family, consisting of two parents and a small number of children (Coontz 1992). Regarding marital dissolution as a reflection of the growing individualism of American culture, the divorce rate grew steadily throughout the twentieth century. By 1980, it was five times higher than it had been in 1900. With the advent of no-fault divorce laws in the early 1970s, initially in California and then expanding to include many other states, people in unhappy marriages could exit them far more readily than in the past and without the stigma attached to such a decision.

Liberals tended to support this development, stressing that the happiness and well-being of marital partners was of primary importance. If one or both parties to a marriage were no longer happy in their relationship, the argument went, there was no good reason for the marriage to continue. In response, conservatives argued that marriages ought not to be dissolved easily and disagreed with the individualistic character of the liberal position. Thus, marital dissolution was perceived to be a reflection of the erosion of traditional values. In short, the family became one of the major battlegrounds in the culture wars. Connected to this were questions associated with the character of families. Liberals stressed the importance of an egalitarian form of decision making in which both adult partners occupied an equal footing. This was most forcefully articulated among feminists, who called for the end of the patriarchal family and the emergence of a democratic one. Conservatives, on the other hand, stressed the importance of tradition and argued—often using religious arguments—that there were innate differences between men and women and these differences ought to be reflected in a division of labor and authority in families where men were viewed as the "head of the household."

Although in part a separate issue, clearly women's work outside the home represents challenges to the family as well as calling attention to changes in the public sphere. Again, this change served as a source of considerable tension and conflict. First published in the early 1960s, Betty Friedan's *The Feminine Mystique* (1997) constituted a manifesto of sorts for homemakers, especially those with college educations, who found their lives in the domestic sphere of the mid-twentieth-century United States to be stultifying and unrewarding. Despite the hyperbolic language at times (for example, describing the suburban home as a concentration camp), the main message of the book was clear: Rather than simply entering the workforce because of economic necessity, women wanted to do so because it was in the world of white-collar professional careers that women could best develop their potential and find meaning and purpose in their lives.

An irony involved in this claim is that it was advanced at approximately the same time that social scientists and social critics such as William H. Whyte (1956) and C. Wright Mills (1951) were writing influential books that depicted work in corporate America as the realization of Weber's nightmare of the bureaucratic "iron cage" come to life. This was depicted as the era of the gray flannel suit, where yes-men gave up their individuality for the sake of the organization. Whether feminists tended to idealize the world of nondomestic work, or whether these critics were overly harsh in their indictments of the same world, need not concern us here. The point from the feminist perspective is that women wanted to have available to them the same opportunities as men. Interestingly, it was only at a somewhat later phase of the women's movement that the reverse became a real issue, as calls were made for men to begin to assume an equal share of domestic responsibilities.

For their part, conservatives were prepared to depict the entry of women into the workforce as an assault on the integrity of the family and on the traditional gender division of labor wherein women's sphere was the domestic or private, while men were to assume their proper roles in the public realm. The conservative countermovement to feminism placed particular blame for the presumed decline of the family—the rise in divorce, youth problems such as those revolving around sex and drugs, and associated issues—on the decision of many women to enter the world of paid work. Career women, particularly those with young children, were often depicted as selfish individuals who put their own desires above the needs of their families.

Unlike their failure to cut off legal access to abortion, conservatives succeeded in stopping the passage of the Equal Rights Amendment (ERA) in the 1970s. Their opposition to the amendment was predicated on the fear that it would lead to a culture in which sharply demarcated male and female roles disappeared. This was seen as a clear and present threat to traditional authority patterns. It was, of course—and that is precisely why the women's movement was so intent on passing the ERA: It was viewed as an important legislative remedy to a patriarchal society.

The reality is that most women work outside the home. No longer is the stay-at-home mother the norm. Often women leave the workforce when their children are very young (as do, to a considerably lesser extent, fathers) but reenter it when the children reach school age. Women in fundamentalist churches, particularly if they are college-educated and live in comfortable middle-class communities, are increasingly inclined to work outside the home, though to a lesser extent than their liberal counterparts. Thus, the idea of the preservation of the private and public spheres as gendered ones in which women remained in the former while men occupied the latter has increasingly broken down throughout society.

As a result, American society as a whole has become considerably more tolerant of diverse family arrangements. Thus, people who do not marry—individuals who in the past were seen as having a character defect that prevented them from entering into marriage, which was seen as a natural stage of the life cycle—are not scorned as spinsters and bachelors. Likewise, childless couples are accepted as valid partnerships, as children are not an essential element in a couple's decision to marry. In addition, single-parent families are seen as legitimate. It is important to realize that while these arrangements still may be frowned upon in some quarters, their level of acceptance today contrasts markedly with what it was as little as a half-century ago. Today, for example, we see the Episcopal Church considering liturgical formularies for publicly acknowledging (hence blessing) committed unions that are nonmarital. One might suggest that the main beneficiaries of this new tolerance are women, who have more rights and opportunities than they had in the past.

Not surprisingly, one of the concerns voiced by those most uncomfortable with these changes involves the role of the male in the family today. Some conservatives believe that men have lost their sense of who they are and what their appropriate role in the family ought to be. This sentiment is vividly expressed in the group known as Promise Keepers, founded by Bill McCartney, the former head football coach at the University of Colorado. He contended that he had allowed his career ambitions to overshadow his responsibilities to his family and his God, but as a result of a conversion experience, he became convinced of the imperative to reassert himself as the head of his household (McCartney 1997). Initially a loose organization that planned gatherings of committed men in football stadiums and similar kinds of venues, Promise Keepers grew dramatically from an essentially all-volunteer organization to one with a paid staff and formal organizational structure. These rallies amounted to an amalgamation of religious revival and male bonding experience. Embraces, tears, and the like were evidence of the highly charged emotional character of these events, and they conveyed a message than men needed to express their feelings—including the fact that real men can cry (Brickner 1999; Claussen 2000; R. H. Williams 2001).

If it were simply a matter of irresponsible men "getting their act together," Promise Keepers would not have been controversial. But there was another message that disturbed liberal critics, leading them to conclude that Promise Keepers was a profoundly reactionary countermovement attempting to undo the gains women had achieved in the wake of the contemporary women's movement. Central to its traditionalist premises, Promise Keepers placed the blame for the presumed decline of the family on the modern emphasis on egalitarian households. If men were to be blamed for the abrogation of their God-given familial authority, women too could be faulted for their willingness to assume the mantle of headship or coheadship of families. Moreover, if men were actually to assume their rightful roles as the heads of households, women had to be prepared to return to a role of subservience to their husbands.

The men of Promise Keepers were heterosexuals drawn largely from fundamentalist Protestant or conservative Catholic backgrounds. A reflection of the location of this organization on the Religious Right is its antipathy toward homosexuals. Indeed, for them homosexuality is something of a talisman, reflecting all that has gone wrong in our society as a result of moral failures of men to understand and embrace the role God has planned for them. In this regard, the group is but an example of a general conservative reaction to gays and lesbians in American society at a time when society at large has become more tolerant of homosexuals.

GAYS, LESBIANS, AND RELIGION

Janet Folger was for years an activist in the antiabortion movement, but she shifted her focus in recent years to address what she concluded was an equally disturbing fact of contemporary life: the increasing acceptance of what religious conservatives refer to as the "homosexual lifestyle." Her "Truth and Love Campaign" saw the gay rights movement as an affront to Christianity. The open expression of homosexuality, its increased visibility in movies and on television, and the willingness of local governments to enact gay rights ordinances amounted, in her view, to "a slap in the face of tens of millions of Christians" (see E. Freud 2000).

This stance was echoed in conservative Mississippi senator Trent Lott's expressed hostility toward federal legislation designed to grant to gays and lesbians the same civil rights protections guaranteed to people on the basis of race. His argument was simple and straightforward: Unlike racial minorities, who cannot choose their status, homosexuals have in fact made a lifestyle choice. Thus, he wanted to be on record that while he supports civil rights on the basis of race and gender, he does not support similar rights on the basis of sexual preference (E. Freud 2000). This contrast reflects the typical understanding of homosexuality on the part of the Religious Right.

The most virulent manifestations of antihomosexual religiosity can be seen in the case of some fringe fundamentalist groups that actively confront gays and lesbians with a message that they are doomed to hell. They were evident at the funeral of Episcopalian Matthew Shepard, a young man brutally murdered in Wyoming by two other young men who attacked him after they discovered he was gay. Attracting international attention, Shepard's funeral was attended by many who did not know him personally, but who wanted to make a statement against homophobic hate. They were met by a contingent of fundamentalists led by the Reverend Fred Phelps, pastor of the Westboro Baptist Church of Topeka, Kansas—formally identified by the Southern Poverty Law Center and others as a "hate group"—outside the church carrying banners and signs condemning Shepard to hell and claiming that his death was God's judgment on his immoral lifestyle. More recently, Phelps's group has picketed the burials of slain veterans of the Iraq war, regardless of their own sexual preference, on the basis that American military fatalities in this conflict are a sign of God's judgment against the United States for its tolerance of homosexuality.

While most conservative Christian groups disavow such aggressive and ugly tactics, they nonetheless agree with the idea that homosexuality is an affront to Christianity. The selective citation of biblical passages is usually employed as a way of indicating that to be a Christian means to disavow homosexuality. This is in no small part a reflection of the emphasis among the Religious Right on the notion of conversion—being *born again.* Although there is considerable evidence that people do not choose to become homosexual—either because there is a genetic predisposition to same-sex preferences or it is the result of childhood socialization—the conservative response to homosexuality is to ask gays to repent and change their ways, or, in current parlance, their lifestyle. Acting on this position, they have created networks of Christian counselors who work to free homosexuals from the bondage of their sin, transforming them into healthy and happy heterosexuals prepared for marriage and children. The most prominent of these networks is Exodus International.

The significance of the homosexual issue for fundamentalists should not be underestimated. It has emerged as one of the core thematic issues of the Religious Right. An indication of how powerful a topic it is can be seen in the 2000 presidential campaign. Republican George W. Bush, who portrayed himself as something of a fundamentalist but who also said he is committed to tolerance and inclusion, walked a fine line between reaching out to marginalized groups and wholeheartedly embracing the fundamentalist view. Since the Christian Right has been crucial for Republican success since the election of Ronald Reagan, candidates have reached out to its members. At the same time, concerned that their views have put off more moderate Republicans, Bush's talk about inclusion was designed to appeal to this segment of the electorate. The difficulty involved in pleasing both camps was evident when a gay group called the Log Cabin Republicans sought an audience with him. Although his father had met with the group when he ran for president, Bush decided that he would be ill-advised to do so because it might alienate him from fundamentalists.

Although Americans are deeply divided over the matter of gay and lesbian rights—seen most vividly in recent years in the debates in virtually all states over whether to accord to homosexual couples, through "civil unions," legal rights comparable to those of married heterosexuals—it is clear that tolerance has grown during the last three decades. While many remain opposed to gay marriages, they are less opposed to such notions as the right of gay couples in committed long-term relationships to such things as access to the health and pension plans of their partners. Canada, by contrast, adopted same-sex marriage in 2005. Although the issue was certainly debated there, the decision seems now to have received general acceptance as the law of the land.

Within the mainline churches, the laity and clergy are much divided over homosexuality. Some share opinions not much different from their fundamentalist counterparts, while in other instances congregations actively support gays and lesbians. An example of the latter is the Lutheran parish in the Chicago suburb of Oak Park, where Penny Edgell Becker (1997) conducted an ethnographic study. The parish had been a dying congregation in an older community, but in recent years it has been revitalized in part by reaching out to members of racial minorities and to gays and lesbians. Some have referred to churches like this one, which today exist in most urban centers, as "Gay 90s" churches: members are either gay or in their nineties. Many members of the mainline occupy a middle ground where they believe in tolerance, but not active endorsement of homosexuality (see Wellman 1999).

These divisions have been reflected over the issue of whether gays and lesbians ought to be ordained. This has proved to be a highly contentious issue in almost all the mainline denominations, where liberal leaders have either ordained or hired homosexual clergy in a challenge to both clergy and lay colleagues to accept committed gay/lesbian unions as consistent with the underlying principles

Vicki, Mario, Biology, and Sociology: The Genes Problem

The controversies that currently embroil the Episcopal Church as a result of the consecration of a man who is living in an openly gay relationship point not only to difficulties within a specific religious context, but also to a larger argument over whether or not homosexuality is inborn or learned: that is, whether homosexuality is a matter of choice or a matter of genetic programming.

V. Gene Robinson wishes to argue with regard to himself that his service as a bishop proves that "God thinks I'm *all right* [emphasis added]." The Reverend Mario Bergner, Ph.D., himself a priest of the Episcopal Church, is a former homosexual who considers himself to have been "healed by Jesus," and who now operates Redeemed Life Ministries, a Christian organization where he works with persons who wish to seek a way out of a homosexual lifestyle, into what he considers a Christian lifestyle. Redeemed Life Ministries uses traditional Christian practices of healing prayer, along with Dr. Bergner's academic training, to work with the homosexual to create a renewed identity. Each of the two approaches to people generally—one emphasizing acceptance, the other emphasizing change—has creditability within the Christian tradition. Dr. Bergner, however, also points out that the matter has multiple dimensions: "Homosexuality is not a singular, monolithic condition shared by all people with same-sex attraction. There are many factors in a person's life that will affect the course of healing." Professor Bergner also points out that the older a person becomes, the less likely he or she will amenable to treatment/healing, whether psychiatric or spiritual, in respect to his or her homosexuality/heterosexuality.

Returning to V. Gene Robinson, for example, we find that he was, from his birth in central Kentucky in 1947, "Vicki Gene" Robinson, after his mother and father, because they had expected a girl, who would have been "Vicki Imogene." (The Vicki is, ironically, for his *father*, whose middle name was Victor.) His birth was a difficult one, and it was initially expected that he would not live, which may perhaps explain the odd naming. Nevertheless, he did live, hence a sociologically significant question arises: *How many boys do you know named "Vicki"?* Sociologists recognize that names have social significance, as do other early childhood experiences. One cannot assess Robinson's whole developmental sequence from this one piece of information alone, of course. The point that we would make, however, is that a boy who has grown up named "Vicki" has grown up oddly, so much the more so in the society of 1950s America. In that sense, Vicki Gene Robinson has not been quite *all right* from the day he was born. The same could be said of a girl named Otto.

This brings us directly to the nature/nurture controversy: Was "Baby Robinson" born homosexual or was he immersed in a situation characterized by ambiguous gender expectations almost from the moment of his birth? This is important to assessing the biological and cultural elements of human development that make up the nature/nurture controversy—*and it is important to sociology*. People are not born into vacuums. They are born into families, and those families function within societies. Continuing to reflect something of the incongruity of his life from birth was the Bishop's announcement at a lecture at Florida's Nova Southeastern University in late November 2007 that he intended to enter into a legal union with his partner of twenty years in June 2008: "I always wanted to be a June bride." (See Adams 2006: 10, 282; Bergner 2004; Fournier 2007) of Christian marriage. To date, this position has been formally accepted only by the United Church of Christ, Unitarian Universalism, and Reform and Conservative Judaism, while it has been rejected or sidelined by the Lutheran, Methodist, Presbyterian, and Reformed churches.

A unique situation has occurred in the Episcopal Church, where a gay man in a committed relationship was elected and received the necessary consents from a sufficient number of bishops and jurisdictions within the U.S. church to be consecrated as Bishop of New Hampshire in the fall of 2003. Hence the Right Reverend V. Gene Robinson appears to be a fully authorized member of the U.S. church's hierarchy. Although the Episcopal Church has not officially accepted gay marriage as legitimate, some of its geographic subunits have created rites of union for "trial use." The Robinson consecration greatly hardened the position of the two sides of the debate within the worldwide Anglican Communion. Most of the churches of the African, Asian, and South American provinces have been among the most critical, with the Nigerian church setting up an alternative jurisdiction in the United States and the Ugandan church renouncing all aid from the American church. This position has further hardened with the 2006 election of a new occupant of the Episcopal Church's office of Presiding Bishop, who is not only a woman but who was also a participant in the Robinson consecration. This debate is likely to continue in some measure at least for the remainder of the present decade, and may well ultimately be settled in the United States through legal actions over church property in civil courts rather than within the church structure itself. By contrast, across the same period, the Roman Catholic Church has recently reinforced its position in opposition to homosexuality among the clergy to reach beyond the celibacy requirement that applies to all of its priests and instituted procedures designed specifically to exclude homosexual candidates from the ordination process.

Prayers for Lesbians and Gay Men, Their Families, and Friends

It is important to gays and lesbians that their sexual identity be affirmed in their worship, as this prayer illustrates:

> For the quarter of a million homosexuals murdered in Nazi concentration camps and those who remained imprisoned despite the Allied victory, and now live in history's closet: *We pray, O God, for those who died in closets.* For millions of lesbians and gay men in other countries in which there are no support systems or groups, in which revelation leads to imprisonment, castration, or death: *We pray, O God, for those who fear in closets.* For priests, nuns and ministers and lay church leaders who, to serve the church, cannot come out, while bringing liberation to others who are oppressed: *We pray, O God, for those who liberate from closets.* (Emphasis in the original.)

Source: Chris Glaser, *Coming Out to God: Prayers for Lesbians and Gay Men, Their Families and Friends* (Louisville, Ky: Westminster/John Knox, 1991), 86–87.

More than two decades ago, some gays concluded, by contrast, that rather than struggle to gain a place in these denominations, it would be easier simply to create their own denomination, as they have done in the form of the Metropolitan Community Church. This raises a larger question, not only for gays and lesbians, but also for heterosexual women, about whether existing religious institutions have been shaped so profoundly by patriarchal views that include mandatory heterosexuality that it would be wise to abandon these institutions and instead create a new institutional structure in which a new gendered form of spirituality might manifest itself. In some measure, the problems within the Episcopal Church confirm this view, but on the other hand they enable a more open confrontation of these issues among a wider public.

Images of God and Gendered Spirituality

Feminists have raised questions about the impact of the masculine concept of God characteristic of the Abrahamic religions: Judaism, Christianity, and Islam—so called because each of these major world faiths draws its lineage from the biblical account of Abraham, the man who God in the biblical book of Genesis states would become "the father [patriarch] of many nations." Some have argued that the patriarchal character of traditional religious practice is not simply a reflection of the influence of external societal mores and values, but is rather inextricably tied up with core religious beliefs. Thus the radical feminist theologian Mary Daly has argued that the image of God as an all-knowing and all-powerful male encourages the view of women as unequal to men. She contends, "A woman's asking for equality in the church would be comparable to a black person's demanding equality in the Ku Klux Klan" (Daly 1968: 6).

One response of women sympathetic to this line of argument is involvement with a countercultural social movement that has attempted to construct distinctly women-centered forms of spirituality. The underlying purpose of these endeavors is to create a system of beliefs, symbols, and rituals that are designed to challenge the religious subordination of women in Christianity. The women's spirituality movement tends to be neopagan in a New Age modality. That is to say, there is a focus on nature and with it on divine images of goddesses. The Wiccan movement is intended to be subversive insofar as it takes the witch, which is condemned in the dominant religious culture, and elevates it to a privileged position (Neitz 1990, 2000). According to Helen Berger (1999), the attraction of the Wiccan movement, a topic we take up in greater detail in chapter 11, is due to its capacity to empower. She writes:

> Wiccan rituals are designed to increase women's sense of power and to help them recognize their own will. As Witchcraft is an anti-authoritarian religion that celebrates the lack of a central authority that determines orthodoxy, there is no one set of beliefs or practices about appropriate gender roles within this religion. (1999: 37; see Berger and Ezzy 2007)

Janet Jacobs (1990) has studied a related inversion of cultural stereotypes in the roles of midwives and healers—discredited roles in male-dominated medicine—by the movement. While the research on the various groups that make up the movement has been relatively limited to date, one thing is clear: There is an eclectic, fluid, and highly improvised character to them (see Griffin 2000).

In stark contrast to this rejection of traditional religion, elements of the conservative countermovement attempt to shore up traditional images of God. While feminists understand why this might be attractive to males, they find it more difficult to comprehend why women would also be attracted to the idea of God the Father. Yet for women who find the modern world to be an alienating and bewildering place, tradition—always redefined to meet the needs of the present—is seen as a potential source of comfort. The image of an authoritative and omniscient God offers solace for those who see modernity as the scourge of certainty and stability (Beyer 1994; Davidman 1991).

Between those who reject and those who embrace traditional images of God are members of the Judeo-Christian mainline who take seriously the feminist critique but are not prepared to abandon their tradition outright (Ruether 1985). Here one finds evidence of a significant transformation in the image of God that can be described as the feminization of the deity. The God of the Hebrew Bible has receded into the background, if not entirely disappeared. No longer is the emphasis on a wrathful or punitive God. In its place is a loving God, a caring God, and a nurturing God. Rather than an emphasis on a God looking at us judgmentally, there is instead an emphasis on a God walking with people on their spiritual journeys. In short, God has given up many culturally defined masculine attributes, while simultaneously acquiring feminine attributes.

This shift manifests itself in various ways. Sometimes liturgies are revised to downplay the idea of God as male. Sometimes this is by invoking God as "Her." Other times, it simply involves dropping gendered pronouns wherever possible. In the Catholic tradition, the role of Mary has historically served as something of an antidote to the masculine imagery of God, but Mary is not herself a god, so some critics could claim that her role serves implicitly to reinforce notions of gender inequality. The problem for Christians is not only that Jesus was a male, but that he referred to God as his Father as well. Garry Wills (1998), a devout Catholic who is also a critic of the Church hierarchy, has called for a devaluation of the cult of Mary and in its place an appreciation of the feminine characteristic of the third element of the Trinity, the "Holy Spirit" (a title that is grammatically feminine in the original Greek). What all of this suggests is that within the mainline denominations, there is currently considerable exploration of the imagery of God. Where precisely these explorations will lead is at the moment unclear.

Suggestions for Further Reading

Elizabeth Adams. 2006. *Going to Heaven: The Life and Election of Bishop Gene Robinson.* Brooklyn, N.Y.: Soft Skull Press.

Helen A. Berger and Douglas Ezzy. 2007. *Teenage Witches: Magical Youth and the Search for the Self.* New Brunswick, N.J.: Rutgers University Press.

Mark Chaves. 1997. *Ordaining Women: Culture and Conflict in Religious Organizations.* Cambridge, Mass.: Harvard University Press.

Lynn Davidman. 1991. *Tradition in a Rootless World: Women Turn to Orthodox Judaism.* Berkeley: University of California Press.

Carol Gilligan. 1982. *In a Different Voice.* Cambridge, Mass.: Harvard University Press.

Nancy Nason-Clark and Mary Jo Neitz, eds. 2001. *Feminist Narratives and the Sociology of Religion.* Lanham, Md.: AltaMira.

Mary Jo Neitz. 1990. "In Goddess We Trust." In *In Gods We Trust: New Patterns of Religious Pluralism in America*, 2nd ed., ed. Tom Robbins and Dick Anthony (pp. 353–71). New Brunswick, N.J.: Transaction.

Paula Nesbitt. 1997. *Feminization of the Clergy in America.* New York: Oxford University Press.

Martin Riesebrodt. 1993. *Pious Passion: The Emergence of Modern Fundamentalism in the United States and Iran.* Berkeley: University of California Press.

Rhys Williams. 2001. *Promise Keepers and the New Masculinity: Private Lives and Public Morality.* Lanham, Md.: Lexington Books.

Barbara Brown Zikmund, Adair T. Lummis, and Patricia M. Y. Chang. 1998. *Clergy Women: An Uphill Calling.* Louisville, Ky.: Westminster John Knox.

PART THREE

RELIGION, CULTURE, AND CHANGE

Alamy A8W4R3

CHAPTER 8

Religious Change

THE CASE OF CATHOLICISM IN THE UNITED STATES

A curious student of the sacred would probably not elect to seek enlightenment about religion from a cultural figure like Lenny Bruce, the wildly profane comedian whose popularity in the habitats of "hip" extended through the 1950s and the early 1960s. Yet Bruce, a secular Jew who professed admiration for Jesus Christ and the pope, was sociologically insightful when he admitted that "The only *the* religion, actually, is Catholicism."

Part of the reason for this judgment rested on the comic's sense of the ubiquity of Roman Catholic institutions on the American landscape. "There's more [Catholic] churches and people that work for the church than I think there are courthouses and judges," Bruce once guessed (1970: 40–41). His analogy betrays a keen feeling for the complexities of a huge organization that is consecrated to one central purpose but at the same time is widely scattered and composed of all sorts of people.

Church with a Capital C

In fact, the Roman Catholic Church is the largest single religious body in the United States, counting approximately 70 million people as members. Its presence, though especially obvious in regions like New England and the Middle Atlantic states, is visible in most parts of the country. Roughly forty-three thousand Catholic clergy serve about twenty-three thousand congregations in 195 dioceses, an administrative structure that is spread across every state of the Union. In addition, the Catholic Church in the United States operates nearly 600 hospitals, more than 230 colleges and universities, and almost 200 seminaries—not to mention more than 1,300 secondary schools and about five times that number of elementary schools. Through infant baptisms alone, Catholics now add close to a million new members in the United States each year (*Official Catholic Directory* 2005: 2049). From ethnic parishes that anchor neighborhoods in the most densely populated cities to tiny mission outposts in rural hamlets, the Catholic Church today is very much a fact of American life.

But it was not always so. To be sure, the Roman Catholic Church has maintained a foothold on the North American continent for centuries, since the explorations and conquests sponsored by the Catholic monarchs of Spain and France. However, at the time of U.S. independence, Catholics in the thirteen original colonies were extremely small in number and nearly invisible socially. Not until more than fifty years later did the population of Catholics in the United States swell with large-scale immigration from Ireland and Germany and by the acquisition of vast territories in the West through purchase or annexation.

Resistance to this incorporation, and to later phases of immigration from southern and eastern Europe, was fierce. Hence the history of anti-Catholicism in the United States is long and ugly. Yet the animus of nativists and religious bigots ultimately did not prevent the Catholic Church from expanding rapidly, or its faithful from attaining a degree of material comfort and social acceptance that established them as a twentieth-century success story, a model of "extraordinary economic and social progress" (Greeley 1979b: 94).

The voluminous writing of the priest-sociologist Andrew M. Greeley on the subject across fifty years (see, for example, Greeley 1963: 11–15, 1976b, 1977: 50–68, 1979b: 92–95) clearly demonstrates how far Catholics as a group have advanced in the 150 years since they became a sizable presence in American society. One hundred years ago, to take but a single example, Catholics were the least likely of members of major Christian denominations to have attended a college or university. However, the difference in higher education between Catholics and the national average closed by the outbreak of World War II, and innovations like the benefits for schooling that the G.I. Bill supplied to veterans led to broad postwar educational mobility. More recent statistics confirm that Catholics are now better educated than persons who follow any other major religious tradition except Judaism (Greeley 1977: 40, 54).

An alternative index of social mobility by Catholics is their inclusion in directories of the U.S. elite. Of the more than 16,000 prominent citizens who listed their religious affiliations in the 1930–1931 volume of *Who's Who in America*, only 740 (or 4.5 percent) were Roman Catholics. Within that total, Catholics were better represented in political circles (6.7 percent), but they were noticeably sparse among those who could be identified as elite intellectuals (2.9 percent) (Davidson 1994: 425, 431–34). With the publication of the 1992–1993 edition of *Who's Who*, Catholics accounted overall for 23 percent of the entries—a fivefold increase, but still a small underrepresentation compared to their proportion of the U.S. population and, more specifically, of church members in the United States. And even in the 1990s, Catholics were suspiciously missing from the ranks of "cultural" elites (Davidson, Pyle, and Reyes 1995: 164–69; see also Davidson and Pyle 2005, Pyle and Koch 2001).

Change: From Breeze to Tornado

Many people—not excluding Catholics themselves—think that the Catholic Church is unitary in addition to universal, monolithic as well as monumental, and immutable as much as it is inimitable. Nothing could be farther from the truth. Given the profound depth and the sweeping scope of the changes that have characterized Catholic life in the United States since before the nation's founding to the present, it makes sense to pay closer attention to the details of those shifts: changes in the exercise and reception of religious authority, in the cultivation of devotional practices, and in reforms in the structures of governance (especially in the wake of scandals caused by the misconduct of some clergymen and their superiors in the Church). Changes, too, have marked the absorption of new members, recruitment of professional personnel, and the raising of funds. This scrutiny in turn may yield clues about the nature and course of religious change in American society.

The Catholic Church has sustained a number of rather forceful shocks to its systems of tradition, particularly in the half century since the 1950s. These include (but are not confined to) the reforms of the Second Vatican Council—popularly titled "Vatican II"—and the release of *Humanae vitae*, the 1968 papal encyclical that condemned the use of "artificial" contraception by married Catholics.

When Pope John XXIII convened the Second Vatican Council in 1962, he explained that his intention was to throw open a window and permit a refreshing breeze to enter the stuffy confines of a venerable but ages-old institution. However, as Andrew M. Greeley and Mary Greeley Durkin have remarked, "In the United States, the papal breeze turned into a tornado" (1984b: 3). Using different imagery to the same effect, Dean R. Hoge (1986) spoke of an opening of "floodgates," producing a torrent of change in response to long-building pressures (see also Greeley 2004b; Hoge and Wenger 2003: 7–8; Wilde 2004: 576–81).

Commitment: Loyalty, but Not Obedience

What is amazing about the aftermath of these developments is how little they and the manifold social transformations since the 1960s have interfered with the loyalty of U.S. Catholics to their church and the faith that it guards. Catholics in the final decades of the twentieth century still believed in God (96 percent); still worshiped regularly at Mass (53 percent had done so in the previous seven days, 78 percent in the last month); and still claimed to be "certain" that God provides for the faithful a glorious life after death (70 percent). Conversions to the Catholic faith in aggregate nearly offset defections from the ranks of the Church in the United States (Gallup and Castelli 1987: 26–28; Greeley 1985: 51–53).

What is more, several specific aspects of religious devotion among Catholics have actually risen in frequency in recent decades. Data from the National Opinion Research Center (NORC) in Chicago reveal that half of those who attend Mass weekly receive Holy Communion; in the early 1960s only one in six did. In 1984, 62 percent of adult Catholics prayed each day, up from 52 percent in 1972. And also in 1984, 31 percent of Catholics reported that they had undergone at least one "intense religious experience," up from 25 percent in 1972

(Greeley 1977: 127, 1985: 50–51). In more recent decades (that is, between 1973 and 1998), belief among Catholics in the existence of an afterlife actually rose by 12 percent (Greeley and Hout 1999: 815–16). As the cataloger of these findings from various surveys, Greeley neatly summarized their import: "In a wide variety . . . of devotional, doctrinal, and behavioral matters since the end of the Vatican Council, there has been no change." Further, he noted that "in some matters, frequency of prayer and reception of Holy Communion for example, there has actually been an increase of reported religious devotion" (1985: 53).

But some of the conditions of religious life among U.S. Catholics definitely *have* changed in the years since the closing of Vatican II. An inventory of changes compiled by Richard P. McBrien, a well-known American Catholic theologian and writer, portrays the post–Vatican II Church as "marked by a weakening of its authority structure, . . . by a decrease in attendance at weekly Mass . . . , and especially by a precipitous drop-off in vocations to the ordained priesthood and religious life" (in Hoge 1987: vi). Each of these changes is deserving of further elaboration. In fact, if the survey analyses are correct, the first two developments are closely related.

Devotion: A Collapse of Authority

Amid the "religious revival" of the 1950s, 70 to 75 percent or more of adult Catholics in the United States attended Mass on a weekly basis (D'Antonio 1994: 383). Between 1963 and 1974, however, the percentage of Catholics in the United States who attended church weekly fell from 72 to 50—where, with only minor fluctuations, it has been lodged ever since. The bulk of the decline, data show, occurred in 1969 and thereafter. Also, the rate of weekly church attendance for U.S. Protestants in this interval did not vary greatly above or below 40 percent (Gallup and Castelli 1987: 26–28; Greeley 1976a: 11, 1977: 127, 1979a: 10, 1979b: 96–98, 1985: 55).

Why did church attendance drop for one group alone in the United States, and why did it drop so sharply? The most intensively tested explanation for the steep decline in religious practice among Catholics links the marked deterioration in habits of churchgoing after 1968 to two factors: a loss of confidence in the authority of Catholic leaders after the promulgation of the encyclical *Humanae vitae* in that year, and a liberalized position on sexual ethics that was simultaneously gaining currency among the laity (Greeley 1976a: 15).

In 1963, 70 percent of Catholics agreed that it is "certainly true that Jesus handed over leadership of his church to Peter and the popes." Ten years later, only 42 percent endorsed this statement (Greeley 1976a: 14, 1977: 128, 1985: 54). Also in that time, Catholic church attendance plummeted. Statistical analyses of these concurrent trends reveal that the second moved directly in response to the first—that is, as Catholics abandoned their commitment to the divine institution of papal authority, so they also decreased their church attendance.

In the 1960s, U.S. Catholics who felt a need for guidance in facing a new morality looked to the Church's *Magisterium* (or teaching authority) for some sign of assistance, for some words of advice on how to cope with rapidly changing social circumstances. What they received instead, various commentators contend, was merely repetition and chastisement. The disappointment for many was so acute, the disillusionment so bitter, that their usual religious practices were severely disrupted, sending church attendance—that most visible act of compliance with Church law—into an eight-year tailspin. "The decline in church attendance, in other words, began immediately after the birth control encyclical," according to Andrew Greeley, "and ended when Catholic readiness to accept the Church's teaching on birth control and premarital sex reached rock bottom" (1985: 56).

The decline in attendance at Mass has bottomed out, but it is clear that the Catholic Church's credibility as a teacher in the area of human sexuality has been badly damaged. It is far from clear, though, what the institutional church might do on its own to remedy the problem. For "Once authority itself is in question," note Greeley and Durkin, "it no longer has the ability to reestablish its power by asserting that it has the power. It merely makes itself look ridiculous" (1984b: xvi).

Today, only about 12 percent of Catholics accept the Church's ban on artificial contraception. Surprisingly, however, these are not the only people who are seated in the congregations on Sunday. Indeed, fully 80 percent of regular attenders at Mass nowadays dissent from the birth control teaching (Davidson et al. 1997: 47). They thus form a kind of "loyal opposition" in the pews (Castelli and Gremillion 1987: 45). In the words of Greeley, the opponents who nevertheless attend church loyally are "rejecting any claim by the Magisterium to have a monopoly on God" (Greeley 1985: 70).

The laity's reluctance to back the hierarchy on issues of sexual ethics is reflected with some strength among members of the clergy as well. In 1969, emerging from the immediate aftermath of the encyclical *Humanae vitae*, readers of a national survey could find that 3 percent of priests had become more conservative on the question of the permissibility of contraception, but nine times that fraction—or 27 percent—had shifted in reaction to a more liberal or tolerant position. Overall, the survey revealed that a minority (40 percent) of priests endorsed the official policy of the Catholic Church on birth control, and only 13 percent would deny absolution (that is, sacramental forgiveness of sins) to someone who confessed that he or she used contraception and refused to stop (NORC 1972: 101–15, 312). "We have here," claimed Greeley, "one more case of what happens to an obligation that is imposed by sheer authority at a time when the right of authority to impose obligations without supportive creditable justification is called into question" (1972b: 67).

Governance: Guiding the People of God

The first Roman Catholic diocese in the United States, the See of Baltimore, was established shortly after the red-hot embers of revolution had cooled in the bracing waters of freedom. In some ways more historic than this achievement for Catholics in the new republic was how the episcopal office was filled. Contrary to the present policy of appointment from Rome, the Vatican permitted priests in the fledgling country to meet in 1789 and to elect from their number the first bishop of Baltimore. The assembled U.S.-based clergy chose John Carroll, administrator of the U.S. mission and part of a politically prominent Maryland family that included a delegate to the Continental Congress and a signer of the Declaration of Independence. Also noteworthy, perhaps, is that this occasion was the last time that any such experiment in ecclesiastical democracy for Catholics was to occur on U.S. soil.

Americans, of course, tend to view events like elections as routine and right. Thus, as José Casanova asserts, there arises within the Catholic Church in this country a "tension between the traditional hierarchical (episcopal), clerical, and authoritarian governance structures of the church and the democratic, lay, and participatory principles which permeate both the American polity and the governance structures of most American denominations" (1992: 87). Patriotic Americans idealize the fiery passion of rhetoric from a soapbox orator, the reasoned persuasion of debate during a candidates' forum, and the homespun honesty of decision making at the annual town meeting. The exercise of authority in any manner that does not involve consultation with, and the approval of, those who are subject to it, in contrast, seems to Americans to require explanation and justification.

> In the United States, citizens become accustomed to participatory structures in all institutions traditionally claiming authority; they take part in electoral politics, voluntary associations of all kinds, scientific debates, legal debates, juries, and even public policy commissions. All of this feels normal and proper. Americans participate in elections at all levels, from local horticulture club to national president, and they are accustomed to constitutions at all levels designating terms of office and scope of leaders' power. No one seriously disputes that this is the best way of managing claims to authority. (D'Antonio et al. 1989: 80)

Notwithstanding this disposition, in their religious pursuits U.S. Catholics are told repeatedly that "the Church is *not* a democracy." This is despite a pronounced desire on the part of lay Catholics for more participation in institutional decisions that affect them, especially on the parish level and in the area of finances and expenditures. In one survey, 60 percent of U.S. Catholics said that they wanted "more democratic decision making" in their parishes; 55 percent applied this same wish to their dioceses; and slightly fewer, 51 percent, carried the preference all the way to Rome. In the same study, 81 percent believed that laypersons "have the right to participate in deciding how parish income should be spent," and a majority (57 percent) sought a similar power in "selecting the priests for their parish" (D'Antonio et al. 1989: 108–12, 115–19). In keeping with their democratic spirit, 65 percent of Catholics in the United States said that they would "prefer to have bishops chosen by priests and people in their own diocese" (Greeley 2004b: 94–98).

Leadership: Failures at the Top

The Roman Catholic Church is more than merely undemocratic in its mode of organization: It is also thoroughly hierarchical. All power resides at the top of the formal structure and flows downward from there in a straight line. The Roman pontiff occupies the highest vertical position in the organizational chart (apart from Christ Himself), and all legitimate authority within the Church derives from the pope's acts of delegation.

Although actual practice has varied from time to time and place to place, the current procedure is for all Catholic bishops to be appointed from Rome; they are answerable, in turn, solely to the man who installed them and to his successors. As one European cardinal explained it recently, "The bishops are accountable to no one but the pope. And the pope is accountable to no one but Jesus" (quoted in Pope 2004: 87). Aside from the need for periodic reports to the Vatican and the requirement of a personal visit to the doorstep of the pope (*ad limina*) at least once every five years, bishops of the Catholic Church enjoy wide latitude in how they operate within their dioceses. There are times, however, when this lack of continuing oversight sows the seeds of crises.

Nowhere is this pitfall more obvious than in the behavior of some bishops in response to accusations of misconduct, and especially charges of the sexual abuse of children, against members of the clergy under their supervision. By the mid-1980s, some ominous storm clouds had already gathered on the organization's horizon. A debilitating scandal swirled in southwestern Louisiana, where a popular priest was charged with molesting nearly one hundred young boys; he was ultimately sentenced to a twenty-year term in state prison (Berry 1992, Goodstein 2003). In the 1990s, the Diocese of Dallas, Texas, was similarly convulsed when another priest was accused of sexually victimizing altar boys in three different congregations. At his criminal trial the guilty priest received a life sentence, and the Church later paid civil settlements of $30.9 million to twelve of the victims and their families. The reaction of the Catholic bishops of the United States to these scandals was to approve, in 1992, a series of recommended guidelines for dioceses to follow when the laity lodged credible allegations of predatory behavior by priests (Goodstein 2003; Pope 2004: 79).

But the true dimensions of the crisis, and of the hierarchy's complicity in it, did not begin to become apparent until the first weeks of 2002, when news media in Boston reported on official documents that had emerged in the trial of a lone priest, the Reverend John Geoghan, for child molestation. The papers established definitively that Geoghan's colleagues and superiors in the clergy had known for years of his pattern of misbehavior, but had persisted in reassigning him to local churches. There, in his pastoral role, he repeatedly had easy access to unsuspecting minors. Before he was arrested and sentenced to prison (where he was eventually murdered), Geoghan was held responsible for the molestation of more than 130 children across three decades of service in six Boston-area parishes (*Boston Globe* 2002; Goodstein 2003).

When, in the midst of the Geoghan case, an influential lay Catholic in Boston confronted the archbishop, Cardinal Bernard F. Law, wanting to be told how many more such cases may be in the offing, Law is reported to have said "there may be one or two" (quoted in Paulson 2003c). Whether the cardinal was deceitful or merely ill-informed, the truth was far, far worse. More victims came forward, more suits were filed, attempts to block discovery were deflected, and reams of internal church records cascaded from the chancery into the waiting hands of plaintiffs' attorneys. "The documents reveal that church officials knew far more then than they were believed to have known," wrote a columnist for the *Boston Globe* at the time. "And they strongly suggest," he continued, that persons in charge "simply didn't care very much" about the injured, for "the real issue was how best to cover their backs." The writer's understated conclusion: "That is far from any defensible concept of ministry" (Walker 2002).

Cardinal Law reiterated excuses for his ministry throughout the scandal in Boston. Initially, he blamed "inadequate record-keeping" for the consistent reassignment of abusive priests. He admitted that his "emphasis" on confidentiality in dealing with priestly personnel may have been misplaced and might be misunderstood by the laity. His supporters in turn accused the *Globe* of conducting a "witch-hunt" against the Church (quoted in Pope 2004: 75–77). Prominent Catholics on the political right intimated that dissident theologians were actually to blame for the crisis, because over the years such figures purportedly had fostered what one conservative termed a "subculture of infidelity" in the Church (quoted in Paulson 2003a).

As the lawsuits piled up, the archdiocese engaged in a last-ditch effort to elude liability and its enormous expense: It hired an appellate litigator to argue the radical position that the hundreds of claims of abuse should be dismissed because the constitutional doctrine of separation of church and state forbade any court from issuing a civil judgment against a religious body. (The position of the archdiocese was that to deem it liable for the misconduct of some of its priests was to suggest a proper standard for the supervision and oversight of church employees, a regimen that no secular authority was competent, it held, to fashion.) The presiding judge was not swayed. "Church doctrine and canon law do not conflict with civil law on the subject of sexual abuse," she wrote, "particularly the sexual abuse of children" (quoted in Gelzinis 2003; see also Zoll 2003). On the criminal side, after a sixteen-month investigation, a grand jury impaneled by Thomas Reilly, the attorney general of Massachusetts, was to find in 2003 that, between the years 1940 and 2000, evidence implicated no fewer than 235 priests in forty-five cities and towns of the Archdiocese of Boston in the abuse of a total of more than one thousand vulnerable children (Lavoie 2003a).

When the ensuing clamor finally subsided, Cardinal Law had relinquished his post in Boston. After a quiet interlude spent living at a small convent in Maryland, Law moved to Rome, where he situated himself at the St. Mary Major Basilica. The Church in Boston first paid $10 million in 2002 to 86 victims of Father Geoghan, and then in 2003 settled the claims of 552 additional victims of clergy abuse for $85 million, the largest diocesan payout on record to that date (Lavoie 2003b). Succeeding settlements eventually elevated the penalty for the misdeeds of priests and their superiors to more than $150 million. To initiate payment on this debt, the Church sold off the ornate mansion that the archbishops of Boston had used as their home, as well as forty-six acres of land in the suburb of Brighton (Zoll 2007).

However, by far the most sizable civil settlement in claims of sexual abuse by Roman Catholic priests was reached in 2007 between the Archdiocese of Los Angeles, the most populous Catholic community in the United states, and more than five hundred plaintiffs. The Church in that case agreed to pay the staggering sum of $660 million to avoid fifteen trials that were pending at the time, avoiding as well the likelihood, in some or all of these proceedings, that Cardinal Roger M. Mahony would be called to testify about the Church's enabling of clerical violators, and thus run the risk of punitive damages being assessed against the institution. Added to the $114 million that the Los Angeles archdiocese had already committed to victims in a series of previous settlements, its total liability thus exceeded three-quarters of a *billion* dollars. Nationwide the financial toll for litigation over claims of sexual abuse against the Catholic Church has now shot above $2 billion. Five smaller dioceses in turn sought the protection of bankruptcy as a result. Yet "I didn't file it for the money," one survivor in California said of her suit. "I would give back the money if I could have my childhood back" (quoted in Mozingo and Spano 2007).

The year of the scandal in Boston, the Cardinal's Appeal, an annual fundraising drive to support archdiocesan operations, collected only half of its usual amount, with receipts plummeting from more than $16 million in 2001 to $8.6 million in 2002 (Paulson 2003b); the drive was promptly relaunched as "The Catholic Appeal." In 2003, the year following the revelations about sexual abuse, St. John's, the seminary of the Archdiocese of Boston, enrolled no beginning students for the first time in its modern history (Russell 2003).

In 2002, the United States Conference of Catholic Bishops reacted collectively to the abuse crisis with the formal adoption of a *Charter for the Protection of Children and Young People* (USCCB 2002), a self-imposed code of conduct that featured a controversial provision mandating "zero tolerance" for allowing accused priests to remain in service while their cases are investigated. The bishops also appointed a National Review Board of lay Catholics to oversee their compliance with the *Charter* and established an Office of Child and Youth Protection within the Church's central bureaucracy.

A nationwide audit of U.S. dioceses that the National Review Board commissioned, carried out by independent researchers from the John Jay College of Criminal Justice in New York in 2004, discovered that in the half-century between 1950 and 2002, more than 4,000 Catholic priests and deacons were accused of abuse against more than 10,000 minors. Calculated differently, allegations had been lodged against 4 percent of diocesan priests who served in that period and about 3 percent of priests from religious orders (John Jay College 2004: 6–7, 26–28). However, a quarter of all incidences of sexual abuse that had been asserted nationally were attributed to fewer than 150 recidivist clergy (Pope 2004: 73). In 2002 alone, more than 400 priests resigned, retired, or were suspended from practicing their ministry after charges of abuse (Goodstein 2003).

Frustration with the Catholic Church's tactics in fending off scores of lawsuits over sexual abuses by priests led first to criticism from—and shortly thereafter the resignation of—one of the Church's key lay monitors: Frank Keating, a former FBI agent, federal prosecutor, Republican governor of Oklahoma, and the inaugural chair of the National Review Board. During a freewheeling interview in mid-2003, Keating compared the no-holds-barred legal strategies of some U.S. dioceses to the workings of the organized-crime syndicates that he had pursued while in law enforcement. "I have seen an underside that I never knew existed," he reflected (quoted in Stammer 2003).

Bishops demanded Keating's firing from the Review Board, and he answered quickly with his resignation. However, in the letter that transmitted his decision, he expanded on his description of what he had witnessed. "Our church is a faith institution, a home to Christ's people," Keating (2003) wrote to the head of the bishops' conference. "It is not a criminal enterprise. It does not condone and cover up criminal activity. It does not follow a code of silence. My remarks, which some bishops found offensive, were deadly accurate. I make no apology. To resist grand jury subpoenas, to suppress the names of offending clerics, to deny, to obfuscate, to explain away: that is the model of a criminal organization, not my church."

Every profession harbors within it persons who would transgress ethics and law. In this respect the clergy are no different from doctors, lawyers, teachers, and others—and the Roman Catholic clergy are unexceptional when compared to ordained ministers of other faiths (Shupe 2007). But what makes it possible for these individuals to offend is not only their personal demons, but the structure of the situations in which they routinely find themselves. In the Catholic Church, as one lay publication, the *National Catholic Reporter*, editorialized, "the sex abuse crisis is no longer mostly about sexual abuse. It is more enduringly a crisis of authority and accountability" (2005). The absence of accountability was abetted, in this instance, by the unchallenged deference that was accorded to priests and the arrogance that it bred (see Appleby 2002), by the secrecy in which the clergy customarily operated, and by the pressures of clerical careers that elevated an insistence on orthodoxy and the defense of the Church as an organization from public "scandal" above potentially disruptive truth-telling.

In short, priests and bishops who, when presented with complaints of wrongdoing, upheld "the primacy of institutional loyalty were rewarded with promotion and institutional power, which in turn reinforced moral myopia. The decision-makers were able to function in secret, in part because they were in no clear and systematic way accountable to the laity, or even the immediately affected parishioners in the parishes victimized by abusive priests" (Pope 2004: 77).

Given all that members of the Church in the United States have been forced to endure during these years of crisis, they continue to hold a remarkably firm grip on their identity as Catholics (*National Catholic Reporter* 2006). A painstaking review of data in national surveys from 2001 through 2005 shows that there has been no wholesale exodus from the Catholic Church in the wake of the revelations of abuse and cover-up, nor has there been a lasting drop-off in attendance at Mass. Parishes report, further, no declines in receipts from collections. Instead, Catholics targeted their ire narrowly against their bishops: rates of participation in annual diocesan appeals for funds displayed a sharp dip, and a majority of those who said that they had ceased donating money to their dioceses mentioned the sexual abuse scandal as a cause (Gray and Perl 2006: 11–15).

Membership: Problems in the Pews

The great twentieth-century author James Joyce is supposed to have observed that when one utters the phrase "the Catholic Church," one really means, "Here comes everybody." (In fact, the phrase is from his novel *Finnegans Wake*.) Be that as it may, the fact that Catholicism attracts a diverse body of believers does not also establish that everybody is treated equally or reacts in a uniform manner on his or her arrival in the arms of the Catholic Church. In particular, the Catholic Church in the United States harbors special tensions in accommodating the religious and social needs of racial or ethnic minorities and of women. For African Americans and for members of the Latino community, affiliation with the Catholic Church functions in different ways, although in each context membership (or its abandonment) is associated with striving for social position as well as with religious dedication.

AFRICAN-AMERICAN CATHOLICS

The vast majority of black Christians attend Protestant churches, usually in denominations that were founded during the nineteenth and early twentieth centuries as havens from racial discrimination in the white world. These groups survive and sometimes thrive in the integrated religious marketplace today in their role as modern-day "ethnic" churches.

Yet somewhere between 5 and 10 percent of African Americans report their current religious preference as Catholic (Hunt 1996: 846). Of this number, it is estimated that half were reared in one or another branch of Protestantism (Cavendish, Welch, and Leege 1998: 407n). For African Americans, several sociologists have theorized, the largely white Catholic Church constitutes a prime destination for religious switchers as they realize social mobility through educational and occupational advancement. "Black persons who desire to attend integrated churches befitting [a] middle-class life-style often find themselves in Catholic parishes in their neighborhoods," explain Hoge, McGuire, and colleagues (1981: 60–61), "when the Protestant churches are less racially integrated or less appealing." Becoming a Catholic, according to this view, places distance between previously deprived blacks and their origins in poverty, and helps ease newly mobile African Americans into a refined and reserved religious setting that is more compatible, socially and culturally, with middle-class status. "The Catholic Church," reflected Joe R. Feagin (1968: 191), "may well provide some

Note the U.S. flags hanging from the classroom windows of this Catholic school. Francis P. Clark Collection (GFCL 38), UNDA. Reproduced with permission of the University of Notre Dame.

middle-class Negroes with an escape route from social ties with their lower-class brethren." Larry L. Hunt and Janet G. Hunt noted not too much later: "Catholicism is a 'deviant' form of affiliation embraced by a small minority of the black community. As such it implies and symbolizes change of life-style and a break with traditional objects of identification—both social and symbolic" (1976: 375).

Urban Catholic parishes, Hunt and Hunt (1978) speculated, draw into their confines African Americans who, rather than staying segregated in inner-city black churches, endeavor to integrate themselves into the majority white society. When joining the mass migration to the suburbs was out of the question, blacks who could not or would not separate from other blacks geographically used the "institutional space" that the Catholic Church afforded to act on their motivations. "Conversion to Catholicism placed these blacks in predominantly white congregations, symbolized their apartness from other blacks, and altered their life chances by providing increased association and identification with whites" (Hunt and Hunt 1978: 666, 669). In addition, attendance at the ritualized liturgy of the Catholic Church removed blacks from exposure to the stigma that the well educated and accomplished often attribute to highly emotional expressions of faith.

Empirical research bears out the correlation of Catholic membership and higher social standing for blacks. Data from surveys conducted by organizations such as Gallup show that African Americans who are Catholic have occupations with greater prestige and more income and education than those in Protestant denominations (Feigelman, Gorman, and Varacalli 1991). For example, black Catholics drop out of high school at only about half the rate of other African Americans (Polite 1992: 212).

These findings were replicated in analyses of data on schoolchildren from the National Institutes of Mental Health (Hunt and Hunt 1975). African-American Catholics from social backgrounds above the lower class and for whom religion was important exhibited higher aspirations than Protestants for educational and occupational achievement, as well as a less tenacious identification with the black community in the United States. In a related study, black Catholics, not surprisingly, were also more likely to prefer a staid style of worship (Nelsen and Dickson 1972: 157–60).

A further incentive for African Americans to participate in—and perhaps convert to—Roman Catholicism is the availability to them, under the auspices of the Catholic Church, of a comprehensive system of low-cost, high-quality, safe, and well-managed schools for their children (Hoge, McGuire, et al. 1981; Nelsen and Dickson 1972: 154). Many parochial schools, particularly those for primary students, were started in cities across the country to meet the basic educational needs of immigrant European populations. As immigrants and their descendants learned and worked, strove and achieved, their families in many instances relocated to the suburbs. But their schools, diminished somewhat in number, remained behind in aging neighborhoods to embrace and educate new generations of students—now including many who are not European, not white, and not Catholic. In an era when publicly funded schools must cope with crumbling facilities and a deteriorating social climate, Catholic education stands out as an option for children to which quite a few African-American parents are committed (Polite 1992).

The documented worldly success of African-American Catholics notwithstanding, the latest research harbors signs that the period of advantage for U.S. blacks in conversion to Catholicism may be ending. Larry Hunt (1996, 1998a) has outlined how, in the last century, religious conversion elevated African Americans above their segregated and subordinated beginnings and spurred secular accomplishment. But for younger blacks, a generation now facing crucial decisions about identities and opportunities, it is only those who were born and reared in families that are already Catholic who maintain that edge in achievement. As Hunt summarizes the transition, "Catholicism is no longer the major channel through which blacks seeking change in their personal lives move" (Hunt 1998a: 191).

HISPANIC CATHOLICS

"The American Catholic Church has become to such a large extent a white-European middle-class institution," in the opinion of José Casanova, "that it is finding [it] very difficult to meet the spiritual and social needs of Hispanics, in the same way in which it has been unable either to attract or to meet the needs of African Americans" (1992: 90). The seriousness of this inability is immediately evident in that people of Latino background in the United States, an expanding population of about 40 million persons who once were thought to profess Roman Catholicism almost universally and exclusively are adopting new religious identities to an increasing degree. The best estimates from surveys today place the proportion of adult Hispanics who have retained a birthright affiliation with the Catholic Church at slightly over 70 percent (Perl, Greely, and Gray 2006: 430). Around 20 percent of Hispanics identify with one or another Protestant body, and 8 percent claim to have no religion (Espinosa 2004: 307, 317).

Evidence from both polls (for example, D'Antonio et al. 1989: 39–43) and observations (for example, Deck 1994; Weigert, D'Antonio, and Rubel 1971) attests to the relative detachment of Hispanic Catholics from the rites and rigors of the official church. Indeed, no ethnic minority anywhere along the broad spectrum of cultural, linguistic, and national-origin backgrounds that make up Catholicism in the United States is at once so thoroughly immersed in Catholic religious symbols and so markedly estranged from the organization that is their custodian. For some, this alienation is so severe that it has caused them to look for a more comfortable religious environment outside the Catholic Church. This phenomenon has been described as the "binary" between institutional and popular religion that runs throughout Latino religion—that is a widespread, deep-seated tendency within Hispanic Catholic populations to use the symbolic apparatus of institutional Catholicism primarily in noninstitutional, popular, or "domestic" contexts (see Lopez-Pulido 2007). For at least some Hispanic Catholics, some of these popular traditions can be successfully reintegrated into Protestant forms of religious expression.

The first published examination of data on Hispanic departures from Catholicism, by Andrew Greeley (1988), calculated that in the fifteen years between 1973 and 1988 more than a million Latinos and Latinas left the Catholic Church, mostly in favor of varieties of conservative Protestantism. Although much research on this topic is anecdotal and patchy at best, the appeal of Protestant churches for Hispanics has been credited to their smaller size, their lack of hierarchy, a warmer and more personal atmosphere, a less stilted and more popular style of worship (especially in Pentecostal congregations), nonprofessional clergy who have in common with those whom they serve an everyday language and ethnic culture, and a stress on behavioral norms that contribute not only to holiness but also to the acquisition of economic well-being and social respectability (see Deck 1994: 413–24; Marín and Gamba 1993; Roof and Manning 1994: 177–81; Weigert, D'Antonio, and Rubel 1971). This last aspect may be uniquely compelling to Hispanic women (Hunt 1999, 2001).

As an interesting contrast to the historic pattern of African-American attraction to Catholicism with rising social status, the road to higher social status for Latino Americans appears to lead away from the Catholic Church toward various versions of Protestantism—Pentecostalism foremost among them. Greeley (1988, 1991, 1997; see also Hunt 2001) has traced a connection between conversion of Catholic Latinos to Protestantism and aspirations on their part to upward social mobility (see also Espinosa 2004: 315–18). The results may already be apparent: Hispanic Americans who switch religious affiliation have greater amounts of education and income than those who remain Catholic, and they are more likely to hold employment in white-collar or managerial jobs.

Likewise, there is a strong association among Hispanics between gravitation to Protestantism and assimilation into the majority culture. Larry Hunt (1998b), for one, determined that Catholic losses of Latino members to Protestantism were especially pronounced among those Hispanic Americans whose families had lived in the United States for three or more generations, who spoke English, and who were residentially removed from others of their ethnic background. Conversion to moderate-to-liberal, or "mainline," Protestantism seems to confer a status advantage on Hispanics who began life as Catholics (Hunt 2000). So, too, does conversion to conservative Protestantism elevate the status of Hispanic men, but it does not behave similarly for women from that background. "In sum," writes Hunt, "conversion appears to move men into the broader public world in distinctive behavioral and ideological ways, but, for women, it ideologically confines them to the domestic world and/or its extensions in church settings" (2001: 155).

WOMEN IN THE CHURCH

No person with any exposure to the operations of a Christian denomination in the United States—neither prelate nor pastor, lay trustee nor member—would underestimate the importance of the work of women to the day-to-day life of their congregations. Of course, on Sundays the pews are normally filled with spouses and families, the elderly, and the occasional single. During the rest of the week, however, a local church is discernibly the domain of adult women.

Overwhelmingly, it is women who organize the liturgies, rehearse the choir, teach in the religious education program, edit the bulletins, convene myriad committees of the congregation, plan the fund-raisers, trigger the "telephone tree," circulate e-mails, handle outreach to the indigent and to youth, run the carpools, preside over child care, clean the sanctuary, launder the altar linens, sell the raffle tickets, gather donations of goods for parish bazaars, and bake the cakes that are for sale in the vestibule of the church after services. For instrumental reasons if not out of a commitment to equality, therefore, any denomination that gives short shrift to its female members is asking for trouble (Gribble 2005: 10).

Nevertheless, the Catholic Church in the United States is notorious in some circles for seeming to alienate otherwise faithful women. As Greeley and Durkin have written, "The 'good Catholic wife and mother' so beloved in clerical homilies is, on the average, madder than hell at Church leadership" (1984b: 11). On top of that, the pair note, "Church leadership is monumentally insensitive to the dimensions of its 'women problem'" (1984a: 143). In addition to the Catholic Church's refusal to make priestly ordination accessible to female candidates, Catholic women bear the weight of omission from many other areas of ecclesiastical power and control. Indeed, Mary Greeley Durkin, a lay theologian and mother, insists, "All but the most naive women recognize they are excluded from most of the important decision-making situations in the parish, diocesan and universal Church" (Greeley and Durkin 1984a: 117; cf. Bannah, Farrell, and Howarth 2007; Manning 1997: 376).

It is interesting to record how relatively few Catholic women in the United States, in spite of such conditions, deliberately distance themselves from the Catholic Church (Dillon 1998: 124–25). To be candid, some women *do* recoil from the male dominance that prevails in official quarters of the Catholic Church and "in some instances, even . . . sever all relationships with patriarchal religions." However, the great majority, whether of conservative or liberal leanings, remain attached to the institution. They persist in movement toward a participatory ideal in what is still a hierarchical structure. "Why is it," inquire Greeley and Durkin, "that some women experience this incongruity between the image of the Church as the 'people of God' and the reality of woman's place in the Church and still continue active involvement in the Church?" (1984a: 118).

The beginnings of an answer to that question have surfaced from ethnographic studies of Catholic women—both those who hold traditional views about church and society (Manning 1997, 1999) and those who are deeply engaged in attempts to liberalize Catholic norms and practices (Dillon 1998, 1999; Loseke and Cavendish 2001). What these studies have found is that the Catholic tradition is so robust and vital on a personal level, and sufficiently variegated and flexible as an ideology (Dillon 1999: 13), that its many followers, opposed though they may be in theory, can appropriate its symbols and stories for ends that are relevant to them. To borrow the words of Michele Dillon, they "combine a need for membership in a larger community with a stress on individual differences, and illustrate the feasibility of grafting new ways of being onto old traditions" (1999: 243). In the same vein, the spirituality of the Catholic women whom Elaine Howard Ecklund interviewed did not pull her "respondents away from organized religion. Rather, believing that personal understandings of doctrines were possible even *allowed* them to remain committed to a Church and a congregation that had doctrines with which they disagreed" (2003: 523).

As a result, religious rules about gender, sexuality, and family life do not behave in the main as tools of regulation (which seldom is imposed from without). Rather, for the believer who is highly aware but not scrupulously observant of these rules, they symbolize sympathy with the values of a specific religious culture (Manning 1999: 161). In this process, then, even the most orthodox members exercise a kind of informal (but not untutored) realism about what deference they should give to the Church, and so settle on a notion of what the Church can properly expect of them. In one example, "Barbara," the pseudonym that Christel Manning gave to a conservative Catholic daycare operator whom she interviewed in California, took a stand on power sharing in the home that sliced through much formal teaching:

> She admits that "I get upset" every time the priest discusses biblical passages relating to female submission. "Submit is a hard word. I couldn't submit to something I felt was morally wrong. I think husbands and

Bishops' Memorial Hall Collection (GBMH 1/25), UNDA. Reproduced with permission of the University of Notre Dame.

> wives need to work together." . . . Barbara does not believe her husband is the spiritual head of the family. "I see it as the opposite. Not in all cases, but in the families I know the women are really the spiritual leaders." (Manning 1999: 24)

Even among Catholic wives and mothers who object to ordaining women, Manning discovered a pride in the numerous nonordained ministries, such as lector and Eucharistic minister, that have opened up to the talents and gifts of their gender. She reports that "several conservative Catholics with whom I spoke would gladly expand women's role as far as Church law will allow." Another of Manning's informants, to whom she refers as "Bridget," for example, revealed:

> I don't see any reason why women can't function within the parish and have various leadership positions without sacrificing their families. That's all just fine. I mean, I don't have a problem with that. I think it's great. I don't see why they can't lector, why they can't cantor, can't be teachers, or can't head committees. (quoted in Manning 1999: 119)

But what about those women who believe that the current state of gender relations in the Catholic Church is too restrictive? Something of a similar habit, it turns out, acts to connect those who would challenge and thus change the Catholic Church not only to a hazy aspiration to equality in the future, but to the messy organizational politics of the institution in the present day (Ecklund 2003, 2005; Leming 2006, 2007). Ironically, argues Dillon in her analysis of Catholics who campaign for the morality of homosexual relationships, priestly ordination for women, and legal resort to abortion, it is precisely their knowledge of Catholic ideas and idioms that imparts to such critics of the Church their standing in debates of the moment.

> Respondents' participation in the Catholic tradition and their experience of its "higher truths" gives them a doctrinally informed authority to contest the church hierarchy's stance. By the same token, their commitment to what they experience as the "essential" meanings of Catholicism provides them with symbolic resources to which they apply their interpretive autonomy in a doctrinally reflexive manner. (Dillon 1999: 185)

This individualized approach, further, is not confined to laypersons. Clergy in the Catholic Church, whether by conviction or necessity, have become experts in interpreting doctrine so that "pastoral" considerations might take precedence over the letter of moral or religious law. Indeed, Mark R. Kowalewski (1993) suggests that the hierarchical structure of the Church encourages a brand of "good cop/bad cop" bargaining between the laity and their ministers, wherein authorities at the episcopal level can insist from a distance on stringent enforcement of doctrinal discipline, while priests in the parishes perform ready alterations to policy in order to suit emergent needs of average members. As Kowalewski notes, "[p]riests are not simply bearers of the official directives of the organization, they also exercise their ministry in the context of individual pastoral experience—an experience which often calls for compromise and negotiation." Accordingly, "priests selectively use official teaching and respect the moral decisions that clients make in conscience" (1993: 210, 212). An astute bishop has stated the identical point less formally: "It is a long way from Rome to most rectories" (the Most Reverend John Blackwood "Blackie" Ryan, quoted in Greeley 2000: 146).

In the end, the very structure of the Catholic Church, the forms of Catholic culture (see Burns 1996) and the methods of interpretation that Catholics themselves have adopted consign the institution to a stimulating if tumultuous future. Minorities and the marginal, those deprived of voice and volition, and dissidents of all stripes within the Catholic Church are more inclined to stand and fight than to retreat or renounce their membership. The "collective memory" of Catholics "reminds them that their genealogy is entwined with a historically continuous church rather than a history of sectlike divisions. There is a disposition therefore to stay, rather than to leave, and to work toward transformation from within the tradition" (Dillon 1998: 132).

In America, Catholics, at least, will be living in what the Chinese supposedly cursed as "interesting times" for some time to come.

Personnel: People without Priests

Another change that is of immense significance for the future of the Catholic Church in the United States is the declining number of volunteers whom the organization deems suitable for ordination to the priesthood. Sacramental activity is central to the Catholic tradition, and Catholic theology puts the highest priority on the regular sacrifice of the Mass. Only a priest can preside at the Eucharistic celebration and legitimately pronounce the words of consecration over the offerings of bread and wine.

But the net supply of active-duty Catholic clergy in the United States has not grown appreciably in the last three decades. To the contrary, it has begun a precipitous slide, the end of which is nowhere in sight. According to one series of projections that employs the latest data and the most advanced techniques of forecasting (Schoenherr and Young 1993; Young 1998: 15), numbers of Catholic priests in 2015 will have plummeted to roughly half their level a half-century earlier, in 1966. What Andrew Greeley (1972b: 16) wrote thirty years ago thus endures to the present day as a fair summary of the outlook for U.S. priests: "The Catholic priesthood in the United States has many strong, positive assets," he admitted, "but also some critical problems which, if they are not resolved, make the long-run prospects for the priesthood look rather bleak."

Official statistics on the shortage of Catholic priests in the United States are likely to understate the magnitude of the problem (Greeley 1977: 36, 165–66). The primary source for statistics on personnel and membership in the Roman Catholic Church in the United States by year is *The Official Catholic Directory*, published annually by P. J. Kenedy and Sons, now of New Providence, New Jersey. However, counts of priests in the *Directory* include a proportion—estimated for 1980 at approximately 14 percent (Hoge, Shields, and Verdieck 1988: 265)—who, through infirmity or because of retirement or pending resignation, are no longer active in full-time assignments. If this fraction has changed over three decades, it most probably has risen.

Further, *Official Directory* figures for the Catholic population in the United States, which are summed from ecclesiastical reports, consistently yield markedly lower totals than those that are derived from nationwide polls (Greeley 1963: 11; Stark and McCann 1993: 117). When used to determine ratios of Catholic people to priests, then, these numbers overestimate the corps of available clergy and underestimate the size of the Catholic constituency to be served by the staff of ordained ministers, and so diminish the apparent severity of the clergy shortage.

Nevertheless, unadjusted statistics on the matter speak clearly enough. In 1960, 53,796 priests served a Catholic population of approximately 40 million. After twenty-five years, in 1985, the number of Catholic priests had increased slightly to 57,317, but the flock that they were to tend expanded enormously—to somewhere between 52 million and 64 million, depending upon whether one believes the lower figures supplied by chancery offices around the country or the higher ones produced by sample surveys (Hoge 1987: 228–29).

A better measure of the growing burden on the clergy is furnished by calculations of the ratio of total Catholics to priests. Ponder this hypothetical situation: If all the priests in the United States were engaged in pastoral work, and they were distributed evenly among the nation's Catholic population, for how many church members would each priest be responsible? In 1944, the answer to that question would have been 593; by 1960, the number had risen to 726; by 1985, it had increased again, to 912 (Hoge 1987: 228–29); and in 1997, the count of parishioners that each priest would have to handle had reached 1,294. Today the official member-per-priest ratio exceeds 1,530. Altogether, these statistics depict a leap in the human load for priests of more than 150 percent in a little more than sixty years. Furthermore, as the statistical data on denominational growth presented in chapter 4 showed, the Catholic Church continues to be a "growth church" in the United States. Hence, even if the present number of priests can be maintained, the member-per-priest ratio will continue to rise.

The problem is evidently not one of retention, for departures from the clergy, once a serious problem, are now less common. In total, approximately one out of every seven diocesan clerics resigned from the priesthood between 1970 and 1985; rates of resignation were marginally higher for priests from religious orders (Greeley 2004c: 62; Hoge, Shields, and Verdieck 1988: 266–67). Most of the departures were concentrated toward the start of this period (Hoge, Shields, and Griffin 1995: 196). Resignations from active ministry slowed from 11.7 per thousand diocesan priests in 1974 to 3.9 per thousand in 1983 (Hoge 1987: 232–33; but cf. Schoenherr and Young 1990: 468–69). In research, the reason for leaving given most frequently by those who intended to resign from the Catholic clergy, whether in times of high turnover or low, was a desire to marry (NORC 1972: 258–66). All the same, this motivation may have functioned "as a channel for other causes," such as individual loneliness (NORC 1972: 266; see also Greeley 2004c: 63–65).

Because resignations are more likely to happen in the careers of younger and more theologically liberal clergy (Schoenherr and Young 1990: 471–72), their impact is not solely to draw down the numbers of available priests, but also to paint a group portrait of the priesthood—that is, first, old and increasingly gray, and second, notably more conservative than the laity. In 1966, about half (48 percent) of diocesan priests in the United States were forty-four years old or younger; in 1985, only a third of that group were younger than forty-five; by 1995, the percentage of younger priests was lower still, at 29 (Young and Schoenherr 1992: 25; Young 1998: 16). Combine this aging trend with the orthodoxy and obedience of the few men who are newly ordained (Greeley 2004a; Hoge, Shields, and Griffin 1995: 206, 212; Hoge, Shields, and Verdieck 1988: 267; Hoge and Wenger 2003: 66–69; Young and Schoenherr 1992), and without any changes in policy on the horizon, the Catholic Church is left with a class of parochial leaders who are mostly out of step both theologically and demographically with those who fill the pews.

As the ratios suggest, the more pressing reality for personnel in the Catholic Church is that numbers of ordinations in recent decades simply have not kept pace with numerical growth in the U.S. Catholic laity. More than forty years ago, in excess of 1,000 men were ordained to diocesan service in each of two successive cohorts, 1967 and 1968. By 1980, the corresponding count had fallen to 593 (Hoge, Potvin, and Ferry 1984: 7). A decade ago, in 1997, it fell to 509. This represents an absolute drop of greater than 50 percent in annual numbers of new priests available to U.S. dioceses. The declines in ordinations to ministry in religious orders during this period were even more drastic (Hoge, Potvin, and Ferry 1984: 15). The most recent classes of ordinands, diocesan and religious, in the United States are smaller still—numbering around 450 (Greeley 2004c: 7).

Were these statistics insufficient to dramatize the extent of the "vocations crisis" in the Catholic Church, a brief look at the situation in the Church's seminaries, the institutional seedbeds of future clergy, should be convincing. Ordinations may yet trickle from these centers of priestly formation, to join in the dioceses and parishes of the United States a still quite sizable pool of ordained men serving the Catholic Church. However, people who are oriented toward the future should be advised that the flow has practically dried up at its source. In a recent thirty-year period, to cite one example, the total number of seminarians who were enrolled in theologates (that is, postbaccalaureate courses) in the United States fell from close to eight thousand in 1967 to a little more than three thousand in 1997 (Schuth 1999: 58–59).

This is merely the latest stage in a long-term decline. At the conclusion of World War II, Catholic seminaries in the United States were actually crowded with students: In 1946, there was one seminarian for every 3,918 U.S. Catholics. Fifteen years later, in 1961, there were 4,965 Catholics for each seminary student. But twenty years after that, in 1981, with seminary enrollments dwindling, it took 13,210 Catholics to produce a single candidate for the priesthood (Hoge

1987: 228–29). By now the ratio has jumped to approximately 21,000 Catholics to one seminarian. The meager return from this harvest is worse when considered against the increasing size of cohorts of young Catholic males, the group from which priests-to-be would historically be recruited. In 1960, there were sixty-seven seminarians for every thousand Catholic males of about twenty years of age; by 1980, that number was down to just nine (Hoge, Potvin, and Ferry 1984: 11).

An analysis of data from the United States as well as several other Western countries by Rodney Stark and Roger Finke (2000) asserts that the collapse in vocations to the Catholic priesthood and religious life was a by-product of a shifting cost-benefit calculation in the minds of potential candidates. Simply put, they contend, reforms in the Catholic Church since the 1960s have deprived priests and nuns of many of the status gratifications, unique to those in the religious life, that they would have enjoyed in an earlier era. At the same time, the largest burdens to be borne by Catholics pursuing religious careers (such as the requirement of celibacy) were left in place. The outcome was to make entry into these positions much less attractive to young people who were considering service to the Catholic Church. A decline in vocations was thus "self-imposed, not merely incidental to the process of modernity" (Stark and Finke 2000: 132). However, Stark and Finke follow these observations with an even more controversial claim. They insist that in those religious communities and individual dioceses that have piloted a "return to tradition," rewards to clergy and sisters have increased, and greater-than-expected numbers of new vocations have resulted (see also Yuengert 2001).

Sociologist Lawrence A. Young has warned, in the abstract language of social science, that the worsening shortage of priestly personnel in the Catholic Church "has important ramifications for the polity and the normative or cultural structure of the Church and wider society" (1998: 8). More concretely, he describes a future in which imminent choices of how and where religious professionals will be recruited, trained, and allocated "will lead to changes in the distribution of power, formation of coalitions, determination of goals, and other political processes in the Catholic Church."

Following the simplest possible scenario (but not therefore a painless one), if the downward trend continues in the new century and the Catholic Church's hierarchy makes no changes in policy to address it, the all-but-inevitable result will be a radical alteration in the nature of communal religious life among Catholics. Either parishioners will be denied regular access to the fullness of the Eucharist for lack of a priest to officiate, or the function of the priest will be reduced to that of a sacramental circuit rider (Zech 1994: 246–48), with the balance of parish life maintained and controlled by teams of lay persons (Davidson and Williams 1997: 516–17).

Public opinion data indicate that neither possibility is attractive to Catholics in the United States. In the former case, the centerpiece of Catholic liturgical life would be truncated or lost, surely with tragic consequences for spirituality and even membership. For many contemporary parishioners, "going to Mass" not only signifies but also virtually defines what it means to be a Catholic. In the latter case, local congregations would be deprived of traditional, full-time, professional religious leadership—and the range of inspirational, psychological, and practical services that they have long enjoyed from priests who were more than masters of ceremonies (Zech 1994).

An array of impediments stands in the path to greater numbers of vocations to the Catholic priesthood, but research on clergy recruitment across the denominational spectrum in the United States conducted by Dean Hoge suggests that the critical factors in the Catholic context "must be due to differences in institutional rules concerning clergy." Young Catholic Americans mature in the same middle-class cultural environment as young members of moderate and liberal Protestant denominations. Yet as early as 1983 the data would show that "all the middle-class Protestant denominations have a surplus of clergy," while "the Catholic Church alone has a shortage" (Hoge 1987: xiii). Two potential explanations in this Protestant-Catholic contrast are the restriction of ordination to men and the requirement of clerical celibacy.

Most prominent among the factors deterring young Catholic men from choosing the priesthood as a career are the requirement of clerical celibacy and the necessity of making a lifetime commitment to service in the Catholic Church (Hoge, Potvin, and Ferry 1984: 48–49). More than 60 percent of Catholic males enrolled in college who admitted that they were not interested in becoming priests listed as the biggest block the fact that priests are "not allowed to marry." About one in eight (12 percent) in this uninterested group said that he would change his mind and seriously consider the priesthood were the demand for celibacy repealed (Hoge 1987: 120–29). Indeed, projections made from NORC data imply that compulsory celibacy reduces annual ordinations in the United States by approximately fifteen hundred. An intermediate change, retaining celibacy but limiting periods of service to a fixed term, would generate perhaps one thousand more priestly vocations per year (Greeley 1985: 118–19). This could produce enough clergy to make feasible a return to staffing levels of ordained ministers that prevailed in the United States during the middle of the twentieth century.

Priests as well as lay people in the Catholic Church for decades have favored, above other arrangements, a rule of optional celibacy for their ministers. Most priests added that they personally had no plans to marry—only about 20 percent could envision themselves as husbands (Greeley 2004c: 62, 67; NORC 1972: 246)—but they did not want to deprive their peers of this choice. When the initial measurements of these attitudes were taken, in the late 1960s, a large majority of diocesan priests in the United States expected to witness a change in Catholic church law on celibacy for clergy within five years (65 percent), or within ten years (75 percent) at the outside (Greeley 1972b: 77–78). In almost forty years, however, no such change has come.

The institutional turmoil surrounding the Catholic Church's teaching authority on a range of matters unfortunately may have suppressed one of the most effective means of recruitment to the priesthood, namely, encouragement from

The Globalization of Vocations

Fifty years ago, young Irish men facing few prospects in their own desperately poor homeland flocked to the priesthood, far exceeding Ireland's needs. They turned up in parochial schools and parishes in Chicago, Boston, New York—and all over Africa, including Nigeria, where entire regions were taught Christianity by Irish priests.

Today, Ireland, its economy roaring, is short of priests. Not only has it stopped exporting them, it can't fill vacancies at home created by retiring clergy. So Nigerians are coming to help.

This is not just a Christian thing to do, but an aspect of globalization, too. Nigeria, an English-speaking country, has what economists call a comparative advantage when it comes to priest production. It costs as little as $500 a year to educate, feed, and house a priest in Nigeria, a tiny fraction of the annual cost of producing a priest in Ireland or the U.S. . . . While India and a few other nations produce greater numbers of priests, Nigeria probably exports more than any other country today. The Vatican doesn't compile statistics on priest exports by country, but the U.S. Conference of Bishops estimates that Nigerian priests are the most mobile.

Hundreds work in Catholic dioceses in the United States, filling a growing number of vacancies. Nigerians are also prominent in Britain and Germany, where vacancies have risen.

Source: G. Paschal Zachary, "Parish the Thought: A Nigerian Priest Finds an Irish Home," *Wall Street Journal*, May 11, 2000, A1, A10.

the families of potential candidates and reinforcement from priests themselves. Most active priests, in particular, recall favorably the personalities of priests whom they knew in their youth, and this example influenced their own decisions to seek ordination (Hoge, Potvin, and Ferry 1984: 38–39, 44–50). But much of the impromptu framework of emotional support and career advice for would-be priests withdrew into uncertainty and confusion after the 1960s (NORC 1972: 267–73) and has not fully reemerged (Greeley 2004c: 119–23). Almost two-thirds (64 percent) of priests in the United States remembered that, in the mid-1960s, they vigorously encouraged young men to contemplate going to the seminary; no more than five years later, that proportion was cut in half (33 percent) (NORC 1972: 268–69). The halfheartedness of priests as recruiters of their successors in the profession, according to one analysis, "represents an extremely serious problem for the Catholic priesthood in the United States" (NORC 1972: 269).

In any event, evidence shows that there is a pent-up impulse for service to the Catholic Church in the United States that current rules do not release. Catholic youth as a whole identify strongly with the faith, and an impressive minority stands ready to assist the church in ministerial capacities that do not require ordination and the permanent sacrifice of options in life associated with that status.

So far, the Vatican and the U.S. bishops have resisted any serious examination of alternatives to the current requirement that candidates for the priesthood be celibate males. In fact, Pope John Paul II went to the extraordinary length of declaring, in his apostolic letter *Ordinatio sacerdotalis* (1994), that the ordination of women is forever forbidden in the Catholic Church, and thus the possibility of such a change ought not to remain open to discussion. His successor, Pope Benedict XVI, has restated this position several times. The year after his election, for instance, he told German interviewers (Bellut et al. 2006) that "we believe that our faith and the constitution of the College of the Apostles binds us and does not allow us to confer priestly ordination on women. But," he was quick to add, "we should not think either that the only role of importance one can have in the Church is that of being a priest." The continued intransigence of the hierarchy probably explains why there has been no large-scale, systematic research to discern how many Catholic women of comparable age and position to those men studied in recent research would be willing to accept the norm of lifelong celibacy were the priesthood opened to them.

The steadfast opposition of the hierarchy notwithstanding, U.S. Catholics are growing gradually more comfortable with the prospect that they may someday see changes in the qualifications that are necessary for ordination. A survey by Louis Harris in 1967 placed "a bare majority" of the Catholic laity in the camp tolerating optional celibacy for priests (Greeley 1972b: 85). According to NORC data (see Greeley 1977: 153, 161), this proportion rose through the 1970s so that, eventually, 80 percent of lay Catholics arrived at the point where they could "accept" a married clergy, and 62 percent actively endorsed the idea. By 1985, a national telephone poll conducted under the direction of the Gallup Organization found that 63 percent of adult Catholics thought that it would be "a good thing" for the Catholic Church to permit the ordination of married men. More recent statistics place endorsement of a married clergy at more than three quarters (76 percent) of Catholics (Davidson et al. 1997: 26).

In the Gallup sample from 1985, 47 percent of Catholics said the possibility of ordination for women would qualify as "a good thing" (Hoge 1987: 144). Trend data from NORC and others indicate that this proportion has been rising consistently over time, from 29 percent approval of women priests in 1974, to 44 percent in 1982 (Greeley 1977: 161, 1985: 182), to a 63 percent majority in 1993 (Davidson et al. 1997: 26), and to 65 percent approving today (Greeley 2004b: 96–97). In addition, slightly less than half (48 percent) of those Catholics who were surveyed in Gallup's 1985 effort favored the voluntary return to active duty of resigned priests who have married, as well as the opportunity for an "honorable discharge" for priests after a stipulated length of service (Greeley 1972b: 87–88, 2004c: 122–23; Hoge 1987: 144, 234–35).

Finances: Expanding Mission, Declining Resources

During his long tour of duty in the Roman Curia, the Catholic Church's bureaucracy, U.S.-born archbishop Paul Marcinkus gained a reputation as a tough-talking Midwesterner. Marcinkus headed the Institute for Religious Works, which is better known colloquially as the Vatican Bank. Yet this bank has no branches or automated teller machines, and it does not advertise free checking for a minimum deposit. Instead, the Institute is a "bank" solely in that it invests the assets of the Catholic Church's central units at a profit. After all, Marcinkus insisted with his trademark bluntness, "You can't run the Church on Hail Marys."

That harsh message is as true on this side of the Atlantic as on the other. In the United States, survey research on earning and spending during the 1960s suggests that Christians—Protestants and Catholics alike—made monetary contributions to their churches at the same general level: approximately 2.2 percent of income. With the passage of years, the Protestant rate of giving has remained stable. Yet even as real incomes of Americans (that is, incomes after accounting for the impact of inflation) grew considerably over the last third of the twentieth century, the relative size of Catholic contributions to the Church shrank, displaying a loss of one-quarter by 1974 and one-half by 1984. Without a doubt, today's Catholic parishes receive greater amounts of revenue, in absolute numbers of dollars, than they did previously, but Catholic giving has lagged behind the increments to income that both chronic inflation and growth in productivity cause (Greeley and McManus 1987: 38, 52–53). Catholics in the United States on the whole have gotten richer in the preceding forty years, but their parishes on average have not benefited to a like degree from this prosperity.

To be more explicit, Andrew Greeley and William McManus, a retired bishop, calculated that U.S. Catholics, as families and unrelated individuals, in 1984, contributed less than 1.2 percent of their annual incomes to the Church. In comparison, the typical Protestant gave much more—a constant 2.2 percent of income—although Protestants posted somewhat lower earnings, and therefore would have had less "disposable" income, than did Catholics (Greeley and McManus 1987: 18; Forbes and Zampelli 1997: 22; Hoge and Yang 1994: 124–25; Hoge, Zech, et al. 1996: 20–23; Rexhausen and Cieslak 1994: 222; Zech 2000: 551). Moreover, the widest gaps in giving between Catholics and their Protestant fellow Christians were detected primarily in the upper regions of the economic and educational distributions. As a proportion of income, Catholic contributions equaled or exceeded those of Protestants only among families in near poverty whose members had never graduated from high school (Greeley and McManus 1987: 28, 34–35). In other words, the main responsibility for the gross difference from Protestants in donations resides among Catholics who are better off. Indeed, other data indicate that as a Catholic household's income rises, the proportion of its income that is contributed to the parish dips (see Forbes and Zampelli 1997: 24–25; Hoge and Yang 1994: 130; Rexhausen and Cieslak 1994: 222).

Subsequent investigations have sustained the impression that Catholics are less generous to their churches than are Protestants. For example, studies in the mid-1990s by Hoge and several colleagues fixed mean per-member gifts to Catholic churches at merely $160 annually (see Hoge and Yang 1994: 129–31;

Hoge, Zech, et al. 1996: 31–32). Whether measured as members, households, or attenders, Catholics gave less money on average than persons in any of the four comparison groups of Protestants in the analysis. Contributing most of all were respondents in the sample who belonged to the Assemblies of God, a loose affiliation of Pentecostal churches. In each category of measurement, Christians in the Assemblies donated to their congregations from *at least three to more than four times* the absolute amounts that Catholics contributed to theirs.

Are the revenue expectations for Catholic churches in the United States improving over time? The evidence is that changes since the beginning of the 1980s have not been dramatic. Data that William V. D'Antonio and his colleagues collected in 1987 depict lay Catholics donating 1.9 percent of their incomes, closer to the consistently higher level for Protestants. The authors are aware, nonetheless, that this figure may be an overstatement, and are convinced that the true percentage probably lies between 1.5 and 1.7 (D'Antonio et al. 1989: 153).

The logical next step is to ask what changes to Catholic culture in the United States since the middle of the last century might have caused such erosion in monetary support for the institutional work of the Catholic Church. Some students of religious finances maintain that, in the same manner that members of any organization may "vote with their feet" and stride toward the exits when official proceedings plunge to a critical negative threshold, so may members "vote with their dollars" and withhold economic aid from undertakings of policy of which they disapprove. In keeping with this theory, one ought to search for explanations for declining religious contributions in those domains of ecclesiastical life that foster the greatest conflict or spawn the most widespread alienation.

A likely suspect in this search is controversy over the moral teachings of the Catholic Church. D'Antonio and coauthors, for example, discovered that rates of religious giving suffered most among Catholics who adopted liberal postures on sexual issues (1989: 155–61). For their part, Greeley and McManus (1987: 45, 62–64) charted a steep drop in giving by Catholics who reject the official teaching of the Church that bans contraception for married couples. Together, this opposition on sex issues and the alienation that it produces, they say, account statistically for half of the recorded decline in Catholic contributions.

Newer research, however, questions this conclusion. In their comparative data, Hoge and his collaborators could discover no relationship between disagreement with teachings of the Catholic Church on birth control, homosexuality, or the ordination of women and lower levels of giving. Catholics who regarded premarital sex as wrong and who shared the Church's condemnation of abortion, on the other hand, were more prone to generous contributions (Hoge and Yang 1994: 136; Hoge, Zech, et al. 1996: 74–75, 164–65). While the majority of Catholic respondents to the survey expressed discontent with the lack of control they had over decisions in the Church that pertain to money (just 48 percent reported that they possessed "enough influence" in such matters), this attitude seemed not to determine strongly the sizes of their contributions (Hoge, Zech, et al. 1996: 41–42, 87–96). "Democracy in itself is not a predictor of giving," argue the investigators, "but dissatisfaction with leadership *is* a predictor" (Hoge, Zech, et al. 1996: 94; cf., Miller, Parfet, and Zech 2001).

Several more mundane factors appear to enjoy an undisputed statistical relationship with rates of donations to churches. The first is the sheer size of membership in the local congregation, and here the effect is negative (Cieslak 1984; Miller, Parfet, and Zech 2001; Zaleski and Zech 1992). Roman Catholic parishes are often *eight times* as large as their Protestant counterparts in a community (Hoge, Zech, et al. 1996: 20, 29). Religion on such a large scale necessarily forces contact with members to cross broad social distances and to assume an impersonal style. The intensity of religious commitment presumably slumps as a result: Rather than generating further attachment to one's fellow believers, participation in church under these circumstances simply isolates and distances individuals and families from the institutional whole. This detachment thus weakens sentiments of individual responsibility for the financial welfare of the church—what has been dubbed "ownership" in the shorthand terminology of congregational studies (Hoge and Augustyn 1997; Rexhausen and Cieslak 1994: 224–28).

Another explanation for reduced contributions that holds up empirically is the lower importance that is imparted to giving as an element of membership in Catholic churches. Put another way, Catholic pastors (the objections of parishioners notwithstanding) are in fact less inclined to emphasize sharing material gifts as a religious obligation of members. They are correspondingly less likely to have executed a formal program in their parishes to promote stewardship or "sacrificial giving" (Hoge, Zech, et al. 1996: 36–37), which can increase revenues to the church to levels higher than otherwise would have occurred (Cieslak 1984; Forbes and Zampelli 1997; Harris 1994; Hoge and Augustyn 1997: 56–57; Sullivan 1985: 317–18; Zech 2000: 554–55).

Suggestions for Further Reading

William V. D'Antonio, James D. Davidson, Dean R. Hoge, and Mary L. Gautier. 2007. *American Catholics Today: New Realities of Their Faith and Their Church*. Lanham, Md.: Rowman & Littlefield.

James D. Davidson. 2005. *Catholicism in Motion: The Church in American Society*. Liguori, Mo.: Triumph Books.

Michele Dillon. 1999. *Catholic Identity: Balancing Reason, Faith, and Power*. Cambridge: Cambridge University Press.

Jay P. Dolan. 1992. *The American Catholic Experience: A History from Colonial Times to the Present*. 1985. Reprint, Notre Dame, Ind.: University of Notre Dame Press.

Bryan T. Froehle and Mary L. Gautier. 2000. *Catholicism U.S.A.: A Portrait of the Catholic Church in the United States*. Maryknoll, N.Y.: Orbis Books.

Chester Gillis. 1999. *Roman Catholicism in America*. New York: Columbia University Press.

Andrew M. Greeley. 2004. *The Catholic Revolution: New Wine, Old Wineskins, and the Second Vatican Council*. Berkeley and Los Angeles: University of California Press.

Dean R. Hoge, Mary Johnson, William D. Dinges, and Juan L. González. 2001. *Young Adult Catholics: Religion in the Culture of Choice*. Notre Dame, Ind.: University of Notre Dame Press.

Mark S. Massa. 1999. *Catholics and American Culture: Fulton Sheen, Dorothy Day, and the Notre Dame Football Team*. New York: Crossroad.

Charles Morris. 1997. *American Catholic: The Saints and Sinners Who Built America's Most Powerful Church*. New York: Times Books.

Richard A. Schoenherr, with David Yamane. 2002. *Goodbye, Father: The Celibate Male Priesthood and the Future of the Catholic Church*. New York: Oxford University Press.

Leslie Woodcock Tentler, ed. 2007. *The Church Confronts Modernity: Catholicism Since 1950 in the United States, Ireland, and Quebec*. Washington, D.C.: Catholic University of America Press.

Photograph courtesy of William H. Swatos, Jr.

CHAPTER 9

The Globalization Dynamic

HISTORIC ANIMOSITIES OR POSTMODERN POLITICS?

It is difficult to think of an occurrence that caught Western students of religion more by surprise than the worldwide resurgence of religion—*political religion*, no less—that occurred with increasing visibility as the 1970s wore on. New religious movements (NRMs) had already appeared, but many of the leading theorists of religion in modernity, as we have seen, merely attempted to accommodate these into an existing secularization paradigm by citing the apparently bizarre character of these movements as popularly portrayed. The highly eclectic character of the religious marketplace seemed only to confirm the privatization thesis. Such religious controversies as did reach political proportions, as in Northern Ireland and Israel/Palestine, were often "explained" (that is, explained away) by social scientists as merely symbolic expressions of socioeconomic variables. The idea that there were concerted groups of people taking religion seriously enough to affect the order of global society gained little credence, in fact, until the appearance of the Ayatollah Khomeini in revolutionary Iran. He meant business, and the simple explanation that he was a mere figurehead for those really in power fell into greater and greater disrepute as the heads of one after another of those "really" in power rolled before the Ayatollah's revolutionary justice.

Standard social scientific models of change seemed ill equipped to account for worldwide religious resurgence. The two primary theories of "modernization"—development (a functionalist derivative) or exploitation (a Marxist derivative, sometimes termed "dependency" or "world-system" theory)—both proceed from the assumption that religious "prejudices" hamper "progress" and are disappearing throughout the world. Secular education, secular armies, secular economics, secular politics combine to create the modern state. The only real difference between these two models of modernization is whether capitalism is viewed as a friend or foe to nation-state growth and the good order of the international system of states. According to either of these theories, then, religious resurgence represents a "deviant" occurrence in the broad sweep of history.

If, indeed, only an isolated instance of religious resurgence were now to be observed, one could hardly quarrel with such theoretical presuppositions. We have deviants within our own local communities, after all, so why not expect the same at the political level in the international system of states? The problem, however, is that the resurgence phenomenon is *global* in character—so much so that it strains credulity to accept an argument that worldwide religious resurgence represents some form of mass delusion.

Globalization theory provides an approach to the present world situation that addresses these developments. Although rooted in the materialist analyses of Fernand Braudel and Immanuel Wallerstein, generally known as *world-system theory*, globalization has been reshaped by the later work of John Meyer and especially Roland Robertson to incorporate important cultural components, including religion (cf. Beyer 1994). What *globalization* refers to is most simply conceptualized by Robertson's phrase that the world is seen as "a single place" (see R. Robertson 1992). As Frank Lechner observes in a recent survey of the field, "Globalization refers to the worldwide diffusion of practices, expansion of relations across continents, organization of social life on a global scale, and growth of a shared global consciousness," but not only this. For "globalization also recasts the agenda of social theory. . . . [W]hereas social theory once focused on the rise of individual, state-organized societies, it now must address the implications of change of scale in supraterritorial social relations. While modernization could once be treated as change within a single civilizational arena, students of globalization must now examine how world order can arise in the face of civilizational differences" (2004: 330).

Globality stands over against locality (or localism), but since the local is always within the global, the two are in constant relationship (which may be positive or negative). The global is universalistic, while the local is particularistic. In practice, however, there can be both particularistic universalism and universalistic particularism, giving rise, among other things, to the phenomenon of religious resurgence often popularly dubbed "fundamentalism."

Strictly speaking, the word *fundamentalism* refers to a specific theological movement that originated in American Protestantism at the turn of the twentieth century. A group of Protestant leaders, concerned about what they considered to be a process of "modernism" that was shaking the foundations of the Christian religion, set forth a list of "fundamentals" that they considered to be essential to the Christian faith (see Dixon, Meyer, and Torrey 1910–1915; Marsden 1980). People who subscribed to these were subsequently termed—first by their detractors, later by themselves—*fundamentalists*.

When the worldwide religious resurgence of the 1970s gained attention, however, the term *fundamentalist* was seized in a more extensive fashion. It was now expanded to include all contemporary religious movements that display what Eugen Schoenfeld (1987) has demarcated "exclusive militancy." In a definition that rivals Robertson's "seeing the world as a single place" for simplicity, T. K. Oommen (1994) has similarly defined fundamentalism as "text without context." What this means is that religious texts (or scriptures) that were originally written in a specific historical and cultural context, hence a specific *social* setting, are decontextualized and held to be applicable without regard to local circumstances. At the same time, however, all other competing texts are rejected as having any corresponding claim to truth. Yet another helpful marker is provided by Laurence Coupe's phrase "the myth of mythlessness" (1997: 9). Fundamentalists claim that their

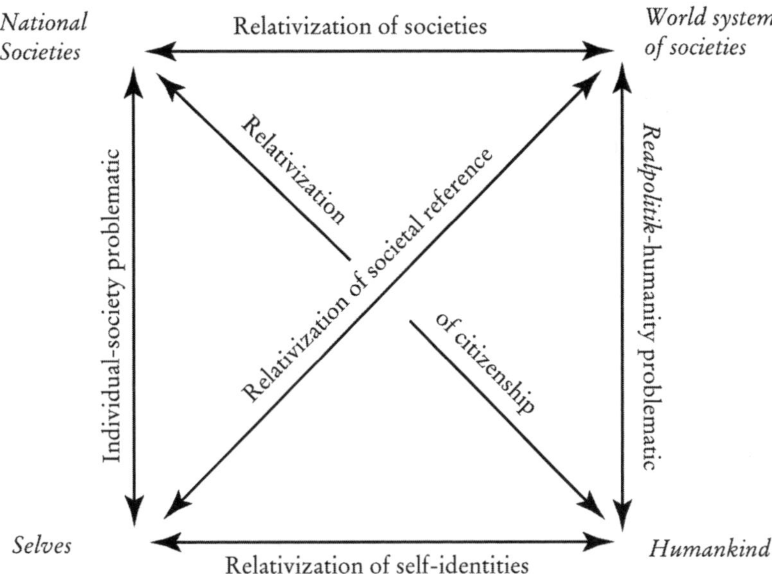

Figure 9.1. The Global Field. Source: Roland Robertson, Globalization: Social Theory and Global Culture *(London: Sage, 1992), 27.*

religion is objectively "true," while others are based on "myths" or "falsehoods," whereas scholars of religion recognize that all belief systems (including secular belief systems, such as Marxism, scientism, and humanism) are based on myths or stories with unprovable baselines, which are more or less integrated into one's own biography, as mediated by one's culture. For example, none of us objectively knows what happened at the Creation, because none of us was there. Similarly, even if the crucifixion of a man named Jesus of Nazareth was performed in the time and place that Christians believe, no objective historical evidence will ever be able to prove that he died "for our sins." As another example, the myth of the social scientific study of religion is meaningfulness, "the meaning of meaning" being nonobjective.

It is important to recognize that all fundamentalisms, as they are advanced around the globe today, are *specifically modern products* and heterodox faith traditions (see Lechner 1985). This claim is never made, of course, by fundamentalists themselves, but is easily documented by historical surveys of the faith traditions they claim to represent. The majority of those in the world today who claim to be Christians do not belong to fundamentalist churches—and never have. The majority of Muslims do not belong to fundamentalist (or "Islamicist") sects of that faith. The historic creeds to which the majority of those who call themselves Christians assent are not used by most fundamentalist Christians; the central concerns of fundamentalist Muslims are not the essential "Five Pillars" of Islam. Ultraorthodox Jews are more orthodox than the Orthodox, which is an obvious contradiction in terms. All religious fundamentalisms as we know them today were constructed during the twentieth century as responses to the modern world-system, which had its beginnings in the sixteenth century but has come to fruition in the global project that has progressed with increasing certainty ever since World War II.

Global Culture

If we are to understand the relationship between the seemingly conflicting dynamics of globalization and fundamentalism, we need to reflect on the culture of modernity itself. "Modern world culture is more than a simple set of ideals or values diffusing and operating separately in individual sentiments in each society," Meyer observes. "[T]he power of modern culture—like that of medieval Christendom—lies in the fact that it is a shared and binding set of rules exogenous to any given society, and located not only in individual sentiments, but also in many world institutions" (1980: 117). These institutions, like the United Nations, the World Court, and world financial institutions that make a world economy work, involve an element of *faith*: that is, they rest on a certain belief that what they do is both *right* and *natural* (these two conditions being bound together, for example, in the phrase "human rights").

This worldview (in the double sense) has not characterized human history, taken as a whole, even into our own day. Consider the following vignette from social historian Agnes Heller:

> About thirty years ago I became acquainted with the middle-aged owner of a little trattoria in Rome's Campo dei Fiori. After a lively conversation I asked him to advise me about the shortest way to Porta Pia. "I am sorry, but I cannot help you," he answered. "The truth of the matter is I have never ever in my life left the Campo dei Fiori." About one and a half decades later, on the board of a jumbo jet en route to Australia, I discussed the then-current political affairs with my neighbour, a middle-aged woman. It turned out that she was employed by an international trade firm, spoke five languages, and owned three apartments in three different places. Recalling the confession of the trattoria owner, I asked her the obvious question: "Where are you at home?" She was taken aback. After awhile she responded: "Perhaps where my cat lives."
>
> These two people seemingly lived worlds apart. For the first, the Earth had a center, it was called Campo dei Fiori, the place where he was born and expected to die. He was deeply committed to the geographic monogamy that wedded him to his tradition. His commitment stretched from the remote past, the past of the Campo, up to a future beyond his own, the future of the Campo. For the second, the Earth had no center; she was geographically promiscuous, without pathos. Her whereabouts made no difference to her. My question surprised her because the loaded concept "home" seemingly had no significance for her.
>
> This was confirmed by her wittingly unwittingly ironical answer. As long as there is something called home, our cat lives in our home. So when my interlocutor said, in reversing the signs, that "My home

> is where my cat lives," she had deconstructed the concept "home." Her geographic promiscuity symbolized something uncanny (*unheimlich*), namely the abandonment of, perhaps, the oldest tradition of the homo sapiens, privileging one, or certain, places against all the others. (1995: 1)

Not surprisingly, commentators on this condition of modernity (or "postmodernity") have spoken of both "the homeless mind" (Berger et al. 1973) and "the absent center" (Lemert 1975).

This illustration by Heller can help us understand particularly well the potential problems of globalization. To move from the worldview of the man of Campo dei Fiori to the woman of the "jumbo jet" is to move from one way of *knowing* to another; it is a total shift in *epistemology*, the technical term philosophers apply to systems of knowledge. All ways of knowing, however, rest on systems of *beliefs* about the universe that are themselves unprovable to observation. One can make logical assertions about creation and evolution, for example, but one can also make logical assertions about the existence of God, as St. Thomas Aquinas did almost one thousand years ago. But none of us has observed either one directly, hence we ultimately accept one or another account "on faith": the arguments as a whole have a ring of consistency or plausibility that convinces us that they are inherently worthwhile to getting on with life in the present. In short, the worldview of globalization has an essentially *religious* character in that it requires us to accept beliefs about "the ways the world works" that may be in conflict with other beliefs—not only beliefs of the existing formally organized religions, such as Christianity or Islam, but also beliefs of the popular or implicit religions on the basis of which people have constructed their lives for centuries (see Glock 1988).

Globalization particularly flies in the face of the belief in absolute nation-state sovereignty—what Frank Lechner (1989) terms "institutionalized societalism"—which, ironically, reached its apex as the very capstone of the globalization process that now threatens its undoing. On the one hand, the globe appears as a union of sovereign states, recognized by world institutions as having transcendent integrity. On the other hand, the sovereignty of these states as political actors is circumscribed by a set of principles—a "higher law"—that in fact rests on beliefs generated by specific world orientations that are themselves metaphysical; that is, the principles of global society are generated by accepting some kinds of faith propositions and not others. In general, these propositions reflect Anglo-American utilitarian-pragmatic philosophy since the eighteenth century, which lacks absolutes, hence is subject to contradiction as circumstances change.

Before we turn back to religious fundamentalism, let us look at another formally nonreligious vignette. The nation-state of Iceland has been one of the greatest beneficiaries of the principle of institutionalized societalism; though numbering little more than 250,000 people, it has virtually all of the privileges in world institutions that are accorded to the United States or Japan, and perhaps more than China. Part of the process of the creation of an independent Iceland, however, was the enshrining of the Icelandic language as the keystone of its claim to distinction—so much so that Icelandic sociologist of religion Pétur Pétursson (1988) has described it as characterized by a "language fundamentalism." A manifestation of the Icelandic fascination with Icelandic is a law that all Icelanders must have Icelandic names. One of the by-products of globalization, however, is a world-openness that allows the relatively free exchange of peoples and goods across national borders—a relatively fluid view of citizenship (that is, world citizenship).

Consider now the case of "Eternal Peace" Cabrera Hidalgo/Edgarsson. In the late 1980s, Jorge Ricardo Cabrera Hidalgo came to Iceland from Colombia. "After attending college and working for some time, he decided to start his own business, upon which he was informed that bureaucratically speaking it would be much easier for him if he were an Icelandic citizen" (*Iceland Reporter* 1996: 2). After being granted Icelandic citizenship in the mid-1990s, however, he was required to take an Icelandic name, which he considered "a violation of basic human rights." To settle the matter temporarily, he chose from the list of authorized names "Eilífur Friður," Eternal Peace, to which was then added the patronymic Edgarsson, since Edgar was his father's Christian (first) name. But this did not solve his problems:

> To complicate matters even further, Eilífur Friður had met an Icelandic woman prior to the citizenship adaptation, with whom he has a daughter, Freyja María Cabrera. Little Freyja María is permitted to keep her name . . . but any sisters or brothers she may subsequently receive will have a surname different from hers: namely Eilífsdóttir [for a girl] or Eilífsson [for a son], which, as Eilífur Friður points out, is sure to raise questions when the family travels abroad, and will be outright rejected in his native country.
>
> "My purpose in choosing the name" [Eternal Peace], he says, "is to call attention to the laws and make people question whether or not they are just. . . . I do not find it just to be forced to change my name." (*Iceland Reporter* 1996: 2)

Nor does the matter end here for Icelanders, for Icelandic naming laws now also permit children to take or be given their mother's Christian name to form their last name (matrinymic). This is an interesting evidence of the ways in which particularisms and universalisms interact: Iceland has traditionally been relatively egalitarian with respect to gender, and this has been enhanced as this norm has been given greater positive sanction in world institutions; hence Icelandic laws have simultaneously been changed to reflect this universalistic norm but correspondingly have become even more particularized in regard to naming. (Of course, just as anywhere else in the world, in everyday interaction people may use whatever name [nickname] they please; at issue is one's *legal* or citizenship name, hence the right of the nation-state to exercise authority over citizens.)

In this curious case of naming we see the strange collisions of globalization and localization, of the world-system and institutionalized societalism, that on a larger scale can lead to intrasocietal and intersocietal tensions, and even to open hostilities. A single dynamic simultaneously facilitates cooperation and conflict.

When violence is sanctioned by the transcendent norms of religious belief, it becomes a far more attractive option than the irony of "eternal peace."

Excursus on the History of Religions

A few words about the historical circumstances that surround the three great Western religious traditions—Christianity, Judaism, and Islam—may help set the religious context for the appearance of contemporary fundamentalisms. These are not the only religions to have produced religious fundamentalisms in our time, but a good case can be made that the other fundamentalisms that have emerged have used these religious traditions as the models for their programs (for example, that "Hindu fundamentalism" is reactive to Islamic fundamentalism and would not otherwise have existed). These three great traditions all find their root in a single place, namely, the account of the call by God of the patriarch Abraham and his response, as detailed in chapters 12–21 of the biblical book of Genesis. Historians of religions thus often call these three religious traditions the Abrahamic religions.

Students sometimes ask how it is that three religions, and their hundreds of subparts, that worship "the same God" can have so much conflict. The answer is that it's really quite easy, since each has a different conception of that same God; hence it may perceive the others as perverting the truth. Because each tradition harks back to a common narrative recorded in a written form that it considers to be "the Word of God," differences of interpretation (or hermeneutics [in Arabic, *ijtihad*]) can become *either* magnified *or* reduced through culture contact. This is precisely the problem that globalization highlights in the contrast of universalistic particularism and particularistic universalism. Consider some alternatives that different configurations of religions offer.

Suppose we live in a world in which we think there are many different gods: We have our god; you have your god. We could fight over whose god is more powerful, and people certainly have done that. Usually, however, when such a conflict occurs, it is relatively localized, and the winners' god displaces the losers' god. We could also, however, agree to disagree, and peace might prevail. We could worship our god; you could worship your god. In many respects, what were once known as the "religions of the Orient" allowed easily for these possibilities, as do other folk religions. We might call them "preglobal," however, in the sense that they don't see the world as a "single place." As they persist in modernity—from Voodoo to Zen—they are primarily clientelistic, inasmuch as they are organized to cater to the needs of individual believers or practitioners, hence they represent countermodern tendencies.

On the other hand, the Abrahamic traditions all begin with the assertion of a single, universal God (monotheism). Such is the first commandment of Judaism, the summary of the law given by Jesus of Nazareth, and the first pillar of Islam. There is *only* one God over all the universe, including every human being, and every human being should honor Him. (Note that all Abrahamic religious fundamentalisms insist on referring to God in the masculine only.) We know, however, that there has been considerable variety within and among the Abrahamic traditions in regard to how God is understood and what fidelity to God means. Again, there are two alternatives. The peaceful alternative allows one to say, in effect, "There is only one God over all the world, but each of us (or each community of us) may come to that God in different ways. We should respect this diversity of approaches." A militant alternative says, "There is only one God over all the world, and there is only one way correctly to come to and live under Him. Anyone who does not conform to this standard must be brought to do so; anyone who persists in acting otherwise is an enemy (both to us and to God)." The first of these alternatives particularizes the universal, while the second universalizes the particular. The universalization of the particular at the world level sets the stage for global fundamentalisms.

Until relatively recently, culture contact even within Abrahamic traditions was narrowly circumscribed. Consider, for example, that when the sociologist Émile Durkheim published his famous study on suicide only one hundred years ago, he was able to compare "racial" differences between the French and the Germans without any real criticism of his definition of race. Likewise, when Lutherans from various European locales came to North America, they quickly formed congregations for each variation of cultural practice (principally, but not only, language), rather than homogenizing around a common Lutheranism; this persisted until the end of the twentieth century. Much the same way, Jews in major urban areas are as likely to refer to synagogues as Russian, German, Sephardic, or Polish as they are Conservative, Reform, or Orthodox. The Roman Catholic Church also learned at the end of the nineteenth century that if it did not accommodate ethnic differences by establishing ethnic parishes (termed "national parishes") in North America, the institutional loyalty of its people was not going to hold (see, for example, Ciesluk 1947; Shaw 1991). These are the parishes the Catholic Church is now being forced to close as specific Euro-American ethnicities—such as Czech, Latvian, Lithuanian, and Polish—move out of historic neighborhoods and blend into the general population.

Globalization and Fundamentalisms

Globalization, however, breaks across cultural barriers through finance, media, and transport. Anglo-America is the preeminent global societal actor. English is the language of air traffic control and much of the Internet. The dollar and the euro are the measures of world economic value. But these technical systems do not speak to the "soul": that is, the human personality seems to have, at some times and for some people more strongly than others apparently, something we call a "spiritual" dimension. This dynamic is not, however, purely psychological; spirituality involves an element of *power*. Although each of the Abrahamic traditions contextualizes divine power differently, none fails to assert that the presence of God is the presence of power. In the global setting, specifically, the nature of Abrahamic monotheism coupled with the hegemonic position of Anglo-American "know-how" provides a potential resource for confrontation both within our own society and across societies.

In the ensuing pages we will look at three encounters between "the globe" and fundamentalist agendas, none of which can be separated from the joint issues of messiahship and the state of Israel. Although the specifics are different in each case, note that in each as well there is a significant commonality in the direction of hostilities, whether rhetorical or physical, against national political leaders who favor global peace on the basis of a universal value of human worth. These conflicts are generated by people within their own countries who demand acknowledgment of a particularist view of human action based on transcendent realities. In other words, current religious-political crises are not so much based on different *ideas* about "God" as they are on different claims about how God expects human beings to *behave*.

THE RELIGIOUS RIGHT IN THE UNITED STATES

"Mixing politics and religion" is not new in the United States or other nations influenced by American thinking. Not only the civil rights and antiwar movements of the recent past but also both prohibitionism and abolitionism mixed heady doses of politics and religion. In all of these cases, too, social stratification mixed with cultural considerations, including religion. This no more means that economics "causes" religion than that religion "causes" economics; the two can interact, as can other aspects of human experience, and sometimes these interactions have profound civilizational effects—as, for example, occurred at the Reformation in the sixteenth century.

One of the differences between some earlier religio-political alliances in the United States and the contemporary Religious Right is the global dimension of our experience. Exactly when this began may be debated for generations to come, but we might profitably start with the 1950s and the "Communist menace." Clearly some Christian Americans were skeptical of socialism in the nineteenth century, but others embraced it. After McCarthyism at home and Stalinism abroad, however, "godless Communism" became a major foe for Christian combat. Although there was certainly a Catholic anticommunism, fundamentalist Protestants particularly attempted to identify Soviet Marxism with biblical prophecy. At the center of this religious historiography was the newly founded (or refounded) state of Israel. Marxism was laid over against the restoration of Israel as a nation-state as part of a grand theological plan to herald the end of time, the return of Christ, and the judgment of the world. Elaborate explanations, often with increasingly technologically sophisticated visual representations, were constructed to announce a religious end of history. Atomic and hydrogen weaponry only enhanced the cataclysmic drama that would attend Armageddon, the great final battle. Did every Christian in the United States believe this? Certainly not. But we did hear enough of the great arms race of the superpowers, the launching of satellites, espionage, and counterespionage not to dismiss all of it as pure craziness either.

The 1967 attack on Israel by a coalition of Muslim Arab states enhanced further the fundamentalist argument. Whether true or not, the Arabs were perceived as working with Soviet backing—both philosophically and materially.

The Israeli triumph was enthusiastically received across the United States. A sudden alliance of good feeling and mutuality came to prevail among liberals, moderates, and fundamentalists. The victory in Israel was taken as an *American* victory; it justified U.S. principles and served to give a tentative point of unity to a nation otherwise divided over civil rights issues at home and the Vietnam War abroad. As the years passed, this picture changed. Further military conflict in 1973 and Palestinian problems, the dragging on of a settlement, the rise of militant Islam in Iran, battles in Lebanon, and so on, increasingly tried U.S. patience. The fall of the Soviet empire beginning in 1989 without any apparent resolution of the situation in the Holy Land began to make fundamentalist biblical exegeses of prophetic texts less gripping. A new religious coalition in the United States was building over "family values," and a new missionary thrust to the formerly Communist countries had more immediate success.

Today's American Religious Right or Christian Right emerged in its present form in response to an appeal made by U.S. president Richard Nixon to the "silent majority." Amid the protests of the Vietnam War era, Nixon was sure that a "silent majority" of Americans (sometimes called the "silent generation") agreed with him and his handling of the situation. Before too many years had passed, Jerry Falwell, an independent Baptist pastor in Virginia with a simply formatted television worship service, formed a political action group, the Moral Majority, that attempted to move the silent generation at least to send money to allow Falwell to lead the nation to righteousness. The formation of Falwell's group coincided fairly closely with the election of the nation's first bona fide "born-again" or evangelical president, Southern Baptist Jimmy Carter. But in fact, Falwell's vision was quite different from Carter's. The Moral Majority would support the casually Christian Ronald Reagan, not Carter, in the 1980 presidential election.

What were the sins of the Carter administration that irked the Religious Right? Clearly, no single act can be designated as the cause of Carter's rejection; his years were ill fated. He followed on and did not actively work to use his administrative power or legislative influence to alter the effects of the Supreme Court decision in *Roe v. Wade* (1973), which opened the way for legal abortions. The economy fell into deep recession. The Panama Canal had been, according to the perception of many Americans, given away. But when we look at the global situation, two other aspects also emerge: First, Carter and many of his advisers on international affairs were part of a global think-tank known as the Trilateral Commission. For right-wing activists, the Trilateral Commission represented a form of Communist appeasement on the one hand and something of a betrayal to Japanese business interests on the other. Carter was labeled as soft on Communism, while selling out U.S. industry. Carter was perceived as not really believing in the United States, an apostate to our civil religion. Second, Carter allowed Americans to be taken hostage by an infidel regime in Iran and proved impotent as commander in chief. Carter was perceived as having failed Christian America on virtually all fronts. His humanism was demonized both at home and abroad—and he was not helped by the fact that his vice president, Walter Mondale, whom Reagan absolutely trounced in 1984, was the half brother of a signer of the Humanist Manifesto.

Ironically, the Religious Right gained very little of its specifically religious agenda during the years of its favorite sons, Ronald Reagan and the elder George Bush. Though both of these presidents talked the right language on abortion and school prayer, neither was able to effect any significant changes. The fall of the "evil" Soviet empire may have been hastened by the Reagan-Bush line, but it was so entirely unanticipated in the West that this can hardly have been a major factor. Wise investors used these years to internationalize the U.S. economy even further, rather than the reverse, and China became a significant economic player in U.S. markets. Reagan and Bush proved virtually powerless to resolve Holy Land crises—indeed, the worst single loss of American lives in the Middle East, the bombing of the Marine barracks in Lebanon, occurred during the Reagan years. The nation was plunged ever further into debt.

One might think, therefore, that a joint slate of Southern Baptists, in the persons of Bill Clinton and Al Gore, would have rallied the evangelical-fundamentalist cadre. Hardly so: lukewarm Episcopalian George H. W. Bush was by far their choice. Indeed, a demonization process can again be said to have operated with respect to Clinton-Gore, who found themselves not only in trouble with the Christian Right but also precariously positioned in relation to the traditionally Democratic Jewish constituency, which has been divided over the "peace process" in Israel. Rather than embrace such men, the Religious Right first put its hopes in 1996 on populist Catholic Republican Pat Buchanan, only to eke out a weak compromise with Bob Dole. While both Al Gore and George W. Bush made explicit religious affirmations in 2000, and Gore chose an observant Jew as his running mate, it was nevertheless Bush who continued to hold the Christian Right by making explicit statements about the role of Jesus in his life and promoting a platform that honored the particulars of the Christian Right agenda. Although a far less aggressive figure than Buchanan, Bush consistently supported core tenets of the Christian Right agenda and directly rewarded Christian Right initiatives through the concept (and programs) of Charitable Choice, blurring the once-strict separation between governmental and religiously based programs for assistance to Americans in poverty or other circumstances of deprivation. Bush has also appealed indirectly to Christian conservatives with his rhetoric in the conduct of the Iraq war and his support of legislation that restricted expenditures of government funding on abortion, and has expressed at least tacit support for amendments to the U.S. Constitution that would prohibit both abortion and same-sex marriage.

The idea of a Catholic president would have utterly horrified U.S. fundamentalists when that movement was founded at the start of the twentieth century, but a look at Buchanan's candidacy helps us see the interplay between globalization and religion for today's American Religious Right. The issues now are not over the pope as a "foreign power" having control over the United States; rather, the Religious Right wants to assert *authority* in contradistinction to negotiation. The Religious Right is looking for leadership that will uphold "traditional Judeo-Christian" moral principles as unassailably true. What Buchanan offered was an "America First" agenda that was palpably uncompromising. Buchanan's concerns about foreign influences were aimed at international capital and the might of

Globalization in a Different Key

One of the by-products of rising fundamentalisms has been a new recognition of religion as a factor with which world peacemaking bodies must reckon to achieve their goals. The following account by William K. Piotrowski, who was an undergraduate student at Trinity College in Hartford, Connecticut, at the time he wrote it for *Religion in the News,* indicates how politics still plays into the peace agenda:

> [S]ummoned to participate in the Millennium World Peace Summit, more than 1,000 religious leaders from around the world attended a four-day summit in New York City, beginning August 28 [2000].
>
> The brainchild of a meeting between U.N. Secretary General Kofi Annan and Ted Turner, the summit was supposed to spread a common agreement that religions should be a force for peace around the globe. That was the plan.
>
> What actually happened, with the enthusiastic assistance of American journalists, was a savvy intervention by the Dalai Lama that gave a boost to his continuing campaign against the Chinese occupation of Tibet—and demonstrated his mastery of the media.
>
> At root, the story caught hold because of the U.N.'s flagrant ambivalence. On the one hand, the organization wanted to hold a conference on religion and world conflict. On the other, it wanted to respect the sensibilities of powerful member governments like China, which have less than ideal track records on religious liberty.
>
> As early as October 9, 1999, Jonathan Petre of the London *Telegraph* wrote an article suggesting that it would be difficult to meet both objectives. He noted that conference planners seemed to be hedging on the question of who should attend. "The gathering will not include politicians but it should feed into the General Assembly," principal conference organizer Bawa Jain told Petre. . . . [R]eading between the lines, Petre observed, "[O]ne notable absentee, however, is likely to be the Dalai Lama, the Tibetan spiritual leader, because his presence at the summit might inflame the Chinese, who hold one of the five permanent seats on the UN Security Council."
>
> The role or nonrole of the Dalai Lama at the summit remained an internal debate until early August, about a month before the conference was scheduled to begin. At that point, the Dalai Lama's staff made public a letter that rejected an offer to speak to delegates at the end of the conference, rather than participating himself. Laurie Goodstein of the *New York Times* wrote on August 3 that the conference planners had asked the Dalai Lama to "deliver the keynote address at the closing session, to be held not at the United Nations but at the Waldorf-Astoria."
>
> From this point forward the media fixed their attention on the missing lama [monk]. . . .
>
> In response to Goodstein's story, human rights leaders sprang into action in support of the Dalai Lama. Desmond Tutu [retired Anglican archbishop of Capetown, and like the Dalai Lama, a Nobel Peace Prizewinner] took to the pulpit to proclaim that the Dalai Lama's disinvitation "compromises the integrity of the United Nations, and the credibility of the summit." Furthermore, Tutu said, "Apart from anything else, the Dalai Lama is the spiritual leader of a major religion, and it just doesn't make sense that he has not been invited." . . .
>
> From that point on, the Dalai Lama succeeded in taking a ho-hum conference about the virtues of peace and turning it into a high profile forum for Tibetan freedom and China bashing. . . .
>
> As it turned out, the Dalai Lama made sure that he had his own say at the conference. A delegation of four high-ranking Tibetan monks representing

him read a statement from him that spoke of . . . "forgiveness and reconciliation." At that, the official China delegation walked out. Later, according to the *Daily News*, Master Shenghui, vice president of the government-controlled Buddhist Association of China, "called the Dalai Lama's absence a 'clever' ploy, and accused him of 'dishonoring' religion."

Ultimately, media coverage strayed half-heartedly back to the original objective of the conference. . . .

The planners hoped that delegates would act as satellites of the U.N., bringing the message of peace to their corner of the globe. But on August 29, George Melloan of the *Wall Street Journal* reported that "shortly after one Chinese delegate was proclaiming a 'golden age' of religion in China, Chinese police arrested 130 evangelical Protestants in central China."

Source: William K. Piotrowski, "Monastic Spinmeister," *Religion in the News* (Fall 2000): 21–22.

multinational corporations that owe fealty to no flag. He was, at least then, not a politician—and that has an appeal among a sector that increasingly has come to feel that politics as "the art of compromise" is also an act of betrayal.

Why is this so? Again, no single reason accounts for any sociocultural complex; nevertheless, we cannot ignore in the growth of the Religious Right the operation of status variables in social stratification. As we have noted earlier, James D. Davidson and his colleagues have shown that religious groups in the United States are dramatically disproportionately represented among U.S. elites, and that among Protestants there has been very little change in this proportion over time. Fundamentalist Christians, for whatever reason, are people who are not getting their fair share of the political-economic pie. Although they may earn a decent living, they are at increasing distance from economic elites, and they perceive themselves to have little political control, even—perhaps *especially*—in their local communities (for example, in schools, housing projects, and so on). Faceless bureaucracies and court jurisdictions far from their locales mandate systems of action (or prohibit countervailing action) contrary to fundamentalists' perceptions of right and wrong. The more globalization advances, the more a sense of "place" in society recedes. At the same time other religious groups, most notably Reform Jews, along with the religiously unaffiliated, advance ahead of the Christian fundamentalists into the political-economic elite.

Hence, evangelical-fundamentalist Protestants, traditionalist Catholics, and Orthodox Jews form a loose political alliance that attempts to assert citizen control over local issues. The aim of the "stealth" candidacies of the Christian Coalition in the early 1990s, for example, was to place religious conservatives on hundreds of *local* boards of education, city councils, and county commissions. And it is certainly the case that George W. Bush's embrace of faith-based programs and Charitable Choice was early on especially directed toward this constituency rather than the historic Protestant or Catholic mainstream, while it has more recently also attempted to court African-American congregations within geographic sectors where they constitute a significant voting bloc (see Sager 2007).

This notwithstanding, research by Mark Chaves (1999) has shown that at least in its earliest years the actual flow of money from Charitable Choice programs was primarily to the benefit of institutionalized service programs that were for the most part run by mainline churches.

ISLAMIZATION

Many Muslims would prefer, because of the historically Christian associations of the word *fundamentalist*, that the movement often termed *Islamic fundamentalism* instead be called *Islamization* and its adherents *Islamicists*. The movement's roots are varied, but they can probably be traced to reactions toward the British colonial presence in Egypt and in that part of India now known as Pakistan. Until the Six-Day War of 1967, however, these movements had little effect, though, for different reasons, they were largely as sidelined as the Christian fundamentalists in the United States. The failure of the Arab alliance to succeed in defeating the Israelis, however, began to give new urgency to Islamic conservatives.

The attack on Israel was the dream of Egyptian (later, United Arab Republic) president Gamal Abdel Nasser, largely a secularist, who enticed other secular Arab leaders to join his plan. When it failed, this began to allow an opening for conservative Muslim preachers to claim that the basis for the defeat was not Jewish military superiority but the failure of Muslims to immerse themselves adequately in Islam. In this view, human pride rather than submission to Allah was at the heart of the Arab defeat. The momentum for Islamization built slowly, as most secular Arab leaders were reluctant to allow the mullahs opportunities to promulgate their critiques. Economic pressures often intervened. An increasing disparity between those largely secular Arabs who benefited from the oil trade and the rest of the population sent the disenfranchised looking for alternative explanations for their plight. University students, small business owners, craftsmen, and some parts of the old middle class (not least those who produced men with vocations to Muslim ministry) provided fertile soil for the seeds of Islamization. Palestinians who were termed "terrorists" in the West were considered heroes in the Muslim world. Nevertheless, such activities remained relatively marginal to the world-system until 1978–1979, with the rise of the Ayatollah Khomeini in Iran.

Perhaps no more perfect case of both the interaction of and confrontation between globalization and local intransigence could be imagined than Iran; indeed, in some ways it stretched the imaginations of many social scientists who gave inadequate weight to the religious dimension when they attempted to predict Iranian outcomes. Mohammad Reza Shah Pahlavi, who ascended to the throne at age twenty-two and ruled Iran for almost four decades before the Iranian Revolution, was a dedicated modernist. He rejoiced in the political-economic support of the United States and enjoyed a Western lifestyle. He saw his vocation as bringing Iran into the forefront of global geopolitics. "Iran could be the showcase for all of Asia," he claimed. "America cannot spread its assistance in every country everywhere. Here is the place with the best prospect for a great transformation" (quoted in Kimmel and Tavakol 1986: 106). Perhaps the Shah was correct in his analysis, but in hindsight we can see that he made at least three mistakes in implementation:

1. *Economically*, he placed too much emphasis on oil and did not demand sufficient diversification of U.S. assistance to share the benefits of Iran's oil resources and geopolitical setting adequately throughout the population.
2. *Socioculturally*, he demanded changes that exceeded the prerequisites of the project of modernization (such as not permitting the wearing of the veil by women attending universities, reducing support for the mosques, implementing policies to displace small shopkeepers).
3. *Politically*, he created a secret police force (SAVAK) that used extreme cruelty to attack those who disagreed with his policies.

By the late 1970s, spiraling inflation, population pressures in the cities, and a crisis on the world oil market had clearly put the Shah in trouble. That was not too much of a surprise to U.S. social scientists savvy in Middle Eastern studies. What was a surprise was the role that came to be played by the Islamicist Ayatollah Ruhollah Khomeini in the foundation of the Islamic Republic of Iran. Why? Preeminently because secular social science had totally overlooked the persistence of the religious dimension as a possible trajectory for the demonstration of human resentment against oppression—this in spite of the fact that practically every foundational social theorist, including Karl Marx, had recognized the religious dimension as integrally connected to deprivation, though not merely a reflection of deprivation. "We did not want oil, we did not want independence, we wanted Islam," was the Ayatollah's explanation of his appeal and success (quoted in Kimmel and Tavakol 1986: 112).

What did he mean by that? The Shah was a professing Muslim, but this was not enough. What the Ayatollah meant was a lifeworld-level affirmation of *stability*, a continuation of "things the way they always ought to have been." Note carefully the use of the word *ought*; it is important to understanding the fundamentalist dynamic, since what fundamentalism protests against as much as anything in the internationalist vision of globalization is the *relativization of cultural values* that seems to be part and parcel of impersonal market forces that drive high-technology multinational capitalism. Only the most naive fundamentalist would claim that in some past time everyone was religious, or moral, or both. What the fundamentalist would claim was that in the past there was a religious-ethical core within sociocultural systems that was generally acknowledged: sin was sin and truth was truth. Ironically, the preglobalization world of the nation-state, whether in the Arab world or Christian Europe, provided a buffering device that established cultural prerogatives. The Reformation principle of *cuius regio, eius religio* (roughly: the religion of the ruler is the religion of the people) and Muslim principles surrounding the caliphate had a commonsense reality for everyday activity, particularly when language separated major cultural groups. People who "talked different" *were* different. Every culture knew it was right and others were wrong. Common language and common religion went hand-in-hand.

Globalization changed this simple worldview; accommodation and compromise became the order of the day. When we look at Islamization efforts, for example, we see that with few exceptions they are directly proportional to involvement by a Muslim leader in the "ethic" of globalization; that is, in that "shared and binding set of rules exogenous to any given society" of which John Meyer (1980) speaks. The murder of Egyptian president Anwar Sadat in 1981 is an excellent, but not the sole, example. This was similarly the set of values to which the Shah of Iran was at least giving lip service, and it is the basis on which the Pakistani female leader Benazir Bhutto, murdered in 2008 in an effort to return to power there after a military coup had removed her, ultimately attempted to base her claim to legitimacy. While Americans often see specific acts of Islamicist terrorism directed against the United States, the bigger picture clearly shows the primary targets to be Muslim leaders themselves. It is not "the American way of life" that is under attack by Islamicists, but attempts to harmonize—which they see to be compromise, hence weaken, and even deny—Islam with that way of life. Unlike the New Christian Right, most Islamicists are quite willing to let the United States go to hell if it wants to; what they resist are attempts by the global system of states, of which they see the United States as the principal economic and cultural actor, to alter their own lifeworld.

Nowhere are the contradictions between the global system of states and the Islamic lifeworld more pronounced than in the place given to the state of Israel, particularly by the United States. The state of Israel is an "offense" to Muslims not because the Jews are people of a different religion—for Islam has generally been tolerant toward Jews, indeed in many cases far more so than Christianity. Rather, the state of Israel places into juxtaposition irrational and rational political policies, which themselves result from a unique religious configuration in the United States between Jews and the Christian Right. The creation of the state of Israel undermined the secular ideology of the nation-state in the Muslim world because, in a Western betrayal of its own commitments to the secular state, a religious ideology was used to justify the creation of Israel. The establishment of the state of Israel was clearly a response to the Holocaust, but it was also intimately related to fundamentalist Protestant understandings of the necessity for the reunion of the Jewish peoples at Jerusalem prior to some form of millennial return and reign of Jesus Christ. Inseparable from this is the demographic fact that from World War II to 2007 the United States was the largest Jewish country in the world, and that U.S. citizens can hold dual citizenship in both the United States and Israel, a condition that created a unique relationship between the two countries inasmuch as most other nations in the global system refused to grant Israel full diplomatic recognition. In some respects, then, Israel came to be perceived as a client state of the U.S. in the Middle East and among the most radical Muslims was used to reawaken images of the Crusades.

Muslims thus see a moral fissure in the ethic of globalization along these lines: The state of Israel has been established in the center of the historic Islamic world as an outpost for a new campaign to blot out the Islamic way of life. Like the medieval Crusades, this effort seeks to impede the practice of Islam through other standards of behavior to which Muslims will be forced to conform or else by which they will be excluded from the benefits of global citizenship. From the Muslim point of view, by contrast, *Islam* itself provides a set of principles for universal world government. Here, then, we come to the center of the conflict between Islamization and globalization: As preeminently a system of rules, not beliefs, Islam claims to offer a universal alternative to the dominant model of "secular," high-technology multinational capitalism that forms the basis for the global system of states in late modernity. Islamization proposes the universalization of the particular, and by contrast, it sees the Western system as doing nothing but the same. That is, the Islamicist sees the Western system of globalization as the implementation *not* of relatively universal human values, but rather of specifically Western values. The Islamicist might find some support for his position sociologically in Talcott Parsons's claim (1963) that the West has not been secularized, but rather has been so permeated by the core values of the "Judeo-Christian ethic" as to render itself sacralized. Consider simply as an example U.S. postage stamps that carry the message "love."

This observation highlights one of the central propositions of globalization theory, particularly as articulated in the work of Roland Robertson and his colleagues; namely, the role of *ethics* (ethoses) in constructing systems of interaction. Derived from the work of both Max Weber and Parsons, this point of view suggests that systems of *valuing*, whether or not they originate in material conditions, have an influence, perhaps a determinative influence, on subsequent political-economic relationships. Peoples whose worldviews continue to be shaped by Islam, which is founded on a "warrior ethic," according to Weber, will be essentially at variance from the core values of globalization (see Swatos 1995). Failure to recognize the depth to which these cultural components structure political organization leads Westerners to think that the assumptions of modern rationalism can provide a basis for reasonable *compromise*, when in fact they do not. Instead, the warrior ethic sees *standoff* as a transcendent scenario in which different "strong men" contend for power. This view "came home" to Americans most powerfully in the events of September 11, 2001, with the al-Qaeda attacks on the World Trade Center—perhaps no more dramatic symbol of international capitalism could have been chosen for a *Star Wars*–esque scenario wherein the hub of globalization was attacked by the forces of an almost mythical strong man domiciled in one of the most remote parts of the world, governed by the most religiously reactionary of regimes.

A fascinating Weberian study of religion and political democracy by James Duke and Barry Johnson (1989) takes up a variant of Weber's Protestant ethic thesis to demonstrate that Protestantism has acted causally with respect to the development of political democracy. More to the point presently, however, is that, using four indicators of democracy, Islamic nations appear, in that research, at the bottom of five major religious groups on two of the four indicators and next to the bottom (higher only than tribal religions) on the other two. This is intensified by the fact that, whereas in the poorest nations (per capita GNP less than $399) democracy is weak across the board, states with tribal religions drop out of the picture at the uppermost end of the GNP spectrum, but Islamic nations do not. In addition, the undemocratic nature of Islamic regimes is unrelated to whether or not a previous colonial regime was of a more or less democratically oriented religion (for example, French Catholicism or English Protestantism), something that is not true in former colonies whose original tradition was some non-Christian religion other than Islam.

We might turn this around and say that from the Islamicist viewpoint, Muslim leaders who adopt the ethic of globalization, as Meyer summarizes it, have already betrayed the faith; that is, the warrior ethic mediates between "upstream" doctrine and day-to-day practice. This dynamic runs throughout the bulk of Islamic history, though the specific terms have differed across time. Ironically for the West, movements toward democratic pluralism on the global level have actually allowed Islamicist activities to grow in both local and international influence. The same means of communication, transport, and exchange that provide the infrastructure to globalization can be used for the deployment of Islamicist values (much the same way, for example, as Christian televangelists in the United States use the very media of which they are hypercritical as the means for propagating their own views). The Ayatollah Khomeini himself sent audiotape cassettes to Iran while a refugee in France, just as Osama bin Laden appears in televised messages to continue to provoke his adversaries and encourage his followers. Those societies of Muslim heritage that have most intentionally aped Western democratic models have created the conditions for the growth of Islamicist parties, which in their extremism simply reinforce the tendencies that are already latent in the warrior ethic. This is particularly the case when the fruits of the globalization project are inequitably distributed—as they were, for example, in Iran.

FUNDAMENTALISM, GLOBALIZATION, AND AMERICAN CIVIL RELIGION

"God Bless America" reflects not only the most popular slogan of the responses to the events of 9/11 as they appeared across the United States, but also the diffuse quality of American civil religion, which stands alongside of, and both complements and is complemented by, the specific traditions that compose the American religious milieu. "God Bless America" was simultaneously slogan and song. It gave voice to American emotions—and it has a history of association with national resurgence and the sociological corpus: Columbia University sociologist Robert Merton and colleagues performed research on the mass radio audience stimulated by singer Kate Smith, who had introduced the song to an immediately successful national reception in 1938, on the occasion of the twentieth anniversary of the World War I armistice, and subsequently used it to sell bonds during a World War II radiothon (Merton et al. 1946). Written by Irving Berlin during his own military service in 1918, the song was rejected for publication at that time, but would become at the radio voice of Smith a powerful rallying cry in the midst of World War II—nor, of course, was the fact that Berlin was Jewish lost in the midst of Nazi anti-Semitism (cf. http://katesmith.org/gba.html).

Popularizing Political Prophecy in America: Dispensationalism

Why do conservative Americans hate the United Nations—a position whose intensity shocked even presidential hopeful George W. Bush when he was seeking the Republican nomination?

"Part of the answer," writes Paul Boyer, an emeritus professor of history at the University of Wisconsin, "lies in the powerful grip on many evangelicals and fundamentalists of premillennial dispensationalism," a theological doctrine of the "end of the world" that was first developed in the mid-1800s by John Darby, a founder of the Plymouth Brethren sect in Great Britain, and which was popularized in the United States both by his own work and by inclusion in the highly influential *Schofield Reference Bible* of 1909 (which continues to be published).

"Depending on the precise question," Boyer notes, "opinion pollsters find that from 40 to 60 percent of contemporary Americans embrace key elements of Darby's end-time scenario: the imminent Rapture of the saints; the seven-year Tribulation dominated by the Antichrist; the Battle of Armageddon, when Christ and the raptured saints will defeat Antichrist and his earthly armies," and so on. "Following Darby's lead, dispensationalists also attentively monitor the 'signs of the times'—a convergence of events, many centering on the Jews, signaling the terminus of the present dispensation, the Church Age." These views underlie the plots of the *Left Behind* series as well as Hal Lindsey's *The Late Great Planet Earth* (1970), "a kind of 'Dispensationalism for Dummies' [that] was *the* nonfiction bestseller of the 1970s."

> For dispensationalists, the United Nations is at least a forerunner of Antichrist's regime. Earlier prophecy writers found Antichrist tendencies in Saladin, Napoleon, Hitler, Mussolini, and even Juan Carlos of Spain. In current dispensationalist fiction, however, including the *Left Behind* series and Hal Lindsey's 1996 novel *Blood Moon*, the U.N. secretary-general is unmasked as the Evil One. Saturated in such propaganda, dispensationalists understandably recoil in horror when contemplating the United Nations and its penumbra of international organizations. . . .
>
> During the Cold War, Russia preoccupied the prophecy popularizers. . . . Lindsey's *Late Great Planet Earth* described with ill-concealed glee the annihilation awaiting Moscow's armies.
>
> Such images retain their pornographic fascination for today's popularizers, as in the description of the Second Coming in *Glorious Appearing* (2004) . . . of the interminable *Left Behind* series: . . . Born again Christians excepted, millions meet their doom. . . .
>
> The apocalyptic wishful thinking has persisted, but the Cold War's end shifted attention from Russia to the Muslim world. . . .
>
> With 9/11 and the Iraq War, the anti-Muslim theme reached feverish levels. In *Beyond Iraq: The Next Move* (2003), prophecy-writer Michael Evans labeled Islam "a religion conceived in the pit of hell." Televangelist John Hagee, preaching at his Cornerstone Church in San Antonio, called the Iraq War "the gateway to the Apocalypse" and a sign of Christ's immanent Second Coming. [Former U.S.] House majority leader Tom DeLay [who was ultimately forced to resign from Congress for financial misconduct], present in the audience, then rose to proclaim, "Ladies and gentlemen, what has been spoken here tonight is the truth from God."
>
> Lt. General Jerry Boykin, a top Pentagon intelligence official, delivered sermons in full-dress uniform in fundamentalist churches portraying the

> war on terrorism in apocalyptic religious terms: "Why do [radical Muslims] hate us so much? . . . [B]ecause we're a Christian nation." For Boykin, the real enemy "is a spiritual enemy, . . . called Satan," and his earthly agents will be defeated only "if we come against them in the name of Jesus." As for domestic politics, George Bush is "in the White House because God put him there for a time such as this."
>
> Source: Paul Boyer, "Give Me That End-Time Religion: The Politicization of Prophetic Belief in Contemporary America," *Reflections* 92, no. 1 (Spring 2005): 24–29.

When examined in a religious rather than a sociopolitical context, what is most immediately obvious is that the song actually says almost nothing about God other than a providential personalism. It primarily exalts in the goodness of the nation even as it affirms the existence of the deity as an ally for her good. Indeed, various commentators, for example, have noted that if the song were theologically authentic the title would be something along the lines of "America Bless God." This observation underscores the important theoretical distinction between theological and religious use of language. Inasmuch as more than 90 percent of the U.S. population still acknowledges belief in God (in relatively simplistic surveys), an appeal to God in this undefined way is an appeal to a singularly unifying religious symbol of high generality.

It is significant, however, that this song, rather than the national anthem, became the expressive focus of American reaction. Within hours of the attacks, when members of Congress sang "God Bless America" on the steps of the Capitol, and certainly by the time of the memorial observance at the National Cathedral, the essentially religious character of American nationhood was increasingly articulated. In the popular vein, Lee Greenwood's 1983 song "God Bless the U.S.A." was also added to this movement—and is now incorporated into the naturalization ceremony of new U.S. citizens (see Meizel 2006; Swatos 2006). The Puritan "errand into wilderness" to found a "city upon a hill" was reaffirmed: The United States began as a religious project—the product of a search for "freedom." The American Way of religious freedom, in this mythological re-creation—which, as Robert Bellah (1999) has pointed out, is actually far more to be associated with Roger Williams than with the "Pilgrim fathers"—was set over against a "foreign" way of religious tyranny and oppression. Civil religion in America thus is not as entirely diffuse as it seems at first blush, for there is an aura within which it operates, what Catherine Albanese has termed *American "public Protestantism"*—the characteristic of Americanism that led to G. K. Chesterton's observation that in the United States "even the Catholics are Protestants." Today we could add other groups as well (e.g., "Protestant Buddhism"). Complementing this public Protestantism is the moral code of the Judeo-Christian ethic.

When the moment came for the institutionally religious and the civilly religious to intersect after the events of 9/11, a crucial choice had to be made as to who should utter the prophetic word. Neither the liberal female bishop of Washington Episcopalians, nor the onetime leader of the Moral Majority, but a man who would embody for the bulk of Americans the public Protestantism that they had encountered the most throughout their lives: Billy Graham mounted the steps of Washington's National Cathedral. Though technically a Baptist, Graham has always been noted as a public figure, both in the United States and abroad, associated neither with a specific church nor with an ostensibly commercial enterprise. In his sermon, Graham interrelated doctrinally specific religion and civil religion as he had done throughout his career. In calling America to repentance and renewal, Graham also renewed his own cultural capital as the living icon of the public Protestantism that forms the specifically religious basis for the diffuse civil religion of America. And did it occur to no one that Billy Graham spent the bulk of his evangelistic ministry conducting *crusades*?

Public Protestantism and American civil religion particularly coalesced because the attacks of 9/11 constituted *moral outrages* inasmuch as they failed to conform to the norms of civil societies in regard to the conduct of public conflicts. By acting outside the norms of structured national conflicts, the perpetrators of these actions were seen to represent persons who had overstepped the bounds of toleration that are inherent in American civil religion. They both violated the norm of taking religion "too seriously" and simultaneously provided evidence of what happens when people take religion "too seriously." For there is within American civil religion a juxtaposition of freedom for and freedom from religion: The latter was outrageously breached on 9/11. The breaching of this norm means that American civil religion itself was attacked. The events of 9/11 did not simply attack America in general; they attacked the American civil-religious principle of laissez-faire—which is also a political-economic worldview, theoretically the American economic worldview. This interplay of laissez-faire religion and laissez-faire economics allows constant ultimate value reinforcement for practical behavior. The appeal of Billy Graham is always to bring people to make their "own decision" about religious commitment—*Decision* being, in fact, the title of his magazine for supporters. The attacks on the World Trade Center and the Pentagon thus were cast not merely as military offenses, but as assaults on core American values, including the religious value of freedom for/from. Not surprisingly, American Muslims had to distance themselves quickly from the contrary values enacted by the terrorists.

The renewal of American civil religion thus can be projected to have an ironic consequence: namely, the decline of the influence of right-wing religious extremism in the political sector with the United States, even as there is a more general turn to religious articulation of central values. This became quickly apparent in the days after the events of 9/11 when attempts by Christian Rightists to associate the attacks with such phenomena as gay/lesbian rights and feminism rang hollow and received scant hearing—or were heard and quickly condemned. American civil religion is not the worship of America, but it is an assertion of central values for the separation of religions from politics even as it asserts the religiousness of the core value of the nation as an instrument of divine intent, if not action. Hence 9/11 served to knit together a stronger conservative Judeo-Christian core while paring away the fringes. Issues that once animated the extreme are being addressed within the core in a spirit of a search for reinvigorated central values, albeit in the context of a specific threat that may in fact obscure the root causes of the problems in question. The contradictions of multinational capitalism, for example, continue to be largely off the agenda of American political and religious discourse.

Not as apparent in the experience of 9/11 was the relationship between the attacker's priorities—the destruction of the state of Israel—and American civil religion. Perhaps because the initial military assaults against Israel in the 1960s by the likes of Egypt's Nasser were fully secularist—Nasser being a great foe of Islamicists, as was the Baath Party that brought Saddam Hussein to power in Iraq—American policy-makers and military strategists largely missed or misread the buildup of Islamicist politics during the 1970s. The United States backed democratic efforts where they seemed viable while accepting the leadership of "strong men" as long as they did not threaten American "interests"—specifically oil resources. Human rights issues were clearly secondary priorities. On the surface of it, for example, one might have thought Jimmy Carter and the Ayatollah Khomeini would have been great friends as advocates of moral high ground; instead they became mortal enemies. Because the state of Israel is intertwined with the Promised Land myth of America, on the one hand, and because of the millennial expectations of American Protestants on the other, American leadership failed to understand the extent to which Islamicists view Israel both as an invasion of their sacred space and, more specifically, as an American client state. Americans by and large continue to fail to see that the Israeli presence in Palestine appears to Islamicists as an American "resettlement project" not essentially different from Soviet resettlements among, for example, the Baltic nations after World War II. Regardless of the high motives out of which they were born, the establishment of the state of Israel, the resettlement of Jews in that territory, and the lack of adequate regard for the people already living there nevertheless represent a Western incursion of unique significance entirely counter to the decolonization that otherwise characterized the post–World War II era. Hence, by its apparent ignorance and arrogance, the United States becomes, in Islamicists' eyes, the final superpower to be undone.

Undergirding these claims and counterclaims are biblical myths of ownership that extend thousands of years into the past, before either Christianity or Islam was ever named. The Promised Land—which is precisely what God is claimed to have given Abraham—was already populated when the children of Israel arrived. Palestinians claim a pre-Israelitic ancestry. The claims of modern Jews, furthermore, are historically corrupted by the fact that, if the term *Semitic* has any genuinely biological concomitants—rather than its fast-and-loose use by anti-Semites—then many, perhaps most, present-day Jews cannot possibly be biological descendants of those who occupied Judea at the time of the Roman destruction of Jerusalem. Hence, the Jewish claim to land rights in historic Israel is a spiritual claim, rooted in religious myth—a myth ironically shared in part with the majority of actual occupants at the time of the creation of the modern state of Israel—i.e., Muslims. Jerusalem thus becomes the epicenter of myths of eternal significance with practical consequences. In this context, the specifically Judeo-Christian roots of American Public Protestantism become quite clear. The claim to the "right of the Jewish people to a nation-state of their own" is shot through with specifically modern American Public Protestant thinking about the nature of the world order. Neither Catholics nor Muslims in a world-historical context, for example, would think this way. The process by which American history has been thought and taught in the United States is retrospectively applied as a universal world history of eternal significance. Manifest destiny is extended as a result of American participation in World War II from a "doctrine" regarding the development of the Western Hemisphere to a universal law based on a specific civil-religious reading, which is also a political-economic reading, of the purpose of the United States as a nation of eternal significance: "In God We Trust"—you can read it on all our money.

At the same time, because of the public Protestantism that pervades the United States, the *successes* of the medieval Crusades are often minimized. The Latin Kingdom of Jerusalem, by contrast, can teach important lessons to those who would too quickly dismiss the persistence of Islamicist forces. Depending on how its boundaries are evaluated, it can be said to have lasted from forty-five to two hundred years. The modern state of Israel only recently celebrated its sixtieth anniversary: As Americans fight the current war against Islamicist terrorism, a perspective on what Max Weber called the "warrior ethic" of Islam needs to be laid over against the work ethic that is enshrined within American civil religion (see Swatos 1995). These ethics represent two competing worldviews of "universal historical" significance. The Islamicist worldview presents a challenge to the United States entirely different in kind from that of the Soviet empire, against which American civil religious defenses were primarily constructed over the last half century. The terrorists who struck on 9/11 could have chosen many different targets. The specific choices they made need to be seen in their symbolic significance, and the importance of the consequences attached to those choices needs to be addressed in a renewed civil religion in America in the era of globalization.

ULTRAORTHODOXY

For the past thirty years Americans have come to anticipate various forms of Palestinian-Islamicist terrorism in and adjacent to the territory now occupied by the state of Israel. Bus bombings, airplane hijackings, suicide attacks, and so on are recurrent copy for television and newspaper headlines. Thus it was with surprise that Americans learned that the assassin of Israeli prime minister Yitzhak Rabin was not a Muslim, or even a Palestinian sympathizer, but a Jew, who proclaimed: "I did this to stop the peace process. . . . We need to be cold-hearted. . . . When you kill in war, it is an act that is allowed." As the story developed, furthermore, it became clear that there was an intimate connection between the inspiration of assassin Yigal Amir and Orthodox Jewry in New York City. Specifically, New York rabbi Abraham Hecht, leader of Brooklyn's largest Syrian synagogue, had publicly ruled the previous June that Rabin and his colleague Shimon Peres were in a state of *moser*, the condition of someone who surrenders his people. "A Jew who hands over Jewish land or wealth to an alien people, Hecht said, is guilty of a sin worthy of the death penalty. And what is more, he went on, Maimonides, the greatest of all Jewish philosophers, said that if a man kills such a person he has done a good deed" (Remnick 1995: 37).

This prominent murder among the thousands committed in the twentieth-century battle for the Holy Land uniquely highlights the intersecting dynamics of globalization and fundamentalism: A local congregational pastor in one part of the world, thousands of miles from a law student elsewhere, inspires the death of a major figure not only in the Middle Eastern peace process but potentially in the entire global system—thanks to media of communication and transport that brought his remarks into one of the crucial value articulations of globalization, a free press. So much was this the case, indeed, that Israelis immediately after the assassination attempted to formalize laws that would actually restrict the publication of such "opinions" as those of Hecht (who was fired by his New York congregation shortly after Rabin's murder).

In the assassination of Yitzhak Rabin the global norms of freedom of religion and freedom of the press, written, for example, into a whole series of world-institutional documents, yielded antiglobal results, enabled by the very technologies that advance the globalization to which Islamicists object. Indeed, one might argue that from an Islamicist viewpoint the assassination of Rabin could be taken as evidence that globalization will be its own gravedigger.

But there is a counterargument to which we have already alluded: namely, that the creation of the state of Israel as it was effected by the Allies following World War II, and especially by the United States, was in conflict with and contrary to the norms of globalization; hence we should anticipate ongoing actual conflict over this sociopolitical fact. The United States will be especially immediately involved in this conflict because of the comparably high proportion of Israelis who retain U.S. citizenship. Put another way, the world-systemic conflict in and about the state of Israel is the "exception that proves the rule" of globalization theory precisely because the foundation of the state of Israel essentially violates the "value-neutral" or "secular" politics that is the norm of global society.

From the restriction of the Papal States within the walls of the Vatican, to the transformation of the Ottoman Empire into modern Turkey, to the de-deification of the emperor of Japan, to the disestablishment of one state church after another, the entire trend of globalization has been away from the particularizing of politics by intrasocietal cultural norms associated with historical religions. How could the state of Israel possibly be founded in contradistinction to this trend? The answer involves a combination of interacting elements.

First, the psychodynamics of guilt over the Holocaust must be acknowledged. The genocide inflicted on European Jews by the Nazi regime—when the majority of "liberal" politicians of all Western democracies stood largely deaf, dumb, and blind—yielded in due time its legitimate emotional remorse. The state of Israel was a global irrational response to an even more overwhelming irrational system of oppression. It flew in the face of the politics of the world-system, but those political principles were themselves still in the stage of formal institutionalization in such bodies as the United Nations. The League of Nations, which originated after World War I, for example, failed. One reason that it failed was the lack of membership of the United States. Inasmuch as the United States had become the largest Jewish nation in the world by 1945 as a result of the Holocaust, a group of sufficient size and prominence within the American population had grown to articulate the case for an international response to the treatment of Jews through independent nationhood in what was considered to be their historic biblical homeland in a region that at the time was largely under British control.

Second, the Jewish people themselves were disarrayed by the Holocaust. Many of the proponents of the idea of a "Jewish homeland" (that is, the modern state of Israel) articulated the concept in *secular* terms. In other words, when the concept of a free-standing state of Israel was discussed in political circles, it was not advanced as a religious cause but an efficient political solution to a world *political* problem of refugee peoples and a resolution to colonial control of a portion of the Middle East. In apparent ignorance of the actual population of Palestine—indeed, a saying at the time about the founding of the state of Israel was "a land without people for a people without a land"—many Western politicians saw the creation of the state of Israel as an act of political self-determination consistent with world-societal principles. The British were keen to withdraw from the region and saw U.S. support for the state of Israel as the ideal avenue for their own exit.

Third, the same infrastructural developments that have allowed the Christian Religious Right and Islamicism to move from life-world conditions to system actors have allowed the development of a Jewish religious form—Ultraorthodoxy—that was heretofore unknown in Judaism. Whereas ultraist forms of Judaism have previously been privatizations of the spiritual dynamic, the open market of globalization has allowed the conditions for the appearance of a public spirituality making political demands. Among the Jews especially, who have traditionally been what Max Weber (1952) terms a "pariah people," only the free conditions of globalization have allowed the politicization of action that could result in the assassination of a world political leader. Maimonides may well have *said* that killing a *moser* would be doing a good deed and meant it, but that Maimonides ever thought that he was saying that killing a prime minister of Israel for participating in the global peace process was a good deed is quite inconceivable. Maimonides was speaking to a global situation in which Jews were a pariah people, not actors in the world-system of states.

This final observation brings us to the heart of globalization theory as an explanation and demonstrates its value in understanding the "resurgence of religion" in our time. It is to be found in the simple definition of fundamentalism from T. K. Oommen that we introduced earlier: "text without context." What happened between Maimonides and Yigal Amir was that *the context changed*. Maimonides probably said what Rabbi Hecht said he said, and Maimonides probably meant what he said. In addition, a fairly creditable argument can be made that in the context in which he was writing—namely, that of Jews as a pariah people—Maimonides was morally justified in what he said. Today, however, it can also be creditably argued that Rabbi Hecht was *absolutely wrong* in his application of the text; he was wrong because he chose to discount context, which is morally unjustifiable given the availability of sociological knowledge today.

We speak rather forcefully for sociologists here, perhaps, but we do so quite intentionally, because as we move toward concluding this chapter on fundamentalism we want to make it as clear as we can that social theory—at least globalization theory—has direct, practical application, and that by studying sociology one actually does learn something useful. Making the point as simply as we can: *Sociology teaches us that all sociocultural products arise out of sociocultural contexts.* The words of Maimonides are sociocultural products. This does not mean that they are not true. It does mean that *all truth is mediated by context.* To say this is not the same thing as saying "everything is relative," but rather to assert that sociocultural context is integral to the truthfulness of any proposition about social relations. This is most succinctly epitomized in sociology in W. I. Thomas's phrase "the definition of the situation" (see Thomas and Thomas 1928). Situations by their very nature have always been historically particular; hence the universalizing dynamic of globalization creates an inherently perilous setting for misinterpretation, when the particular is universalized—that is, text is taken out of context. Precisely this led to the death of Yitzhak Rabin. By way of example in this chapter, we want to show that globalization theory within sociology can make a crucial contribution to human welfare by demonstrating how understanding context is essential to the application of prescriptive texts, religious or otherwise.

The murder of Yitzhak Rabin—set in the context not only of the rise of political Ultraorthodoxy in Judaism but also in relation to the other movements in Christianity and Islam at which we have looked—lets us return also to an aspect of the secularization controversy, specifically the supposed privatization of religion. Acknowledging that all of these terms admit of definitional manipulation, nevertheless what we want to indicate is that the process of globalization itself has created a new publicization of religion (the resurgence of religion) that is at variance from the dominant chord of secularization theories. At the same time, however, the "resurgent" forms of at least the Abrahamic traditions that we have examined in this chapter are also *new* forms of these religions.

Globalization theory can in this respect help us out of the quagmire of "secularization": that is, secularization theories themselves are, generally speaking, *unsociological* in the same way that most fundamentalisms are unsociological: in that they tend to minimize context. Secularization theories generally treat religion as something *fixed rather than flexible.* We argue, by contrast, using the definition-of-the-situation concept, that if we understand that, sociologically speaking, religions as forms of worship and ethical orientation are cultural products of infinite variability precisely because they refer to a transcendent realm, hence are not subject to the same constraints as sociocultural systems rooted in material objects, then as sociologists we should expect religions to *change.* While, for example, Jesus Christ may be "the same, yesterday, today, and forever," Christianity is going to change. These changes may be dramatic or gradual, great or small, but they will occur as long as humans practice the religion.

Negotiating Religious Peace

David Smock holds a doctorate in anthropology as well as a degree in theological studies and is vice president of the United States Institute of Peace (USIP) Center for Mediation and Conflict Resolution. In a 2007 briefing for President George W. Bush he outlined a series of insights he has garnered across years of observing successes and failures at peacemaking efforts across religious divides. These include:

> 1. Contrary to popular notions, ethnic conflict usually does not derive from ancient hatreds.
> 2. So-called religious conflict is rarely purely religious. The issues at stake . . . are only tangentially related to theological disputes.
> 3. Religion can be a force for good: Invoking religious traditions of healing and compassion can bring adversaries together. . . . For example, religious leaders from Iran originally refused to meet with political leaders in the United States; they did agree, however, to meet at a National Prayer Breakfast.
> 4. When dealing with ethnic and religious conflict, it is vital to address the underlying issues of social justice and fairness.
> 5. Joint action plans can help adversaries come together . . . via the challenge of addressing shared problems.
> 6. One can delegitimize extremists by buttressing traditionalists. . . . [R]eligious extremists often misquote traditional religious texts.
> 7. Constituencies for peace can be developed by building a coalition of like-minded people [to achieve religiously neutral goals].
> 8. It is critical to talk to your enemies.

Source: "Institute Vice President David Smock Advises President Bush," *PeaceWatch* (United States Institute of Peace) 13, no. 2 (July/August 2007): 4–5.

Indeed, repeating an observation from early in this text, the only religions that will not change are religions that cease to be practiced.

The global resurgences of religious traditions in new forms are evidence for both the truth of the relation of context to religion, which is inherent to the participation of human beings in religion, and the essential error of the secularization concept. Sociology teaches us that *all religion is secular*, because all religion exists in relation to both system and life-world. How specific religions orient and reorient themselves to system and life-world will vary as systems and life-worlds change, but at the same time, systems and life-worlds will include religious considerations in the total matrix of experience and interpretation that leads to specific action, hence to changes in patterns of action. The very processes that create the sociocultural contexts in and through which globalization theory becomes good theory also create the contexts for the resurgent religious forms that we tend to characterize as fundamentalisms. This dialectic between material and ideal culture is inherent in all sociocultural processes. A complete globalization theory will predict countersystem tendencies by the very nature of the dynamics that create the system itself. Globalization theory explains both why the systems of religion that are rising are rising and why those that are falling are falling. It also explains why those forms that are rising are probably unlikely to achieve their ultimate goals, and why those that may appear to be falling may not experience the "withering" that either their critics or their mourners expect.

Suggestions for Further Reading

Geneive Abdo. 2006. *Mecca and Main Street: Muslim Life in America after 9/11*. New York: Oxford University Press.

Joseph Alagha. 2007. *The Shifts in Hizbullah's Ideology: Religious Ideology, Political Ideology, and Political Program*. Amsterdam: Amsterdam University Press.

Peter Beyer. 2007. *Religions in Global Society*. London: Routledge.

Terence E. Fretheim. 2007. *Abraham: Trials of Family and Faith*. Columbia: University of South Carolina Press.

Philip Jenkins. 2007. *God's Continent: Christianity, Islam, and Europe's Religious Crisis*. New York: Oxford University Press.

Mark Juergensmeyer. 2003. *Terror in the Mind of God: The Global Rise of Religious Violence*, 3rd ed. Berkeley: University of California Press.

George M. Marsden. 2006. *Fundamentalism and American Culture: The Shaping of Twentieth-Century Evangelicalism, 1870–1925*, 2nd ed. New York: Oxford University Press.

Michael Scheuer. 2008. *Marching Toward Hell: America and Islam after Iraq*. New York: Free Press.

Ruth R. Wisse. 2007. *Jews and Power*. New York: Knopf.

Photograph courtesy of William H. Swatos, Jr.

CHAPTER 10

Mediating Meaning

RELIGION IN—AND AS—CONTEMPORARY CULTURE

The anthropologist Clifford Geertz, a renowned interpreter of Islam in both Indonesia and Morocco, once wrote that a human being "is an animal suspended in webs of significance he himself has spun" (1973: 5). Like the lowly spider, we humans create the "homes" in which we dwell. Yet there is a crucial difference in this residency that distinguishes us from insects and other creatures—and it is not just that we are a lot bigger and, for the most part, better looking. Humans live in settings that are much more than their material surroundings. They live, first and foremost, not in the cement-and-steel or bricks-and-lumber products of modern construction techniques, but in a collection of symbolic structures that they have endowed with some meaning.

Stated somewhat differently, the important fact of your day so far may not be that you walked out your front door at ten minutes before nine this morning (and accidentally slammed the door behind you), but instead that you were on your way to a certain place, trying to arrive on time, to see the people with whom you study or work, and to do the things that you and they value enough to devote your time and energy to them. Purposes and plans, schedules and tasks, ambitions and dreams: Such strands of our lives, when taken together, are the cultural environment in which we live—an atmosphere no less essential and consequential than the air we breathe. Although the physical demands of our bodies may prompt us to quench our thirst or to bundle up against a chill, *how* we accomplish natural aims like these is largely a question about which we refer to *culture* for answers.

Religious culture may be culture of merely one type, but it is a type that for believers is primary, for it comes close to defining identity and purpose for them in this existence. The symbols of religion—and the ritual actions that, when repeated, catalyze their meanings—give places to people in this world, orienting them to self and others. In addition, they forecast for people what they can expect in this life and in the next. Culture of this type thus tells those who craft and consume it who they are and where they fit, both in society and across the broader sweep of history.

Sacred and Profane Culture: Leap of Faith or Extreme Recreation?

Whether society regards an item of culture—a word or gesture, an idea or practice—as sacred is not a static and unchanging judgment. Rather, as the great sociological thinker Émile Durkheim observed in *The Elementary Forms of the Religious Life* nearly a century ago, "in the present day just as much as in the past, we see society constantly creating sacred things out of ordinary ones" (1965: 243). Moreover, the religious process to which Durkheim alluded works equally as often in the opposite way, to strip objects and actions of their sacred meanings.

The Canadian essayist and critic Douglas Fetherling, who signed on to an English merchant ship for a cruise across the oceans of the world, learned of several examples of Durkheim's dynamic in the island nations of the Pacific:

> The core idea behind the South Pacific cargo cults is that "natives" discover or are given "cargo" (western manufactured goods) and, extrapolating from this, develop a belief that a sort of messiah will reappear from overseas and shower them with the trappings of materialism. No one is certain how far back these recurring folk beliefs extend, but in this form, probably not before the arrival of Christian missionaries in the early nineteenth century. The island of Tanna, one of Vanuatu's most popular destinations, is home to the Jon Frum cult, which came alive again during World War II on Efate, the capital island. Local Melanesians employed by the U.S. armed services saw African American GIs being issued the same materiel as whites, an experience that led somehow to a revival of old (pre-missionary) traditions and beliefs. These found expression in the idea that one Jon Frum (that is, John *from* America) would appear to distribute western goods among the poor. Such cults had clear anti-colonial subtexts, and the British imprisoned the cult leaders at Port Vila on Efate—in the long run, to little avail. After Prince Philip visited the New Hebrides in the 1970s, one group on Tanna, about three hundred strong at present, came to see HRH [His Royal Highness] as the reincarnation of Jon Frum. There is even an altar to him.
>
> Cargo cults are not confined to Vanuatu. New Hanover in Papua New Guinea [PNG] is renowned as home to a cargo cult that worships Lyndon Johnson, of all people. Not Hubert Humphrey or Walter Mondale, *Lyndon Johnson*. What's most remarkable, though, is the way the cultural tide ebbs and flows. Some anthropologists are cargo cultists in reverse; they see themselves enriching us all by getting in touch with "primitive peoples." Pentecost in PNG, for example, is famous as the island where bungee jumping (using vines tied to the jumper's ankle) originated as an ancient rite. Just as it took the Melanesians to find religious significance in old Coke bottles and the other detritus of western culture, so it took Euro-Americans to transform the sacred into a mere sport through the application of modern bungee technology and marketing.

Source: Douglas Fetherling, *Running Away to Sea: Round the World on a Tramp Freighter* (Toronto: McClelland and Stewart, 1998), 144–45.

Mass Faith: The Media of Religion

Related to any discussion of churches in a technologically advanced society like the United States is an assessment of the media that disseminate religious culture to the population: A massive market in religious artifacts; a flood of books from religious presses; videotapes, CDs, and DVDs from religious producers; a flourishing of religious devotions on the nation's radio and television airwaves; and an eruption of religious messages of every possible description on the Internet all demonstrate how ideal for Americans is the marriage between the venerable appeals of faith and their concurrent fascination with the gadgetry of modern technology.

Much of this creativity is the work not of mainline churches and the religious organizations that they sponsor, but instead of what communications researcher Stewart M. Hoover has dubbed "the informal (but highly organized) transdenominational parachurch":

> This parachurch exists in an amazing variety of services and organizations identified generally with the conservative side of the two-party dimension and largely independent of formal, denominational religion. There are recording companies and Christian record labels, book publishers, bookstore chains, magazines, newsletters, tract publishers, manufacturers and distributors of "Christian kitsch" artifacts, film producers and distributors, broadcasters, advertising agencies, consulting firms, radio and TV format syndicators, and a plethora of specialized and general ministries. . . . These parachurch institutions rely on communication technology to a greater extent than do conventional churches. The newsletters, magazines, mailing lists, recordings, motion pictures, and cassettes marketed by these organizations far outstrip, in volume and in sophistication, the combined output of the conventional churches. Even "person-to-person" ministries, such as traveling revivalists and musical groups, rely heavily on modern marketing and public relations techniques. (Hoover 1988: 90, 110)

This chapter is intended to give the reader a small glimpse into the sprawling activities of many of these entities, and to portray how religious culture in and beyond American society is conceived, perceived, and received.

Religion in Material Culture: Faith in the Flesh

Sometimes religious culture takes the form of concrete objects. This embodiment of belief is part of what scholars distinguish by the phrase "material culture." As historian Colleen McDannell observes:

> People build religion into the landscape, they make and buy pious images for their homes, and they wear special reminders of their faith next to their bodies. Religion is more than a type of knowledge learned

> through reading holy books and listening to holy men. The physical expressions of religion are not exotic or eccentric elements that can be relegated to a particular community or a specific period of time. Throughout American history, Christians have explored the meaning of the divine, the nature of death, the power of healing, and the experience of the body by interacting with a created world of images and shapes. (1995: 1)

Everything that is equally sacred and solid—from the largest shrines to which pilgrims might process, down to the smallest talismans they could grip in their hands—helps to rescue religion from the thin mists of pure intellect and hold and convey religious meaning in the physical world. A good example is provided in a description of the symbolic functions of a medieval church by the artist and art historian Gregor T. Goethals. She writes:

> In the Middle Ages, cathedrals were decorated with images that described the significant happenings that governed and ordered life. One of the ambulatory stained glass windows at Chartres depicts events in the life of the emperor Charlemagne; its various sections illustrate his importance to the development of the church. On the exterior, three portals give an overview of history. Sculpted figures represent the heroes of the Old Testament and historical circumstances which culminate in the reign of Christ. Leading up to the doorways on the southern entrance are images of the saints, martyrs, and servants of the church since the time of Christ. Selected by an ecclesiastical hierarchy and executed by artisans, the stone and glass symbols of Chartres, like the sculptures on the facade of the Parthenon, are visual constructions of meaning. (1990: 121–22)

Without a doubt, it is a long way from Chartres to your local shopping center. Nevertheless, for a much more contemporary manifestation of religious meaning being captured in objects, pay a visit to one of the estimated thousands of stores, both adjacent to churches and in commercial retail spaces such as malls, that sell religious (or more specifically "Christian") goods (see Garrett and Reiss 2005; Kiesling 2005: 18; McDannell 1995: 222–69). A reporter from the *Wall Street Journal* did just that at a suburban Catholic church in Arizona, and was a bit surprised at what she found:

> "If more parishes did this, they'd have a lot more funding for programs," says store manager Dolly Splawinski.
>
> St. Timothy's hired her to manage its store five years ago, and she attributes the outlet's success mostly to a larger, unconventional inventory and to more-sophisticated merchandising displays. One miniature heaven scene displayed Christian stuffed bears, each floating on its own little puffy cloud. Most Christian stores are "very tacky and ugly," says Ms. Splawinski. (L. Miller 1999: B4)

St. Timothy's in Mesa is by no means special in either its goals or its methods. People, it appears, are happy to find outlets where they can purchase visible and

Diet as Devotion

[T]reating diet as a matter of religious concern reaches back thousands of years. . . . The practitioners of Judaism, Islam and Hinduism live under strict dietary rules. But the American Protestant variant is more recent. It could be said to begin with the Presbyterian minister Sylvester Graham, who in the early 19th century preached against overindulging the appetites, especially for alcohol, tobacco, spices, and meat.

Such intemperance, Graham warned in 1833, would lead to "diseased irritability and inflammation, painful sensibility, and, finally, disorganization and death." Graham's longest-lasting legacy is a form of whole wheat known as Graham flour—the main ingredient of Graham crackers.

Graham's beliefs spread through various religious movements of the time—not least the Seventh-day Adventists. . . . [T]he church founded a network of hospitals, most prominent among them the Western Health Reform Institute in Battle Creek, Mich. In 1876, John Harvey Kellogg, a member of the church, became the director. He described himself as "a sort of umpire as to what was true or correct and what was error in matters relating to hygienic reform, a responsibility which has often made me tremble."

Kellogg blamed many of Americans' worst problems on their heavy, grease-laden breakfasts of meat and pies. In 1895 he and his brother invented the cornflake, a grain-based food meant to replace meat on the breakfast table. It soon made Kellogg and Battle Creek famous.

Source: Daniel Sack, "Feeding the Soul," *Wall Street Journal*, September 29, 2000, W12.

tangible symbols of their innermost commitments. Indeed, a huge market has developed for material representations of religion, and while stonemasons and glaziers may have fewer commissions these days than in ages past, manufacturers of everything from calendars to coffee mugs have raced to fill an artistic void with their products.

This trade has advanced so substantially that operators of Christian bookstores now report that as much as 70 to 75 percent of their revenue in a given year can derive from the sale of merchandise other than books, the inverse of the proportion that was generated in this way thirty years ago (Borden 2007: 68; Garrett and Reiss 2005; McDannell 1995: 259). And because retailers are permitted higher markups on these items, they also realize heftier profits from sales of "kitsch" (also derided as "Jesus junk") than on purchases of books. Aside from gifts like stuffed animals and plush toys, picture frames and plaques, this category of goods includes greeting cards and postcards, videos for entertainment and edification, jewelry with religious symbols and charms, and unique products like "'Scripture keepers,' table-top card-holders decorated with bears or angels that hold daily Scripture verses printed on business-size cards" (Winston 2000: 28). While the evangelical Protestant publisher Zondervan (owned lately by media mogul Rupert Murdoch) has had great commercial success selling an unglamorous product—durable covers for Bibles and hymnals—competitor Thomas Nelson inaugurated a line of religious toys and games for children under the brand name "Tommy Nelson."

Also growing strongly are sales of recorded religious music, whether it is of a traditional sort like Gregorian chant or an adaptation of secular styles as in Christian rock (Howard and Streck 1999; Powell 2002). Here one finds few apologies for the commercialization of the once sacred. "What people are asked to do most of the time they are in church is sing," explained a music producer for a label geared to Catholic audiences. "No one walks out humming the homily" (quoted in Winston 2000: 29).

Religious Publishing: Words and *The Word*

Among the most common items for sale in religious retail outlets across the United States are books: scriptures, devotional tracts, compilations of prayers,

Faith and Fleas: An Alter Altar?

Churchgoing is not the only activity recognized as a potential Sunday commitment by Americans. For others, flea markets represent a similarly regular Sunday life-event. Religion scholar Arthur Farnsley spent two years in the period from 2004 to 2006 trying to bridge the statistical gap between the more than 60 percent of Americans who claim affiliation with a religious congregation and the more than 90 percent who say they believe in God. His research subjects were self-employed persons who worked in the markets and reported they attended worship services less than twice a year.

What he found was an interesting mix of evangelicalism and eclecticism. For example, less than five percent of his subjects did not believe in God. Many, by contrast, reported stories of personal miracles. Fewer than ten percent read the Bible regularly or could recount favorite Bible stories or passages. Yet most "believed in" the Bible. Specifically, more than 80 percent believed in a literal Adam and Eve who lived in a primal garden, as well as both the Virgin Birth and bodily resurrection of Jesus. They also had a strong belief that they could experience God without the necessity of church attendance. Very few knew of any leading evangelical figure other than Billy Graham, and only five percent had read such books as the *Left Behind* series. Only 20 percent considered themselves "born again."

At a more practical level, Farnsley's flea-market faithful lacked any apparent allegiance to the political alliance of evangelical Christianity and right-wing politics. They were largely issue-oriented and tended to be skeptical of the programs of both major political parties. As Farnsley phrases it, "Without the institutional connections provided by churches and media, these biblical literalists do not become red-state Republicans." The question that remains is whether and how these noninstitutional believers are or can be motivated to become voters or whether their noninstitutionalized religiosity is a reflection of a more overarching distrust of institutions that causes them to absent themselves from the ballot box just as much as from the pew. What this research does show sociologically, however, is that simply considering beliefs without also looking at institutional connections may well overstate the size of a too-glibly labeled "evangelical" constituency as a political bloc in U.S. politics.

Source: Arthur E. Farnsley II, "Flea Market Believers," *Christianity Today* (October 2006): 114–21.

and high-minded entertainment to boot. Christian science fiction? Righteous romance? Self-help for the saved? As unusual as some of these labels may sound, they all represent categories of products in the thriving industry of religious publishing (Christopherson 1999). The chairman of the Frankfurt Book Fair, a major international exhibition for publishers and their wares, once quipped about the contemporary book business as a whole, "The industry depends on two young men: Jesus Christ on the one hand and Harry Potter on the other" (quoted in Marty 2003: 8).

Religious publishing is an industry that sold more than $685 million worth of books in 1986 (Ferré 1990: 100). Less than fifteen years later, total sales showed an extraordinary increase. Statistics for 1999 gathered by the Association of American Publishers revealed that sales in the religion column, at $1.22 billion, had come close to doubling. By 2004, this total had mushroomed to about $4.34 billion (Ammerman 2005: 91; Borden 2007: 68; O'Driscoll 2005). Sources in evangelical Christian publishing contend further that their own sector of the book market *alone* actually accounts for $2.5 billion of this commerce (M. Nelson 2000: 39). All "religious products" together are said to enjoy sales in the United States of more than $8 billion (*Economist* 2005).

An obvious reason why estimates of the expanding market for religious books vary so widely is that it is not clear which titles in the data count as religious works. Publishers traditionally have avoided tagging their own products with the label "religion" for fear that these books would be consigned without thought to that dusty nook in the rear of most general-interest bookstores where are deposited self-published cookbooks from the church auxiliary and oversized Bibles with gilt edges and white imitation-leather covers. Accordingly, the practice of a former editor was that "[e]verything got called adult nonfiction, unless it was clearly about the Bible" (quoted in M. Nelson 2000: 38; see also Charles 2004; M. Nelson 2003: 27, 2004).

What is more, many unchurched readers seem to be averse to the strictures of traditional faiths and to the well-worn language that imposes them. To employ the term *religion*, then, says Marcia Nelson, a longtime observer of the book industry, evokes "connotations that are at best limiting in the marketplace" (2000: 38). Having said that, no matter what it is called or how its measurement is gauged, the business of publishing religion—or, as is preferable today, *spirituality*—is burgeoning.

Any religious publishing company, whether it came to life under the auspices of a particular denomination, to circulate the works of a certain sect's founder, to give voice to one faction of an independent tradition like evangelical Protestantism, or simply to meet the demands of readers and thereby make money, is "increasingly run like a business instead of a jubilant ministry" (Ferré 1990: 101). Indeed, the numbers of people, products, contracts, and dollars involved today are too great to allow any less rationalized an enterprise. This imperative is unlikely to change, although it makes for some memorable collisions of Christianity and commerce. An extreme case was the promotional appearance by evangelical author Charles R. ("Chuck") Swindoll at a convention of religious booksellers, for which Swindoll assumed the guise of an

The photographs on this page and the opposite, both intended to give artistic expression to Christian sentiments, also show two very different approaches to the material dimension of religious devotion. Photograph above courtesy of William H. Swatos, Jr.; opposite, Francis P. Clark Collection (GFCL 38), UNDA, reproduced with permission of the University of Notre Dame.

Arnold Schwartzenegger clone, "The Sermonator." Behind dark glasses and mounted on the back of a Harley-Davidson motorcycle, Swindoll spent an afternoon posing for pictures with delegates (Shattuck 1993: 128).

Not all moneymaking ideas in religious publishing need to be so flashy. Certain categories of books—Bibles and other sacred texts, for example—are perennial sellers, requiring little marketing push. Moreover, many versions or translations of scriptures lie in the public domain. (That is, if they ever were copyrighted, the protections of intellectual property law have expired, so no royalties are owed on sales.) They thus are relatively cheap to produce, with costs of production barely extending beyond the price of the raw materials necessary for printing and binding.

In addition, certain faith traditions, such as Roman Catholicism, feature sacramental events that occur regularly over the life cycle (baptisms, confessions, communions, confirmations, ordinations, weddings) and that often call for the presentation of religious gifts. Thus, publishers of religious books and the stores that sell them can rely on a stable, though rather small, flow of predictable purchases. At retailers that carry Catholic titles, for instance, the steadiest sales are of items like *The New Jerusalem Bible* (a version from Doubleday, a commercial publisher, that many Catholics prefer for personal study) and *The Catechism of the Catholic Church* (see M. Nelson 1999: S5; Winston 2000: 30).

Nevertheless, the true news in religious publishing in the last decade has been the growth of sales fueled by people, many of them middle-aged baby boomers, who have embarked on inner journeys in search of a faith that personally suits them, whether or not it resides within the doctrinal boundaries of a conventional church (Roof 1999; Roof, Carroll, and Roozen 1995). These new seekers after enlightenment are predominantly affluent and highly educated. This means that they have time and money to spend on self-discovery and improvements to their lifestyles, but also that they understand the benefits of a little advance research.

Professing scant religious experience or depth of theological conviction themselves, they resolve to plan ahead and read up on the self-assigned task. One publishing executive thus speaks of "a large number of believers in exile who are getting their spiritual meaning not from the Church but from books" (quoted in Carrigan 1995a: 36). Like potential visitors to a foreign terrain, the would-be devout stop first at the bookstore to browse the volumes that offer to guide them in their travels across the world's religious geography.

Stroll into practically any bookseller of moderate size these days and you will be confronted with the result of this demand: shelf upon shelf and aisle after aisle of published works on "Faith," "Devotion," "Spirituality," "Eastern Beliefs," and "The New Age"—but seldom a label as prosaic as "Religion," and almost never "Theology." What, you may inquire, is situated in these sections? The answer is no single thing, but some of everything; it is as if one had poured the accumulated wisdom from ages of religious thought and practice into a lidless electric blender, switched on the rotors, and splattered the walls with the mixture. Here is a book of inspirational addresses from the late Pope John Paul II; over there is a volume based on the mystical Jewish Kabbalah; right behind you, a collection of sermons on marriage and the family to exhort and sustain evangelical Protestant parents. Do you want classics? To the left, the *Summa* of Thomas; at right, *The Institutes* of Calvin; in the center, *The Confessions* of Augustine.

Around the corner, you might spot an anthology of reflections to comfort the bereaved Christian widow or widower, a history of Islam's diffusion throughout the Middle East, a scholarly study of American Hindus, a plea for peace from the Dalai Lama of Tibet, or a how-to manual for Zen meditation. At the far end of the floor, look for Celtic mythology, Native American ethnology, and the Doctors of the Church. Have an appetite for *Chicken Soup for . . .* your or someone else's soul? Check the freestanding display. Thanks to Health Communications, the Florida-based publisher of these ubiquitous handbooks of present-day parables and proverbs, bookstores now stock more than 120 varieties—and counting (M. Nelson 2000: 38).

Having traveled full circle, the sheer diversity of religious products has attracted the attention and analysis of the book industry, the firms that, each responding in its own fashion, created it. Notes *Religion Update*, a supplement to the trade journal *Publishers Weekly*, "the past ten or fifteen years have demonstrated in very concrete ways the strength of the religious impulse. The bottom-line evidence of book sales has spoken of a continuing spiritual hunger, albeit one that has taken on new shapes and names" (M. Nelson 1999: S4).

One area of religious publishing that has undergone a veritable explosion in recent times has been the writing and sale of "inspirational" fiction. Admittedly, religious stories have tumbled from the presses for as long as there have been books in print and literate persons to read them. Yet, with many of these stories, a didactic purpose overwhelms whatever merits they may possess as literature. Thus, regardless of their value as aids to instruction in the faith, many if not most explicitly religious novels, frankly, were not worth reading. With only a few exceptions, "Christian fiction of the twentieth century," confesses communications specialist John Ferré, was "notorious for its heroes-and-villains plots and lobotomized characters" (1990: 106). Writing in *Library Journal*, a magazine for library professionals, Henry Carrigan, Jr., concurs: "In the past, Christian fiction has been marked by insipid writing and sentimental theology" (1995a: 39). But the current popularity of novels with religious themes is probably without precedent in scale and certainly unique as a business venture.

An especially successful example of the prevailing crop of titles in the widening market for religious fiction is the *Left Behind* series of millennial thrillers from the creative duo of Tim LaHaye (better known formerly, along with his wife, Beverly, for political activism on the Christian Right) and the veteran author Jerry B. Jenkins. The original novel, published in 1995, and each subsequent episode in the series are oriented around the vivid drama of biblical prophecies about the end-times.

The *Left Behind* series, now completed, runs to a total of sixteen volumes (twelve books in the body of the series, a three-book "prequel," and one sequel). Together, these titles have sold a combined 62 million copies—a truly astounding figure for religious books—and have registered more than $650 million in sales for Tyndale House, their fundamentalist Protestant publisher (*Economist* 2005). Numbers five through nine in the series even landed on the national bestsellers list of the stately (and secular) *New York Times*, alien territory to nearly all conservative Christian authors (Winston 1999: 32). Almost three-quarters of all copies that Tyndale sold were purchased in "mainstream outlets" outside the markets of Christian booksellers. In addition, the books spun off four direct-to-video movies starring television actor Kirk Cameron (Bowles 2006), a series of works for young-adult readers (*Left Behind: Kids*), and even a video game, *Left Behind: Eternal Forces* (Gundersen 2006). The next project for coauthors LaHaye and Jenkins is *The Jesus Chronicles*, a series of fictionalized accounts of the lives of the authors of the four Gospels (Memmott 2006). *John's Story: The Last Eyewitness* (2006) is the first volume; *Mark's Story* follows (2007). So at the start of the new millennium, *Publishers Weekly* could credit innovations like *Left Behind* for the fact that religious fiction "happens to be going apocalyptic gangbusters right now" (M. Nelson 2000: 38).

"That Old-Time Religion": Broadcast Faith in the United States

"IN THE BEGINNING . . ."

Religious broadcasting in the United States is nearly as old as broadcasting itself, and it is almost as varied. The initial attempt to cast the words of humans out into the heavens, in fact, featured the Word of God. The first successful wireless voice broadcast, on Christmas Eve 1906, included a reading of the narrative of Jesus's birth from the Gospel according to Luke.

In the next two decades, as the technology of broadcasting spread, radio stations sprang up around the country. More than half of them, it is estimated, carried some religious programming; more than one-tenth were actually owned by churches. KDKA in Pittsburgh, the radio station that inaugurated regular broadcast service, was also the first to air, in 1921, a weekly program of worship: vespers from Calvary Episcopal Church in that city. (An employee of the station's parent company was a member of the Calvary congregation.) The broadcast's engineers, to avoid obtrusiveness in church, wore choir robes while on the job (Armstrong 1979: 19–20).

After World War II, religious broadcasting again flourished, this time with the advent of television. In the early stages of this medium, as with radio, networks and individual stations set aside blocks of free airtime, usually on Sundays, to be shared by representatives of the major denominations (and by them alone). The motivation for this action was to fulfill a legal obligation, assumed with the awarding of a broadcast license, that a station operate with policies based on the "public interest, convenience, and necessity" (quoted in Armstrong 1979: 25).

The Federal Communications Commission (FCC), the government panel that regulates broadcasting in the United States, grants to each license holder an effective monopoly over the use of an assigned frequency. In return, it is expected that each station, as a public trustee, will direct a portion of its programming toward the cultivation of the common good. Carrying religious programs that were produced in conjunction with the largest church bodies was a safe way to satisfy this requirement (Hadden and Swann 1981: 56–57).

Thus, before 1960, the bulk of religious programming along the wide center of the broadcast band consisted of somewhat tame pulpit lectures and sermons, standard Sunday services, uplifting discussions, and interviews without controversy. Sectarianism on the airwaves was averted by an electronic ecumenism that locked out of the studios the more strident voices in religion. Those independent preachers who made it onto the air, mainly evangelicals and fundamentalists, did so by purchasing time (when and where policies permitted such sales) around the edges of the broadcast schedule (Alexander 1994: 57–59).

The cozy cooperation between broadcasters and the major American faith communities came to an abrupt end in 1960, when the FCC ruled that stations could count commercial programming toward their "public interest" quotas. With this change, there was no longer an incentive for station managers to give away broadcast slots to spokespersons for the mainline denominations in order to appease the government—not, at least, when other ministers were standing in line, cash in hand, waiting to purchase that same airtime. In the ensuing competition for control of the religious airwaves, the advantage naturally went to the conservative churchmen, who had already acquired substantial experience in plumbing an audience for contributions to keep a program afloat in the broadcast ocean (Hadden and Shupe 1987: 65–66).

So was born that parallel religious institution, the contemporary "electronic church," a name which itself is a variant on that originally coined by Ben Armstrong and elaborated in his *The Electric Church* (1979). Years later, the U.S. Catholic Conference, the public policy arm of the nation's Catholic bishops, undertook a study to gauge the impact of the change. In 1959, the year before the FCC policy shift, about half of all religious programming in the United States was broadcast on time that was paid for. By 1977, the study showed, more than 90 percent aired on purchased time (Hadden and Shupe 1988: 51–52). Today, more than two thousand radio and television stations in the United States are devoted primarily or exclusively to religious programming (Blake 2005: 32).

THE MESSAGE: "HIS MASTER'S VOICE"?

The image of religious broadcasting that is presented in the press is one designed to provoke pity and anger: Masses of people residing beyond the reach of local churches turn in dissatisfaction and need, from the loneliness of their living rooms, to a motley band of broadcast ministers. Using dubious theology, cheap theatrics, and crass appeals to physical wants, these manipulators ultimately sink their audiences into a grim condition that is every bit as much a spiritual poverty as it is an economic one.

Among the critics of this image is Bobby C. Alexander: "The stereotypic view of televangelism turns viewers into caricatures. It reduces viewers to passive spectators or victims of fraudulent religion. It obscures the active participation in the television programs of viewers who are already committed to the religion promoted there" (1994: 2). Alexander continues:

> Televangelism's negative image has led some to doubt that it offers anything positive to viewers. The negative image has left the impression that televangelism must win viewers by presenting false images, or false promises. It is often assumed that viewers only tune in and give their financial support because the televangelists manipulate their audiences, holding them hostage to promises of pie in the sky by and by or promises of heaven on earth. . . . It is assumed that televangelists merely prey upon viewers by selling a quick-fix religion of magic and wish fulfillment.
>
> Such promises are said to blind viewers to the televangelists' political ambitions, business interests, and ego interests. . . . The problem with the assumption that televangelism wins its audience only by manipulation is that it reduces viewers to grist for the televangelists' mill. The assumption renders them passive consumers of a prepackaged and phony religion. (1994: 23)

Such a view also disregards the multitudes of people in the audience for religious broadcasting who find that watching the programs of evangelists like Oral Roberts or Pat Robertson enhances their lives of faith. They may eagerly embrace the messages of hope and inspiration that are transmitted to them, participate (if merely vicariously) in the good works that the ministry undertakes, and feel an affinity with the larger quasi-community of followers that adheres to the preaching of an individual evangelist (S. Bruce 1990: 133–39; Wright 1989: 748–56).

THE MESSENGERS: THE RETURN OF ELMER GANTRY?

Media coverage of the growth in fundamentalist and evangelical churches in the United States during the 1970s and 1980s focused attention on a concomitant expansion in the activities of religious broadcasters, especially the stars of Sunday morning, the televangelists. Revelations of scandals involving sexual misconduct and/or financial misrepresentation by some of the best-known television preachers, such as the Reverends Jim Bakker and Jimmy Swaggart, served to fix the popular gaze firmly on the operations of religious broadcasters.

Regrettably, unnuanced and even derisive reporting of these scandals also reinforced persistent stereotypes concerning the rather diverse ministries that jointly inhabit the airwaves. Chief among these misconceptions is the impression that all religious broadcasters are modern-day Elmer Gantrys—Gantry was a fictional revival leader whose unscrupulous and hypocritical behavior is at the center of a famous Sinclair Lewis novel by that title (1927). (For the benefit of social scientists, Jeffrey K. Hadden and Anson D. Shupe [1990] have provided an analysis of this stereotype.) In conformity to this popular image, today's broadcast preachers are presumed to be money-hungry opportunists, accountable to no higher authority, who promise miracles in the name of the Lord in order to lure huge numbers of the desperate and the gullible—and their financial contributions—away from the sounder fellowship of mainline congregations.

A more fittingly sociological approach to religious television both drains the topic of some grounds for conflict and anchors its insight in aspects of the roles that broadcast ministers perform and the economic and organizational constraints within which they must work. Put more directly, the viewer of televangelism perceives an industry that is focused on the larger-than-life stature of the preacher and the temptations to which he is continuously subject. Yet this is *not* because humans with unregulated drives toward avarice and lust dominate television ministries, but because their operators labor under unusual, though readily identifiable, circumstances. The electronic church in the twenty-first century, like so many other U.S. institutions, is voluntaristic, diverse, market-oriented, entrepreneurial, technologically advanced, and activated by vast amounts of time and money. This is as it has been for a long time, and probably as it will remain for a long time to come.

To start at the beginning, there simply is no ministry without money. With broadcasting, in a different sense than is normally intended, time is money—that is, time *costs* money, and lots of it (Schultze 1991: 154). Producing a religious program and getting it broadcast is a phenomenally expensive proposition. Unless contributions arrive in amounts sufficient to pay stations, cable systems, and satellite distributors to keep the religious broadcast on the air, it is as if the preacher and his message no longer existed. (If a televangelist runs out of money and falls from the broadcast schedule, does he make a sound?)

Thus, the head of a broadcast ministry, virtuous or not, must preach always with one eye glued to the bottom line and one foot planted a step ahead of his creditors. What he says and does on the air is crucial, for if his words or deeds cause thousands to tune out his program, his survival as an on-air presence is threatened. Whatever other good the televangelist may intend with his preaching to some, and with his service to them and to others, none of it will happen without funds for next week and the week after that. Hence the seeming obsession during religious broadcasts with talk of raising and spending money.

Additionally, the very evangelistic nature of religious commitment among conservative Christians reinforces this entrepreneurial style. To their way of thinking, a faith that is not actively being passed on is a faith that is indolent and moribund. As "Bible-believing" Christians, the leaders of broadcast ministries and their supporters are convinced that two thousand years ago, the risen Jesus charged his disciples to bring to every corner of the globe the Gospel's message of sinfulness within the human heart and salvation through the Son of God (see Matt. 28:19; Mark 16:15; Luke 24:47; Acts 1:7–8). If on top of this conviction is added the belief that one can know neither the day nor the hour when the time for achieving the conversion of the world will expire (Matt. 24:36; Mark 13:32), one can appreciate why the preachers one sees on television are so excited and impatient—and perpetually needy.

There is work to be done: God has commanded it. Time is wasting: God has limited it. The need is great: God's Word still must reach millions. At the logical conclusion to this line of thought are the incessant appeals for money to retire yesterday's debt, which is now coming due; to underwrite today's tasks, whose full dimensions are as yet uncalculated; and to make possible tomorrow's plans, which must be of a magnitude that is commensurate with the Lord's expectations of us.

The principal spokesperson for these appeals is, of course, the televangelist himself. Because very few broadcast ministries are the projects of denominations, it is almost always an individual (most frequently the founder) who comes to embody the spirit of a religious program. As a consequence, and for better or worse, much attention finally rests on the personality and character of the preacher. He becomes the focal point for all that his ministry is and does; for all practical purposes, to many he *is* his organization. Moreover, being the center of attention for all who look to the ministry creates enormous pressures and accompanying temptations to abuse position and privilege.

Televangelists are not above turning this condition around, however, and using it to cultivate loyalty among their followers. After all, it is harder for people to trust an institution than a person, and even harder for them to endorse the worth of an abstract idea. So their scrutiny settles naturally on the profile of the preacher at center stage. Viewers knew that they were watching the late Jerry Falwell, but not necessarily *The Old-Time Gospel Hour*; or Robert Schuller, not necessarily *The Hour of Power* (Schultze 1991: 69–71). For this reason, if not for others, did the most famous twentieth-century evangelist assure listeners to his periodically televised crusades that "Billy Graham, Minneapolis, Minnesota" was his a-cinch-to-remember mailing address. "That's all the address you need," they were told from the podium, to write to what is actually a large and inevitably impersonal religious organization.

THE AUDIENCE: PREACHING TO THE CONVERTED?

Needless to say, the resources behind the electronic church are enough to alarm some in the mainline denominations who perceive television ministries to be a threat. Might not the televangelists siphon away from local churches the allegiance of parishioners, the energies of volunteers, and the donations of benefactors? Clergy of the mainline churches in particular fear that large numbers of alienated believers would avoid the communality of weekly worship in favor of a privatized form of religious inspiration, delivered to isolated believers individually in front of the television set. Not insignificantly, members of a television "congregation" would subsequently express their appreciation for the work of the ministry by dropping their contributions into a mailbox—and not into the collection plate that is passed on Sunday morning.

Research, however, fails to corroborate these common suspicions. First, despite the sometimes outlandish claims of the broadcast preachers themselves, the size of the regular audience for religious television in the United States is rather modest (Alexander 1994: 32–33, 189–90). Arbitron, a private television ratings service, released statistics from 1980 showing that the weekly number of viewers for sixty-six syndicated programs on religious television *combined* totaled between 20 million and 21 million. By 1985, that number had grown to almost 24 million; in 1986, it had fallen again to 19 million. Since many people are normally viewers of more than one religious show, they are counted in this total more than once. Alternative estimates of *unduplicated* viewers of religious television place the true tally at between 10 million and 14 million, or less than 5 percent of the total U.S. population (Hadden and Shupe 1988: 157).

While even this reduced figure is impressive for its absolute magnitude, it is dwarfed by the average ratings for the most popular talk shows and situation comedies on broadcast television and its cable counterparts (Hadden and Shupe 1988: 154–57). By one estimate, twenty times more viewers follow the exploits of *CSI*'s pathologists than tune in to watch CBN's preachers (Blake 2005: 35). Furthermore, the audience for religious television is concentrated heavily in the southern states, where religious convictions have long been thought to be strong (S. Bruce 1990: 110). One analyst who has reviewed the statistics on religious television in the United States summarizes the situation by stating that the audience for the message of mass-media ministers is "quite small by conventional standards." Moreover, viewing of religious programming on television is typically "infrequent" and lasts only for "very short periods of time." In addition, the viewers are not ordinarily unchurched, but are comparatively religious in the first place (Hoover 1987: 135).

Nor is there much of a basis for the concern that Christians in the United States would watch religious television in private as a substitute for worshiping with a congregation (Schultze 1991: 204). In an opinion survey conducted by the Gallup Organization, just one in seven viewers of religious television admitted to watching a devotional broadcast rather than going to services. Most of those who did engage in this practice were persons who have difficulty attending church: the elderly, the immobile, and the chronically infirm. Viewers of reli-

9/11, Media, Meanings, Mormons, Money

By choosing to attack the Twin Towers of the World Trade Center, the perpetrators of the September 11, 2001, attack on the United States handed video media a scene that no amount of money could have bought: an almost surreal collapse of buildings that theretofore had never been able to be shown "for real." Various films across time had staged similar attacks, but this event brought video reality to a new level. If it is the case that Vietnam brought war into our living rooms as never before, then 9/11 brought terror into our living rooms as never before. Parents could no longer tell their frightened children, "Oh honey, don't be afraid, don't cry, it's only make-believe."

But 9/11 also imprinted itself on our brains as a number combination. Like 20/20, it now carries meaning. One recent result of that meaning for Hollywood was to return through film to another 9/11 event, probably known to less than one percent of the American population: the Mountain Meadows Massacre, of September 11, 1857, when 120 American men, women, and children traveling west in a wagon train from Arkansas were murdered by paramilitary forces upon entering the new Mormon territory of Utah. Released in 2007 as *September Dawn*, the film offers itself as an example of "religious fanaticism," and in the process takes aim at such Mormon leaders as Joseph Smith and Brigham Young as potential holy warriors. That this event took place has never been in doubt and has been regretfully acknowledged by Mormon leaders, though never with an admission of complicity on the part of Young. (Smith himself had been lynched in Illinois well prior to this time. Nevertheless the film does portray him prior to his death as proclaiming himself a "New Mohammet" and threatening a holy war against his enemies.) The film fails to show persecution of Mormons prior to their settlement in Utah, and in the absence of definitive evidence one way or the other, chooses to implicate Young explicitly as ordering the massacre. Although the film had been in the works for months and failed to make its first release date, the time of its actual release also coincided with Mormon Massachusetts governor Mitt Romney's rise to prominence as a candidate for the 2008 Republican presidential nomination.

While *September Dawn* opened to weak reviews and does not seem destined to make a lasting impression on the American consciousness, on the one hand it can serve to remind Americans that the perpetration of violence in the name of religion knows no boundaries of race, religion, creed, or time. On the other hand, a comparison of the regrets expressed by Mormon leadership to the events of 9/11/1857 stands in marked contrast to some Muslim reactions to events of today. As one commentator remarks: "In part, preference for Mormons over Muslims as targets of cinematic scorn stems from reasonable concerns for personal safety. Islamic communities have proved more than a mite touchy over media depictions of their faith: Consider the deadly worldwide riots [in early 2007] over a dozen Danish cartoons, or the taking of more than 100 American hostages [in Iran in 1979] and bans in Muslim countries inspired by the respectful 1977 film *Mohammad, Messenger of God. . . .*" (Medved 2007: 13A). Media and the tradition of media freedom are not universally shared human rights but, rather, are societally specific. In part, the war on the "Great Satan of the West" is neither more nor less than a war on freedom of speech.

gious television, in addition, were no less likely than nonviewers to volunteer to help others in their local churches (see Wuthnow 1987, 1989: 115–41).

Neither was there evidence of a net loss in donations to local congregations. "The money given to religious television programs," writes Robert Wuthnow, a sociologist who participated in the study, "appears to result from extra donations that would not likely be given at all were it not for these programs" (1987: 129). Finally, people do not seem to be resorting to the electronic church out of frustration with their own congregations. The study detected no markedly greater dissatisfaction with local churches among viewers of religious programs than among nonviewers. Believers, Wuthnow concludes, "still overwhelmingly look to the churches instead of religious television for spiritual guidance." No tradeoff in loyalty exists between churchgoing and television viewing, because "the two modes of religious expression produce different kinds of gratifications" (1987: 130).

Cyber-Faith: Religion on the Internet

At the height of their popularity during the 1960s, John Lennon boasted that the Beatles were "more popular than Jesus." More than thirty years later, a technology of communication that none of the mop-topped Liverpudlians could have envisioned, the World Wide Web, would prove him wrong. By 1998, Internet search engines could locate nearly 300,000 instances of texts invoking the name of "Jesus," and 154,000 with the word "God" (Connell 1998), but merely 40,000 or so for the Beatles (Chidley 1997: 46). No more than a year later, the Fab Four lagged farther behind, as mentions on the Web for "Jesus" had leaped to more than 2 million, with 3.6 million references to "God" (McCormick 1998: 46). After still a few more years, Jesus made 5.7 million appearances on the Web, while mentions of God more than quadrupled to 16.2 million. (However, "hell," which Web pages mentioned 3.9 million times, beat out "heaven" at 3.5 million! [Stockler 2000].) As of 2008 (and amid the ongoing explosion of content on the Internet), "hell" still surpassed "heaven" (378 million to 234 million uses), and both "God" (a whopping 642 million mentions) and "Jesus" (229 million) remained far ahead of Sir Paul McCartney's old band at a mere 77.4 million mentions.

According to a 1997 survey designed by George Barna, 12 percent of adults with Internet access reported that they go online for religious purposes (Davies 1998). In 2001, just four years later, a different survey organization discovered that 21 percent of Internet users sought religious information online, while by 2004, the contingent of spiritual surfers had grown to 64 percent of the "wired" public (Campbell 2005: 312). These percentages reflect enormous numbers of people—more, in fact, than have used online banks and brokerages or Internet auctions and computer dating services (Helland 2002: 299–300).

As a thoroughly unregulated environment, the Web is a fertile ground for the many flowerings of faith (see Bainbridge 1997: 149–55; Hadden and Cowan 2000). From scriptures to scribbles, holiness to hilarity, it is *all* there—and more. The Internet is nothing less than an unlimited and uncharted universe awash

Falun Gong (Falun Dafa): New Religion in an Old Culture

Western consumers of international news reporting probably first became aware of the movement called Falun Gong (or Falun Dafa, a reference to the "Buddhist Wheel of Law") in 1999, after a peaceful demonstration of ten thousand of its followers in Beijing, outside the government ministry that houses the bureaucrats who license religious activities in China. In retaliation for this defiance, the People's Republic outlawed the group and has subjected leaders of Falun Gong within China to ridicule, surveillance, harassment, and arrest. Organizations that monitor human rights in Asia, such as Human Rights Watch (Spiegel 2002), report that scores of Falun Gong practitioners have died in Chinese jails from beatings and other forms of mistreatment (I. Johnson 2000, 2004: 185–292). Other nations, in turn, have reacted to the official campaign of repression against Falun Gong with strong diplomatic condemnations (I. Johnson 1999).

Falun Gong emerged in 1992 from the preaching of Li Hong Zhi, a forty-year-old former government clerk from Gongzhulin, a town in northeast China. The group maintains no membership rolls, so assertions about numbers of followers are guesses at best. Nevertheless, estimates of its size range from 2 million to 10 million in China (Wyse 2000: 281) to 100 million worldwide (Craig Smith 1999a: A46). During the early years of the group in the United States, persons of Chinese birth or Chinese-American background predominated among members. Now, some leaders report that almost half of Falun Gong's members in the United States are not Chinese (Sawano 2000).

Falun Gong's teachings are a lightly folded blend of Taoist precepts, Buddhist practice, and traditional Chinese beliefs about health and harmony resulting from individual mastery over the "vital energies" (*qi*) of the body. Added to these elements, however, are some novel streaks concerning higher orders of matter and contact with space aliens. Because Falun Gong fuses a number of Asian cultural strains, it has attracted practitioners of several meditative disciplines, devotees of alternative medical therapies, and even veterans of training in the martial arts (Sawano 2000).

Notwithstanding the ancient quality of some of its teachings, Falun Gong is in many respects a very modern creation. Born of an entrepreneurial impulse that an unsympathetic analyst has characterized as "too close to fake TV evangelism" (Wyse 2000: 281), it has heavily exploited such technologies as videotaping (at first) and the Internet (later) to spread its beliefs across oceans and continents. The movement distributes its founder's writings and lectures through publishing houses in Hong Kong and the United States; to promote its beliefs further it held a convention in New York City at the Jacob K. Javits Center, home to large-scale trade shows.

To an outsider, those beliefs, regardless of their origins, seem distinctively—dare one say it?—American. For here is a religion that resists calling itself that, for people more proudly "spiritual" than conventionally pious. It claims to have no constitution and no detailed records of its operations. "The added benefit of Falun Gong," as one reporter paraphrases a Chinese scholar, "is that practicing it requires little effort" (Sawano 2000). Its main text can be downloaded quickly from the World Wide Web. Its followers can meet in a public park (if they like to meet) to conduct their slow and methodical breathing exercises, or they can just stay home; no one keeps track (except, perhaps, a few spies for the Chinese government [Gillis 2007]). Neither does anyone enforce uniformity in personal devotional practices. Falun Gong emphasizes physical fitness and advises members to practice self-help and healing to the point where self-care risks becoming self-absorption. Finally, Li Hong Zhi, its acknowledged master, has migrated to the United States. Under pressure from the authorities, he left China in 1998 and lives in wealthy seclusion in the New York metropolitan area (Craig Smith 1999a, 1999b).

with every conceivable form of religious presence—what one journalist has dubbed "a digital Tower of Babel" (Chidley 1997: 46) and what another observer has called "a temple without bounds" (quoted in Incandela 1997: 31).

In this figurative temple, for example, the more literate seeker, with a few keystrokes, can engage sacred writings from the Bible (in a variety of translations), to the Book of Mormon, to the Bhagavad Gita. Within just a single conventional denomination, Roman Catholicism, the Web is overflowing with relevant texts: papal encyclicals, the revised Code of Canon Law, the documents of Vatican II, *The Catechism of the Catholic Church*, and *The Catholic Encyclopedia*, to name but a few (Incandela 1997: 31). Moreover, the diversity of Catholic destinations for point-and-click pilgrimages across the Internet is astounding. It extends, at the right edge of the ideological spectrum, from the home pages of the conservative group Opus Dei (www.opusdei.org)—oddly enough, an organization notorious in part because of its penchant for secrecy—and Mother M. Angelica's cable satellite system, the Eternal Word Television Network (www.ewtn.com), to those on the left for the various Web presences of the pacifist Catholic Worker (www.catholicworker.org).

Religious uses of the wide-open spaces on the Internet range from the highly spiritual to the purely pragmatic. An example of the former is the site www.sacredspace.ie, which a group of Jesuit priests in Ireland erected to foster daily meditation among harried office workers. Their simple pages furnish readers with excerpts from the Christian scriptures and suggestions for how to initiate prayer (Elwood 2000). An illustration of the latter is the home on the Web of Congregation Or HaTzafon, a Jewish community in Fairbanks, Alaska (www.mosquitonet.com/~orhatzafon), that describes itself as "the farthest north synagogue in the world." The congregation's online Judaica store sells shirts emblazoned with its nickname, "The Frozen Chosen," so that it might accumulate sufficient funds to engage a rabbi full-time ("Deus ex Computer" 1997).

Indeed, several religious organizations not only have been the subjects of Web pages but also are professional creators of digital art and designs on the Web for outside customers. These Internet entrepreneurs include the Monastery of Christ in the Desert, an abbey of contemplative Benedictines in the remote terrain of New Mexico (www.christdesert.org), who regard their work in computing as a continuation of the monastic craft of manuscript "illumination" (Riggs 1996: 28). Included as well is Higher Source (Dawson and Hennebry 1999: 17–20, 25–26), a Web design firm that was operated by principals of the infamous UFO cult known as Heaven's Gate (see Frezza 1997; Hall 2000; Wessinger 1991). Most of the group's U.S. members cast off their earthly "vehicles" in 1997, committing simultaneous suicide in the hope of beginning an ascent to "The Evolutionary Level Beyond Human" by rising from their rented mansion in southern California to a spaceship obscured in the tail of the passing Hale-Bopp comet.

The Internet also features a huge variety of relatively centrist denominational offerings. For example, I-Church is sponsored by the Diocese of Oxford in the Church of England. The site contains the Book of Common Prayer, as well as daily prayers, sermons, and reflections. I-Church members also post

Evangelicals and the Web

Mark U. Edwards, Jr., president emeritus of St. Olaf College in Northfield, Minnesota, and the author of *Printing, Propaganda, and Martin Luther* (1994), provides this assessment of the current role of evangelical Christians on the World Wide Web:

> By one estimate, evangelical Christians account for more than eighty percent of the Christian presence on the World Wide Web. The explosive daily growth in Web content renders such estimates instantly obsolete, but evangelical Christians have clearly embraced the Web with far greater enthusiasm than their mainline (including Catholic) competitors. Why is this, and what may it mean for the future of American Christianity?
>
> A look at the past may throw light on a possible future.
>
> For three decades in the early sixteenth century, Protestants outpublished their Catholic rivals by incredible percentages. One writer, Martin Luther, assisted by enterprising printers who were not handicapped by copyright laws, swamped the market with five pamphlets for every one by "all" the Catholic publicists combined! . . . For more than thirty years . . . Protestant writers overwhelmingly dominated the recently invented printing press. By the time the Catholic authorities found a way to use the new media to their own advantage, the religious landscape of Europe had been utterly and, as history would prove, irreversibly transformed.
>
> Why did this happen?
>
> Pre-Reformation Catholicism had used the press to do more efficiently what they had been doing with manuscripts for centuries: multiplying documents needed by priests and the hierarchy in the normal performance of their duties. . . .
>
> In contrast, the Protestants, bubbling over with missionary zeal, wanted to convert readers and hearers to their new understanding of the Christian gospel. They saw the press as a God-given means to a crucial end: a dramatic reform of the church. They were zealous proselytizers. . . .
>
> What does this suggest for the twenty-first century?
>
> A plausible case can be made that the technologies of the Net, the Web, and television are more compatible with evangelical understandings of theology and worship. The Good News may be mediated by technology, and individuals can come to faith apart from other believers (but not, most would agree, apart from the Holy Spirit). But with its breakdown of traditional propinquity in space, time, and vivid relationships, the virtual world of the Web raises perplexing questions for denominations that understand themselves in terms of physical presence, whether in corporate worship or in the use of the sacraments. More of the mainline than evangelicals are likely to have theological problems with the virtualities of Web-mediated religion.
>
> But then as now, the key difference lies not in theology but in motivation. Today's evangelicals, like sixteenth-century Protestants, seek to proselytize and convert. Today's mainline (including Catholicism) largely does not. There are good theological reasons for evangelical missionary zeal and mainline ecumenical diffidence. But the sixteenth-century example does suggest that the mainline will be ill-advised to allow today's evangelicals to monopolize the educational potential of the Net and the Web.
>
> While the mainline need not reenter the mission business, it needs to recognize that the Net and the Web are opening up a new world. Like the Catholics of the sixteenth century with the printing press, the mainline of today will need to assess the positive educational potential of the Internet and the Web and put it to good use for its own faithful. Or like in the sixteenth century, today's mainline may find itself with a religious landscape irreversibly transformed by its competitor's more effective use of the new information technology.

Source: Reprinted from *Sightings* (November 1, 2001), an Internet newsletter of the Martin Marty Center at the University of Chicago Divinity School.

their own thoughts. One writes, for example, "I-Church is somewhere I can 'do church' when I want and in an exciting new way." Another writes that he is a deaf person and that I-Church provides a way that he "can relax and chat, debate and find the support of many friends in time of need." Persons can also post their pictures along with their comments. The Internet Church of Christ is an online church that accepts members who accept in their "heart" the words, "I declare that Jesus Christ is the only-begotten Son of God, risen from the dead, and I accept Him as my personal Lord and Savior. I desire to join Internet Church of Christ." The site also advertises the King James Bible and a picture of Jesus from AllPosters.com. Some Internet "churches" are outgrowths of already existing real-time churches, while others exist only in the virtual realm. Almost all major denominations have some forms of Internet presence that extend beyond the purely informational and provide means whereby persons can connect with both institutional and individual expressions of their faith tradition.

Without any known parallel, however, is the "virtual diocese" of Bishop Jacques Gaillot, whom the Vatican deposed in 1995 from the See of Evreux in France, after twelve years of service, for "inappropriate" behavior and "inadequate" presentation of Catholic teachings (see Englund 1995). When Gaillot refused an order to resign, his throne was declared "vacant." But Roman Catholic bishops, once they attain that rank, retain it for life. Moreover, the Catholic Church is in theory a territorial organization: A bishop must be a bishop *of someplace*—"there is no room for spare bishops to be knocking around" (Starrs 1997: 194). So Gaillot immediately was given another assignment, this one *in partibus infidelium* (Latin for "in the land of the unbelievers"). It was the nonexistent titular diocese of Partenia, an ancient realm located on the modern map somewhere near Oran in Algeria.

This new responsibility in fact bears no real pastoral duties, as the historical Partenia lies beneath hundreds of feet of shifting sand in North Africa and has not hosted an active community of Christians since the fifth or sixth century. On top of that, no human—believer or unbeliever—has lived there permanently since the eighth century. The bishop had his work cut out for him, reports Paul F. Starrs, a geographer:

> As of mid-1996 his diocese lacked a single living follower [of Catholicism] but was extant because, whereas dunes and camels come and go, a Divine flower can afford to wait through mere centuries until humans may manage to reclaim a chunk of desert. Meanwhile, the need for someone to minister for souls past and potential is presumed to continue unimpeded and intact. At hand was a supreme revenge, the execution of a smoothly realized Vatican passive aggression and a tactic tested through time and never before found wanting—the seconding of a troublesome senior cleric to what in effect amounted to an ecclesiastical nonplace. (1997: 194–95)

A "nonplace" indeed: Within the diocese of Partenia today live "only the scorpions, lizards, and flies that crawl over its sands," adds author Jeff Zaleski, "plus some Muslims, who couldn't care less about what Gaillot might say. There, the Vatican must have reasoned, Gaillot could preach as much as he liked to a congregation of one: himself" (quoted in Weeks 1997: D5).

As grim as such a future would have sounded, before he left his old job Bishop Gaillot availed himself of one more opportunity to preach in Normandy. Less than ten days after his removal, thousands of the faithful stood outside the cathedral of Evreux in a cold rain, while others—including four fellow Catholic bishops and the Communist mayor—packed the old church for Gaillot's final Sunday Mass in his former diocese (Englund 1995). In his farewell homily, Gaillot reassured his listeners, "When people start expressing their thoughts, there is no more fear, no more dread; new energies are deployed everywhere" (Gaillot 1995: 3).

But Gaillot had every reason to dread his fate. After all, the Vatican had handed over to the French bishop a domain that is, in the words of Zaleski, "as close to nowhere as possible" (quoted in Weeks 1997: D5). It did not foresee how Gaillot would seize upon a technology of communication that transcends place, that is simultaneously "nowhere" and "anywhere," in order to minister to a newly gathered flock of cybernautic nomads.

What could have been the bishop's parting words to the public turned out to be prophetic. For however hasty the Congregation for Bishops in Rome may be to discipline, it is undoubtedly slow on the electronic uptake. Bishop Gaillot did not head to North Africa; in fact, titular bishops are forbidden to function in their dioceses, which fall within some other ordinary's actual jurisdiction. Instead he withdrew to shabby lodgings among urban squatters in Paris. Before a year elapsed, however, he had reconstructed his early Christian diocese in cyberspace, turf hardly more solid than the Sahara. With assistance from a Web guru named Léo Scheer and some Swiss designers (Starrs 1997: 195–97), the bishop launched a Partenia home page.

Through its portals, the site (www.partenia.org) draws to Gaillot's "Diocese without Borders" Catholics and others from around the world who converge on "a place of liberty" (quoted in Fox 1997: 297–98). "The primitive church was a kind of Internet in itself," the Bishop of Partenia submits, "which was one of the reasons it was so difficult for the Roman Empire to combat it. The early Christians understood that what was most important was not to claim physical power in a physical place, but to establish a network of believers—to be on line" (quoted in Riggs 1996: 30).

The Partenia Web site extends to visitors the chance to express themselves, on an infinity of subjects and in a variety of languages, by joining an ongoing forum. In contrast, noted one critic (S. Martin 1996: 8), the official home page of the Vatican (www.vatican.va) "is, not surprisingly, very strong on icons but communication appears to be one-way only: from the top down" (see also Dawson and Hennebry 1999: 38n; Helland 2002: 294–98) In the relatively short time since its inception, the upstart site has grown in both size and popularity. It currently contains hundreds of pages of content, and it is linked to scores more sites. In just its inaugural year online, the virtual Partenia logged more than two hundred thousand visits from users (Starrs 1997: 215).

In his own time, the psalmist wondered how to "sing the Lord's song in a strange land" (Ps. 137:4). More puzzling still is how to cope, in our time, with a religious landscape that defies placement and obliterates distance. Yet waves and waves of digital missionaries have already colonized this space, giving new meaning, both technical and theological, to the term *server*.

Suggestions for Further Reading

William Sims Bainbridge. 1997. *The Sociology of Religious Movements*. New York: Routledge.

Brenda E. Brasher. 2004. *Give Me That Online Religion*, 2nd ed. New Brunswick, N.J.: Rutgers University Press.

Lynn Schofield Clark. 2003. *From Angels to Aliens: Teenagers, the Media, and the Supernatural*. New York: Oxford University Press.

Lorne L. Dawson and Douglas E. Cowan, eds. 2004. *Religion Online: Finding Faith on the Internet*. New York: Routledge.

Jeffrey K. Hadden and Douglas E. Cowan, eds. 2000. *Religion on the Internet: Research Prospects and Promises*. Amsterdam: JAI.

Heather Hendershot. 2004. *Shaking the World for Jesus: Media and Conservative Evangelical Culture*. Chicago: University of Chicago Press.

Stewart M. Hoover and Lynn Schofield Clark, eds. 2002. *Practicing Religion in the Age of the Media: Explorations in Media, Religion, and Culture*. New York: Columbia University Press.

Ian Johnson. 2004. *Wild Grass: Three Stories of Change in Modern China*. New York: Pantheon Books.

Colleen McDannell. 1995. *Maternal Christianity: Religion and Popular Culture in America*. New Haven, Conn.: Yale University Press.

R. Laurence Moore. 2003. *Touchdown Jesus: The Mixing of Sacred and Secular in American History*. Louisville, Ky.: Westminster/John Knox Press.

David Morgan. 1998. *Visual Piety: A History and Theory of Popular Religious Images*. Berkeley: University of California Press.

Quentin J. Schultze, ed. 1990. *American Evangelicals and the Mass Media: Perspectives on the Relationship between American Evangelicals and the Mass Media*. Grand Rapids, Mich.: Zondervan.

Robert Wuthnow. 1994. *Producing the Sacred: An Essay on Public Religion*. Urbana: University of Illinois Press.

Jeff Zaleski. 1997. *The Soul of Cyberspace: How New Technology Is Changing Our Spiritual Lives*. San Francisco: HarperCollins.

Photograph courtesy of William H. Swatos, Jr.

CHAPTER 11

Boundary Issues

CHURCH, STATE, AND NEW RELIGIONS

As American society grows more complex, it generates especially trying dilemmas in the task of locating the boundaries between sacred and secular. In particular, a strict reading of the U.S. Constitution mandates a degree of separation between church and state. All students of the U.S. legal tradition would be likely to agree, in keeping with the Constitution's Establishment Clause (which is actually a "no establishment" clause), that the state has no business sponsoring an existing faith or imposing on citizens one of its own creation. In response to the document's Free Exercise Clause, all likewise would extend to individuals the liberty to put into practice their own particular religious beliefs—at least to the extent that they do no physical harm to another. Because this pair of principles is fraught with internal tension, however, disagreement arises in drawing a line between which official acts impartially *protect* religious convictions and which ones inadvertently or intentionally *aid* them. Courts must identify the secular initiatives that infringe on the sanctity of conscience, as well as the sectarian habits that attempt to ride to prominence on the back of the state.

In the United States, the course of judicial reasoning on religious matters is convoluted, to say the least. For example, judicial interpretations currently allow public grants of textbooks to religious schools, but do not permit the provision of wall maps or globes. There is some evidence, in fact, to suggest that from the very first there were two different interpretations of the Establishment Clause: The one that ultimately prevailed was the broad reading that there would be no established religions anywhere in the United States. Yet Stephen Carter points out that at least some supporters of the amendment at the Constitutional Convention apparently saw it as a way to "protect the state religious establishments [such as that in Massachusetts, which lasted until 1833] from disestablishment by the federal government" (1993: 118). In the early years of the republic, the courts seemed to see no inconsistency between a de facto Protestant establishment and the Establishment Clause. Rather, it was the waves of immigrant Catholics that encouraged Protestants to advocate a more separatist view of constitutional rights.

Phillip Hammond (1999) has detailed four critical steps in the U.S. Supreme Court's interpretive style with respect to the First Amendment's Free Exercise Clause. These are:

1. *Reynolds v. United States* (argued 1878, decided 1879), the first significant case of this sort in constitutional history, wherein the Court held rather conservatively that the amendment prohibited government attempts to control *belief*, but did allow the government to restrict *action* based on that belief—specifically, in this case, polygamy on the part of a Mormon man in the Utah territory, in violation of a federal statute that made plural marriages illegal in U.S. territories.
2. *Cantwell v. Connecticut* (1940), wherein the Court somewhat reversed itself in supporting the rights of a Jehovah's Witness who was held to be violating a breach-of-peace ordinance by playing a religious message on a portable phonograph. The Court held that some religiously motivated behavior was subject to constitutional protection, even though the same behavior is not protected when otherwise motivated. This opened a difficult foreground for subsequent actions, because it clearly did not extend to all religiously motivated behavior (for example, human sacrifice); hence the Court would have to decide limits in specific cases.
3. *United States v. Ballard* (1944), in which Guy Ballard and his family, leaders of the I AM movement, were accused of fraud for seeking funding to effect spiritual cures that they claimed they could produce for otherwise incurable ailments. In this case, the Court upheld a lower court acquittal of the Ballards on the basis that the Ballards *believed* that they could do what they said they could do, so it could not be proved that they were engaging in intentional deception.
4. *United States v. Seeger* (1965), wherein protections for conscientious objectors were extended to those who had a purely ethical, nontheistic creed that prohibited participation in acts of military violence (a decision reinforced in *Welsh v. United States* five years later).

Federal courts continue to be inconsistent in applying the Establishment and Free Exercise clauses. There are some signs that members of the federal judiciary are currently more tolerant of contact between church and state than has historically been true. During the 1980s and 1990s, for example, the U.S. Supreme Court permitted, among other configurations, the inclusion of religious symbolism in public school Christmas decorations, the erection of Nativity displays at public expense, the employment of official chaplains by state legislatures, and some forms of tax relief for parents who pay the expenses of children enrolled in religious schools. In addition, in *Rosenberger v. University of Virginia* (1995), it ordered that a public university subsidize a religious magazine from student funds, based on equity and free-speech considerations. On the other hand, 1990 also brought the *Employment Division v. Smith* decision, which overturned the standing policy of the Court that a "compelling state interest" (CSI) must be demonstrated before a public regulation that "burdens" religious practice can be legitimately enforced.

At issue in *Smith* was whether members of a Native American peyote religion fell under state drug-free hiring regulations, hence could be either dismissed from their jobs or not hired. *Smith* upheld the implementation of the drug-free regulations, claiming "that uniform, across-the-board ([that is], nondiscriminatory) regulations are not to be viewed as presumptively invalid and do not require a showing of a CSI" (Robbins 1998: 88). This case and related instances led to the successful passage of the Religious Freedom Restoration Act by Congress in 1994, which was subsequently overturned by the Supreme Court in a Texas case, *City of Boerne v. Flores* (1997), involving a historic Roman Catholic church that wanted to make alterations to its building so as to serve its present congregation better. That action, along with continuing concerns about school prayer and other religious speech acts, in turn occasioned the Religious Freedom Amendment to the Constitution in the late 1990s, which would have, among other things, inserted the word *God* into the Constitution for the first time. It failed to receive the necessary two-thirds vote for passage in the House of Representatives in 1998, thus putting at least a temporary end to this effort.

We should note, however, that in the period since the mid-twentieth century, some of the most significant court decisions for church-state and religion-society relations in the United States have not directly involved religious organizations or the religious practices of individuals at all. These issues began with efforts to establish civil liberties and privacy rights in general. Clearly there can be

Thinking about Marketplace Religion

In an article titled "Suffering and God's Love: Given to the Just and the Unjust Alike," John Garvey raises questions about how the separation of church and state affects religion's ability to deal with pressing existential problems in a market-oriented society. He writes:

> The separation of church and state has at least freed religion from its alliance with coercive power, and where no particular [political] advantage can be gained from religious affiliation, a faith may be chosen cleanly and honestly.
>
> But the price paid for this is that we see religion placed in the realm of the subjective, a matter of taste. The differences involved in religion divide us, and what unites us is considered much more important—but what is that, in our secular society? The marketplace, not only of ideas but of commodities—or rather, ideas become commodities, and the ones we like best are the ones we accept as true. The successful sale of a commodity demands that the thing we are being sold—cars, whiskey, brand-name clothes, bottled water, religion—can satisfy us and make us whole now, and we will not be happy (being happy is all-important) unless we buy, or buy into, what is being offered for sale.

Source: John Garvey, "Suffering and God's Love: Given to the Just and Unjust Alike," *Commonweal* 124, September 12, 1997, 7.

no decision that is more important to the history of religion in the United States in the last quarter of the century than the "pro-choice" decision of *Roe v. Wade* in 1973 that allowed women the right to choose whether to carry a fetus to term. (In other words, it legalized abortion in those states that had not already liberalized access to the procedure.) In the wake of this decision, a conservative religious coalition of significant proportions assembled for political action in the United States. Randall Balmer (2007) has recently spoken of this account as "the abortion myth," and instead cites as the real beginning of the "Christian right" the 1975 Court threat that would have removed the tax-exempt status of Bob Jones University for its failure to treat blacks in the same way as whites. Nevertheless, in the debate as it is both framed and embodied today, myth or not, "abortion" is the rhetorical fulcrum upon which "conservative" versus "liberal" social policies hang in the balance. While *Roe v. Wade* has not been overturned, and in fact has been set back only slightly in subsequent actions, by appeal to it the conservative religious lobby has largely set the agenda for much of U.S. politics since that time (see Simpson 1996). This can be seen most clearly in gay rights and right-to-die legislation and adjudication, where the logic that justified *Roe v. Wade* in the eyes of the Court has been laid aside (Hammond 1999).

Religious Novelty

Among other sources of continual tension in church-state relations in the United States are the activities of religious movements that are novel in their appearance on the American scene. We know them generally as new religious movements, or NRMs. (The public is more likely to apply to them a pejorative term, *cults*, about which we will say more later.) As we have already seen in the litigation involving the Mormons and the I AM movement, crucial cases often emerge when what seems to be a new religious movement emerges. Whether these movements are or are not really new, however, does not seem to matter as much as whether or not they challenge the religious status quo in U.S. society. Charles L. Harper and Bryan F. Le Beau (1993), for example, suggest that we might better term these movements "marginal religious movements" and understand them as outside the existing mainstream. Following their argument, for example, Roman Catholicism in the nineteenth-century United States would have been a marginal religious movement. The ways in which it was treated then, including the ways the Protestant establishment sought to use the Establishment and Free Exercise clauses to maintain the status quo, are consistent with this characterization. Indeed, in an article titled "The Tnevnoc Cult" ("convent" spelled backward)—a satirical tour de force at the time of the NRM controversies of recent decades—David G. Bromley and Anson D. Shupe (1979b) used anti-Catholic materials from the late nineteenth century to show that many of the same kinds of wild allegations that were used in the 1970s and 1980s against NRMs were used against Catholics a century earlier. The historian David Brion Davis (1960, 1971) has provided thorough analyses of the use of these kinds of allegations against unpopular religious groups throughout U.S. history.

In fact, as we indicated in chapter 1, the NRMs that began to influence the sociology of religion—especially from the 1970s on—were not a radical departure from the whole of American religious history, but rather from the general homogeneity that was effected in the 1950s. Harper and Le Beau note that religious historian Sydney Ahlstrom identified more than 120 such movements in the antebellum nineteenth century alone, and today there may be between 500 and 600 such movements. NRM activity is actually part of a "venerable tradition" in U.S. society. In their own research, using the 1989 edition of J. Gordon Melton's *Encyclopedia of American Religions*, Harper and Le Beau identified 822 marginal religious movements, of which only "32 (about 4 percent) are noted to have had any external controversy or conflict" (1993: 176). From this perspective, the "cult scare" that was associated with NRMs in the 1970s and 1980s was clearly disproportionate. The cultural innovation that is reflected in the emergence of NRMs is actually to be expected in a free society. In particular, the U.S. Constitution promises freedom of religion. The intention behind this promise is to make church affiliation in this country wholly voluntary. Stated simply, no power of government is legally to be brought to bear against individuals to force them to declare allegiance, render service, or pay fees to religious organizations that they do not in conscience support. In addition to excluding the government from purely religious decisions, though, Americans have come to embrace the idea that individual spiritual convictions should always be formed without the interference of a heavy hand, no matter to what larger social body it may be attached.

The "cult scare" was generated by critics of some NRMs who charged that these groups frequently violate the volition of prospective members by using exotic techniques of "brainwashing" in their recruitment programs. These tools are thought to include practically irresistible methods of mind control or, in extreme cases, physically coercive adjuncts to persuasion. Moreover, suspicions of psychologically or physically coercive recruitment on the part of new religions have led periodically to calls for governmental investigation and even regulation of unconventional religious bodies—a demand that places the state back in the middle of the religious conflict from which it is supposed to remain aloof. Although this has not happened in the United States, it has happened in other liberal democratic societies such as contemporary France and Germany (Richardson 1999; Richardson and Introvigne 2001).

Exactly how, according to sociological accounts, do NRMs go about adding to their numbers? Although NRMs may have as one of their goals the wholesale transformation of the world, their appeals are usually rather narrowly targeted. Most of the people who are contacted by these movements in various recruiting efforts have some characteristics in common. They are young, affluent, educated, unmarried, and geographically mobile. Such persons make ideal novices, for they bring energy and intelligence to the movement, and they demand little in the way of domestic normalcy or a settled lifestyle in return. They are often fervent in their commitment, but sufficiently flexible in their situations to accommodate the sometimes arbitrary dictates of religious leaders.

Yet sociologists report that few people, even in these prime categories of sensitivity to countercultural messages, eventually become permanent members of unconventional religions. To be sure, some will express momentary curiosity about a new religion; a smaller group will seriously investigate the requirements for membership; a few persons will actually join. However, a large portion of the joiners will "leak" away from the movement after a relatively brief period of involvement.

A typical sequence in this process of attrition was documented by Eileen Barker in her study of the British branch of the Unification Church. Although the setting for this research was in England, a similar pattern would pertain in the United States as well. One of the most famous of the NRMs of the 1960s and 1970s, the Unification Church was founded by a Korean-born evangelist, the Reverend Sun Myung Moon. The press has hence dubbed his followers "Moonies," though some members of the Unification Church take offense at this colloquialism. Barker gained access to church records that permitted her to trace the careers as Unificationists of 1,017 persons who applied to attend "workshops" on Moon's theology in the London area during 1979. Her analysis of these records revealed that 90 percent of those who underwent at least a part of the initial Unification indoctrination failed to join the church. Indeed, there was considerable evidence of desertion at each step in the measured march to membership. She wrote:

> There were more who left before the end of the initial two-day course than there were eventual converts. Roughly a third of the applicants went on to a seven-day workshop, about a fifth to a twenty-one-day course, and just over half of these then declared that they would join, although in fact they did not all do so. Out of the original 1,000, a *maximum* of 50 (19 of whom were British) were full-time members of the Church by the beginning of 1981. This number had dropped to a maximum of 36 by March 1982. (Barker 1985: 67)

Even these estimates, Barker admitted, may be an overstatement of the yield from the preliminary workshops. Clearly, if the performance that these statistics portray is the result of "brainwashing," the Unification Church uses an exceedingly mild detergent. (We also hasten to add that sociologists of religion reject the concept of "brainwashing" as lacking any empirical evidence in these applications [Richardson 1996; Robbins 1984; Robbins and Anthony 1979a, 1982].)

Cult and Anticult: Social Science and Social Movements

From time to time a concept used in sociology seems to take on a life of its own through the media, which may well pervert its social scientific usage. *Charisma* is one example. This term was introduced into political sociology by Max Weber to describe a specific type of authority structure. Today it is applied to everything from restaurants to perfumes to neckties. In general, however, its application is positive: Hardly anyone seems to be hurt by having charisma. The word *cult* has a similar origin but a different outcome, which is bound up with the history of NRMs since the mid-1960s.

Cult has a standard meaning in religious studies as referring to a set of beliefs and practices associated with a specific god or group of gods (in polytheistic religions), a saint, or even an enlightened living person. These beliefs and practices function as a subset within a larger religious tradition. Hence one may find the cult of the Blessed Virgin Mary in Catholicism (the Marian cult) or of Krishna or Sai Baba within Hinduism. Until the mid-1960s, as far as we know, the word *cult* excited no one.

A specific, equally unexciting, use of *cult* occurred in the sociology of religion beginning in 1932, when Howard Becker attempted an extension of church-sect theory to include what Troeltsch had described as "spiritual and mystical religion." Becker's cult type was used to describe a religious grouping whose beliefs were unorthodox, possibly to both secular and religious authorities, and that had a very loose organizational structure. Subsequent authors elaborated the concept in different ways, most notably Bainbridge and Stark (1979, 1980), while others (D. Martin 1966; Swatos 1981b) argued that the concept really confused church-sect theory more than it helped, and thus belonged elsewhere than in this typology.

Colin Campbell spoke of a "cultic milieu" to include a whole variety of movements including "the worlds of the occult and the magical, of spiritualism and psychic phenomena, of mysticism and new thought, of alien intelligences and lost civilizations, of faith healing and nature cure" (1972: 122). To this he added the notion of "seekership," first proposed by John Lofland and Rodney Stark in a pioneering article on the Unification Church, defining it as "floundering among religious alternatives, an openness to a variety of religious views, frequently esoteric, combined with failure to embrace the specific ideology and fellowship of some set of believers" (1965: 870).

As this work was being done, an extraordinarily diverse set of religious movements was appearing on the U.S. scene. Some were imports from abroad—particularly from Asia, as immigration statutes changed, the Vietnam War escalated, and transportation and communication on a world scale became easier. Not all were truly new—Zen and Hare Krishna, for example, have centuries-old roots (older, for example, than Methodism, the Salvation Army, the Disciples of Christ, or Mormonism)—but some, like the Moonies, were new. As we have already indicated—and, again, just as Campus Crusade for Christ or the Intervarsity Fellowship or TEC or Chrysalis—they tended to target younger, more thoughtful people on college campuses or in other receptive settings. Other "new" religions were radical Jesus Movement groups that challenged the mainstream churches in a variety of ways, including interrupting their worship.

Just as Roman Catholics and Mormons in an earlier era, these groups were met by an organized opposition, which was in at least some cases aided and abetted by both the establishment Protestant-Catholic-Jewish coalition and establishment academics, who had accepted a broadly sketched model of secularization. This opposition coalesced as what sociologist of religion Anson Shupe was the first to term the *anticult movement* (ACM; see Shupe and

Scientology has been among the most controversial of NRMs and has been prosecuted and persecuted in much of Western Europe. The argument against Scientology, however, shows one of the important contributions of NRMs generally to the study of religion: namely, that these movements have reasserted the strength of the concept of "religion" in the face of secularizing elites. The most consistent argument lodged against Scientology is that it uses the label "religion" to make money while practicing a bogus "therapy." But isn't this curious: If "religion" were as dead as secular elites would like to claim it is, why would anybody who wanted to take people's hard-earned secular money pose as a religion? Scientology and other NRMs demonstrate the continuation of strong religious longings among people across social classes in contemporary society. Photograph courtesy of William H. Swatos, Jr.

Bromley 1980). Within the ACM there were both overtly religious and manifestly secular components. Those groups that were overtly religious came primarily from conservative Christian organizations. The Southern Baptist Convention, for example, established an influential bureau to deal with "cults," and the Missouri Synod Lutherans added printed literature on the new cults to their existing stock of materials concerning such groups as the Jehovah's Witnesses and the Mormons.

The activities of the ACM extended far beyond literature, however. First, based on now-discredited "brainwashing" theories, the ACM developed not only a network of mental health professionals to offer "rehabilitative" counseling to persons who leave NRMs, but also a cadre of "deprogrammers" who resorted to a variety of tactics, ultimately reaching the level of kidnapping, that forcibly removed NRM converts from their new religious choice. The deprogrammers engaged in an intensive experience of psychological coercion and physical restriction, far closer to what was supposed to have constituted "brainwashing" than what had actually occurred in NRM settings. Once an acceptable level of deprogramming had been reached, the "deconvert" was then turned over to counselors and/or support groups of others who had deconverted. Deprogrammers justified both their illegal activities and their subsequent treatment programs on the basis of the putative brainwashing that had already occurred on the part of the NRMs (much as chemotherapy or radiation therapy, for example, are justified, despite their severity, in light of the nature of the cancer that has already invaded a patient's body). Ultimately, the most active of the ACM groups, the Cult Awareness Network (CAN), was sued into bankruptcy—its logo and name, ironically, purchased by the law firm of a member of one of the most controversial NRMs, the Church of Scientology (see Van Duch 1996). The defeat of CAN and other cases, virtually all of which have held coercive deprogramming to be illegal, have largely put an end to this form of anticult activity.

Asceticism and Mysticism

The church-sect typology was not the only one Max Weber developed in the sociology of religion; indeed, he developed many. Another one that can help us understand how it is that "cults" fit into the picture of religious organization is that of asceticism-mysticism (1978: 541–56). This is a typology of *soteriology*, or the means by which people understand themselves to come into or to remain in a right relationship with the Beyond. Soteriology refers to the ways that a religion prescribes for one of its practitioners to be in a right relationship to its perceived power (for example, God). From the viewpoint of the practitioner, it is the kinds of things he or she ought to do in order to be in that relationship.

Additionally, however, Weber points out that these two poles can refer to two different settings: other-worldly or inner-worldly. Other-worldliness basically refers to life-after-death states, while inner-worldliness refers to the conduct of life in the here-and-now. Someone who is other-worldly in his or her asceticism, for example, may have as a major motivation earning merit in heaven (or avoiding hell), while someone who is inner-worldly may speak in terms of "bringing the kingdom of God on earth." An other-worldly mystic may go into a trance state, "proving" that she or he has transcended the bounds of this world, while an inner-worldly mystic will look for a healing miracle or some other charismatic "gift." There is all the difference in the world, religiously speaking, between the Islamic self-flagellant who shows how he is willing to suffer for the cause of Allah and the Hindu guru who lies on a bed of nails to show that he feels no pain. Figure 11.1 shows these two intersecting typological elements and notes as examples traditions that particularly embody them.

Weber suggests that ideal-typically religions tend toward one of two poles: They are either ascetical or mystical. In the simplest terms, ascetical soteriologies involve giving (often phrased as "giving up" something), while mystical soteriologies involve getting. Forms of giving and getting may be quite simple (like giving a small sum of money to a local religious congregation during a worship service or feeling a sense of inner peace) or quite dramatic (like engaging in self-flagellation or experiencing what otherwise appear to be convulsions). People from one soteriological orientation often view the experience of the other as not religious. For example, people with an ascetical religious orientation may criticize clergy of a different background as being too worldly: "He's not very religious. He drinks." People with a mystical orientation may criticize a worship service that satisfies the ascetical soul as: "Not very good. I didn't get anything out of it." (To which the ascetic would reply: "You're not supposed to get anything out of it. You're supposed to give to it.")

The historically dominant Western form of soteriology is *asceticism*: that is, being religious is often equated with some form of self-denial or pain. One can give up drinking, sex, jewelry; one can crawl up stairs to a holy site on one's knees or beat oneself with chains; or one can devote time to good works with little or no financial return, caring for the shut-in, the indigent, the homeless, and

SOTERIOLOGICAL LOCUS	MYSTICAL	ASCETIC
OTHER-WORLDLY	Classical Hinduism	Medieval Catholicism
INNER-WORLDLY	Contemporary Pentecostalism	Protestant Ethic

Figure 11.1. A Typology of Soteriology

so on. Similarly in the West, people who profess to be, say, good Christians but who live a luxurious lifestyle are often suspect or criticized as hypocrites. In the alternate form of soteriology, the unmediated experience of the Beyond known as *mysticism,* a person seeks mystical union or a mystical experience. Speaking in tongues, trance states, healings, experiences that overcome bodily limitations (as do advanced states of yoga) all are mystical types of soteriological experience.

Weber would note, in addition, as we can see from these examples, that these two soteriological styles can operate in reference to two different world orientations: They can be other-worldly or inner-worldly. Other-worldliness means that people's ascetical or mystical strivings are intended to achieve something on a plane of existence beyond the present one. In the Christian West, for example, virtually all ascetical practice until the time of the Reformation—and much even in the present day—was intended to achieve merit in heaven. At the time of the Reformation, however, a change took place within some forms of Protestantism that began to emphasize making this world a better place—or "bringing about God's kingdom on earth." Similarly, classical Hindu mystical practice was intended to detach the yogi from this world; more recently, mysticisms have promised this-worldly effects and benefits—emphasizing, for example, various health benefits associated with meditation.

Because the ascetical style is the predominant one in the West, it should not be surprising that most religious groups in the West have something of this kind of expression in their origins. NRMs tend to arise as ascetical reactions to what is perceived as the apparent laxity of things as they are. Historically in Catholicism, for example, religious orders formed the way in which the ascetic impulse was channeled within the Church. Some Protestant bodies have analogues to orders (or actual orders), but most do not. The result is that if the ascetic impulse cannot be channeled in this way, a schism (split) is likely to occur and a new sect will be formed. The basis for order spirituality Weber calls *virtuoso religiosity.* The religious virtuoso is someone who takes the demands of his or her *existing religion* to a level that surpasses that of normal devotion, but the religious virtuoso's appeal is always to the original intent of his or her religious tradition (see Wittberg 1994).

Mystical religion, by contrast, finds its root in charisma rather than in virtuosity. The appeal of a charismatic is always to specific gifts of grace that she or he has, and the promise of a charismatic is something *new.* The charismatic offers something in his or her person that he or she claims is unique: The Reverend Moon is the Lord of the Second Advent, Christ returned to claim His world. Of course other people before have claimed to be the returned Christ, but they have not also claimed to be the Reverend Moon. In this sense, the Reverend Moon brings a new revelation. Joseph Smith, the Prophet Muhammad, and Jesus also all brought new revelations. Some succeed; some fail. The sociological irony is that virtually all mystical movements that succeed to the point of organization eventually turn into sects—unless they jump right to being churches by converting a ruler and becoming an established religion.

Most of the post-1960s NRMs are mystical in character. They have a charismatic founder and offer an experience of the Beyond in the here and now. This is what, at least in their initial stages, makes them appear so countercultural to the dominant U.S. experience of sect formation rooted in asceticism. A new, more-conservative-than-the-last-one Baptist church is born every day. That's the American way. What is not the American way is a religion stressing this-worldly gratification and an appeal to the person of a leader rather than to historic teachings. Movements of this-worldly gratification have existed as an "underside" of religion in the United States since at least the nineteenth century (see Albanese 1990), but they have always been treated with some suspicion. These include religions of healing, nature religions, those using psychedelic substances, some forms of spiritualism, and such African-American religions as Father Divine's Peace Mission. A more recent example of this style is that practiced by the Reverend Frederik Eikenrenkoetter, "the Rev. Ike" of the United Church and Science of Living Institute of New York City: "Don't wait for pie in the sky by and by when you die." To some extent, this is changing in light of the challenge of the NRMs, along with the institutionalization of some NRMs in forms more akin to the U.S. denominational experience, on the one hand, while on the other, some of the historic Christian denominations—like the Episcopal Church and Roman Catholicism—are finding within the Christian tradition aspects of mysticism that were long blunted. These are giving rise to expressions of such charismatic "gifts" as speaking in tongues and "miracles" of healing.

The Attraction of the Margin

In late November 1978, news began to arrive in the United States, first slowly and then with tragic rapidity, that a semireligious and socialistic colony in the South American nation of Guyana headed by the Reverend Jim Jones—founder of the California-based Peoples Temple—had been the scene of one of the most shocking murder-suicide rites in recent times. The bizarre tales appearing in the media prompted many people to ask how this group's members could have become involved in something like that. (Similar questions rose again with the Branch Davidian, Solar Temple, and Heaven's Gate incidents in the 1990s.)

Some tried to answer these questions by dismissing the participants as ignorant or mentally unbalanced individuals. But as more news came out, it became known that many of the members were fairly well-educated people, and that Jones, for example, was trusted and respected by part of the California political establishment. We also learned that such events, although rare, have occurred before. Early Christian martyrs were willing to be torn apart by lions rather than toss a pinch of incense to a Roman god; the Book of Maccabees tells of pious Jews who allowed themselves to be slaughtered rather than break the Sabbath by fighting to defend themselves; Buddhists set themselves on fire to protest the Diem regime in Vietnam during the early 1960s.

Why are people willing to go to these extremes? Sociology of religion cannot totally answer this larger question, but it can help us understand why people may join marginal religious groups as one solution to specific social conditions.

During sociology's formative years, W. I. Thomas noted "four wishes" that people seem to share: the desire for recognition, the desire for new experience, the desire for mastery, and the desire for security (Thomas and Znaniecki 1926). These needs are usually met by mediating structures—families, neighborhoods, traditional religious organizations, schools (see Berger and Neuhaus 1977)—that provide individuals with links to society and simultaneously fulfill the needs about which Thomas wrote.

As rapid transportation and communication have effectively made society more global, ties to historic local mediating structures have become quite loose—even nonexistent—for many individuals. If these basic needs cannot be satisfied in customary ways, some people turn to unconventional alternatives. Poet and author Peter Marin quotes from a letter from a friend who joined Guru Maharaj Ji's Divine Light Mission: "After a bad relationship, a disintegrated marriage, a long illness, a deep searching for an answer, I was ripe. I was always impulsive anyway. So, I bought in. That feeling of love, of community. The certainty that you are submitting to God incarnate. It creates a wonderfully deep and abiding euphoria which, for some, lasts indefinitely" (1979: 44).

Harvey Cox (1977a, 1977b) has isolated four reasons why some in the United States were drawn to Eastern religious movements. These reasons correspond quite closely to Thomas's four wishes and can be generalized to most other NRM experiences.

First: Most of the converts to Eastern religions are looking for friendship, companionship, acceptance, warmth, and recognition. The group provides a supportive community that helps overcome past loneliness and isolation. Cox paraphrases this motive: "They seem to care for me here. I was bummed out, confused, just wandering around. . . . They took me in. They made me feel at home. Now I feel like a part of it, an important part, too. I belong here" (1977a: 39). In other words, these religious groups provide emotional ties that converts do not find at home, school, church, or work. Many of these groups even adopt kinship terms to give recruits new identities to set them apart from their former existence—sister, brother, krishna. Often a convert is renamed entirely.

Second: Most NRMs emphasize immediate experience and emotional gratification rather than deliberation and rational argument: "All I got at any church I ever went to were sermons or homilies about God. . . . Words, words, words. It was all up in my head. I never really felt it. It was always abstract, never direct, always somebody else's account of it. . . . But here it really happened to me. I experienced it myself. I don't have to take someone else's word for it" (Cox 1977a: 39). Converts, then, report *experiencing* religion rather than merely thinking about it. Whether by meditation, speaking in tongues, prolonged chanting, or sexual expression, adherents have frequent, relatively intense emotional experiences they could not find in mainstream religion.

Third: NRMs also emphasize authority. By having a firm authority structure and a clear, simple set of beliefs and rules, they offer converts something and someone to believe in. Converts profess to exchange uncertainty, doubt, and confusion for trust and assurance. Cox puts it this way: "They hunger for an authority that will simplify, straighten out, assure; something or somebody that will make their choices fewer and less arduous. For some, the search for authority ends at the swami's feet" (1977a: 39).

Fourth: Marginal religious groups purport to offer authenticity and naturalness in an otherwise "artificial" world. By emphasizing natural foods, communal living apart from "civilization," a uniform dress code, and sometimes nudity, these groups show they are not part of the "plastic society." In fact, some comments indicate that converts are not so much turning *to* the East as turning *from* the West: "Western civilization is shot. It is nothing but technology and power and rationalization, corrupted to its core by power and money. It has no contact with nature, feeling, spontaneity. What we need to do now is learn from the oriental peoples who have never been ruined by machines and science, who have kept close to their ancestors' simplicity. Western religion has invalidated itself" (Cox 1977a: 39).

Just as the original four wishes proposed by Thomas contain some contradictions—new experience versus security, for example—there are also contradictions within these new religious groups. In a number of cases, these contradictions have reached the point of serious concern. Indeed, the contradictions with NRMs indicate that they may not be able to meet their adherents' needs any better than the outside world they claim to reject. Cox fears that many of the NRMs will lead to disillusionment, frustration, and bitterness when members realize that they must ultimately exist in the outside world, which is full of uncertainty, confusion, fuzzy choices, and shades of gray. Moreover, Cox points out, many NRMs have joined the consumer society they allegedly deplore by attractively packaging and selling their teachings and disciplines to the public. In other words, not only do the NRMs not in themselves necessarily solve the problems people in modern society must face, but many have themselves also become as "inauthentic" as the world from which they claim to stand apart.

There are some key questions that can be used to evaluate the authenticity of any religious organization's claims. These can be applied equally well for both personal and academic purposes:

- Does it demand that its adherents cease to think critically and evaluate rationally?
- Does it require—implicitly or explicitly—that its adherents cut themselves off from family and friends outside the group?
- Does it argue that religious experiences cannot be attained except through the use of drugs or that drugs are a major vehicle for true religious experiences?
- Is corporal punishment or intensive, hours-long psychological conditioning a part of its program?
- Does it claim to have special knowledge that can be revealed only to insiders?

A positive answer to any of these questions should arouse concern. Positive answers to several should lead to caution.

Illustrations of NRM Dynamics

In the remaining pages of this chapter, we want to look at three NRM constellations. First, we present a detailed look at the Unification Church, one of the most controversial of the NRMs emanating from Asia to win the early notice of sociologists. Our presentation is adapted from the work of Eileen Barker, to whom we have already referred. Barker, a professor at the London School of Economics, is the world's authority within the sociology of religion on Unificationism. She is also the founder of INFORM, a British-based network that seeks to provide accurate information on NRMs and to work, for example, with families whose members have entered NRMs, to help the families understand better what the religious organization is and what the likely outcomes are to be of their loved one's "conversion." The material presented here was originally prepared by Barker for, and appears in slightly different form in, the *Encyclopedia of Religion and Society*.

In the second case, we actually turn the tables and look at anti-Satanism. What we are trying to show here is how a putative NRM ("Satanism") can be imaginatively constructed by a combination of religious, media, criminal-justice, and mental-health practitioners to the point where society responded to it as if it actually existed. Without wishing to minimize the possibilities for real evil in any society, we want to show how it can be the case that some of the NRM scares that were part of the dynamics of the 1970s and 1980s can be overrated and overstated by social groups when these groups find it in their interest to have an opposition. Indeed, in this respect it is interesting to contrast putative Satanism with the very real deaths (by suicide) of the Solar Temple and Heaven's Gate groups in the mid-1990s. These groups were "flying saucer" or UFO cults whose basic characteristics were described in the sociology of religion by Robert Balch as early as 1980. Unlike putative Satanism, which created a national scare for some years, these groups were so trivialized that their potential negative consequences were ignored. Thus it is largely the case that the social significance of NRMs is much more in the eyes of their beholders than in the groups themselves. Even in the two worst cases of NRM effects—the Peoples Temple and the Branch Davidians—the disastrous scenarios were both occasioned by outside interference by agents of the U.S. government. This is an important element to keep in mind as we think about the relationship between boundary issues of religions and the state even in our own "free" society.

The third case that we examine is neopaganism. It might be argued that since paganism is a term that refers generally to religions that predate the named traditions that neopaganism is not strictly speaking a "new" religion at all. The discontinuities of time and culture between early paganisms and contemporary expressions are so dramatic that their present manifestations cannot be directly connected to on-going religious practices. We treat the neopagan case as an example of an NRM that has gained relative acceptance in contemporary Western societies and try to delineate sociologically why this is so.

UNIFICATIONISM

Known officially as the Holy Spirit Association for the Unification of World Christianity, the Unification Church has its roots in Korea in the 1940s. The founder, Sun Myung Moon, was born in 1920 in a rural part of what is now

Lessons from Waco

In the aftermath of the conflagration at the Branch Davidian compound at Mount Carmel, near Waco, Texas, in 1993, which continues to inspire television docudramas, the U.S. Justice and Treasury departments selected Nancy T. Ammerman, a sociologist of religion now associated with Boston University, as one of ten experts to provide recommendations on how best to address Waco-type situations in the future. She wrote the following observations in 1994 for *Footnotes*, the professional newsletter of the American Sociological Association:

> What sociologists and others who have studied religion in American society have to offer in the midst of the current debate are insights that might have led the agents in charge in Waco to act differently. These observations are not intended to absolve the Davidians of guilt, but they are offered . . . as an alternative way of understanding the dozens, if not hundreds, of non-mainstream religious groups that exist throughout the country.
>
> 1. We must understand the pervasiveness of religious experimentation in American history. We simply have been a very religious people. From the days of the first European settlers, there have always been new and dissident religious groups challenging the boundaries of toleration, and the First Amendment to our Constitution guarantees those groups the right to practice their faith. Only when there is clear evidence of criminal wrong-doing can authorities intervene in the free exercise of religion, and then *only with appropriately low levels of intrusiveness.*
> 2. We must understand that new groups almost always provoke their neighbors. By definition, new religious groups think old ways of doing things are at best obsolete, at worst evil. Their very reason for existing is to call into question the status quo. They defy conventional rules and question conventional authorities. The corollary is that they themselves are likely to perceive the outside world as hostile—and it often is. New groups frequently provoke resistance, in recent years often well-organized through the "Cult Awareness Network."
> 3. We should also understand that many new religious movements ask for commitments that seem abnormal to most Americans, commitments that mean the disruption of "normal" family and work lives. While it may seem disturbing to outsiders that converts live all of life under a religious authority, it is certainly not illegal (nor particularly unusual, if we look around the world and back in history). No matter how strange such commitments may seem to many, they are widely sought by millions of others.
> 4. We must also understand that the vast majority of those who make such commitments do so voluntarily. The notion of "cult brainwashing" has been thoroughly discredited by the academic community, and "experts" who propagate such notions in the courts have been discredited by the American Psychological Association and the American Sociological Association. While there may be real psychological needs that lead persons to seek such groups, and while their judgment may indeed be altered by their participation, neither of those facts constitutes coercion.
> 5. People who deal with new or marginal religious groups must understand the ability of such groups to create an alternative world. The first dictum of sociology is "Situations perceived to be real are real in their consequences." No matter how illogical or unreasonable the beliefs of

a group seem to an outsider, they are the real facts that describe the world through the eyes of the insider.

6. People who deal with the leaders of such groups should understand that "charisma" is not just an individual trait but a property of the constantly-evolving relationship between a leader and followers. So long as the leader's interpretations make sense of the group's experience, that leader is likely to be able to maintain authority. These interpretations are not a fixed text, but a living, changing body of ideas, rules, and practices. Only in subsequent generations are religious prescriptions likely to become written orthodoxies.
7. Finally, authorities who deal with high-commitment groups of any kind must realize that any group under siege is likely to turn inward, bonding to each other and to their leader even more strongly than before. Outside pressure only consolidates the group's view that outsiders are the enemy. And isolation decreases the availability of information that might counter their internal view of the world. In the Waco case, negotiating strategies were constantly undermined by the actions of the tactical teams. Pressure from encroaching tanks, psychological warfare tactics, and the like, only increased the paranoia of the group and further convinced them that the only person they could trust was Koresh.

No one can say whether a better understanding of groups like the Davidians would have changed the outcome in Waco. But decisions based on research evidence that takes human social and religious dynamics into account—something that the people in charge at Waco never sought—would certainly seem preferable to decisions based on tactical necessity alone.

Source: Nancy T. Ammerman, "Lessons from Waco," *ASA Footnotes* 22, January 1994, 3.

North Korea to parents who had converted to a Presbyterian version of Christianity when he was ten years old. On Easter Day 1936, it is claimed, Moon received a message from Jesus telling him that he had been chosen to fulfill the special mission of establishing God's Kingdom of Heaven on earth. During the next nine years, Moon is said to have received further revelations through prayer, study, and a number of conversations with important religious leaders such as Moses and Buddha and, indeed, with God. The teachings, which came to be known as the *Divine Principle*, were eventually written down by Moon's followers, the first version being published in Korean in 1957. They were later translated into English and other languages in a number of editions.

Moon enrolled as an electrical engineering student in Japan in 1941. Two years later he returned to Korea and found work as an electrician, but was arrested by the Japanese police for alleged involvement in underground political activities in support of Korean independence. Later he was to be arrested more than once by the Communists on a variety of counts, including "teaching heretical doctrines." There are several accounts of the torture to which he was subjected and about the time he spent in a labor camp during the Korean War. Released by U.N. forces in 1950, Moon made his way to Pusan and then, with a small group of followers, moved to Seoul. His problems with the authorities continued, but the movement started to attract a growing membership and began sending missionaries to other parts of the world. In 1959 an erstwhile college professor, Dr. Young Oon Kim, took the teachings to the United States, and the small group that she set up on the West Coast became the subject of John Lofland's *Doomsday Cult*, first published in 1966.

Official Beliefs. The *Divine Principle*, which is based on Moon's interpretation of the Old and New Testaments, is one of the more comprehensive and systematic of the belief systems to be found among contemporary NRMs. It teaches that God created Adam and Eve intending that they would marry and, with their children, establish a God-centered family. Moon's special interpretation of the Fall is that, before Adam and Eve had matured sufficiently to be blessed in marriage, the Archangel Lucifer, jealous of God's love for Adam, developed a relationship with Eve that culminated in an illicit spiritual sexual relationship. Eve then tempted Adam to have a physical sexual relationship with her. The consequences were that the family arising from this union, instead of being God-centered, was Lucifer-centered, and that "fallen nature" (a Unification concept with some similarities to that of "original sin") has been passed from generation to generation. Thus it is that not merely disobedience, but also the misuse of love, the most powerful of all forces, continued to be responsible for the evil to be found throughout the world.

According to the *Divine Principle*, the whole of history can be interpreted as God's attempts to work with key figures to restore the Kingdom of Heaven on earth. Ultimately, this is possible only through a messiah faithfully playing the role that Adam failed to perform—to establish a God-centered family. This was the mission of Jesus, but partly because John the Baptist did not encourage the people to follow him, Jesus was murdered before he had the opportunity to marry. A Unification reading of subsequent history reveals remarkable parallels between the time of Jesus and the past two thousand years. It encourages us, furthermore, to recognize that the Lord of the Second Advent was born in Korea between 1917 and 1930. Unificationists believe Moon is that messiah and that he laid the foundation for the restoration of God's kingdom when he married his present wife in 1960.

A further elaboration of Unification beliefs, not contained in the *Divine Principle*, is found in the speeches that Moon has delivered to his followers through the years. These beliefs center around the person of Moon and his family, and explain the important role that they have played and continue to play. Moon and many of his followers have always had a close association with spiritualist beliefs and mediumship, and after the death of one of Moon's sons, Heung Jin Nim, a number of people reported having received messages from him from the spirit world; then, for some months, a young member from Zimbabwe conducted what appeared to be a revivalist movement within the Unification Church, being widely accredited as being a "second self Heung Jin Nim." Eventually, however, the young man's authority and statements showed signs of conflicting with those of Moon, and the young man returned to Africa, where he set up a schismatic movement.

Life in the Movement. In the early 1970s, Moon moved to the United States. Within a few years, his had become a household name, and the "Moonies," as they became known, developed a highly visible profile, selling candles, flowers, literature, and other goods in public places, and inviting thousands to attend public rallies and residential Unification seminars where potential converts could learn about the movement. New members in those days typically lived in Unification centers or with mobile fund-raising teams, working full time for the movement either raising funds or "witnessing" to potential members.

After having been in the movement for some time, members may be "matched" to partners chosen by Moon and whom they might never have met before—who might not even speak the same language. Although they can reject Moon's suggestion (and several have done so), the majority have gone on to what is probably the most important Unification ritual, the Holy Wine Ceremony, when the members believe their blood lineage is purified, followed by a mass wedding ceremony, known as the Blessing, with thousands of other couples. It is believed that the children born into these families are without fallen nature.

Although Unificationism does not practice as many rituals as some other new religions, its members do perform a short Pledge ceremony at 5:00 a.m. on the movement's Holy Days, and on the first day of each week and month. Couples go through special ceremonies when they consummate their marriage and when their children are born. A number of other practices include, for example, the use of holy salt and the establishment of a number of holy places throughout the world.

Literally hundreds of organizations have been associated, often through overlapping membership, with the Unification Church. Among the better known of these are the student arm of the movement, CARP (Collegiate Association for Research into Principles); several political organizations, such as CAUSA and, in the early days, the Freedom Leadership Foundation; the International Religious Foundation; the International Cultural Foundation; and various projects connected with the arts, such as the Korean Folk Ballet. Another project is the building of an international highway around the world, starting with a tunnel between Korea and Japan. On the academic side, there are the Little Angels school and a new university in Korea; the Unification Theological Seminary in suburban New York City; ICUS (the International Conference on the Unity of the Sciences); the Professors World Peace Academy; the University of Bridgeport (Connecticut), which is operated through a board controlled by the Professors World Peace Academy; and the Washington Institute.

Controversies. As in Korea and Japan, a number of voices in the West have been raised against Moon and his followers. In the 1970s, disquiet was expressed about various political activities arising out of Moon's stridently anticommunist stance, these ranging from his support of Nixon's continuing presidency at the time of the Watergate affair to the movement's coming under the scrutiny of the Fraser Committee's *Investigation of Korean-American Relations* (1979). Later, Moon had widely publicized meetings with Soviet president Mikhail Gorbachev and North Korean president Kim Il Sung. Questions were also raised about the vast sums of money that the movement seemed to have at its disposal and the number of properties that it bought in the United States, South America, and elsewhere (see Bromley and Shupe 1979a, 1980; Richardson 1988). Unification businesses, such as an extensive fishing industry and the Il Hwa Pharmaceutical Company, seemed to prosper, and the organization appeared to be extending its influence through extravagant dinners and conferences to which influential persons were invited, and through such ventures as Paragon House Publishers, the *Washington Times*, and *The World and I*, a glossy magazine published through the *Washington Times* company.

In the early 1970s, incomprehension and fear were expressed about the numbers of disproportionately middle-class, well-educated young people who were giving up college studies and careers to work for as many as eighteen hours a day on the streets collecting money for the movement. Several anxious and angry parents began to organize, and a number of anticult groups came into existence throughout the West. Accusations of deceptive and exploitative practices and of brainwashing and mind-control techniques being used to recruit helpless victims became widely reported in the media, and in response the illegal but frequently condoned practice of deprogramming (including kidnapping recruits from the movement) became a not uncommon occurrence.

The influence that the Unification Church has wielded over potential and actual members has not, however, ever been nearly as effective as its opponents have claimed—or even as its members might have wanted. The overwhelming majority of those subjected to the so-called brainwashing techniques have not joined the movement, and most of those who have joined have not only been capable of leaving but have also left it of their own free will within a couple of years (Barker 1984; Galanter 1980; S. Levine 1984). By the mid-1990s the movement had no more than a few hundred full-time members in any Western society, and at most a few tens of thousands worldwide. There is, however, a greater number of people (but probably no more than one hundred thousand) who feel some allegiance to the movement while leading "normal" lives, living in their own homes, and working in non-Unification jobs.

Changes. The movement has undergone a number of changes throughout the past few decades. Demographically, it is no longer predominantly comprised of youthful idealists with few responsibilities, eager to travel around the world at a moment's notice and to work for long hours with little or no remuneration in order to bring about the imminent restoration of the Kingdom of Heaven on earth. By the late 1990s, a sizable proportion of the membership has been born into the movement, and the young converts of the 1970s and 1980s are middle-aged and frequently facing financial and other responsibilities. Many, having sacrificed educational qualifications and careers for the movement, are—at least according to socioeconomic criteria—in a considerably lower position than their parents.

As with any new religion moving into a phase of second- and even third-generation membership, initial enthusiasms have waned, expectations have been disappointed, and several long-term rank-and-file members have become disillusioned with the leadership and less certain about several aspects of the belief system. Years of negative publicity and a number of court cases—including Moon's conviction in 1982 by a U.S. federal court jury of conspiracy to evade taxes (*United States of America v. Sun Myung Moon and Takeru*

Kamiyama) and his subsequent imprisonment—have taken their toll on the movement in North America and Europe. Moreover, by the late 1990s, there were several indications that many of the movement's business ventures were facing substantial difficulties.

The Future. Although Moon successfully undertook a 120-city world speaking tour as recently as 2005, questions are inevitably asked about what will happen to the movement in the future. Moon's wife and children have been playing an increasingly important role since the 1990s, but none of them has his charismatic authority, while the behavior of some of his children has given rise to alarm among even committed Unificationists (see Hong 1998). In addition, there have always been potential factions among the Korean leadership. It is possible that there will be a number of schisms once the Unification messiah is no longer here on earth to provide a unifying focus for the movement. It is, however, also likely that the Unification Church will continue, albeit in a somewhat different form, well into the twenty-first century (see Shupe 1990).

"SATANISM" AND ANTI-SATANISM

Kindled especially by a Geraldo Rivera television special, "Devil Worship: Exposing Satan's Underground," broadcast in October 1988, the attention of a broad sector of the U.S. public became inflamed by the prospects of organized "Satanism" in its midst. This interest was maintained by a series of mass-media news items on purported Satanic cults and Satanically inspired antisocial activities in the ensuing years. These reports represented a new outbreak of excitement over Satanic-labeled phenomena that appeared in several variants since the early 1970s.

The Reconstruction of Satanism. "Satanist" is a label applied to a variety of groups that are diffuse in character but are said to claim a focus on worship of and service to a power of evil, whom Christians have historically personified as Satan or the Devil. Of these groups, Anton LaVey's Church of Satan, founded in 1966, is the most visible, because LaVey's *The Satanic Bible* (1966, with its sequel, *The Satanic Ritual* [1972]), distributed to a mass market by the general paperback publisher Avon, serves as a core text for fledgling participants (for others, see Melton 1986). This may be supplemented by various dictionaries of the occult, all of which can be found in most cities in mainstream bookstores such as Borders or Barnes and Noble.

It is *The Satanic Bible*, however, that provides the first critical indicator of the thrust of contemporary Satanic expression, for *The Satanic Bible* is obviously conceived in relation to the Christian or Holy Bible. *The Satanic Bible* is *not* a "sacred text" in any usual sense of that concept. It lacks both the historicity and the inspirationist claims of the Old and New Testaments, the Qur'an, the Bhagavad Gita, or even the Book of Mormon. It is thus conceived as an anti-Bible directly in reference to and with assumptions about the Christian Bible. Much purportedly Satanic symbolism is similarly conceived vis-à-vis that of Christianity. Similarly, Stephen Kent (1993), in research on testimony by people claiming Satanic child abuse from the 1930s to the 1980s, shows that the Bible and biblical themes provide the primary references for the articulation of abuse. Purported cult ceremonies particularly used biblical references and metaphors.

This relationship is hardly coincidental. Satanic phenomena in the deliberate sense—as distinct from pagan survivals in newly or weakly Christianized or Islamized regions—are reactive in character and follow a period of decadence in the dominant tradition. Thus the historian Jean Delumeau (1978), for example, has shown that interest in Satan in French art and letters did not occur in the high medieval period but in its decline in the fifteenth and sixteenth centuries. The Church of Satan appeared in the historical wake of the "God is dead" controversy of the mid-1960s, but the growth of discussion of "Satanism" as a movement did not accelerate until after the rise of the new evangelicalism that also came in the wake of the spiritual bankruptcy of mainline denominational liberalism in the 1960s. Satanism shares the same religious and moral universe as evangelicalism. This is not at all to say that there is an intentional relationship between Satanism and evangelicalism; indeed, quite the contrary. It is the unintentional, implicit, or latent relationship of the two that makes them interesting. What the two share is a high concept of Satan's power as an active agent in the world of everyday life. Both evangelicalism and Satanism proclaim a "living" Satan. For evangelicalism, Satan is in conflict with the living God and Christ's people; for Satanists, Satan personifies the true power of this world.

Heretofore in the Western world, putative Satanism has been connected primarily with the rituals of the Black Mass. Here, too, the reactive mode is quite clear: The already highly formalized Catholic Eucharistic rite is turned back on itself. This is very different, for example, from pagan revivalism. It is also different from religions such as the Tibetan Bon or the Kurdish Yezidi, where evil spirits play a significant role in a larger cosmology. Although recent Satanic activity in the United States purportedly uses sacrificial elements, the explicit structure of the Mass seems to have been abandoned. Inverting the Ten Commandments—breaking all ten is one of the most significant achievements of putative Satanist spirituality—takes greater prominence. Not surprisingly, according to the explanatory structure we are proposing, evangelical Christians are highly moralistic, whereas the Mass is not a part of their religious practice.

There is more to the relationship than this; indeed, the Satanism-evangelicalism tie is fully symbiotic. Not only does Satanism feed off evangelicalism, it also legitimates evangelicalism, for Satanism is taken by evangelicals as concrete evidence that their claims are true. Satanists fit into the evangelical religious structure; they do not undermine the evangelical ethos but actually reinforce it by bringing the Devil closer to everyday experience. In the present guise, both are also responses to modernity. Both deny the essentially aspiritual quality of modernity, and both give vent to emotional forces within the human personality that are thwarted by instrumental rationality; hence both are expressions of the culture of emotions characteristic of postmodernity (see Hervieu-Léger 1990). LaVey writes early in *The Satanic Bible* that "Satan is the best friend the Church has ever had, as he kept it in business all of these years" (1966: 3). This is only slightly hyperbolic, but it is also only half the picture; for it is equally true that Christianity has kept Satan alive when Satan has suited its purposes.

Satanists and Satanism. One way to address the appearance of current Satanic involvement is to make an important conceptual distinction between Satan*ists*, those who appear to practice some beliefs related to the power of Satan in the world, and Satan*ism* as a putatively organized social movement. It is quite possible for there to be individual Satanists, for example, without organized Satanism. This is one part of the case we are making here. The other side, by contrast, is that not only are there anti-Satanists, but there is also a social movement, anti-Satanism, which was largely responsible for creating and perpetuating the social mythology of "Satanism" in the United States today. Organized Satanism, in short, exists primarily in the *rhetoric* of its opposition. A strikingly analogous argument to this one has been made by Lester R. Kurtz with respect to the fear of "modernism" within the Roman Catholic Church at the turn of the twentieth century (see Kurtz 1986; Lyng and Kurtz 1985). Before discussing anti-Satanism, however, two observations may be helpful.

The first of these points has been well put by Rodney Stark, namely, that "the origins of ideas and of movements need not be, and often are not, the same" (1991: 85). That is, if by *Satanism* we mean an idea system—beliefs about Satan or even beliefs about how Satan might be worshiped—this is properly matter for theology, intellectual history, and the sociology of knowledge. Certainly this belief exists. In a 1990 poll, for example, the Gallup Organization found that 55 percent of Americans believe in the devil, and 49 percent believe that "people on this earth are sometimes possessed by the devil." People claim to "know" what Satanism is. We can, if we wish, trace out the origins and developments of this knowledge system. Elliot Rose (1962) has done so already to a considerable extent and demonstrated that Satanism is preeminently Christian—that is, it was made up and perpetuated by Christians at differing times and places to serve various needs. This in no way proves that there has ever been a social movement that may be termed *Satanism*, any more than knowing all about the Hobbit proves the existence of Middle Earth.

The reality of the idea system, however, does help explain the second observation: that is, the existence of Satan*ists*. In a pluralistic, literate culture, it is possible for a broad spectrum of the population, individually or in groups, to access a variety of philosophical and theological worldviews, and claim them fully or partially as their own. In short, you may call yourself, for instance, Christian or Satanist or Buddhist or atheist, and your profession may be only partially gainsaid. Thus, there *are* Satanists. To deny this is as empirically ungrounded as to accept the existence of Satan*ism* as a social movement.

There are people who claim they worship Satan, either by themselves or in groups. Some may actually do so, and some may do harm to others in the process of doing so (see Kent 1993), as was seen in some cases of violence in schools. These devotees may range from dabblers to philosophers, from sane to insane. Conceivably there are as many possible reasons to worship Satan as any number of other god figures, malevolent or benign. That some of these individuals may at times act out their beliefs proves nothing more than that some individuals act out beliefs. There is, for example, a clinical literature on bodily self-mutilation (see Goldenberg and Sata 1978; Greilsheimer and Groves 1979) that shows that a proportion of individuals who commit these acts give as their reason Matthew 5:29–30 ("If thy right hand offend thee, cut it off . . .") or other biblical texts, but these behavioral aberrations are never responsibly said to "prove" anything about Christianity as a social movement.

Similarly, although we remain skeptical about the Satanic bases of putative ritual murders (consider for example, the Matamoros "ritual murder" scare of 1989), even if such a claim were to be empirically sustained, it would prove nothing except that certain people, upon perceiving certain stimuli, are led to act in certain ways. Individual Satanists or a group of Satanists meeting together or even groups of Satanists scattered across the United States or the Western world are inadequate evidence of a social movement. Satanism in anything other than the ideational sense constitutes something along the lines of rumor or urban legend, with an occasional dose of mass hysteria (see Richardson, Best, and Bromley 1991; Richardson 1997; Shupe 1998; Victor 1993). But it is inadequate to dismiss "the Satanism scare" with this observation. To do so minimizes the force of *anti-Satanism* as a *genuine* social movement—indeed, as the very *producer* of "Satanism," a point that, as we come close to ending this chapter, takes us back to both Durkheim and W. I. Thomas.

Anti-Satanism in the West is a Christian movement that has appeared with vigor at least twice previous to its current vogue. The first centered on the Albigensian heresy during the Inquisition and received its formal articulation at the Fourth Lateran Council of 1215—later to be much adumbrated in the fifteenth century in the manual *Malleus Maleficarum* of Kramer and Sprenger, two Dominican priests under the patronage of Pope Innocent VIII. The second occurred during the rise of Puritanism in the seventeenth century and is associated with, among other things, the Salem witch trials. The Inquisition and Puritanism were, of course, movements of quite different purposes, and the construction of Satanism in each was correspondingly different, though built on a common foundation. The contemporary "scare" was likewise not a simple reappearance of the past. Satanism is a theological *invention*, sociologically speaking, and thus contemporary Satanism was a reinvention of an older tool to fit current needs. Anti-Satanism was a revitalization movement (see A. Wallace 1956) in contemporary Christianity, particularly among the new evangelicals, but reaching out into almost all branches of Western Christendom.

Old Problems, Old Solutions, New Networks. Why was Satanism worth redoing to many Christians? One answer is that Satanism gives the institutional church a renewed claim to authority in speaking to empirical problems. If we use the term *postmodern* here to denominate our own era, then in the modern era we can show that the church lost authority on a whole series of issues. Marriage, divorce, contraception, abortion, health, dying, burial, education, employment, preferment, and so on were all removed from the church's purview of authority. The church could, of course, continue to speak on and to these issues—and to new issues that it previously may not have contemplated (for example, the environment, nuclear weapons, geopolitics)—but it lost any unique claim to control these dynamics and the power to implement its authority.

The world's problems, however, have not gone away. New problems have arisen and old problems remain unsolved. Bad things still seem to happen to good people, and sometimes bad things even appear to be done by good people. The lack of goodness of fit between theory and practice seems to hit particularly hard at the level of violent crime and behavioral aberrations including, but not limited to, those done in connection with substance abuse and in relation to children.

Mental-health professionals and law-enforcement agents are pressed by a distraught larger society to explain why these events occur so uncontrollably, and the larger society is kept informed of their occurrence by media that recognize the social fascination with the unusual. Clients and criminals are also pressed to give accounts of why they have done what they have done. It is assumed—in a rather naive kind of Kantianism—that people know why they do what they do and that they will give a motive account that is honest. Satan ("the Devil made me do it") may likewise be invoked as either motivation or legitimation—or pure fantasy. Max Weber, by contrast, cautions us to the contrary that "in the great majority of cases, actual action goes on in a state of inarticulate half-consciousness or actual unconsciousness of its subjective meaning. The ideal type of meaningful action where the meaning is fully conscious and explicit is a marginal case" (1978: 21–22).

Satanism thus creates happy bedfellows: Mental-health and law-enforcement professionals are partly relieved of their failures to control the population, while the church gets a new lease on life by a respiritualization of empirical problems. Thus, in his account of the police and the occult, Hicks (1991) shows how the Satanic model of criminality reduces to simple formulae complex social problems such as teenage suicide, substance abuse, and sexual molestation to create an expedient and economical "explanation" that is underwritten by evangelical Christianity. Satanism becomes a vehicle for alternately fomenting and displacing public fears based on speculation and misinformation that is especially attractive to sensationalist news media.

The church also has an enormous ideological resource advantage (Kniss 1990: 154–55) from which not only it but also allied professionals may draw. The church, quite simply, wrote the book on Satanism. Intentionally or not, the church creates both the problem and its solution. In the long term, of course, the solution is no solution because the problems are inaccurately diagnosed. This may or may not cause a loss of face for anti-Satanism, however, because other circumstances can intervene that cause a redefinition of the situation so that the matter simply fades away. "Real news"—a tornado or a coup or a plane crash—intervenes. Elliot Rose (1962) shows how this happened historically when the Black Death effectively solved the surplus clerical-intellectual labor problem that created a disenfranchised, hence resentful, clerical underclass that formed the basis for Inquisitorial attacks, the goliards. Thus it may be the case that institutional Christianity can both recapture and retain lost ground long after the purportedly Satanic events have passed.

Extensive survey evidence shows that the new evangelical (or "conservative") churches are the growth churches in the United States. A "living Satan" is part of the "Gospel message" of many of these groups. The mainline liberal Protestant churches—along with the bulk of Roman Catholics—do not absolutely deny the existence of Satan, but the Devil is generally taught as more of a logical possibility than a present, personal reality. Whereas Glock and Stark (1965) found that belief in a real Satan was one of the first theological propositions to be jettisoned by denominational liberals, Swatos (1988) found that virtually all members of a national sample of local leaders of an antipornography protest, organized in 1984 by the National Federation of Decency (now the American Family Association [AFA]), believed in the Satanic causation of pornography. The Devil was also very real to the Catholic charismatics studied by Mary Jo Neitz (1987).

With respect to what we know about NRMs generally, it is especially important to recognize the this-worldly character of the "new" Satan in the anti-Satanism of the new evangelicals. Historically many denominations have used the fear of hell (and the consolation of a heavenly alternative) as a way to persuade some persons to accept the value of Christian belief and action. People were free to choose to accept or reject this message of salvation (and, indeed, even the idea of eternity). Anti-Satanism as a social movement, however, shifts from this end-time level of argument to the much more immediate context of everyday life. Anti-Satanism is thus much closer to the Inquisition and the witch trials than it is to traditional religious claims. Anti-Satanism fingers specific individuals in this world as the agents of Satan's power and sees certain incidents and behaviors (for example, drug use, sexuality, rock music) as arenas for Satan's work. Some anti-Satanists have even targeted *Harry Potter* books in this respect.

Furthermore, the mythic quality of anti-Satanists' claims makes them almost impenetrable to normal standards of evidence. Unlike members of most NRMs, for example, who are only too willing to profess their new faith, Satanists are said by anti-Satanism to be secretive. Thus the Satanic conspiracy is ever present. If anyone denies it, this may be taken by anti-Satanists as prima facie evidence that she or he is either an agent of the Devil or has come unwittingly under Satan's power. As a conspiracy theory, anti-Satanism's "Satanism" is utterly beyond any falsifiability criterion. Again, many theories of mental illness or crime may be tested and found wanting, to the great embarrassment particularly of practitioners. Putative Satanism is never going to come under such condemnation, and Satanism so constructed demands only that one acknowledge its possibility. It is not like positive theology that might demand that a believer institute changes in his or her own life as a result of a new religious commitment.

Through their already-established network of congregations, publishers, clergy, motivational speakers, interdenominational agencies, and so forth, the new evangelicals have a strong resource base for launching anti-Satanism. Anti-Satanist agencies network among themselves and franchise their "courses" to and through new students-become-teachers, sometimes on something very close to a pyramid system. Professional anti-Satanists have offered "instruction" to and through law-enforcement personnel, health-care and mental-health agencies, and some accredited two- and four-year colleges. Through the alliance between evangelicalism and psychology that has grown over the years (see Balswick 1987), anti-Satanism has a structure of professional credibility beyond theology narrowly conceived. Indeed, putative Satanism stands strongest in the absence of careful, rational theology.

Putative Satanism thus blends well with the culture of the emotions characteristic of postmodernity and with the emotional religion it generates. Anson D. Shupe (1998) as well as Robert W. Balch and Margaret Gilliam (1991) have shown in specific local cases how many resources can be mobilized by anti-Satanism and the polymorphous character of its structure. Unlike specific moral crusades against liquor or pornography, anti-Satanism combats an unseen enemy. Thus, if its attack appears to falter on one front, it can simply open another. Any thing, any activity, and any person is a potential target for anti-Satanist labeling.

Because there are and probably always will be Satanists—thanks to the informational resources at hand (provided indirectly by anti-Satanists)—anti-Satanism retains a continuing possibility for erupting as a social movement in Western society. To the extent that the religion of the mainstream allows belief in Satan within its creeds (even though it may not require this belief), it aids and abets anti-Satanism and all of its consequences. In bureaucratized society, for example, the Satanism construct could become a weapon for the government to intervene further and further into the lives of its citizens, for example, with respect to parent-child relationships, child-care institutions, or freedom of religious expression.

NEOPAGANISM: OF GODS AND GODDESSES

One of the most significant religious developments in the last twenty years has been the rise of neopagan worship in contemporary societies. Whether or not this is, strictly speaking, a "new" religion, it is certainly a new religious *movement* in its numbers and contemporary character. Exactly what falls under the heading of *neopagan* can be debated endlessly, as the movement is diverse, but in general it may be said to consist of revivals and adaptations of shamanic, wiccan, gnostic, and druidic forms of worship on an international scale. It has had particular reinvigoration by feminism and "woman-oriented" spiritualities, but by no means are all neopagan groups to be considered feminist. Popular novels like *The Da Vinci Code* also have added interest in aspects of survivals of historic alternative religious movements paralleling orthodox Christian theologies, while the New Age movement in general also figures into contemporary manifestations. "Nature" plays a significant conceptual role in neopaganism, often by taking on, semantic contradictions notwithstanding, a supernatural character. Divinity is seen within the created order.

Neopaganism today draws from a variety of sources. Some of these were works produced by both amateur and professional scholars in the late nineteenth and early twentieth centuries. The Romantic movement in literature and the arts contributed to a wide revival of interest in legends and myths from the pre-Christian era. While the accuracy of these scholars' research has been debated, it nevertheless provided important source materials and concepts for subsequent developments. These increased in number in the 1980s and 1990s and were especially reinvigorated by the growth of the Internet as an opportunity to transcend the limits of geography. The Internet served as both an informational and communicative resource: People could not only find out more about neopagan resources and events, they could also make direct contact with others and in certain cases create, in effect, Internet religions (see, e.g., Krogh and Pillifant 2004). Because neopaganism is also nature religion, its practitioners do not have the same needs as the historical world religions to build physical structures as worship sites. Although some neopagans find it meaningful to visit sites of historic pagan temples through organized international travel programs (see, e.g., Rountree 2006), others are as likely to want to visit natural sites with relative economies of effort and expenditure.

Origins and Ironies. Neopaganism is especially significant as a new movement in the way in which it has been facilitated and globalized by cyber-technology. Nevertheless, important developments in the movement were already taking place in the late 1960s and early 1970s, more or less in the wake of the civil rights and anti–Vietnam War movements, both broadly conceived as anti-establishment and youth movements. It would be wrong, however, to think that these neopagan movements were entirely "invented" by disenchanted youth. A variety of figures in Western Europe and the United States had been writing and speaking about these issues for at least fifty years before the current wave of interest appeared. At the same time as well, the discipline of religious studies was being increasingly introduced into university settings, and this gave greater academic legitimation to the study of alternative religious movements, as distinct from earlier approaches to the teaching of religion, which tended to take an established religion as its point of departure.

One particularly interesting case of the rise of neopaganism is to be found in the case of Ásatrú, the "religion of the gods" in Iceland. For a variety of reasons, Iceland has been relatively more open to new religious ideas since the end of the nineteenth century than many other European societies. Additionally, Iceland has a written culture that antedates its conversion to Christianity and is preserved in the literature of Edda and Saga. Thus there is a continuing link to a pagan past, albeit mediated by a period of Christianization. The average Icelander knows the literature of the nation's pagan past in a way that is unique among his or her European contemporaries. Thus, out of a coffeehouse conversation among four men in 1972 came a proposal to found a group that would revive pre-Christian Norse religion in Iceland.

Events moved swiftly: A journalist first raised the question with the government's Minister of Justice and Ecclesiastical Affairs of whether it might be possible for the group to obtain official recognition as a registered religious body, which would give the Chief Godi (priest) equal legal status with the pastors of Christian bodies in Iceland. The issue having been raised, the Ásatrúarmenn decided to find out and applied for legal status in the fall of that year. By the spring of 1973, Ásatrú had become a "religion" in Iceland: The Chief Godi was thus a legitimate "minister of religion" in the government's eyes, and the

Ásatrúarmenn received tax support in ratio to their numbers. This process aroused considerable international interest, especially due to the formal character of the recognition. The Icelandic case cannot by any means be taken as the "explanation" for the rise of neopagan religious practice in the bulk of the Western world. On the other hand, it did provide a test case in which reasonable people looking at the issue with a measure of objectivity could conclude that neopaganism had a legitimate basis for recognition as a religious practice.

In the United States, where the government does not "approve" religions, neopagans sought other outlets. For some neopagans, one organizational resource came to be found in the Unitarian Universalist Association, a body whose historical roots reach virtually to the founding of the United States. From those days well into the twentieth century, the "UU church," as it's often called, became more and more a bastion of humanistic liberalism, abandoning not merely the formal Christian doctrine of God as the Trinity of Father, Son, and Holy Spirit, but any specific definition of belief in God at all. In the last decades of the twentieth century, however, the theological openness of Unitarian Universalism had something of a blowback, in that it also became a site for both New Age and neopagan devotees (see Lee 1995). Although more recent years have seen the development of increased numbers of freestanding Neopagan groups, the late-twentieth-century period of association between some Neopagans and UU churches provided a context for Neopagans to develop a sense of the kinds of structural considerations that facilitated movement into closer relationships with mainstream religious organization and practice—a first-level institutionalization of Neopaganism as "legitimate" religious expression within the normative structure of American denominationalism.

Aspects of the UU experience combined with university-based religious studies allowed neopaganism to achieve a level of legitimacy in American society that would likely astound persons whose religious awareness stopped at the end of the 1950s. For example, a deceased neopagan soldier in the United States armed forces may now obtain a headstone with the neopagan pentacle symbol, akin to the cross or the Star of David on tombstones provided to deceased Christians and Jews, and U.S. military chaplains must be prepared to facilitate neopagan ceremonies. Within the discipline of religious studies, books on what would historically have been lumped together as "pagan" traditions abound, and in his *Pagan Theology* (2003), Michael York draws together extensive material from multiple traditions in an attempt to create a coherent explanatory structure for "paganism as a world religion." Similarly, Barbara Jane Davy's *Introduction to Pagan Studies* (2006) presents a religious-studies-textbook approach to the topic analogous to treatments of other world religions.

History and Sociology. These developments should not, however, be taken out of context. The percentage of persons declaring themselves pagan in the United States remains extremely small. The percentage *increase* can be made to appear huge, but only because there were virtually no persons who would formally declare themselves pagan fifty years ago—and indeed, only open-ended surveys at that time would have allowed that option, since "Pagan" was not on standard lists of fixed responses at that time. What self-professed pagans there were in that era would likely have been stuck between the forced choices of "Other" and "None." In addition, as paganism formalizes, it remains to be seen whether or not intergroup rivalries will emerge to such an extent that the same forms of dissatisfaction that are sometimes expressed about divisions among Christian bodies will begin to be associated with neopagan groups.

The *neo* of current pagan organizations and activities gives these groups the advantage of no known history to live down and no preexisting conflicts to address. It also fits well with a globalized society, where local traditions can each be appropriated for its own sake, without defection from a claimed single historical "truth" or founder. As such, the history of religions in America would lead us to expect that neopagan adherents will continue to grow in number for at least the remainder of this generation. The following generation will determine much more than the current one whether neopaganism does or does not become a permanent part of the American—and global—religious scene. Many of the "new religions" that caused such debate twenty-five years ago have either simply disappeared or stagnated. Unlike Satanism, however, neopaganism presents a positive religious alternative to the traditions of the American mainline and is not merely a construct of fundamentalist imaginations.

Suggestions for Further Reading

David V. Barrett. 2001. *The New Believers: Sects, "Cults" and Alternative Religions.* London: Cassell.

David Bromley, ed. 2007. *Teaching New Religious Movements.* New York: Oxford University Press.

Bill Ellis. 2001. *Raising the Devil: Satanism, New Religions, and the Media.* Lexington: University Press of Kentucky.

James R. Lewis. 2003. *Legitimating New Religions.* New Brunswick, N.J.: Rutgers University Press.

Lucy Salisbury Payne. 1990. "Uncovering the First Amendment: A Research Guide to the Religion Clauses." *Notre Dame Journal of Law, Ethics, and Public Policy* 4:825–934.

Thomas Robbins and Dick Anthony, eds. 1990. *In Gods We Trust*, 2nd ed. New Brunswick, N.J.: Transaction.

E. Burke Rochford, Jr. 2007. "The Sociology of New Religious Movements," pp. 253–90 in Anthony J. Blasi, ed. *American Sociology of Religion: Histories.* Leiden: Brill.

Rodney Stark, ed. 1985. *Religious Movements: Genesis, Exodus, and Numbers.* New York: Paragon House.

Michael York. 2003. *Pagan Theology: Paganism as a World Religion.* New York: New York University Press.

Benjamin Zablocki and Thomas Robbins, eds. 2001. *Misunderstanding Cults: Searching for Objectivity in a Controversial Field.* Toronto: University of Toronto Press.

References

The principal academic journals in general sociology and the sociology of religion are cited in these references using the following abbreviations:

AJS	*American Journal of Sociology*
Annals	*Annals of the American Academy of Political and Social Science*
ASR	*American Sociological Review*
JCS	*Journal of Church and State*
JSSR	*Journal for the Scientific Study of Religion*
RRR	*Review of Religious Research*
SA	*Sociological Analysis*
SC	*Social Compass*
SF	*Social Forces*
SoR	*Sociology of Religion*

Abramson, Harold J. 1972. *Ethnic Diversity in Catholic America*. New York: Wiley.

———. 1980. "Religion." In *The Harvard Encyclopedia of American Ethnic Groups*, ed. Stephan Thernstrom, Ann Orlov, and Oscar Handlin (pp. 869–75). Cambridge, Mass.: Harvard University Press.

Adams, Elizabeth. 2006. *Going to Heaven: The Life and Election of Bishop Gene Robinson*. Brooklyn, N.Y.: Soft Skull Press.

Alba, Richard. 1985. *Italian-Americans: Into the Twilight of Ethnicity*. Englewood Cliffs, N.J.: Prentice-Hall.

———. 1990. *Ethnic Identity: The Transformation of White America*. New Haven, Conn.: Yale University Press.

Albanese, Catherine L. 1990. *Nature Religion in America: From the Algonkian Indians to the New Age*. Chicago, Ill.: University of Chicago Press.

———. 1992. *America: Religions and Religion*. 2nd ed. Belmont, Calif.: Wadsworth.

Alexander, Bobby C. 1994. *Televangelism Reconsidered: Ritual in the Search for Human Community*. Atlanta, Ga.: Scholars Press.

Althusser, Louis. 1970. *For Marx*. New York: Vintage.

Ammerman, Nancy Tatom. 1987. *Bible Believers: Fundamentalists in the Modern World*. New Brunswick, N.J.: Rutgers University Press.

———. 1990. *Baptist Battles: Social Change and Religious Conflict in the Southern Baptist Convention*. New Brunswick, N.J.: Rutgers University Press.

———. 1994. "Telling Congregational Stories." *RRR* 35: 289–301.

———. 1997a. *Congregation and Community*. New Brunswick, N.J.: Rutgers University Press.

———. 1997b. "Organized Religion in a Voluntaristic Society." *SoR* 58: 203–15.

———. 2005. *Pillars of Faith: American Congregations and Their Partners*. Berkeley, Calif.: University of California Press.

Anderson, Charles H. 1970. *White Protestant Americans: From National Origins to Religious Group*. Englewood Cliffs, N.J.: Prentice-Hall.

Appleby, R. Scott. 1997. "Among Catholics, It's Crisis All Over." *Commonweal* 124 (March 14): 17–20.

———. 2002. "The Church at Risk: Remarks to the USCCB." Washington, D.C.: United States Conference of Catholic Bishops.

Archdeacon, Thomas. 1983. *Becoming American: An Ethnic History*. New York: Free Press.

Armstrong, Ben. 1979. *The Electric Church*. Nashville, Tenn.: Nelson.

Avineri, Shlomo. 1968. *The Social and Political Thought of Karl Marx*. Cambridge, Mass.: Cambridge University Press.

Bader, Christopher, Kevin Dougherty, Paul Froese, Byron Johnson, F. Carson Mencken, Jerry Z. Park, and Rodney Stark. 2006. *American Piety in the 21st Century: New Insights to the Depth and Complexity of Religion in the U.S.* Waco, Tex.: Baylor Institute for Studies of Religion.

Baer, Hans. 1993. "The Limited Empowerment of Women in Black Spiritual Churches." In *Gender and Religion*, ed. William H. Swatos, Jr. (pp. 75–93). New Brunswick, N.J.: Transaction.

Baer, Hans A., and Merrill Singer. 1992. *African-American Religion in the Twentieth Century: Varieties of Protest and Accommodation*. Knoxville, Tenn.: University of Tennessee Press.

Bagby, Ihsan, Paul M. Perl, and Bryan T. Froehle. 2001. *The Mosque in America: A National Portrait*. Washington, D.C.: Council on American-Islamic Relations.

Bailey, Edward I. 1997. *Implicit Religion in Contemporary Society*. Kampen, Netherlands: Kok Pharos.

———. 1998a. "Implicit Religion." In *Encyclopedia of Religion and Society*, ed. William. H. Swatos, Jr. (p. 235). Walnut Creek, Calif.: AltaMira.

———. 1998b. "'Implicit Religion': What Might That Be?" *Implicit Religion* 1: 9–22.

Bainbridge, William Sims. 1985. "Utopian Communities: Theoretical Issues." In *The Sacred in a Secular Age: Toward Revision in the Scientific Study of Religion*, ed. Phillip E. Hammond (pp. 21–35). Berkeley, Calif.: University of California Press.

———. 1997. *The Sociology of Religious Movements*. New York: Routledge.

Bainbridge, William Sims, and Rodney Stark. 1979. "Cult Formation: Three Compatible Models." *SA* 40: 283–95.

———. 1980. "Client and Audience Cults in America." *SA* 41: 199–214.

———. 1981. "Friendship, Religion, and the Occult: A Network Study." *RRR* 22: 313–27.

———. 1984. "Formal Explanation of Religion: A Progress Report." *SA* 45: 145–58.

Balch, Robert W. 1980. "Looking behind the Scenes in a Religious Cult: Implications for the Study of Conversion." *SA* 41: 137–43.

Balch, Robert W., and Margaret Gilliam. 1991. "Devil Worship in Western Montana: A Case Study in Rumor Construction." In *The Satanism Scare*, ed. James T. Richardson, Joel Best, and David Bromley (pp. 249–62). Hawthorne, N.Y.: Aldine de Gruyter.

Balmer, Randall H. 1996. *Grant Us Courage: Travels along the Mainline of American Protestantism*. New York: Oxford University Press.

———. 2007. *Thy Kingdom Come: How the Religious Right Distorts Faith and Threatens America*. New York: Basic Books.

Balswick, Jack O. 1987. "The Psychological Captivity of the Evangelicals." In *Religious Sociology: Interfaces and Boundaries*, ed. William H. Swatos, Jr. (pp. 141–52). New York: Greenwood.

Baltzell, E. Digby. 1966. *The Protestant Establishment: Aristocracy and Caste in America*. New York: Vintage.

———. 1976. "The Protestant Establishment Revisited." *American Scholar* 45: 499–518.

———. 1996. *Puritan Boston and Quaker Philadelphia*. 1979. Reprint, New Brunswick, N.J.: Transaction.

Bannan, Regina, Susan Farrell, and Rea Howarth. 2007. *Status of Women in the U.S. Roman Catholic Church: A Report Card*. http://womensjusticecoalition.org/sites/default/files/WomensJustice-Media-Report&Card.pdf.

Barker, Eileen. 1984. *The Making of a Moonie: Choice or Brainwashing?* Oxford, United Kingdom: Blackwell.

———. 1985. "The Ones Who Got Away: People Who Attend Unification Workshops and Do Not Become Moonies." In *Religious Movements: Genesis, Exodus, and Numbers*, ed. Rodney Stark (pp. 65–93). New York: Paragon House.

Barrow, Logie. 1986. *Independent Spirits: Spiritualism and English Plebeians, 1850–1910*. London: Routledge.

Bartkowski, John P. 1998. "Changing of the Gods: The Gender and Family Discourse of American Evangelicalism in Historical Perspective." *History of the Family* 3: 95–115.

Becker, Gary S. 1976. *The Economic Approach to Human Behavior*. Chicago, Ill.: University of Chicago Press.

Becker, Howard. 1932. *Systematic Sociology*. New York: Wiley.

Becker, Penny Edgell. 1997. "What Is Right? What Is Caring? Moral Logics in Local Religious Life." In *Contemporary American Religion: An Ethnographic Reader*, ed. Penny Edgell Becker and Nancy L. Eiesland (pp. 121–45). Walnut Creek, Calif.: AltaMira.

———. 1999. *Congregations in Conflict: Cultural Models of Local Religious Life*. New York: Cambridge University Press.

Beckford, James A. 1991. "Quasi-Marxisms and the Sociology of Religion." In *New Developments in Theory and Research*, ed. David G. Bromley (pp. 17–35). Greenwich, Conn.: JAI Press.

Bell, Daniel. 1973. *The Coming of Post-Industrial Society: A Venture in Social Forecasting*. New York: Basic Books.

Bellah, Robert N. 1967. "Civil Religion in America." *Daedalus* 96 (Winter): 1–21.

———. 1970a. *Beyond Belief: Essays on Religion in a Post-Traditional World*. New York: Harper & Row.

———. 1970b. "Christianity and Symbolic Realism." *JSSR* 9: 89–115.

———. 1974. "American Civil Religion." In *American Civil Religion*, ed. Russell E. Richey and Donald G. Jones (pp. 255–72). New York: Harper & Row.

———. 1975. *The Broken Covenant: American Civil Religion in Time of Trial*. New York: Seabury.

———. 1989. "Comment." *SA* 50: 147.

———. 1999. "Is There a Common American Culture? Diversity, Identity, and Morality in American Public Life," in *The Power of Religious Publics: Staking Claims in American Society*, ed. William H. Swatos, Jr., and James K. Wellman, Jr. (pp. 53–67). Westport, Conn.: Praeger.

Bellah, Robert N., Richard Madsen, William M. Sullivan, Ann Swidler, and Steven M. Tipton. 1985. *Habits of the Heart: Individualism and Commitment in American Life*. Berkeley, Calif.: University of California Press.

Bellut, Thomas, Gerhard Fuchs, Eberhard von Gemmingen, and Christoph Lanz. 2006. "Interview of the Holy Father Benedict XVI in Preparation for the Upcoming Journey to Bavaria." Vatican City: Libreria Editrice Vaticana.

Benedict, Ruth. 1940. *Race, Science and Politics*. New York: Modern Age Books.

———. 1943. *Race and Racism*. London: Scientific Book Club.

Bensman, Joseph, and Arthur J. Vidich. 1971. *The New American Society: The Revolution of the Middle Class*. Chicago, Ill.: Quadrangle Books.

Berger, Helen A. 1999. *A Community of Witches: Contemporary Neo-Paganism and Witchcraft in the United States*. Columbia, S.C.: University of South Carolina Press.

Berger, Helen A., and Douglas Ezzy. 2007. *Teenage Witches: Magical Youth and the Search for the Self*. New Brunswick, N.J.: Rutgers University Press.

Berger, Peter L. 1954. "The Sociological Study of Sectarianism." *Social Research* 21: 467–85.

———. 1963. *Invitation to Sociology: A Humanistic Perspective*. Garden City, N.Y.: Doubleday.

———. 1967. *The Sacred Canopy*. Garden City, N.Y.: Doubleday.

———. 1981. "The Class Struggle in American Religion." *Christian Century* 98: 194–99.

———. 1992. "Sociology: A Disinvitation?" *Society* 30 (November): 12–18.

———. 1997. "Epistemological Modesty: An Interview with Peter Berger." *Christian Century* 114: 972–75, 978.

Berger, Peter L., Brigitte Berger, and Hansfried Kellner. 1973. *The Homeless Mind: Modernization and Consciousness*. New York: Random House.

Berger, Peter L., and Thomas Luckmann. 1966. *The Social Construction of Reality*. Garden City, N.Y.: Doubleday.

Berger, Peter L., and Richard John Neuhaus. 1977. *To Empower People: The Role of Mediating Structures in Public Policy*. Washington, D.C.: American Enterprise Institute.

Bergner, Mario. 2004. "The Not-So-Gay Lifestyle: Pastoral Care for Homosexuals Who Want Out." http://www.christianitytoday.com/le/2004/001/7.42.html.

Berry, Jason. 1992. *Lead Us Not into Temptation: Catholic Priests and the Sexual Abuse of Children.* New York: Doubleday.

Beyer, Peter. 1989. "Globalization and Inclusion: Theoretical Remarks on the Non-Solidary Society." In *Religious Politics in Global and Comparative Perspective*, ed. William H. Swatos, Jr. (pp. 39–53). New York: Greenwood.

———. 1994. *Religion and Globalization.* London: Sage.

Beyerlein, Kraig. 2004. "Specifying the Impact of Conservative Protestantism on Educational Attainment." *JSSR* 43: 505–18.

Bibby, Reginald W. 1978. "Why Conservative Churches Really Are Growing: Kelley Revisited." *JSSR* 17:129–37.

———. 1987. *Fragmented Gods: The Poverty and Potential of Religion in Canada.* Toronto, Ontario: Irwin.

———. 1995. *There's Got to Be More! Connecting Churches and Canadians.* Winfield, British Columbia: Wood Lake Books.

Bibby, Reginald W., and Merlin B. Brinkerhoff. 1973. "The Circulation of the Saints: A Study of People Who Join Conservative Churches." *JSSR* 12: 273–83.

———. 1983. "Circulation of the Saints Revisited: A Longitudinal Look at Conservative Church Growth." *JSSR* 22: 253–62.

———. 1994. "Circulation of the Saints, 1966–1990: New Data, New Reflections." *JSSR* 33: 273–80.

Billingsley, Andrew. 1998. *Mighty Like a River: The Black Church and Social Reform.* New York: Oxford University Press.

Birnbaum, Norman. 1973. "Beyond Marx in the Sociology of Religion?" In *Beyond the Classics?: Essays in the Scientific Study of Religion*, ed. Charles Y. Glock and Phillip E. Hammond (pp. 3–70). New York: Harper & Row.

Blake, Mariah. 2005. "Stations of the Cross: How Evangelical Christians Are Creating an Alternative Universe of Faith-Based News." *Columbia Journalism Review* 44: 32–39.

Blasi, Anthony J. 1980. "Definition of Religion and Phenomenological Approach: Towards a Problematic." *Les Cahiers du CRSR* 3: 55–70.

———. 1990. "Problematic of the Sociologists and People under Study in the Sociology of Religion." *Ultimate Reality and Meaning* 13: 145–56.

———. 1998. "Functionalism." In *Encyclopedia of Religion and Society*, ed. William H. Swatos Jr. (pp. 193–97). Walnut Creek, Calif.: AltaMira.

Blassingame, John W. 1972. *The Slave Community: Plantation Life in the Antebellum South.* New York: Oxford University Press.

Boas, Franz. 1931. "Race and Progress." *Science* 73 (July 3): 1–8.

Bogardus, Emory. 1959. *Social Distance.* Yellow Springs, Ohio: Antioch College Press.

Borden, Anne L. 2007. "Making Money, Saving Souls: Christian Bookstores and the Commodification of Christianity." In *Religion, Media, and the Marketplace*, ed. Lynn Schofield Clark (pp. 67–89). New Brunswick, N.J.: Rutgers University Press.

Bordin, Ruth. 1965. "The Sect to Denomination Process in America: The Freewill Baptist Experience." *Church History* 34: 77–94.

Borg, Meerten ter. 1991. *Ein Uitgewaairde Enewigheid: Het Menselijk Tekort in de moderne Cultuur.* The Hague, Netherlands: Harm Meijer.

Borowik, Irena. 1994. "Religion in Postcommunist Countries." In *Politics and Religion in Central and Eastern Europe: Traditions and Transitions*, ed. William H. Swatos, Jr. (pp. 37–46). Westport, Conn.: Praeger.

Boston Globe, Investigative Staff. 2002. *Betrayal: The Crisis in the Catholic Church.* Boston, Mass.: Little, Brown.

Boulard, Fernand. 1960. *An Introduction to Religious Sociology: Pioneer Work in France.* London: Darton, Longman, Todd.

Bouma, Gary D. 1973. "Beyond Lenski: A Critical Review of Recent 'Protestant Ethic' Research." *JSSR* 12: 141–55.

———. 1979. "The Real Reason One Conservative Church Grew." *RRR* 20: 127–37.

Bourdieu, Pierre, and Loïc J. D. Wacquant. 1992. *An Invitation to Reflexive Sociology*. Chicago, Ill.: University of Chicago Press.

Bowles, Scott. 2006. "Hollywood Turns to Divine Inspiration." *USA Today* (April 14): 1A.

Brasher, Brenda E. 1997. "My Beloved Is All Radiant: Two Case Studies of Congregational-Based Christian Fundamentalist Female Enclaves and the Religious Experiences They Cultivate among Women." *RRR* 38: 231–46.

———. 1998. *Godly Women: Fundamentalism and Female Power*. New Brunswick, N.J.: Rutgers University Press.

Brewer, Earl D. C. 1952. "Sect and Church in Methodism." *SF* 30: 401–8.

Brewer, Earl D. C., and Douglas W. Johnson. 1972. "Research Documents in the H. Paul Douglass Collection." *RRR* 13: 107–11.

———. 1979. *An Inventory of the Harlan Paul Douglass Collection of Religious Research Reports*. Woodbridge, Conn.: Research Publications.

Brickner, Bryan W. 1999. *The Promise Keepers: Politics and Promises*. Lanham, Md.: Lexington.

Brinkerhoff, Merlin B., and Reginald W. Bibby. 1985. "Circulation of the Saints in South America: A Comparative Study." *JSSR* 24: 39–55.

Brittingham, Angela, and G. Patricia de la Cruz. 2005. *We, the People of Arab Ancestry in the United States*. Washington, D.C.: Bureau of the Census, United States Department of Commerce.

Broadway, Bill. 2001. "Number of U.S. Muslims Depends on Who's Counting." *Washington Post* (November 24): A1.

Bromley, David G., and Anson D. Shupe. 1979a. *Moonies in America: Cult, Church, and Crusade*. Beverly Hills, Calif.: Sage.

———. 1979b. "The Tnevnoc Cult." *SA* 40: 361–66.

———. 1980. "Financing the New Religions: A Resource Mobilization Approach." *JSSR* 19: 227–39.

Brown, Dan. 2003. *The Da Vinci Code: A Novel*. New York: Doubleday.

Brown, R. Khari, and Ronald E. Brown. 2003. "Faith and Works: Church-Based Social Capital Resources and African American Political Activism." *Social Forces* 82: 617–41.

Bruce, Lenny. 1970. "Religions Inc.; Catholicism; Christ and Moses; and the Lone Ranger." In *The Essential Lenny Bruce*, ed. John Cohen (pp. 39–56). New York: Douglas.

Bruce, Steve. 1990. *Pray TV: Televangelism in America*. London: Routledge.

———. 1993. "Religion and Rational Choice: A Critique of Economic Explanations of Religious Behavior." *SoR* 54: 193–205.

———. 1999. *Choice and Religion: A Critique of Rational Choice Theory*. New York: Oxford University Press.

Brzezinski, Zbigniew. 1970. *Between Two Ages: America's Role in the Technetronic Era*. New York: Penguin.

Bukhari, Zahid H. 2003. "Demography, Identity, Space: Defining American Muslims." In *Muslims in the United States: Demography, Beliefs, Institutions*, ed. Philippa Strum and Danielle Tarantolo (pp. 7–20). Washington, D.C.: Woodrow Wilson International Center for Scholars.

Burns, Gene. 1996. "Studying the Political Culture of American Catholicism." *SoR* 57: 37–53.

Cadge, Wendy. 2004. *Heartwood: The First Generation of Theravada Buddhism in America*. Chicago, Ill.: University of Chicago Press.

Calhoun, Craig. 1997. *Nationalism*. Minneapolis, Minn.: University of Minnesota Press.

Campbell, Colin. 1972. "The Cult, the Cultic Milieu, and Secularization." In *A Sociological Yearbook of Religion in Britain* 5, ed. Michael Hill (pp. 119–36). London: SCM.

Campbell, Heidi. 2005. "Making Space for Religion in Internet Studies." *The Information Society* 21: 309–15.

Cantril, Hadley. 1943. "Educational and Economic Composition of Religious Groups." *AJS* 47: 574–79.

Caplow, Theodore. 1982. "Religion in Middletown." *Public Interest* 68 (Summer): 78–87.

Caplow, Theodore, Howard M. Bahr, and Bruce A. Chadwick. 1983. *All Faithful People: Change and Continuity in Middletown's Religion*. Minneapolis: University of Minnesota Press.

Carey, Patrick W. 1987. *People, Priests, and Prelates: Ecclesiastical Democracy and the Tensions of Trusteeism*. Notre Dame, Ind.: University of Notre Dame Press.

Carrigan, Henry, Jr. 1995a. "Reading Is Believing: Religious Publishing toward the Millennium. From Those Returning to the Fold to Those Looking beyond Western Creeds, a Community of Religion Readers Expands the Market." *Library Journal* 120 (May 1): 36–40.

———. 1995b. "Should Christian Fiction Be in Libraries?" *Library Journal* 120 (May 1): 39.

Carroll, Jackson W., Barbara Hargrove, and Adair Lummis. 1983. *Women of the Cloth: A New Opportunity for Churches*. New York: Harper & Row.

Carter, Stephen L. 1993. *The Culture of Disbelief: How American Law and Politics Trivialize Religious Devotion*. New York: Basic Books.

Casanova, José. 1992. "Roman and Catholic and American: The Transformation of Catholicism in the United States." *International Journal of Politics, Culture and Society* 6: 75–111.

Castelli, Jim, and Joseph Gremillion. 1987. *The Emerging Parish: The Notre Dame Study of Catholic Life Since Vatican II*. San Francisco, Calif.: Harper & Row.

Cavendish, James C., Michael R. Welch, and David C. Leege. 1998. "Social Network Theory and Predictors of Religiosity for Black and White Catholics: Evidence of a 'Black Sacred Cosmos'?" *JSSR* 37: 397–410.

Chapman, Mark. 1999. "Identifying Evangelical Organizations: A New Look at an Old Problem." *Studies in Religion/Sciences religieuses* 28: 307–21.

Charles, Ron. 2004. "Religious Book Sales Show a Miraculous Rise." *Christian Science Monitor* (April 9): 11.

Chaves, Mark A. 1994. "Secularization as Declining Religious Authority." *SF* 72: 749–74.

———. 1995. "On the Rational Choice Approach to Religion." *JSSR* 34: 98–104.

———. 1997. *Ordaining Women: Culture and Conflict in Religious Organizations*. Cambridge, Mass.: Harvard University Press.

———. 1999. "Religious Congregations and Welfare Reform: Who Will Take Advantage of 'Charitable Choice'?" *ASR* 64: 836–46.

———. 2004. *Congregations in America*. Cambridge, Mass.: Harvard University Press.

Chaves, Mark A., and James C. Cavendish. 1994. "More Evidence on U.S. Catholic Church Attendance." *JSSR* 33: 376–81.

———. 1997. "Recent Changes in Women's Ordination Conflicts: The Effect of a Social Movement on Intraorganizational Controversy." *JSSR* 36: 574–83.

Chaves, Mark A., and Philip S. Gorski. 2001. "Religious Pluralism and Religious Participation." *Annual Review of Sociology* 27: 261–81.

Chaves, Mark A., and Sharon L. Miller, eds. 1999. *Financing American Religion*. Walnut Creek, Calif.: AltaMira.

Chen, Hsiang-Shiu. 1992. *Chinatown No More: Taiwan Immigrants in Contemporary New York*. Ithaca, N.Y.: Cornell University Press.

Chidley, Joe. 1997. "Jesus on the Net: A New Platform for Believers and Heretics Alike." *Maclean's* 110 (December 15): 46.

Christenson, James A., and Ronald C. Wimberley. 1978. "Who Is Civil Religious?" *SA* 39: 77–83.

Christerson, Brad, Korie L. Edwards, and Michael O. Emerson. 2005. *Against All Odds: The Struggle for Racial Integration in Religious Organizations*. New York: New York University Press.

Christiano, Kevin J. 1986. "Church as a Family Surrogate: Another Look at Family Ties, Anomie, and Church Involvement." *JSSR* 25: 339–54.

———. 1988. "Religion and Radical Labor Unionism: American States in the 1920s." *JSSR* 27: 378–88.

———. 1991. "The Church and the New Immigrants." In *Vatican II and U.S. Catholicism*, ed. Helen Rose Ebaugh (pp. 169–86). Greenwich, Conn.: JAI.

———. 1993. "Religion among Hispanics in the United States: Challenges to the Catholic Church." *Archives de sciences sociales des religions* 83: 53–65.

———. 2000. "Religion and the Family in Modern American Culture." In *Family, Religion, and Social Change in Diverse Societies*, ed. Sharon K. Houseknecht and Jerry G. Pankhurst (pp. 43–78). New York: Oxford University Press.

Christopherson, Neal. 1999. "Accommodation and Resistance in Religious Fiction: Family Structures and Gender Roles." *SoR* 60: 439–55.

Cieslak, Michael J. 1984. "Parish Responsiveness and Parishioner Commitment." *RRR* 26: 132–47.

Ciesluk, Joseph E. 1947. *National Parishes in the United States*. Washington, D.C.: Catholic University of America Press.

Claussen, Dane S., ed. 2000. *The Promise Keepers: Essays on Masculinity and Christianity*. Jefferson, N.C.: McFarland.

Coleman, James William. 2001. *The New Buddhism: The Western Transformation of an Ancient Tradition*. New York: Oxford University Press.

Collins, Randall. 1986. *Weberian Sociological Theory*. Cambridge, Mass.: Cambridge University Press.

Commager, Henry Steele, ed. 1935. *Documents of American History*. New York: Appleton-Century-Crofts.

Connell, Joan. 1998. "Searching for God in Cyberspace." In *Religion & Ethics NewsWeekly Viewer's Guide: With Essays, Discussion Questions and Resources on America's Changing Religious and Ethical Landscape*, ed. Joyce Bermel (p. 4). New York: WNET Television.

Cookson, Peter W., Jr., and Caroline Hodges Persell. 1985. *Preparing for Power: America's Elite Boarding Schools*. New York: Basic Books.

Coontz, Stephanie. 1992. *The Way We Never Were: American Families and the Nostalgia Trap*. New York: Basic Books.

Coreno, Thaddeus. 2002. "Fundamentalism as a Class Culture." *SoR* 63: 335–60.

Cornell, Stephen, and Douglas Hartmann, 1998. *Ethnicity and Race: Making Identities in a Changing World*. Thousand Oaks, Calif.: Pine Forge.

Coupe, Laurence. 1997. *Myth*. London: Routledge.

Cox, Harvey G. 1965. *The Secular City: Secularization and Urbanization in Theological Perspective*. New York: Macmillan.

———. 1969. *The Feast of Fools: A Theological Essay on Festivity and Fantasy*. Cambridge, Mass.: Harvard University Press.

———. 1977a. "Eastern Cults and Western Culture: Why Young Americans Are Buying Oriental Religions." *Psychology Today* 11 (July): 36–42.

———. 1977b. *Turning East: The Promise and Peril of the New Orientalism*. New York: Simon and Schuster.

Cuddihy, John Murray. 1978. *No Offense: Civil Religion and Protestant Taste*. New York: Seabury.

Curtis, Edward E., IV. 2005. "African-American Islamization Reconsidered: Black History Narratives and Muslim Identity." *Journal of the American Academy of Religion* 73: 659–84.

Dahrendorf, Ralf. 1959. *Class and Class Conflict in Industrial Society*. Palo Alto, Calif.: Stanford University Press.

Daly, Mary. 1968. *The Church and the Second Sex*. San Francisco, Calif.: Harper & Row.

Daniels, Roger. 1990. *Coming to America: A History of Immigration and Ethnicity in American Life*. New York: HarperCollins.

D'Antonio, William V. 1994. "Autonomy and Democracy in an Autocratic Organization: The Case of the Roman Catholic Church." *SoR* 55: 379–96.

D'Antonio, William V., James D. Davidson, Dean R. Hoge, and Ruth A. Wallace. 1989. *American Catholic Laity in a Changing Church*. Kansas City, Mo.: Sheed and Ward.

Davidman, Lynn. 1991. *Tradition in a Rootless World: Women Turn to Orthodox Judaism*. Berkeley, Calif.: University of California Press.

Davidson, James D. 1977. "Socio-Economic Status and Ten Dimensions of Religious Commitment." *Sociology and Social Research* 61: 462–85.

———. 1991. *Religion among America's Elite: Persistence and Change in the Protestant Establishment*. Notre Dame, Ind.: Cushwa Center for the Study of American Catholicism.

———. 1994. "Religion among America's Elite: Persistence and Change in the Protestant Establishment." *SoR* 55: 419–40.

Davidson, James D., and Ralph E. Pyle. 2005. "Social Class." In *Handbook of Religion and Social Institutions,* ed. Helen Rose Ebaugh (pp. 185–206). New York: Springer.

Davidson, James D., Ralph E. Pyle, and David V. Reyes. 1995. "Persistence and Change in the Protestant Establishment, 1930–1992." *SF* 74: 157–75.

Davidson, James D., Joseph A. Schlangen, and William V. D'Antonio. 1969. "Protestant and Catholic Perceptions of Church Structure." *SF* 47: 314–22.

Davidson, James D., and Andrea S. Williams. 1997. "Megatrends in 20th-Century American Catholicism." *SC* 44: 507–27.

Davidson, James D., Andrea S. Williams, Richard A. LaManna, Jan Stenftenagel, Kathleen Maas Weigert, William J. Whalen, and Patricia Wittberg. 1997. *The Search for Common Ground: What Unites and Divides Catholic Americans*. Huntington, Ind.: Our Sunday Visitor.

Davies, Tanya. 1998. "Emporium." *Maclean's* 111 (May 25): 12.

Davis, David Brion. 1960. "Some Themes of Counter-Subversion: An Analysis of Anti-Masonic, Anti-Catholic, and Anti-Mormon Literature." *Mississippi Valley Historical Review* 47: 205–24.

——, ed. 1971. *The Fear of Conspiracy: Images of Un-American Subversion from the Revolution to the Present*. Ithaca, N.Y.: Cornell University Press.

Davy, Barbara Jane. 2006. *Introduction to Pagan Studies*. Lanham, Md.: AltaMira.

Dawson, Lorne L., and Jenna Hennebry. 1999. "New Religions and the Internet: Recruiting in a New Public Space." *Journal of Contemporary Religion* 14: 17–39.

Deck, Allan Figueroa. 1994. "The Challenge of Evangelical/Pentecostal Christianity to Hispanic Catholicism." In *Hispanic Catholic Culture in the U.S.: Issues and Concerns*, ed. Jay P. Dolan and Allan Figueroa Deck (pp. 409–39). Notre Dame, Ind.: University of Notre Dame Press.

Delumeau, Jean. 1978. "La peur de Satan." *Histoire* 6: 32–41.

Demerath, N. J., III. 1965. *Social Class in American Protestantism*. Chicago, Ill.: Rand-McNally.

——. 1994. "The Moth and the Flame: Religion and Power in Comparative Blur." *SoR* 55: 105–17.

"Deus ex Computer: How Does a New Medium Tell the Old, Old Story?" 1997. *Economist* 345 (November 15): 11.

De la Cruz, G. Patricia, and Angela Brittingham. 2003. *The Arab Population: 2000*. Washington, D.C.: Bureau of the Census, United States Department of Commerce.

De Vaus, David A. 1982. "The Impact of Children on Sex Related Differences in Church Attendance." *SA* 43: 145–54.

Díaz-Stevens, Ana María. 1993. *Oxcart Catholicism on Fifth Avenue: The Impact of the Puerto Rican Migration upon the Archdiocese of New York*. Notre Dame, Ind.: University of Notre Dame Press.

Dillon, Michele. 1998. "Rome and American Catholics." *Annals* 558: 122–34.

——. 1999. *Catholic Identity: Balancing Reason, Faith, and Power*. Cambridge: Cambridge University Press.

Dixon, A. C., Louis Meyer, and R. A. Torrey, eds. 1910–1915. *The Fundamentals: A Testimony to the Truth*, 12 vols. Chicago, Ill.: Testimony.

Dobbelaere, Karel. 1981. *Secularization: A Multi-Dimensional Concept*. London: Sage.

Dolan, Jay P. 1992. *The American Catholic Experience: A History from Colonial Times to the Present*. 1985. Reprint, Notre Dame, Ind.: University of Notre Dame Press.

Domhoff, G. William. 1967. *The Higher Circles: The Governing Class in America*. Englewood Cliffs, N.J.: Prentice-Hall.

——. 1974. *The Bohemian Grove and Other Retreats*. New York: Harper & Row.

Dorsey, Gary. 1995. *Congregation: The Journey Back to the Church*. New York: Viking.

Dredge, Bart. 1986. "Faith, Hope, or Charity: A Look at Church Sermons and Social Class." *Sociological Inquiry* 56: 523–34.

Drucker, Peter. 1993. "The Rise of the Knowledge Society." *Wilson Quarterly* 17(2): 52–71.

Dubinin, N. P. 1956. "Race and Contemporary Genetics." In *Race, Science, and Society*, ed. Leo Kuper (pp. 68–94). Paris: UNESCO.

Du Bois, W. E. B. 1961. *The Souls of Black Folk*. 1903. Reprint, New York: Fawcett World Library.

Dudley, Carl S., Jackson W. Carroll, and James P. Wind, eds. 1991. *Carriers of Faith: Lessons from Congregational Studies*. Louisville, Ky.: Westminster John Knox.

Duke, James T., and Barry L. Johnson. 1989. "Protestantism and the Spirit of Democracy." In *Religious Politics in Global and Comparative Perspective*, ed. William H. Swatos, Jr. (pp. 131–46). New York: Greenwood.

Durkheim, Émile. 1965. *The Elementary Forms of the Religious Life*. 1912. Reprint, New York: Free Press.

Earle, John R., Dean D. Knudsen, and Donald W. Shriver Jr. 1976. *Spindles and Spires: A Re-Study of Religion and Social Change in Gastonia*. Atlanta, Ga.: John Knox Press.

Ebaugh, Helen Rose Fuchs, and Janet Saltzman Chafetz. 2000. *Religion and the New Immigrants: Continuities and Adaptations in Immigrant Congregations*. Walnut Creek, Calif.: AltaMira.

Ecklund, Elaine Howard. 2003. "Catholic Women Negotiate Feminism: A Research Note." *SoR* 64: 515–24.

——. 2005. "Different Identity Accounts for Catholic Women." *RRR* 47: 135–49.

Eco, Umberto. 1983. *The Name of the Rose*. San Diego, Calif.: Harcourt Brace Jovanovich.

Economist. 2005. "Onward, Christian Shoppers." *Economist* 377 (December 3): 60–62.

Ellison, Christopher G. 1992. "Are Religious People Nice People? Evidence from the National Survey of Black Americans." *SF* 71: 411–30.

——. 1995. "Rational Choice Explanations of Individual Religious Behavior: Notes on the Problem of Social Embeddedness." *JSSR* 34: 89–97.

Ellison, Christopher G., and Darren E. Sherkat. 1995. "The 'Semi-Involuntary Institution' Revisited: Regional Variations in Church Participation among Black Americans." *SF* 73: 1415–37.

Elwood, J. Murray. 2000. "Dublin Jesuits Create Internet Prayer Space." *National Catholic Reporter* (April 28): 12.

Emerson, Michael O., and Christian Smith. 2000. *Divided by Faith: Evangelical Religion and the Problem of Race in America*. New York: Oxford University Press.

Engels, Friedrich. 1968. *The Condition of the Working Class in England*. 1844. Reprint, Stanford, Calif.: Stanford University Press.

Englund, Steven. 1995. "*Provocateur* or Prophet? The French Church and Bishop Gaillot." *Commonweal* 122 (October 6): 12–18.

Erickson, Keith V. 1977. "Black Messiah: The Father Divine Peace Mission Movement." *Quarterly Journal of Speech* 63: 428–38.

Espinosa, Gastón. 2004. "Changements démographiques et religieux chez les hispaniques des États-Unis." *SC* 51: 303–20.

Fass, Paula S. 1989. *Outside In: Minorities and the Transformation of American Education*. New York: Oxford University Press.

Feagin, Joe R. 1968. "Black Catholics in the United States: An Exploratory Analysis." *SA* 29: 186–92.

Feigelman, William, Bernard S. Gorman, and Joseph A. Varacalli. 1991. "The Social Characteristics of Black Catholics." *Sociology and Social Research* 75: 133–43.

Femminella, Francis X., ed. 1985. *Irish and Italian Interaction*. Staten Island, N.Y.: American Italian Historical Association.

Fenn, Richard K. 1977. "The Relevance of Bellah's 'Civil Religion' Thesis to a Theory of Secularization." *Social Science History* 1: 502–17.

Ferré, John P. 1990. "Searching for the Great Commission: Evangelical Book Publishing Since the 1970s." In *American Evangelicals and the Mass Media: Perspectives on the Relationship between American Evangelicals and the Mass Media*, ed. Quentin J. Schultze (pp. 99–117). Grand Rapids, Mich.: Zondervan.

Fichter, Joseph H. 1951. *Dynamics of a City Church*. Chicago, Ill.: University of Chicago Press.

——. 1954. *Social Relations in the Urban Parish*. Chicago, Ill.: University of Chicago Press.

Finke, Roger, and Christopher P. Scheitle. 2005. "Accounting for the Uncounted: Computing Correctives for the 2000 RCMS Data." *RR* 47: 5–22.

Finke, Roger, and Rodney Stark. 1988. "Religious Economies and Sacred Canopies." *ASR* 53: 41–49.

——. 2005. *The Churching of America, 1776–2005: Winners and Losers in Our Religious Economy*. 2nd ed. New Brunswick, N.J.: Rutgers University Press.

Fischer, Claude S., Michael Hout, Martin Sánchez Jankowski, Samuel R. Lucas, Ann Swidler, and Kim Voss. 1996. *Inequality by Design: Cracking the Bell Curve Myth*. Princeton, N.J.: Princeton University Press.

Fitzpatrick, Joseph P. 1987. *Puerto Rican Americans: The Meaning of Migration to the Mainland*. 2nd ed. Englewood Cliffs, N.J.: Prentice-Hall.

Fitzpatrick, Joseph P., and Lourdes Travieso Parker. 1981. "Hispanic-Americans in the Eastern United States." *Annals* 454: 98–110.

Foley, Michael W., and Dean R. Hoge. 2007. *Religion and the New Immigrants: How Faith Communities Form Our Newest Citizens*. New York: Oxford University Press.

Forbes, Kevin F., and Ernest M. Zampelli. 1997. "Religious Giving by Individuals: A Cross-Denominational Study." *American Journal of Economics and Sociology* 56: 17–30.
Formicola, Jo Renee. 2007. "The Further Legal Consequences of Catholic Clerical Sexual Abuse." *JCS* 49: 445–65.
Fournier, Keith. 2007. "Commentary: Male Episcopal Bishop Wants to Be a 'June Bride.'" http://www.catholic.org/national/national_story.php?id=26150.
Fox, Thomas C. 1997. *Catholicism on the Web.* New York: Holt.
Francis, E. K. 1947. "The Nature of the Ethnic Group." *AJS* 52: 393–400.
Francis, Leslie J. 1997. "The Psychology of Gender Differences in Religion: A Review of Empirical Research." *Religion* 27: 81–96.
Frazier, E. Franklin. 1964. *The Negro Church in America.* New York: Schocken.
Fredrickson, George. 1999. "Mosaics and Melting Pots." *Dissent* (Summer): 36–42.
Freud, Emma. 2000. *Sins of the Flesh.* London: BBC1 documentary (September 24).
Freud, Sigmund. 1964. *The Future of an Illusion.* 1927. Reprint, Garden City, N.Y.: Doubleday.
Frezza, Bill. 1997. "Reflections on Heaven's Gate: Religion and the Internet." *Communications-Week* 659 (April 21): 49.
Friedan, Betty. 1997. *The Feminine Mystique.* 1963. Reprint, New York: Norton.
Gaillot, Jacques. 1995. "Farewell Homily: Evreux Cathedral Church, 22nd January 1995." www.partenia.org/english/retrospective-eng.htm.
Galanter, Marc. 1980. "Psychological Induction into the Large Group." *American Journal of Psychiatry* 137: 1574–79.
Gallagher, Sally K., and Christian S. Smith. 1999. "Symbolic Traditionalism and Pragmatic Egalitarianism: Contemporary Evangelicals, Families, and Gender." *Gender and Society* 13: 211–33.
Gallup Poll. 1993. *Gallup Poll Monthly* (August).
Gallup, George, Jr., and Jim Castelli. 1987. *The American Catholic People: Their Beliefs, Practices, and Values.* Garden City, N.Y.: Doubleday.
———. 1989. *The People's Religion: American Faith in the 90s.* New York: Macmillan.
Gamm, Gerald H. 1999. *Urban Exodus: Why the Jews Left Boston and the Catholics Stayed.* Cambridge, Mass.: Harvard University Press.
Garrett, Lynn, and Jana Reiss. 2005. "Convention Coverage: CBA Accentuates the Positive." *Publishers Weekly* 252 (February 14): 15.
———. 2006. "CBA in Nashville: Advancing or Retreating?" *Publishers Weekly* 253 (February 6): 11.
Gates, Henry Louis, Jr. 1996. "The Charmer." *New Yorker* (April 29–May 6): 116–31.
Geertz, Clifford. 1973. *The Interpretation of Cultures: Selected Essays.* New York: Basic Books.
———. 1983. *Local Knowledge: Further Essays in Interpretive Anthropology.* New York: Basic Books.
———. 2002. "An Inconsistent Profession: The Anthropological Life in Interesting Times." *Annual Review of Anthropology* 31: 1–19.
Gehrig, Gail. 1981. "The American Civil Religion Debate: A Source for Theory Construction." *JSSR* 20: 51–63.
Gelzinis, Peter. 2003. "One Priest Laments Lack of Leadership at the Archdiocese." *Boston Herald* (February 20): 6.
Genovese, Eugene. 1972. *Roll, Jordan, Roll: The World the Slaves Made.* New York: Pantheon.
Giddens, Anthony. 1999. *Runaway World: How Globalization Is Reshaping Our Lives.* London: Profile Books.
Gilkes, Cheryl Townsend. 1998. "Plenty Good Room: Adaptation in a Changing Black Church." *Annals* 558: 101–21.
Gilligan, Carol. 1982. *In a Different Voice: Psychological Theory and Women's Development.* Cambridge, Mass.: Harvard University Press.
Gillis, Charlie. 2007. "Beijing Is Always Watching: Chinese-Canadians Say Spies Have Been Monitoring and Intimidating Them." *Maclean's* 120 (May 14): 20–22.
Glasner, Peter. 1977. *The Sociology of Secularisation.* London: Routledge.
Glazer, Nathan. 1957. *American Judaism.* Chicago, Ill.: University of Chicago Press.
Gleason, Philip. 1995. *Contending with Modernity: Catholic Higher Education in the Twentieth Century.* New York: Oxford University Press.
Glock, Charles Y. 1962. "On the Study of Religious Commitment." *Religious Education* 57: S98–S110.

——. 1964. "The Role of Deprivation in the Origin and Evolution of Religious Groups." In *Religion and Social Conflict*, ed. Robert Lee and Martin E. Marty (pp. 24–36). New York: Oxford University Press.

——. 1985. "On Nature, Sources, and Consequences." *Religious Studies Review* 11 (January): 20–23.

——. 1988. "The Ways the World Works." *SA* 49: 93–103.

——. 1993. "The Churches and Social Change in Twentieth-Century America." *Annals* 527: 67–83.

Glock, Charles Y., Benjamin B. Ringer, and Earl R. Babbie. 1967. *To Comfort and to Challenge: A Dilemma of the Contemporary Church*. Berkeley, Calif.: University of California Press.

Glock, Charles Y., and Rodney Stark. 1965. *Religion and Society in Tension.* Chicago, Ill.: Rand-McNally.

Goethals, Gregor T. 1990. *The Electronic Golden Calf: Images, Religion, and the Making of Meaning*. Cambridge, Mass.: Cowley Publications.

Gold, Steven J. 1999. "From 'The Jazz Singer' to 'What a Country!' A Comparison of Jewish Migration to the U.S., 1880 to 1930 and 1965 to 1998." *Journal of American Ethnic History* 18: 114–41.

Goldenberg, Edward, and Lindbergh S. Sata. 1978. "Religious Delusions and Self-Mutilation." *Current Concepts in Psychiatry* 4(5): 2–5.

Goldscheider, Calvin, and Alan S. Zuckerman. 1984. *The Transformation of the Jews*. Chicago, Ill.: University of Chicago Press.

Goodman, Nathan G., ed. 1945. *A Benjamin Franklin Reader*. New York: Crowell.

Goodstein, Laurie. 2003. "Decades of Damage: Trail of Pain in Church Crisis Leads to Nearly Every Diocese." *New York Times* (January 12): 1, 20–21.

Gopnik, Adam. 1996. "The Virtual Bishop: What Does It Take to Get the French to Turn on Their Computers?" *New Yorker* (March 18): 59–63.

Gouldner, Alvin W. 1979. *The Future of Intellectuals and the Rise of the New Class*. New York: Seabury Press.

Gramsci, Antonio. 1971. *Selections from the Prison Notebooks*. New York: International Publishers.

Grasmick, Harold G., Linda Patterson Wilcox, and Sharon R. Bird. 1990. "The Effects of Religious Fundamentalism and Religiosity on Preference for Traditional Family Norms." *Sociological Inquiry* 60: 352–69.

Gray, Mark M., and Paul M. Perl. 2006. *Catholic Reactions to the News of Sexual Abuse Cases Involving Catholic Clergy. CARA Working Papers* 8. Washington, D.C.: Center for Applied Research in the Apostolate.

Greeley, Andrew M. 1963. "Some Information on the Present Situation of American Catholics." *Social Order* 13 (April): 9–24.

——. 1964. "The Protestant Ethic: Time for a Moratorium." *SA* 25: 20–33.

——. 1969. *Religion in the Year 2000*. New York: Sheed and Ward.

——. 1972a. *The Denominational Society: A Sociological Approach to Religion in America*. Glenview, Ill.: Scott Foresman.

——. 1972b. *Priests in the United States: Reflections on a Survey*. Garden City, N.Y.: Doubleday.

——. 1976a. "Council or Encyclical?" *RRR* 18: 3–24.

——. 1976b. *Ethnicity, Denomination, and Inequality*. Beverly Hills, Calif.: Sage.

——. 1977. *The American Catholic: A Social Portrait*. New York: Basic Books.

——. 1979a. "Ethnic Variations in Religious Commitment." In *The Religious Dimension: New Directions in Quantitative Research*, ed. Robert Wuthnow (pp. 113–34). New York: Academic Press.

——. 1979b. "The Sociology of American Catholics." *Annual Review of Sociology* 5: 91–111.

——. 1985. *American Catholics since the Council: An Unauthorized Report*. Chicago, Ill.: Thomas More Press.

——. 1988. "Defection among Hispanics." *America* 159 (July 23–30): 61–62.

——. 1989. *Religious Change in America.* Cambridge, Mass.: Harvard University Press.

——. 1991. "The Demography of American Catholics: 1965–1990." In *Vatican II and U.S. Catholicism*, ed. Helen Rose Ebaugh (pp. 37–56). Greenwich, Conn.: JAI Press.

——. 1997. "Defection among Hispanics (Updated)." *America* 177 (September 27): 12–13.

——. 2000. *The Bishop and the Missing L Train: A Blackie Ryan Story*. New York: Forge.

——. 2004a. "Young Fogeys: Young Reactionaries, Aging Radicals—The U.S. Catholic Church's Unusual Clerical Divide." *Atlantic Monthly* 293 (January): 40–41.

———. 2004b. *The Catholic Revolution: New Wine, Old Wineskins, and the Second Vatican Council.* Berkeley, Calif.: University of California Press.

———. 2004c. *Priests: A Calling in Crisis.* Chicago, Ill.: University of Chicago Press.

Greeley, Andrew M., and Mary Greeley Durkin. 1984a. *Angry Catholic Women: A Sociological Investigation, A Theological Reflection.* Chicago, Ill.: Thomas More Press.

———. 1984b. *How to Save the Catholic Church.* New York: Viking Penguin.

Greeley, Andrew M., and Michael Hout. 1999. "Americans' Increasing Belief in Life After Death: Religious Competition and Acculturation." *ASR* 64: 813–35.

Greeley, Andrew M., and William E. McManus. 1987. *Catholic Contributions: Sociology and Policy.* Chicago, Ill.: Thomas More Press.

Greene, Victor R. 1975. *For God and Country.* Madison, Wis.: State Historical Society of Wisconsin.

———. 1990. "Old-time Folk Dancing and Music among the Second Generation, 1920–1950." In *American Immigrants and Their Generations*, ed. Peter Kivisto and Dag Blanck (pp. 142–63). Urbana, Ill.: University of Illinois Press.

Greenspan, Karen. 1994. *The Timetables of Women's History.* New York: Simon and Schuster.

Greilsheimer, Howard, and James E. Groves. 1979. "Male Genital Self-Mutilation." *Archives of General Psychiatry* 35: 441–46.

Gribble, Richard. 2005. "The Church: Present Reality and Future Possibilities." *American Catholic Studies* 116: 1–17.

Griffin, Wendy, ed. 2000. *Daughters of the Goddess: Studies of Healing, Identity, and Empowerment.* Walnut Creek, Calif.: AltaMira.

Griffith, R. Marie. 1997. *God's Daughters: Evangelical Women and the Power of Submission.* Berkeley, Calif.: University of California Press.

Grimes, William. 1996. "Is It Time for an Epitaph to the Ruling Elite?" *New York Times* (August 25): E3.

Gundersen, Edna. 2006. "GAMES: 'Left Behind' Fans Find Another Reason for Rapture." *USA Today* (April 7): 1E.

Gustafson, Paul M. 1967. "UO-US-PS-PO: A Restatement of Troeltsch's Church-Sect Typology." *JSSR* 6: 64–68.

———. 1973. "Exegesis on the Gospel According to St. Max." *SA* 34: 12–25.

Hadaway, C. Kirk, and Penny Long Marler. 1993. "All in the Family: Religious Mobility in America." *RRR* 35: 97–116.

———. 1998. "Did You Really Go to Church This Week? Behind the Poll Data." *Christian Century* 115: 472–75.

———. 2005. "How Many Americans Attend Worship Each Week? An Alternative Approach to Measurement." *JSSR* 44: 307–22.

Hadaway, C. Kirk, Penny Long Marler, and Mark A. Chaves. 1993. "What the Polls Don't Show: A Closer Look at U.S. Church Attendance." *ASR* 58: 741–52.

———. 1998. "Overreporting Church Attendance in America: Evidence That Demands the Same Verdict." *ASR* 63: 122–30.

Hadaway, C. Kirk, and David A. Roozen. 1995. *Rerouting the Protestant Mainstream: Sources of Growth and Opportunities for Change.* Nashville, Tenn.: Abingdon Press.

Haddad, Yvonne Yazbeck, and Adair Lummis. 1987. *Islamic Values in the United States.* New York: Oxford University Press.

Hadden, Jeffrey K. 1987. "Toward Desacralizing Secularization Theory." *SF* 65: 587–611.

Hadden, Jeffrey K., and Douglas E. Cowan, eds. 2000. *Religion on the Internet: Research Prospects and Promises.* Amsterdam, Netherlands: JAI.

Hadden, Jeffrey K., and Anson Shupe. 1987. "Televangelism in America." *SC* 34: 61–75.

———. 1988. *Televangelism: Power and Politics on God's Frontier.* New York: Holt.

———. 1990. "Elmer Gantry: Exemplar of American Televangelism." In *Religious Television: Controversies and Conclusions*, ed. Robert Abelman and Stewart M. Hoover (pp. 13–22). Norwood, N.J.: Ablex.

Hadden, Jeffrey K., and Charles E. Swann. 1981. *Prime Time Preachers: The Rising Power of Televangelism*. Reading, Mass.: Addison-Wesley.

Haines, Herbert H. 1988. *Black Radicals and the Civil Rights Movement, 1954–1970*. Knoxville: University of Tennessee Press.

Hall, Charles. 1995. "Entering the Labor Force: Ideals and Realities among Evangelical Women." In *Work, Family, and Religion in Contemporary Society*, ed. Nancy Tatom Ammerman and Wade Clark Roof (pp. 137–54). New York: Routledge.

Hall, John R. 2000. "Finding Heaven's Gate." In *Apocalypse Observed: Religious Movements and Violence in North America, Europe and Japan*, ed. John R. Hall, Philip D. Schuyler, and Sylvaine Trinh (pp. 149–82). London: Routledge.

Hammond, Phillip E. 1976. "The Sociology of American Civil Religion: A Bibliographic Essay." *SA* 37: 169–82.

———. 1999. "Can Religion Be Religious in Public?" In *The Power of Religious Publics: Staking Claims in American Society*, ed. William H. Swatos, Jr., and James K. Wellman, Jr. (pp. 19–31). New York: Praeger.

Hammond, Phillip E., Mark A. Shibley, and Peter M. Solow. 1995. "Religion and Family Values in Presidential Voting." In *The Rapture of Politics*, ed. Steve Bruce, Peter Kivisto, and William H. Swatos, Jr. (pp. 55–68). New Brunswick, N.J.: Transaction.

Hammond, Phillip E., and Kee Warner. 1993. "Religion and Ethnicity in Late-Twentieth-Century America." *Annals* 527: 55–66.

Handlin, Oscar. 1951. *The Uprooted: The Epic Story of the Great Migrations That Made the American People*. Boston, Mass.: Little, Brown.

Hargrove, Barbara W. 1986. *The Emerging New Class: Implications for Church and Society*. New York: Pilgrim.

Harper, Charles L., and Bryan F. Le Beau. 1993. "The Social Adaptation of Marginal Religious Movements in America." *SoR* 54: 171–92.

Harris, Joseph Claude. 1994. "An Analysis of Catholic Sacrificial Giving Programs in Seattle, Washington." *RRR* 36: 230–37.

Harris, Rebecca L. 1995. "The Calling of Protestant Women Clergy." Master's thesis, Wright State University, Dayton, Ohio.

Heilman, Samuel C., and Steven M. Cohen. 1989. *Cosmopolitans and Parochials: Modern Orthodox Jewish America*. Chicago, Ill.: University of Chicago Press.

Helland, Christopher. 2002. "Surfing for Salvation." *Religion* 32: 293–302.

Heller, Agnes. 1981. *Renaissance Man*. New York: Schocken.

———. 1995. "Where Are We at Home." *Thesis Eleven* 41: 1–14.

Herberg, Will. 1983. *Protestant-Catholic-Jew: An Essay in American Religious Sociology*. 1955. Reprint, Chicago, Ill.: University of Chicago Press.

Herrnstein, Richard, and Charles Murray. 1994. *The Bell Curve: Intelligence and Class Structure in American Life*. New York: Free Press.

Hervieu-Léger, Danièle. 1990. "Present-Day Emotional Renewals: The End of Secularization or the End of Religion?" In *A Future for Religion?*, ed. William H. Swatos, Jr. (pp. 129–64). Newbury Park, Calif.: Sage.

Hicks, Robert D. 1991. *In Pursuit of Satan: The Police and the Occult*. Buffalo, N.Y.: Prometheus.

Higham, John. 1970. *Strangers in the Land*. New York: Atheneum.

Hoge, Dean R. 1986. "Interpreting Change in American Catholicism: The River and the Floodgate." *RRR* 27: 289–99.

———. 1987. *The Future of Catholic Leadership: Responses to the Priest Shortage*. Kansas City, Mo.: Sheed and Ward.

Hoge, Dean R., and Boguslaw Augustyn. 1997. "Financial Contributions to Catholic Parishes: A Nationwide Study of Determinants." *RRR* 39: 46–60.

Hoge, Dean R., with Kenneth McGuire, Bernard F. Stratman, and Alvin A. Illig. 1981. *Converts, Dropouts, Returnees: A Study of Religious Change among Catholics*. Washington, D.C.: U.S. Catholic Conference.

Hoge, Dean R., Patrick H. McNamara, and Charles E. Zech, with Loren B. Mead. 1997. *Plain Talk about Churches and Money*. Bethesda, Md.: Alban Institute.

Hoge, Dean R., Raymond H. Potvin, and Kathleen M. Ferry. 1984. *Research on Men's Vocations to the Priesthood and the Religious Life*. Washington, D.C.: U.S. Catholic Conference.

Hoge, Dean R., and David A. Roozen, eds. 1979. *Understanding Church Growth and Decline, 1950–1978*. New York: Pilgrim.

Hoge, Dean R., Joseph J. Shields, and Douglas L. Griffin. 1995. "Changes in Satisfaction and Institutional Attitudes of Catholic Priests, 1970–1993." *SoR* 56: 195–213.

Hoge, Dean R., Joseph J. Shields, and Stephen Soroka. 1993. "Sources of Stress Experienced by Catholic Priests." *RRR* 35: 3–18.

Hoge, Dean R., Joseph J. Shields, and Mary Jeanne Verdieck. 1988. "Changing Age Distribution and Theological Attitudes of Catholic Priests, 1970–1985." *SA* 49: 264–80.

Hoge, Dean R., and Jacqueline E. Wenger. 2003. *Evolving Visions of the Priesthood: Changes from Vatican II to the Turn of the Century*. Collegeville, Minn.: Liturgical Press.

Hoge, Dean R., and Fenggang Yang. 1994. "Determinants of Religious Giving in American Denominations: Data from Two Nationwide Surveys." *RRR* 36: 123–48.

Hoge, Dean R., Charles E. Zech, Patrick H. McNamara, and Michael J. Donahue. 1996. *Money Matters: Personal Giving in American Churches*. Louisville, Ky.: Westminster John Knox.

Homans, George Caspar. 1958. "Social Behavior as Exchange." *AJS* 63: 597–606.

———. 1974. *Social Behavior: Its Elementary Forms*. Rev. ed. New York: Harcourt Brace Jovanovich.

Hong, Nansook. 1998. *In the Shadow of the Moons: My Life in the Reverend Sun Myung Moon's Family.* Boston, Mass.: Little, Brown.

Hoover, Stewart M. 1987. "The Religious Television Audience: A Matter of Significance or Size?" *RRR* 29: 135–51.

———. 1988. *Mass Media Religion: The Social Sources of the Electronic Church*. Newbury Park, Calif.: Sage.

Hout, Michael, and Claude S. Fischer. 2002. "Why More Americans Have No Religious Preference: Politics and Generations." *ASR* 67: 165–90.

Hout, Michael, Andrew Greeley, and Melissa J. Wilde. 2001. "The Demographic Imperative in Religious Change in the United States." *AJS* 107: 468–500.

———. 2005. "Birth Dearth: Demographics of Mainline Decline." *The Christian Century* 122 (October 4): 24–27.

Howard, Jay R., and John M. Streck. 1999. *Apostles of Rock: The Splintered World of Contemporary Christian Music.* Lexington, Ky.: University Press of Kentucky.

Hudson, Winthrop S. 1987. *Religion in America: An Historical Account of the Development of American Religious Life*. 4th ed. New York: Macmillan.

Hunt, Larry L. 1996. "Black Catholicism and Secular Status: Integration, Conversion, and Consolidation." *Social Science Quarterly* 77: 842–59.

———. 1998a. "Religious Affiliation among Blacks in the United States: Black Catholic Status Advantages Revisited." *Social Science Quarterly* 79: 170–92.

———. 1998b. "The Spirit of Hispanic Protestantism in the United States: National Survey Comparisons of Catholics and Non-Catholics." *Social Science Quarterly* 79: 828–45.

———. 1999. "Hispanic Protestantism in the United States: Trends by Decade and Generation." *SF* 77: 1601–24.

———. 2000. "Religion and Secular Status among Hispanics in the United States: Catholicism and the Varieties of Hispanic Protestantism." *Social Science Quarterly* 81: 344–62.

———. 2001. "Religion, Gender, and the Hispanic Experience in the United States: Catholic/Protestant Differences in Religious Involvement, Social Status, and Gender-Role Attitudes." *RRR* 43: 139–60.

Hunt, Larry L., and Janet G. Hunt. 1975. "A Religious Factor in Secular Achievement among Blacks: The Case of Catholicism." *SF* 53: 595–605.

———. 1976. "Black Catholicism and the Spirit of Weber." *Sociological Quarterly* 17: 369–77.

———. 1978. "Black Catholicism and Occupational Status in Northern Cities." *Social Science Quarterly* 58: 657–70.

Hunter, James Davison. 1988. "American Protestantism: Sorting Out the Present, Looking toward the Future." In *The Believable Futures of American Protestantism*, ed. Richard John Neuhaus (pp. 18–48). Grand Rapids, Mich.: Eerdmans.

———. 1991. *Culture Wars: The Struggle to Define America*. New York: Basic Books.

———. 1994. *Before the Shooting Begins: Searching for Democracy in America's Culture War*. New York: Free Press.

Hurh, Won Moo. 1998. *Korean Americans*. Westport, Conn.: Greenwood.

Iannaccone, Laurence R. 1990. "Religious Practice: A Human Capital Approach." *JSSR* 29: 297–314.

———. 1991. "The Consequences of Religious Market Structure: Adam Smith and the Economics of Religion." *Rationality and Society* 3: 156–77.

———. 1992. "Religious Markets and the Economics of Religion." *SC* 39: 123–31.

———. 1994. "Why Strict Churches Are Strong." *AJS* 99: 1180–1211.

———. 1995. "Voodoo Economics? Reviewing the Rational Choice Approach to Religion." *JSSR* 34: 76–88.

———. 1996. "Reassessing Church Growth: Statistical Pitfalls and Their Consequences." *JSSR* 35: 197–216.

———. 1997. "Rational Choice: Framework for the Scientific Study of Religion." In *Rational Choice Theory and Religion: Summary and Assessment*, ed. Lawrence A. Young (pp. 25–44). New York: Routledge.

———. 1998. "Introduction to the Economics of Religion." *Journal of Economic Literature* 36: 1465–96.

Iannaccone, Laurence R., Daniel V. A. Olson, and Rodney Stark. 1995. "Religious Resources and Church Growth." *SF* 74: 705–31.

Ice, Martha. 1987. *Clergy Women and Their Worldviews*. New York: Praeger.

Iceland Reporter. 1996. "Eternal Peace." *Iceland Reporter* 243: 2.

Incandela, Joseph M. 1997. "In Cyberspace, All Things Catholic." *Commonweal* 124 (December 5): 31.

Jacobs, Janet L. 1990. "Women-centered Healing Rites: A Study of Alienation and Reintegration." In *In Gods We Trust: New Patterns of Religious Pluralism in America*, 2nd ed., ed. Tom Robbins and Dick Anthony (pp. 373–83). New Brunswick, N.J.: Transaction.

———. 1998. "Gender." In *Encyclopedia of Religion and Society*, ed. William H. Swatos, Jr. (p. 206). Walnut Creek, Calif.: AltaMira.

Jacobsen, Douglas, and William Vance Trollinger, eds. 1998. *Re-Forming the Center: American Protestantism, 1900 to the Present*. Grand Rapids, Mich.: Eerdmans.

Jaspers, Karl. 1964. *Three Essays: Leonardo, Descartes, Max Weber*. New York: Harcourt, Brace, and World.

Jasso, Guillermina, Douglas S. Massey, Mark R. Rosenzweig, and James P. Smith. 2003. "Exploring the Religious Preferences of Recent Immigrants to the United States: Evidence from the New Immigrant Survey Project." In *Religion and Immigration: Christian, Jewish, and Muslim Experiences in the United States*, ed. Yvonne Yazbeck Haddad, Jane I. Smith, and John L. Esposito. Walnut Creek, Calif.: AltaMira.

Jewett, Paul. K. 1980. *The Ordination of Women*. Grand Rapids, Mich.: Eerdmans.

John Jay College of Criminal Justice. 2004. *Nature and Scope of the Problem of Sexual Abuse of Minors by Catholic Priests and Deacons in the United States, 1950–2002*. Washington, D.C.: United States Conference of Catholic Bishops.

Johnson, Benton. 1957. "A Critical Appraisal of the Church-Sect Typology." *ASR* 22: 88–92.

———. 1961. "Do Holiness Sects Socialize in Dominant Values?" *SF* 39: 309–16.

———. 1963. "On Church and Sect." *ASR* 28: 539–49.

———. 1971. "Church and Sect Revisited." *JSSR* 10: 124–37.

———. 1977. "Sociological Theory and Religious Truth." *SA* 38: 368–88.

Johnson, Ian. 1999. "Who Ya Gonna Call? In China, Debunkers Hire a Cultbuster." *Wall Street Journal* (August 30): A1, A14.

———. 2000. "Death Trap: How One Chinese City Resorted to Atrocities to Control Falun Dafa." *Wall Street Journal* (December 26): A1, A4.

———. 2004. *Wild Grass: Three Stories of Change in Modern China*. New York: Pantheon.

Johnston, Michael. 1982. "The 'New Christian Right' in American Politics." *Political Quarterly* 53: 181–99.

Jolicoeur, Pamela M., and Louis L. Knowles. 1978. "Fraternal Associations and Civil Religion: Scottish Rite Freemasonry." *RRR* 20: 3–22.

Jones, Dale E., Sherri Doty, Clifford Grammich, James E. Horsch, Richard Houseal, Mac Lynn, John P. Marcum, Kenneth M. Sanchargrin, and Richard H. Taylor. 2002. *Religious Congregations and Membership in the United States, 2000: An Enumeration by Region, State, and County Based on Data Reported for 149 Religious Bodies*. Nashville, Tenn.: Glenmary Research Center.

Karabel, Jerome. 2005. *The Chosen: The Hidden History of Admission and Exclusion at Harvard, Yale, and Princeton*. Boston: Houghton Mifflin.

Keating, Frank. 2003. "Governor Keating Resigns from National Review Board: Letter from Governor Keating." Washington, D.C.: United States Conference of Catholic Bishops.

Keister, Lisa A. 2003. "Religion and Wealth: The Role of Religious Affiliation and Participation in Early Adult Asset Accumulation." *SF* 82: 175–207.

Kelley, Dean M. 1972. *Why Conservative Churches Are Growing*. New York: Harper & Row.

———. 1978. "Why Conservative Churches Are Still Growing." *JSSR* 17: 165–72.

Kennedy, Ruby Jo Reeves. 1944. "Single or Triple Melting Pot? Intermarriage Trends in New Haven, 1870–1940." *AJS* 49: 331–39.

Kent, Stephen A. 1993. "Deviant Scripturalism and Ritual Satanic Abuse, Part One: Possible Judeo-Christian Influences." *Religion* 23: 229–41.

Kent, Stephen A., and James V. Spickard. 1994. "The 'Other' Civil Religion and the Tradition of Radical Quaker Politics." *Journal of Church and State* 36: 373–87.

Kiesling, Angie. 2005. "The Christian Steeple-Chase: Church Bookstores Are One of the Fastest-Growing Segments of Christian Bookselling." *Publishers Weekly* 252 (January 10): 18–21.

Kimmel, Michael S., and Rahmat Tavakol. 1986. "Against Satan." In *Charisma, History, and Social Structure*, ed. Ronald M. Glassman and William H. Swatos, Jr. (pp. 101–12). New York: Greenwood.

Kivisto, Peter. 1993. "Religion and the New Immigrants." In *A Future for Religion*, ed. William H. Swatos Jr. (pp. 92–108). Newbury Park, Calif.: Sage.

———. 2001. "Theorizing Transnational Immigration: A Critical Review of Current Efforts." *Ethnic and Racial Studies* 24: 549–77.

———. 2003. "Social Spaces, Transnational Immigrant Communities, and the Politics of Incorporation." *Ethnicities* 3: 5–28.

———. 2007. "Rethinking the Relationship between Ethnicity and Religion." *Handbook of the Sociology of Religion*, ed. James A. Beckford and N. J. Demerath III (pp. 474–94). Thousand Oaks, Calif.: Sage.

Kivisto, Peter, and Wendy Ng. 2006. *Americans All: Race and Ethnic Relations in Historical, Structural, and Comparative Perspectives*, 2nd ed. New York: Oxford University Press.

Kniss, Fred. 1990. "Toward a Theory of Ideological Change." In *Time, Place, and Circumstance*, ed. William H. Swatos, Jr. (pp. 92–108). New York: Greenwood.

Korman, A. K. 1988. *The Outsiders*. Lexington, Mass.: Lexington.

Kowalewski, Mark R. 1993. "Firmness and Accommodation: Impression Management in Institutional Roman Catholicism." *SoR* 54: 207–17.

Krogh, Marilyn C., and Brooke Ashley Pillifant. 2004. "Kemetic Orthodoxy: Ancient Egyptian Religion on the Internet." *SoR* 65: 167–75.

Kurtz, Lester R. 1986. *The Politics of Heresy: The Modernist Crisis in Roman Catholicism*. Berkeley, Calif.: University of California Press.

Kuykendall, John W. 1982. *Southern Enterprise*. Westport, Conn.: Greenwood.

LaHaye, Tim F., and Jerry B. Jenkins. 1995. *Left Behind: A Novel of the Earth's Last Days*. Wheaton, Ill.: Tyndale House Publishers.

———. 2006. *John's Story: The Last Eyewitness*. New York: Putnam Praise.

———. 2007. *Mark's Story*. New York: Penguin.

Larson, Edward J., and Larry Witham. 1997. "Scientists Are Still Keeping the Faith." *Nature* 386: 435–36.

Larson, Rebecca. 1999. *Daughters of Light: Quaker Women Preaching and Prophesying in the Colonies and Abroad, 1700–1775*. New York: Knopf.

LaVey, Anton. 1966. *The Satanic Bible*. New York: Avon.

———. 1972. *The Satanic Ritual*. New York: Avon.

Lavoie, Denise. 2003a. "Child Abuse Record of Boston Priests 'Staggering,' Attorney General Says. More Than 1,000 Molested by Clergy, Workers: Report." *Ottawa* [Ontario] *Citizen* (July 24): A12.

———. 2003b. "Archdiocese to Pay $85M to Abuse Victims: Boston Priests' Deal Largest Known Settlement for Molestation Charges." *Ottawa* [Ontario] *Citizen* (September 10): A15.

Le Bras, Gabriel. 1955. *Sociologie de la pratique religieuse dans les campagnes françaises*. Paris: Presses universitaires de France.

———. 1956. *De la morphologie à la typologie*. Paris: Presses Universitaires de France.

Lechner, Frank J. 1985. "Fundamentalism and Socio-Cultural Revitalization in America: A Sociological Interpretation." *SA* 46: 243–60.

———. 1989. "Cultural Aspects of the Modern World-System." In *Religious Politics in Global and Comparative Perspective*, ed. William H. Swatos, Jr. (pp. 11–17). New York: Greenwood.

———. 1991. "The Case against Secularization: A Rebuttal." *SF* 69: 1103–19).

———. 2004. "Globalization." In *Encyclopedia of Social Theory*, ed. George Ritzer (pp. 331–33), Thousand Oaks, Calif.: Sage.

Lee, Martha F. 1988. *The Nation of Islam, An American Millenarian Movement*. Lewiston, N.Y.: Mellen.

Lee, Richard Wayne. 1995. "Strained Bedfellows: Pagans, New Agers, and 'Starchy Humanists' in Unitarian Universalism." *SoR* 56: 379–96.

Lehman, Edward C. 1985. *Women Clergy*. New Brunswick, N.J.: Transaction.

———. 1993. *Gender and Work: The Case of the Clergy*. Albany, N.Y.: State University of New York Press.

Lemann, Nicholas. 1991. *The Promised Land: The Great Migration and How It Changed America*. New York: Knopf.

Lemert, Charles C. 1975. "Social Structure and the Absent Center: An Alternative to the New Sociologies of Religion." *SA* 36: 95–107.

Leming, Laura M. 2006. "Church as Contested Terrain: 'Voice of the Faithful' and Religious Agency." *RRR* 48: 56–71.

———. 2007. "Sociological Explorations: What Is Religious Agency." *Sociological Quarterly* 48: 73–92.

Lenski, Gerhard E. 1961. *The Religious Factor: A Sociological Study of Religion's Impact on Politics, Economics, and Family Life*. Garden City, N.Y.: Doubleday.

Leonard, Karen I., Alex Stepick, Manuel A. Vásquez, and Jennifer Holdaway, eds. 2005. *Immigrant Faiths: Transforming Religious Life in America*. Walnut Creek, Calif.: AltaMira.

Leuba, James. 1921. *The Belief in God and Immortality*. Chicago, Ill.: Open Court.

Levin, Jeffrey S., ed. 1994. *Religion in Aging and Health: Theoretical Foundations and Methodological Frontiers*. Thousand Oaks, Calif.: Sage.

Levin, Jeffrey S., and Harold G. Koenig, eds. 2005. *Faith, Medicine, and Science: A Festschrift in Honor of Dr. David B. Larson*. Binghamton, N.Y.: Haworth Press.

Levine, Lawrence W. 1977. *Black Culture and Black Consciousness*. New York: Oxford University Press.

Levine, Saul V. 1984. *Radical Departures*. San Diego, Calif.: Harcourt Brace Jovanovich.

Levitt, Peggy. 2001. *The Transnational Villagers*. Berkeley, Calif.: University of California Press.

———. 2007. *God Needs No Passport: Immigrants and the Changing American Religious Landscape*. New York: The New Press.

Lewis, I. M. 1986. *Religion in Context: Cults and Charisma*. Cambridge: Cambridge University Press.

Lewis, Sinclair. 1927. *Elmer Gantry*. New York: Harcourt, Brace.

Lienesch, Michael. 1991. "'Train Up a Child': Conceptions of Child-Rearing in Christian Conservative Social Thought." *Comparative Social Research* 13: 203–24.

Lincoln, C. Eric. 1973. *The Black Muslims in America*. Boston, Mass.: Beacon.

Lincoln, C. Eric, and Lawrence H. Mamiya. 1990. *The Black Church in the African-American Experience*. Durham, N.C.: Duke University Press.

Linder, Eileen W., ed. 2003. *Yearbook of American and Canadian Churches: 2003*. Nashville, Tenn.: Abingdon Press.

Lindsey, Hal, with Carole C. Carlson. 1970. *The Late Great Planet Earth*. Grand Rapids, Mich.: Zondervan.

Lindsey, Hal, with Cliff Ford. 1998. *Facing Millennial Midnight: The Y2K Crisis Confronting America and the World*. Beverly Hills, Calif.: Western Front.

Lipset, Seymour Martin. 1959. "Religion in America: What Religious Revival?" *RRR* 1: 17–24.

Little, David. 1969. *Religion, Order, and Law: A Study in Pre-Revolutionary England*. New York: Harper & Row.

Livingstone, Frank B. 1962. "On the Non-Existence of Human Races." *Current Anthropology* 3: 279–81.

Lofland, John. 1966. *Doomsday Cult: A Study of Conversion, Proselytization and Maintenance of Faith*. Englewood Cliffs, N.J.: Prentice-Hall.

Lofland, John, and Rodney Stark. 1965. "Becoming a World Saver." *ASR* 30: 862–75.

Lopreato, Joseph, and Timothy Crippin. 1999. *Crisis in Sociology: The Need for Darwin*. New Brunswick, N.J.: Transaction.

López-Pulido, Alberto. 2007. "A Sociological Analysis of Latino Religions: The Formation of the Theoretical Binary and Beyond." In *American Sociology of Religion: Histories*, ed. Anthony J. Blasi (pp. 223–51). Leiden, the Netherlands: Brill.

Loseke, Donileen R., and James C. Cavendish. 2001. "Producing Institutional Selves: Rhetorically Constructing the Dignity of Sexually Marginalized Catholics." *Social Psychology Quarterly* 64: 347–62.

Luckmann, Thomas. 1967. *The Invisible Religion: The Problem of Religion in Modern Society*. New York: Macmillan.

———. 1990. "Shrinking Transcendence, Expanding Religion?" *SA* 50: 127–38.

Lukács, Georg. 1971. *History and Class Consciousness: Studies in Marxist Dialectics*. Cambridge, Mass.: MIT Press.

Luke, Timothy W. 1987. "Civil Religion and Secularization: Ideological Revitalization in Post-Revolutionary Communist Systems." *Sociological Forum* 2: 108–34.

Luker, Kristin. 1984. *Abortion and the Politics of Motherhood*. Berkeley, Calif.: University of California Press.

Lummis, Adair. 1994. "Feminist Values and Other Influences on Pastoral Leadership Styles." Paper presented at the annual meeting of the Society for the Scientific Study of Religion.

Lynd, Robert S., and Helen M. Lynd. 1929. *Middletown*. New York: Harcourt, Brace.

———. 1937. *Middletown in Transition*. New York: Harcourt, Brace.

Lyng, Stephen G., and Lester R. Kurtz. 1985. "Bureaucratic Insurgency: The Vatican and the Crisis of Modernism." *SF* 63: 901–22.

Mack, Raymond W., Raymond J. Murphy, and Seymour Yellin. 1956. "The Protestant Ethic, Level of Aspiration, and Social Mobility: An Empirical Test." *ASR* 21: 295–300.

Manning, Christel J. 1997. "Women in a Divided Church: Liberal and Conservative Catholic Women Negotiate Changing Gender Roles." *SoR* 58: 375–90.

———. 1999. *God Gave Us the Right: Conservative Catholic, Evangelical Protestant, and Orthodox Jewish Women Grapple with Feminism*. New Brunswick, N.J.: Rutgers University Press.

Marcum, John P. 1999. "Measuring Church Attendance: A Further Look." *RRR* 41: 121–29.

Marín, Gerardo, and Raymond J. Gamba. 1993. "The Role of Expectations in Religious Conversions: The Case of Hispanic Catholics." *RRR* 34: 357–71.

Marin, Peter. 1979. "Spiritual Obedience." *Harper's* (February): 43–58.

Marler, Penny Long, and C. Kirk Hadaway. 1999. "Testing the Attendance Gap in a Conservative Church." *SoR* 60: 175–86.

Marsden, George M. 1980. *Fundamentalism and American Culture: The Shaping of Twentieth-Century Evangelicalism, 1870–1925*. New York: Oxford University Press.

Marshall, Gordon. 1982. *In Search of the Spirit of Capitalism: An Essay on Max Weber's Protestant Ethic*. New York: Columbia University Press.

Martin, David. 1962. "The Denomination." *British Journal of Sociology* 13: 1–14.
———. 1966. *Pacifism*. New York: Schocken.
Martin, Seamus. 1996. "In a Virtual Parish: A Rebel Catholic Bishop Has Turned the World Wide Web into His Diocese." *Irish Times* [Dublin] (February 5): 8.
Marty, Martin E. 1959. *The New Shape of American Religion*. New York: Harper & Row.
———. 1970. *Righteous Empire: The Protestant Experience in America*. New York: Dial Press.
———. 1981. *The Public Church: Mainline, Evangelical, Catholic*. New York: Crossroad.
———. 1986a. *Protestantism in the United States: Righteous Empire*. Rev. ed. of *Righteous Empire*. New York: Scribner.
———. 1986b. Review of *The Future of Religion*, by Rodney Stark and William Sims Bainbridge. *Journal of Religion* 66: 208–09.
———. 1987. *Religion and Republic: The American Circumstance*. Boston, Mass.: Beacon.
———. ed. 1992. *Civil Religion, Church and State*. Munich, Germany: Saur.
———. 1997. "An Exuberant Adventure: The Academic Study and Teaching of Religion." *Religious Studies News* (September): 20, 48.
———. 1998. "Is That a Fact?" *Context* 30 (January 1): 1.
———. 2003. "Taken Out of Context." *Context* 35 (February 1): 8.
Marx, Gary. 1967. "Religion: Opiate or Inspiration of Civil Rights Militancy among Negroes?" *ASR* 32: 64–72.
Marx, Karl. 1963. *Theories of Surplus Value*. 1862–1863. Reprint, New York: International Publishers.
———. 1964. *Early Writings*, ed. T. B. Bottomore. New York: McGraw-Hill.
———. 1967. *Capital*, 3 vols. 1867. Reprint, New York: International Publishers.
———. 1974. *The Grundrisse: Foundations of a Critique of Political Economy*. 1857–1858. Reprint, New York: Random House.
Marx, Karl, and Friedrich Engels. 1975. *On Religion*. Moscow: Progress Publishers.
Massey, Douglas S., Camille Z. Charles, Garvey F. Lundy, and Mary J. Fischer. 2003. *The Source of the River: The Social Origins of Freshmen at America's Selective Colleges and Universities*. Princeton, N.J.: Princeton University Press.
Mathisen, James A. 1989. "Twenty Years after Bellah: What Ever Happened to American Civil Religion?" *SA* 50: 129–46.
Mayer, Albert J., and Harry Sharp. 1962. "Religious Preference and Worldly Success." *ASR* 27: 218–27.
Mazlish, Bruce. 1984. *The Meaning of Karl Marx*. New York: Oxford University Press.
McAdam, Doug. 1988. *Freedom Summer*. New York: Oxford University Press.
McAllister, Ronald J. 1998. "Research Methods." In *Encyclopedia of Religion and Society*, ed. William H. Swatos, Jr. (pp. 413–20). Walnut Creek, Calif.: AltaMira.
McCartney, Bill. 1997. *Sold Out: Becoming Man Enough to Make a Difference*. Nashville, Tenn.: Word.
McCleary, Rachel M., and Robert J. Barro. 2006. "Religion and Economy." *Journal of Economic Perspectives* 20: 49–72.
McClelland, David C. 1961. *The Achieving Society*. Princeton, N.J.: Van Nostrand.
McCloud, Sean. 2007. *Divine Hierarchies: Class in American Religion and Religious Studies*. Chapel Hill: University of North Carolina Press.
McCormick, Patrick. 1998. "Catholic.com: Surfing for Salvation." *U.S. Catholic* 63 (October): 46–48.
McDannell, Colleen. 1991. "Interpreting Things: Material Culture Studies and American Religion." *Religion* 21: 371–87.
———. 1995. *Material Christianity: Religion and Popular Culture in America*. New Haven, Conn.: Yale University Press.
McGreevy, John T. 1996. *Parish Boundaries: The Catholic Encounter with Race in the Twentieth-Century Urban North*. Chicago, Ill.: University of Chicago Press.
McGuire, Meredith B. 1982. *Pentecostal Catholics: Power, Charisma, and Order in a Religious Movement*. Philadelphia: Temple University Press.
McMahon, Eileen M. 1995. *What Parish Are You From? A Chicago Irish Community and Race Relations*. Lexington: University Press of Kentucky.
McMullen, Michael. 2000. *The Bahá'í: The Religious Construction of a Global Identity*. New Brunswick, N.J.: Rutgers University Press.

McRoberts, Omar. 2003. *Streets of Glory: Church and Community in a Black Urban Neighborhood*. Chicago, Ill.: University of Chicago Press.

Mead, Sidney E. 1954. "Denominationalism: The Shape of Protestantism in America." *Church History* 23: 291–320.

——. 1956. "From Coercion to Persuasion: Another Look at the Rise of Religious Liberty and the Emergence of Denominationalism." *Church History* 25: 317–37.

——. 1963. *The Lively Experiment*. New York: Harper & Row.

Medved, Michael. 2007. "Hollywood's Terrorists: Mormon Not Muslim." *USA Today* (August 13): 13A.

Medwick, Cathleen. 1999. *Teresa of Avila: The Progress of a Soul*. New York: Knopf.

Meizel, Katherine. 2006. "The Singing Citizenry: Popular Music and Civil Religion in America." *JSSR* 45: 497–503.

Melton, J. Gordon, ed. 1978. *The Encyclopedia of American Religions*. Wilmington, N.C.: McGrath.

——. 1986. *The Encyclopedic Handbook of Cults in America*. New York: Garland.

——. 1998. "Modern Alternative Religions in the West." In *A New Handbook of Living Religions*, ed. John R. Hinnells (pp. 594–617). Harmondsworth, United Kingdom: Penguin.

Memmott, Carol. 2006. "'John's Story' Kicks Off 'The Jesus Chronicles.'" *USA Today* (November 16): 1D.

Menjívar, Cecilia. 2000. *Fragmented Ties: Salvadoran Immigrant Networks in America*. Berkeley, Calif.: University of California Press.

——. 2006. "Liminal Legality: Salvadoran and Guatemalan Immigrants' Lives in the United States." *AJS* 111: 999–1037.

Merton, Robert K. 1936. "Puritanism, Pietism, and Science." *Sociological Review* 28: 1–30.

——. 1946. *Mass Persuasion: The Social Psychology of a War Bond Drive*. New York: Harper.

——. 1996. *On Social Structure and Science*. Chicago, Ill.: University of Chicago Press.

Meyer, John W. 1980. "The World Polity and the Authority of the Nation-State." In *Studies of the Modern World-System*, ed. Albert J. Bergesen (pp. 109–37). New York: Academic Press.

Micheelsen, Arun. 2002. "'I Don't Do Systems': An Interview with Clifford Geertz." *Method and Theory in the Study of Religion* 14: 2–20.

Michelat, Guy. 1990. "L'identité catholique des Français: I. Les dimensions de la religiosité." *Revue française de sociologie* 31: 355–88.

Miki, Hizuru. 1999. "Towards a New Paradigm of Religious Organizations." *International Journal of Japanese Sociology* 8: 141–59.

Miller, David L. 1994. "Statement on the AAR." *Religious Studies News* (September): 3.

Miller, Lisa. 1999. "Registers Ring in Sanctuary Stores: Tax-Exempt Church Shops Peddle Stuffed Bears, Tapes and Special Coffee Blends." *Wall Street Journal* (December 17): B1, B4.

——. 2000. "Redefining God." *Wall Street Journal* (April 21): W1, W4.

Miller, Robert J., Robert A. Parfet, and Charles Zech. 2001. "The Effect of Life Cycle and Parishioner Perceptions on Average Household Giving in Catholic Parishes." *RRR* 42: 313–31.

Mills, C. Wright. 1951. *White Collar: The American Middle Class*. New York: Oxford University Press.

——. 1956. *The Power Elite*. New York: Oxford University Press.

——. 1959. *The Sociological Imagination*. New York: Oxford University Press.

Min, Pyong Gap. 1996. *Caught in the Middle: Korean Merchants in America's Multiethnic Cities*. Berkeley, Calif.: University of California Press.

——. 1999. "A Comparison of Post-Intergenerational Mobility and Cultural Transmission." *Journal of American Ethnic History* 18 (3): 65–94.

Min, Pyong Gap, and Jung Ka Kim, eds. 2002. *Religions in Asian America: Building Faith Communities*. Walnut Creek, Calif.: AltaMira.

Morawska, Ewa. 1999. "The Sociology and History of Immigration: Reflections of a Practitioner." Paper presented at the European University Institute, Florence, Italy, May 20.

Morgan, S. Philip. 1983. "A Research Note on Religion and Morality: Are Religious People Nice People?" *SF* 61: 683–92.

Morris, Aldon D. 1984. *The Origins of the Civil Rights Movement: Black Communities Organizing for Change*. New York: Free Press.

Mozingo, Joe, and John Spano. 2007. "$660-Million Settlement in Priest Abuses." *Los Angeles Times* (July 15): A1.

Murrell, Nathaniel Samuel, William David Spencer, and Adrian Anthony McFarlane, eds. 1998. *Chanting Down Babylon: The Rastafari Reader*. Philadelphia: Temple University Press.

Naff, Alixa. 1985. *Becoming American: The Early Arab Immigrant Experience*. Carbondale: Southern Illinois University Press.

Nash, Dennison. 1968. "'A Little Child Shall Lead Them': A Statistical Test of an Hypothesis That Children Were the Source of the American 'Religious Revival.'" *JSSR* 7: 238–40.

Nash, Dennison, and Peter L. Berger. 1962. "Church Commitment in an American Suburb: An Analysis of the Decision to Join." *Archives de sociologie des religions* 7: 105–20.

Nason-Clark, Nancy. 1987a. "Are Women Changing the Image of Ministry? A Comparison of British and American Realities." *RRR* 28: 330–40.

———. 1987b. "Ordaining Women as Priests: Religious vs. Sexist Explanations for Clerical Attitudes." *SA* 48(3): 259–73.

———. 1998. "Sexism." In *Encyclopedia of Religion and Society*, ed. William H. Swatos Jr. (pp. 460–64). Walnut Creek, Calif.: AltaMira.

National Catholic Reporter. 2005. "Law's Power a Symbol of Deeper Crisis." *National Catholic Reporter* (April 22): 28

———. 2006. "Catholics Not Leaving Church Over Sex Abuse Scandal, Survey Finds." *National Catholic Reporter* (May 26): 11.

Neitz, Mary Jo. 1987. *Charisma and Community: A Study of Religious Commitment within the Charismatic Renewal*. New Brunswick, N.J.: Transaction.

———. 1990. "In Goddess We Trust." In *In Gods We Trust: New Patterns of Religious Pluralism in America*, 2nd ed., ed. Tom Robbins and Dick Anthony (pp. 353–71). New Brunswick, N.J.: Transaction.

———. 1998. "Feminist Research and Theory." In *Encyclopedia of Religion and Society*, ed. William H. Swatos Jr. (pp. 184–86). Walnut Creek, Calif.: AltaMira.

———. 2000. "Queering the Dragonfest: Changing Sexualities in a Post-Patriarchal Religion." *SoR* 61: 369–91.

Nelsen, Hart M., and Lynda Dickson. 1972. "Attitudes of Black Catholics and Protestants: Evidence for Religious Identity." *SA* 33: 152–65.

Nelsen, Hart M., and Ann Kusener Nelsen. 1975. *The Black Church in the Sixties*. Lexington: University Press of Kentucky.

Nelson, Geoffrey K. 1969. *Spiritualism and Society*. London: Routledge.

Nelson, Marcia Z. 1999. "The Road Soon Taken: What Might the Next Century Hold for Religious Publishing?" *Publishers Weekly* 246 (November 15): S1–S9.

———. 2000. "Just How Big Is It, Really? Determining the Size of the Religion Book Industry Remains an Elusive Goal for All Publishers." *Publishers Weekly* 247 (March 13): 38–40.

———. 2003. "How Big Is It Redux: Measuring the Religion Publishing Industry Is Still an Imprecise Art." *Publishers Weekly* 250 (November 10): 25–27.

———. 2004. "The Publishing Business: Religion Sells." *Christian Century* 121 (October 18): 8–10.

Nesbitt, Paula D. 1997. *Feminization of the Clergy in America*. New York: Oxford University Press.

Nesti, Arnaldo. 1985. *Il religioso implicito*. Rome, Italy: Ianua.

Nesti, Arnaldo, Paolo Giannoni, and Severino Dianich. 1993. *La religione implicita: Sociologi e teologi a confronto*. Bologna, Italy: EDB.

Neuhaus, Richard John, ed. 1986. *Unsecular America*. Grand Rapids, Mich.: Eerdmans.

Newman, William M., and Peter L. Halvorson. 1980. *Patterns in Pluralism: A Portrait of American Religion, 1952–1971*. Washington, D.C.: Glenmary Research Center.

Newport, Frank. 1979. "The Religious Switcher in the United States." *ASR* 44: 528–52.

Niebuhr, Gustav. 1999. "Debate by Lutherans over Links to Episcopal Church Bares Internal Politics." *New York Times* (August 19): A10.

———. 2001. "Studies Suggest Lower Count for Number of U.S. Muslims." *New York Times* (October 25): A16.

Niebuhr, H. Richard. 1929. *The Social Sources of Denominationalism*. New York: Holt.

Nielsen, Donald A. 1990a. "Max Weber and the Sociology of Early Christianity." In *Time, Place, and Circumstance*, ed. William H. Swatos, Jr. (pp. 87–102). New York: Greenwood.
———. 1990b. "The Inquisition, Rationalization, and Sociocultural Change in Medieval Europe." In *Time, Place, and Circumstance*, ed. William H. Swatos, Jr. (pp. 107–22). New York: Greenwood.
NORC (National Opinion Research Center [Andrew M. Greeley and Richard A. Schoenherr, coinvestigators]). 1972. *The Catholic Priest in the United States: Sociological Investigations*. Washington, D.C.: U.S. Catholic Conference.
Numrich, Paul David, ed. 2008. *North American Buddhism*. Leiden, The Netherlands: Brill.
O'Driscoll, Patrick. 2005. "Religious Retailers Gather to Show Off Wares: Politics Takes Prominent Role at Event." *USA Today* (July 15): 11A.
Official Catholic Directory. Annual. New Providence, N.J.: Kenedy.
Olson, Daniel V. A. 1999. "Religious Pluralism and U.S. Church Membership: A Reassessment." *SoR* 60: 149–73.
Olson, Daniel V. A., and C. Kirk Hadaway. 1999. "Religious Pluralism and Affiliation among Canadian Counties and Cities." *JSSR* 38: 490–508.
Oommen, T. K. 1994. "Religious Nationalism and Democratic Polity." *SoR* 455–72.
Padover, Saul K. 1978. *Karl Marx: An Intimate Biography*. New York: McGraw-Hill.
Park, Robert E. 1950. *Race and Culture*. Glencoe, Ill.: Free Press.
Parot, Joseph. 1981. *Polish Catholics in Chicago, 1850–1920*. DeKalb: Northern Illinois University Press.
Parsons, Talcott. 1937. *The Structure of Social Action: A Study in Social Theory with Special Reference to a Group of Recent European Writers*. New York: McGraw-Hill.
———. 1960. "Some Comments on the Pattern of Religious Organization in the United States." In *Structure and Process in Modern Societies* (pp. 295–321). New York: Free Press.
———. 1963. "Christianity and Modern Industrial Society." In *Sociological Theory, Values, and Sociocultural Change: Essays in Honor of Pitirim A. Sorokin*, ed. Edward A. Tiryakian (pp. 33–70). New York: Free Press.
———. 1974. "Religion in Postindustrial America: The Problem of Secularization." *Social Research* 41: 193–225.
Paterson, John. 1982. *Kildare*. Kildare, Ireland: n.p.
Patterson, Orlando. 1982. *Slavery and Social Death*. Cambridge, Mass.: Harvard University Press.
———. 1997. *The Ordeal of Integration*. Washington, D.C.: Civitas/Counterpoint.
Paulson, Michael. 2003a. "Priest Who Asked Law to Quit Attacked." *Boston Globe* (March 8): A1.
———. 2003b. "Church Refuses Group's Money: Voice of Faithful Decries Decision." *Boston Globe* (April 1): A1.
———. 2003c. "Church Insiders Now on Outside: Say Lennon Does Little to Reach Out." *Boston Globe* (May 25): A1.
Peach, Ceri. 1980. "Which Triple Melting Pot? A Re-examination of Ethnic Intermarriage in New Haven, 1900–1950." *Ethnic and Racial Studies* 3: 1–16.
Peek, Lori. 2005. "Becoming Muslim: The Development of a Religious Identity." *SoR* 66: 215–42.
Perl, Paul, Jennifer Z. Greely, amd Mark M. Gray. 2006. "What Proportion of Adult Hispanics Are Catholic? A Review of Survey Data and Methodology." *JSSR* 45: 419–36.
Perrin, Robin D., and Armand L. Mauss. 1991. "Saints and Seekers: Sources of Recruitment to the Vineyard Christian Fellowship." *RRR* 33: 97–111.
———. 1993. "Strictly Speaking . . . : Kelley's Quandary and the Vineyard Christian Fellowship." *JSSR* 32: 125–35.
Pétursson, Pétur. 1988. "The Relevance of Secularization in Iceland." *SC* 35: 107–24.
Pew Research Center. 2007. *Muslim Americans: Middle Class and Mostly Mainstream*. Washington, D.C.: Pew Research Center.
Polite, Vernon C. 1992. "Getting the Job Done Well: African American Students and Catholic Schools." *Journal of Negro Education* 61: 211–22.
Poloma, Margaret M. 1989. *Assemblies of God at the Crossroads*. Knoxville: University of Tennessee Press.
Pope, Liston. 1942. *Millhands and Preachers: A Study of Gastonia*. New Haven, Conn.: Yale University Press.

——. 1948. "Religion and the Class Structure." *Annals* 256: 84–90.
——. 1957. *The Kingdom beyond Caste*. New York: Friendship Press.
Pope, Stephen. 2004. "Accountability and Sexual Abuse in the United States: Lessons for the Universal Church." *Irish Theological Quarterly* 69: 73–88.
Portes, Alejandro. 1996. "Global Villagers: The Rise of Transnational Communities." *American Prospect* 25 (March–April): 74–77.
Portes, Alejandro, and Rubén G. Rumbaut. 2006. *A Portrait of Immigrant America*, 3rd ed. Berkeley: University of California Press.
Portes, Alejandro, and Min Zhou. 1993. "The Second Generation: Segmented Assimilation and Its Variants." *Annals* 530: 74–96.
Powell, Mark Allan. 2002. "Jesus Climbs the Charts: The Business of Contemporary Christian Music." *Christian Century* 119 (December 18): 20–26.
Powell, Walter, and Paul J. DiMaggio, eds. 1991. *The New Institutionalism in Organizational Analysis*. Chicago: University of Chicago Press.
Purvis, Sally B. 1995. *The Stained Glass Ceiling*. Louisville, Ky.: Westminster John Knox.
Pyle, Ralph E. 1996. *Persistence and Change in the Protestant Establishment*. Westport, Conn.: Praeger.
——. 2006. "Trends in Religious Stratification: Have Religious Group Socioeconomic Distinctions Declined in Recent Decades?" *SoR* 67: 61–79.
Pyle, Ralph E., and James D. Davidson. 2003. "The Origins of Religious Stratification in Colonial America." *JSSR* 42: 57–75.
Pyle, Ralph E., and Jerome R. Koch. 2001. "The Religious Affiliations of American Elites, 1930s to 1990s: A Note on the Pace of Disestablishment." *Sociological Focus* 34: 125–37.
Raboteau, Albert. 1978. *Slave Religion: The Invisible Institution in the Antebellum South*. New York: Oxford University Press.
Rankin, Richard. 1993. *Ambivalent Churchmen and Evangelical Churchwomen*. Columbia: University of South Carolina Press.
Read, Jen'nan Ghazal. 2003. "The Sources of Gender Role Attitudes among Christian and Muslim Arab-American Women." *SoR* 64: 207–22.
Religion News Service. 2004. "Rising Belief in Hell, Angels, Heaven, Devil." *Christian Century* 121 (June 15): 14.
——. 2006. "Gallup: Churches of Christ Have Most Frequent Attenders." *Christian Century* 123 (May 16): 15.
Remnick, David. 1995. "The Jewish Conversation." *New Yorker* 71 (November 20): 37–40.
Research Publications, Inc. 1975. *Social Problems and the Churches: The Harlan Paul Douglass Collection of Religious Research Reports.* [2,785 microfiches, 11 x 15 cm.] Woodbridge, Conn.: Research Publications.
Rexhausen, Jeff, and Michael J. Cieslak. 1994. "Relationship of Parish Characteristics to Sunday Giving among Catholics in the Archdiocese of Cincinnati." *RRR* 36: 218–29.
Ribuffo, Leo P. 1986. "Henry Ford and *The International Jew*." In *The American Jewish Experience*, ed. Jonathan D. Sarna (pp. 175–90). New York: Holmes and Meier.
Richardson, James T., ed. 1988. *Money and Power in the New Religions*. Lewiston, N.Y.: Mellen.
——. 1993. "Definitions of Cult: From Sociological-Technical to Popular-Negative." *RRR* 34: 348–56.
——. 1996. "'Brainwashing' Claims and Minority Religions Outside the United States: Cultural Diffusion of a Questionable Concept in the Legal Arena." *Brigham Young University Law Review* (21): 873–904.
——. 1997. "The Social Construction of Satanism: Understanding an International Social Problem." *Australian Journal of Social Issues* 32: 61–85.
——. 1999. "Public Religion and New Religions." In *The Power of Religious Publics: Staking Claims in American Society*, ed. William H. Swatos, Jr., and James K. Wellman, Jr. (pp. 153–67). New York: Praeger.
Richardson, James T., Joel Best, and David G. Bromley, eds. 1991. *The Satanism Scare*. Hawthorne, N.Y.: Aldine de Gruyter.
Richardson, James T., and Massimo Introvigne. 2001. "'Brainwashing' Theories in European Parliamentary and Administrative Reports on 'Cults' and 'Sects.'" *JSSR* 40: 143–68.

Richey, Russell E., and Donald G. Jones, eds. 1974. *American Civil Religion*. New York: Harper & Row.

Riesebrodt, Martin. 1993. *Pious Passion: The Emergence of Modern Fundamentalism in the United States and Iran*. Berkeley: University of California Press.

Riggs, Brian. 1996. "Do This in Random Access Memory of Me." *U.S. Catholic* 61 (August): 26–33.

Robbins, Thomas. 1984. "Constructing Cultist 'Mind Control.'" *SA* 45: 241–56.

———. 1998. "Church-and-State Issues in the United States." In *Encyclopedia of Religion and Society*, ed. William H. Swatos Jr. (pp. 87–90). Walnut Creek, Calif.: AltaMira.

Robbins, Thomas, and Dick Anthony. 1979a. "Cults, Brainwashing, and Counter-Subversion." *Annals* 446: 78–90.

———. 1979b. "The Sociology of Contemporary Religious Movements." *Annual Review of Sociology* 5: 75–89.

———. 1982. "Deprogramming, Brainwashing, and the Medicalization of Deviant Religious Groups." *Social Problems* 29: 283–97.

Robbins, Thomas, Dick Anthony, Madeline Doucas, and Thomas Curtis. 1976. "The Last Civil Religion: Reverend Moon and the Unification Church." *SA* 37: 111–26.

Robbins, Thomas, and Roland Robertson. 1991. "Studying Religion Today." *Religion* 21: 319–37.

Robertson, Pat. 1991. *The New World Order*. Dallas, TX: Word.

Robertson, Roland. 1970. *The Sociological Interpretation of Religion*. New York: Schocken.

———. 1971. "Sociologists and Secularization." *Sociology* 5: 297–312.

———. 1978. "Biases in the Analysis of Secularization." In *Meaning and Change*, ed. Roland Robertson (pp. 258–76). New York: New York University Press.

———. 1992. *Globalization: Social Theory and Global Culture*. London: Sage.

Robertson, Roland, and JoAnn Chirico. 1985. "Humanity, Globalization, and Worldwide Religious Resurgence: A Theoretical Exploration." *SA* 46: 219–42.

Rochford, E. Burke, Jr. 2007. *Hare Krishna Transformed*. New York: New York University Press.

Rodman, Gilbert B. 1996. *Elvis after Elvis: The Posthumous Career of a Living Legend*. London: Routledge.

Roof, Wade Clark. 1972. "The Local-Cosmopolitan Orientation and Traditional Religious Commitment." *SA* 33: 1–15.

———. 1978. *Community and Commitment: Religious Plausibility in a Liberal Protestant Church*. New York: Elsevier.

———. 1996. "'Thick Gatherings': Congregations in America." *Journal of Religion* 76: 450–55.

———. 1999. *Spiritual Marketplace: Baby Boomers and the Remaking of American Religion*. Princeton, N.J.: Princeton University Press.

Roof, Wade Clark, Jackson W. Carroll, and David A. Roozen, eds. 1995. *The Post-War Generation and Establishment Religion: Cross-Cultural Perspectives*. Boulder, Colo.: Westview Press.

Roof, Wade Clark, with Bruce Greer, Mary Johnson, Andrea Leibson, Karen Loeb, and Elizabeth Souza. 1993. *A Generation of Seekers: The Spiritual Journeys of the Baby Boom Generation*. San Francisco, Calif.: HarperCollins.

Roof, Wade Clark, and Christel J. Manning. 1994. "Cultural Conflicts and Identity: Second-Generation Hispanic Catholics in the United States." *SC* 41: 171–84.

Roof, Wade Clark, and William McKinney. 1987. *American Mainline Religion: Its Changing Shape and Future*. New Brunswick, N.J.: Rutgers University Press.

Roozen, David A., and C. Kirk Hadaway, eds. 1993. *Church and Denominational Growth*. Nashville, Tenn.: Abingdon.

Roozen, David A., and James R. Nieman, eds. 2005. *Church, Identity, and Change: Theology and Denominational Structures in Unsettled Times*. Grand Rapids, Mich.: Eerdmans.

Rose, Elliot. 1962. *A Razor for a Goat: A Discussion of Certain Problems in the History of Witchcraft and Diabolism*. Toronto, Ontario: University of Toronto Press.

Rose, Susan D. 1987. "Women Warriors: The Negotiation of Gender in a Charismatic Community." *SA* 48: 245–58.

———. 1988. *Keeping Them Out of the Hands of Satan: Evangelical Schooling in America*. New York: Routledge.

Rountree, Kathryn. 2006. "Journeys to the Goddess: Pilgrimage and Tourism in the New Age." In *On the Road to Being There: Studies in Pilgrimage and Tourism in Late Modernity*, ed. William H. Swatos, Jr. (pp. 33–60). Leiden, Netherlands: Brill

Royle, Marjorie. 1987. "Using Bifocals to Overcome Blindspots." *RRR* 28: 341–50.

Ruether, Rosemary R. 1985. *Woman-Church*. San Francisco, Calif.: Harper & Row.

Rumbaut, Rubén. 1994. "The Crucible within: Ethnic Identity, Self-Esteem, and Segmented Assimilation among Children of Immigrants." *International Migration Review* 28: 748–94.

Runciman, W. G. 1970. *Sociology in Its Place*. Cambridge: Cambridge University Press.

Russell, Jenna. 2003. "Amid Decline, Nine Ordained as Priests: Drop in Enrollment Worries Catholics." *Boston Globe* (May 25): B1.

Ruthven, Malise. 1988. *The Divine Supermarket*. London: Chatto and Windus.

Ruyter, Wim de. 1996. "Dark, Backward, and Barbarous." *Leiden Institute for the Study of Religions Newsletter* 1: 3–8.

Sager, Rebecca. 2007. "The Cultural Construction of State-Sponsored Religion: Race, Politics, and State Implementation of the Faith-Based Initiative." *JCS* 49: 467–85.

Salomon, Albert. 1945. "German Sociology." In *Twentieth-Century Sociology*, ed. Georges Gurvitch and Wilbert E. Moore (pp. 586–614). New York: Philosophical Library.

Sargeant, Kimon Howland. 2000. *Seeker Churches: Promoting Traditional Religion in a Nontraditional Way*. New Brunswick, N.J.: Rutgers University Press.

Sawano, Nanaho. 2000. "Tracing Falun Gong's Roots in the U.S." *Christian Science Monitor* (January 6): 18.

Schoenfeld, Eugen. 1987. "Militant Religion." In *Religious Sociology: Interfaces and Boundaries*, ed. William H. Swatos, Jr. (pp. 125–37). New York: Greenwood.

Schoenherr, Richard A., and Andrew M. Greeley. 1974. "Role Commitment Processes and the American Catholic Priesthood." *ASR* 39: 407–26.

Schoenherr, Richard A., and Lawrence A. Young. 1990. "Quitting the Clergy: Resignations in the Roman Catholic Priesthood." *JSSR* 29: 463–81.

———. 1993. *Full Pews and Empty Altars: Demographics of the Priest Shortage in United States Catholic Dioceses*. Madison: University of Wisconsin Press.

Schultze, Quentin J. 1991. *Televangelism and American Culture*. Grand Rapids, Mich.: Baker Book House.

Schuman, Howard. 1971. "The Religious Factor in Detroit: Review, Replication, and Reanalysis." *ASR* 36: 30–48.

Schuth, Katarina. 1999. *Seminaries, Theologates, and the Future of Church Ministry: An Analysis of Trends and Transitions*. Collegeville, Minn.: Liturgical Press.

Sennett, Richard. 1998. *The Corrosion of Character: The Personal Consequences of Work in the New Capitalism*. New York: Norton.

Shattuck, Cynthia. 1993. "Religious Publishing: Commentary." *Anglican Theological Review* 75: 127–31.

Shaw, Stephen J. 1991. *The Catholic Parish as a Way-Station of Ethnicity and Americanization: Chicago's Germans and Italians, 1903–1939*. Brooklyn, N.Y.: Carlson.

Sherkat, Darren E. 1997. "Embedding Religious Choices: Integrating Preferences and Social Constraints into Rational Choice Theories of Religious Behavior." In *Rational Choice Theory and Religion: Summary and Assessment*, ed. Lawrence A. Young (pp. 65–85). New York: Routledge.

Sherkat, Darren E., and Shannon A. Cunningham. 1998. "Extending the Semi-Involuntary Institution: Regional Differences and Social Constraints on Private Religious Consumption among African Americans." *JSSR* 37: 383–96.

Sherkat, Darren E., and John Wilson. 1995. "Preferences, Constraints, and Choices in Religious Markets: An Examination of Religious Switching and Apostasy." *SF* 73: 993–1026.

Shiner, Larry. 1967. "The Concept of Secularization in Empirical Research." *JSSR* 6: 207–20.

Shupe, Anson D. 1990. "Sun Myung Moon's American Disappointment." *Christian Century* 107: 764–66.

———. 1998. "The Modern Satanistic Scare in North America." In *Rethinking New Religious Movements*, ed. Michael A. Fuss (pp. 365–80). Rome, Italy: Pontifical Gregorian University Research Center on Cultures and Religions.

———. 2007. *Spoils of the Kingdom: Clergy Misconduct and Religious Community*. Urbana: University of Illinois Press.

Shupe, Anson D., and David G. Bromley. 1980. *The New Vigilantes: Deprogrammers, Anti-Cultists, and the New Religions*. Beverly Hills, Calif.: Sage.

Silk, Mark. 1988. *Spiritual Politics: Religion and America Since World War II*. New York: Simon and Schuster.

Simpson, John H. 1995. "The Mood of America in the 1980s: Some Further Observations on Sociomoral Issues." In *The Rapture of Politics,* ed. Steve Bruce, Peter Kivisto, and William H. Swatos, Jr. (pp. 69–83). New Brunswick, N.J.: Transaction.

———. 1996. "'The Great Reversal': Selves, Communities, and the Global System." *SoR* 57: 115–25.

Sklare, Marshall. 1972. *Conservative Judaism: An American Religious Movement*. New York: Schocken.

Smith, Christian S. 1998. *American Evangelicalism: Embattled and Thriving*. Chicago, Ill.: University of Chicago Press.

Smith, Craig S. 1999a. "American Dream Finds Chinese Spiritual Leader: Large U.S. Home Bought for Wife of Founder of Besieged Discipline." *Wall Street Journal* (November 1): A41, A46.

———. 1999b. "Risking It All: Falun Follower Defies Beijing. Personal Journey Reflects China's Search for Meaning after Marxism." *Wall Street Journal* (December 30): A8–A9.

Smith, Jonathan Z. 1982. *Imagining Religion: From Babylon to Jonestown*. Chicago, Ill.: University of Chicago Press.

Smith, Tom W. 2001. *Estimating the Muslim Population in the United States*. New York: American Jewish Committee.

———. 2002a. "Religious Diversity in America: The Emergence of Muslims, Buddhists, Hindus, and Others." *JSSR* 41: 577–85

———. 2002b. "The Muslim Population of the United States: The Methodology of Estimates." *Public Opinion Quarterly* 66: 404–17.

Smith, Wilfred Cantwell. 1984. "On Mistranslated Book Titles." *Religious Studies* 20: 27–42.

Sorokin, Pitirim A. 1937–1941. *Social and Cultural Dynamics.* New York: American.

Spickard, James V. 1998. "Rethinking Religious Social Action: What Is 'Rational' about Rational-Choice Theory?" *SoR* 59: 99–115.

Spiegel, Mickey. 2002. *Dangerous Meditation: China's Campaign against Falungong*. New York: Human Rights Watch.

Stammer, Larry B. 2003. "Mahony Resisted Abuse Inquiry, Panelist Says." *Los Angeles Times* (June 12): A1.

Stark, Rodney. 1991. "Christianizing the Urban Empire." *SA* 52: 77–88.

———. 1992. "The Reliability of Historical United States Census Data on Religion." *SA* 53: 91–95.

———. 1996. *The Rise of Christianity: A Sociologist Reconsiders History*. Princeton, N.J.: Princeton University Press.

———. 1998. "Live Longer, Healthier, and Better: The Untold Benefits of Becoming a Christian in the Ancient World." *Christian History* 17: 28–30.

———. 1999. "Micro Foundations of Religion: A Revised Theory." *Sociological Theory* 17: 264–89.

———. 2000. "Secularization, R.I.P." In *The Secularization Debate*, ed. William H. Swatos, Jr., and Daniel V. A. Olson (pp. 41–66). Lanham, Md.: Rowman & Littlefield.

Stark, Rodney, and William Sims Bainbridge. 1979. "Of Churches, Sects, and Cults: Preliminary Concepts for a Theory of Religious Movements." *JSSR* 18: 117–31.

———. 1980a. "Networks of Faith: Interpersonal Bonds and Recruitment to Cults and Sects." *AJS* 85: 1376–95.

———. 1980b. "Towards a Theory of Religion: Religious Commitment." *JSSR* 19: 114–28.

———. 1985. *The Future of Religion: Secularization, Revival, and Cult Formation*. Berkeley: University of California Press.

———. 1996. *A Theory of Religion*. 1987. Reprint, New Brunswick, N.J.: Rutgers University Press.

———. 2002. "Physiology and Faith: Addressing the 'Universal' Gender Difference in Religious Commitment." *JSSR* 41: 495–507.

———. 2006. *Cities of God: The Real Story of How Christianity Became an Urban Movement and Conquered Rome.* San Francisco, Calif.: HarperSanFrancisco.

Stark, Rodney, and Kevin J. Christiano. 1992. "Support for the American Left, 1920–1924: The Opiate Thesis Reconsidered." *JSSR* 31: 62–75.
Stark, Rodney, and Roger Finke. 2000. "Catholic Religious Vocations: Decline and Revival." *RRR* 42: 125–45.
Stark, Rodney, and Laurence Iannaccone. 1994. "A Supply-Side Reinterpretation of the 'Secularization' of Europe." *JSSR* 33: 230–52.
———. 1997. "Why the Jehovah's Witnesses Grow So Rapidly." *Journal of Contemporary Religion* 12: 133–57.
Stark, Rodney, and James C. McCann. 1993. "Market Forces and Catholic Commitment: Exploring the New Paradigm." *JSSR* 32: 111–24.
Starrs, Paul F. 1997. "The Sacred, the Regional, and the Digital." *Geographical Review* 87: 193–218.
Stockler, Bruce. 2000. "On the Web, in the Heart." *New York Times* (October 13): A31.
Sullins, D. Paul. 2000. "The Stained Glass Ceiling: Career Attainment for Women Clergy." *SoR* 61: 243–66.
Sullivan, Dennis H. 1985. "Simultaneous Determination of Church Contributions and Church Attendance." *Economic Inquiry* 23: 309–20.
Swartz, Marc, ed. 1968. *Local-Level Politics*. Chicago, Ill.: Aldine.
Swatos, William H., Jr. 1979. *Into Denominationalism: The Anglican Metamorphosis*. Storrs, Conn.: Society for the Scientific Study of Religion.
———. 1981a. "Beyond Denominationalism? Community and Culture in American Religion." *JSSR* 20: 217–27.
———. 1981b. "Church-Sect and Cult: Bringing Mysticism Back In." *SA* 42: 17–26.
———. 1988. "Picketing Satan Enfleshed at 7-Eleven." *RRR* 30: 73–82.
———. 1990. "Renewing 'Religion' for Sociology: Specifying the Situational Approach." *Sociological Focus* 23: 141–54.
———. 1992. "The Feminization of God and the Priesting of Women." In *Twentieth-Century World Religious Movements in Neo-Weberian Perspective*, ed. William H. Swatos, Jr. (pp. 283–95). Lewiston, N.Y.: Mellen.
———. 1994. "Western Hemisphere Protestantism in Global Perspective." In *Religions sans Frontières?*, ed. Roberto Cipriani (pp. 180–96). Rome: Presidenza del Consiglio dei Ministri.
———. 1995. "Islam and Capitalism: A Weberian Perspective on Resurgence." In *Religion and the Transformation of Capitalism*, ed. Richard H. Roberts (pp. 47–62). London: Routledge.
———. 1997. "The Politics of Gender and the 'Two-Party' Thesis in American Protestantism." *SC* 44: 23–35.
———. 2006. "Implicit Religious Assumptions within the Resurgence of Civil Religion in the USA since 9/11." *Implicit Religion* 9: 166–79.
Swatos, William H., Jr., and Paul M. Gustafson. 1992. "Meaning, Continuity, and Change." In *Twentieth-Century World Religious Movements in Neo-Weberian Perspective*, ed. William H. Swatos, Jr. (pp. 3–20). Lewiston, N.Y.: Edwin Mellen Press.
Swatos, William H., Jr., and Lutz Kaelber, eds. 2005. *The Protestant Ethic Turns 100: Essays on the Centenary of the Weber Thesis*. Boulder, Colo.: Paradigm.
Swatos, William H., Jr., and Peter Kivisto. 2007. "The Protestant Ethic Thesis as *American* Sociology of Religion." In *American Sociology of Religion: Histories*, ed. Anthony J. Blasi (pp. 87–119). Leiden, The Netherlands: Brill.
Swenson, Don. 1999. *Society, Spirituality, and the Sacred*. Peterborough, Ontario: Broadview.
Synnott, Marcia Graham. 1979. *The Half-Opened Door: Discrimination and Admissions at Harvard, Yale, and Princeton, 1900–1970*. Westport, Conn.: Greenwood.
TAD. 1999a. "Over 350,000 Christians." *The Anglican Digest* 41 (5): 54.
———. 1999b. "69% of Americans." *The Anglican Digest* 41 (2): 47.
———. 1999c. "The Southern Baptist Convention." *The Anglican Digest* 41 (5): 55.
Tamney, Joseph B. 1979. "Established Religiosity in Modern Society: Islam in Indonesia." *SA* 40: 125–35.
———. 1980. "Fasting and Modernization." *JSSR* 19: 129–37.
———. 1992. *American Society in the Buddhist Mirror*. New York: Garland.

Tamney, Joseph B., and Stephen D. Johnson. 1998. "The Popularity of Strict Churches." *RRR* 39: 209–23.

Taylor, Barbara Brown. 2001. "Faith Matters: A Case of Mistaken Identity." *Christian Century* 118 (September 26): 32.

Thernstrom, Stephan, Ann Orlov, and Oscar Handlin, eds. 1980. *The Harvard Encyclopedia of American Ethnic Groups*. Cambridge, Mass.: Harvard University Press.

Thomas, Keith. 1971. *Religion and the Decline of Magic*. New York: Scribner.

Thomas, W. I., and Dorothy Swain Thomas. 1928. *The Child in America: Behavior Problems and Programs*. New York: Knopf.

Thomas, W. I., and Florian Znaniecki. 1926. *The Polish Peasant in Europe and America*. Chicago, Ill.: University of Chicago.

Tillich, Paul. 1957. *Dynamics of Faith*. New York: Harper.

Tizon, Orlando. 1999. "'Destroying a Marriage to Save a Family': Shifting Filipino American Gender Relations." In *Multiculturalism in the United States*, ed. Peter Kivisto and Georganne Rundblad (pp. 381–93). Thousand Oaks, Calif.: Pine Forge.

Tocqueville, Alexis de. 1956. *Democracy in America*. 1835. Reprint, New York: Vintage.

Touraine, Alain. 1971. *Post-Industrial Society*. New York: Random House.

Troeltsch, Ernst. 1931. *The Social Teaching of the Christian Churches*. New York: Macmillan.

Tschannen, Olivier. 1991. "The Secularization Paradigm: A Systematization." *JSSR* 30: 396–415.

Turner, Victor W. 1967. *The Forest of Symbols: Aspects of Ndembu Ritual*. Ithaca, N.Y.: Cornell University Press.

———. 1974. *Dramas, Fields, and Metaphors: Symbolic Action in Human Society*. Ithaca, N.Y.: Cornell University Press.

———. 1985. *On the Edge of the Bush: Anthropology as Experience*. Tucson: University of Arizona Press.

Tweed, Thomas A. 1992. *The American Encounter with Buddhism*. Bloomington: Indiana University Press.

Ueda, Reed. 1994. "Second-Generation Civic America: Education, Citizenship, and the Children of Immigrants." *Journal of Interdisciplinary History* 29: 661–81.

United States Conference of Catholic Bishops [USCCB]. 2002. Charter for the Protection of Children and Young People. Washington, D.C.: USCCB Publishing Office.

Van Biema, David, with Nadia Mustafa, Mitch Frank, David E. Thigpen, Cathy Booth Thomas, and David Schwartz. 2001. "As American as . . . : Although Scapegoated, Muslims, Sikhs and Arabs Are Patriotic, Integrated—and Growing." *Time* 158 (October 1): 72–74.

Van Duch, Darryl. 1996. "Anti-Cult Group's Assets Bought by Scientologist. Church Gets Foe's Name in Bankruptcy: Are Files Next?" *National Law Journal* (December 23): A6.

Vásquez, Manuel A., and Marie Friedmann Marquardt. 2003. *Globalizing the Sacred: Religion across the Americas*. New Brunswick, N.J.: Rutgers University Press.

Verdieck, Mary Jeanne, Joseph J. Shields, and Dean R. Hoge. 1988. "Role Commitment Processes Revisited: American Catholic Priests, 1970 and 1985." *JSSR* 27: 524–35.

Victor, Jeffrey S. 1993. *Satanic Panic: The Creation of a Contemporary Legend*. Chicago, Ill.: Open Court.

Vidal, Jaime R. 1991. "Proselytism of Hispanic Migrants: A Challenge to the American Church." *Migration World Magazine* 19 (2): 13–16.

Vidich, Arthur, and Stanford M. Lyman. 1985. *American Sociology: Worldly Rejections of Religion and Their Directions*. New Haven, Conn.: Yale University Press.

Vogel, Arthur A. 1966. *The Next Christian Epoch*. New York: Harper & Row.

Wagner, Melinda Bollar. 1990. *God's Schools: Choice and Compromise in American Society*. New Brunswick, N.J.: Rutgers University Press.

———. 1997. "Generic Conservative Christianity: The Demise of Denominationalism in Christian Schools." *JSSR* 36: 13–24.

Walker, Adrian. 2002. "No Excuses for Law." *Boston Globe* (December 5): B1.

Wallace, Anthony F. C. 1956. "Revitalization Movements." *American Anthropologist* 58: 264–81.

———. 1966. *Religion: An Anthropological View*. New York: Random House.

Wallace, Ruth A. 1992. *They Call Her Pastor*. Albany: State University of New York Press.
———. 1993. "The Sociological Construction of a New Leadership Role: Catholic Women Pastors." *SoR* 54: 31–42.
Wallis, Roy. 1975. "Scientology: Therapeutic Cult to Religious Sect." *Sociology* 9: 89–100.
Wallis, Roy, and Steve Bruce. 1984. "The Stark-Bainbridge Theory of Religion: A Critical Analysis and Counter Proposals." *SA* 45: 11–27.
———. 1986. *Sociological Theory, Religion and Collective Action*. Belfast: Queen's University Press.
Walter, Tony, and Grace Davie. 1998. "The Religiosity of Women in the Modern West." *British Journal of Sociology* 49: 640–60.
Walzer, Michael. 1997. *On Toleration*. New Haven, Conn.: Yale University Press.
Warner, R. Stephen. 1988. *New Wine in Old Wineskins: Evangelicals and Liberals in a Small-Town Church*. Berkeley: University of California Press.
———. 1993. "Work in Progress toward a New Paradigm for the Sociological Study of Religion in the United States." *AJS* 98: 1044–93.
———. 1994. "The Place of the Congregation in the Contemporary American Religious Configuration." In *New Perspectives in the Study of Congregations*, ed. James P. Wind and James W. Lewis (pp. 54–99). Chicago, Ill.: University of Chicago Press.
———. 2005. *A Church of Our Own: Disestablishment and Diversity in American Religion*. New Brunswick, N.J.: Rutgers University Press.
Warner, R. Stephen, and Judith G. Wittner, eds. 1998. *Gatherings in Diaspora: Religious Communities and the New Immigration*. Philadelphia, Penn.: Temple University Press.
Warner, W. Lloyd, ed. 1942a. *Democracy in Jonesville*. New York: Harper & Row.
———. 1942b. *Social Class in America*. Chicago, Ill.: Science Research Associates.
———. 1961. *The Family of God*. New Haven, Conn.: Yale University Press.
———. 1973. *Yankee City*. New Haven, Conn.: Yale University Press.
Warner, W. Lloyd, and Paul S. Lunt. 1941. *The Social Life of a Modern Community*. New Haven, Conn.: Yale University Press.
Waters, Mary. 1990. *Ethnic Options: Choosing Identities in America*. Berkeley: University of California Press.
Watts, Jill. 1992. *God, Harlem U.S.A.: The Father Divine Story*. Berkeley: University of California Press.
Wax, Murray. 1971. *Indian Americans: Unity and Diversity*. Englewood Cliffs, N.J.: Prentice-Hall.
Weber, Max. 1946. *From Max Weber*, ed. C. Wright Mills and H. H. Gerth. New York: Oxford University Press.
———. 1949. *Max Weber on the Methodology of the Social Sciences*. 1904–1917. Reprint, Glencoe, Ill.: Free Press.
———. 1952. *Ancient Judaism*. Glencoe, Ill.: Free Press.
———. 1978. *Economy and Society*. 1922. Reprint, Berkeley: University of California Press.
———. 1998. *The Protestant Ethic and the Spirit of Capitalism*. 1904–1906. Reprint, New York: Oxford University Press.
Weeks, Linton. 1997. "Cosmic Congregation." *Washington Post* (September 4): D5.
Weigert, Andrew J., William V. D'Antonio, and Arthur J. Rubel. 1971. "Protestantism and Assimilation among Mexican Americans: An Exploratory Study of Ministers' Reports." *JSSR* 10: 219–32.
Welbourn, F. B. 1965. *East African Christian*. London: Oxford University Press.
———. 1968. *Atoms and Ancestors*. Bristol, United Kingdom: Arnold.
Welch, Michael R., and John Baltzell. 1984. "Geographic Mobility, Social Integration, and Church Attendance." *JSSR* 23: 75–91.
Wellman, James K., Jr. 1999. "Religion out of the Closet: Public Religion and Homosexuality." In *The Power of Religious Publics*, ed. William H. Swatos, Jr., and James K. Wellman, Jr. (pp. 131–51). Westport, Conn.: Praeger.
Wessinger, Catherine. 1999. *How the Millennium Comes Violently: From Jonestown to Heaven's Gate*. New York: Seven Bridges Press.
Whyte, William H. 1956. *The Organization Man*. New York: Simon and Schuster.

Wilde, Melissa J. 2004. "How Culture Mattered at Vatican II: Collegiality Trumps Authority in the Council's Social Movement Organizations." *ASR* 69: 567–602.

Williams, Andrea S., and James D. Davidson. 1996. "Catholic Conceptions of Faith: A Generational Analysis." *SoR* 57: 273–89.

Williams, Raymond Brady. 1996. *Christian Pluralism in the United States: The Indian Immigrant Experience*. New York: Cambridge University Press.

———. 1998. "Asian Indian and Pakistani Religions in the United States." *Annals* 558: 178–95.

Williams, Rhys H., ed. 2001. *Promise Keepers and the New Masculinity: Private Lives and Public Morality*. Lanham, Md: Lexington Books.

Williams, Rhys H., and Susan M. Alexander. 1994. "Religious Rhetoric in American Populism." *JSSR* 33: 1–15.

Wills, Garry. 1998. "The Vatican Monarchy." *New York Review of Books* 45 (February 19): 20–25.

Wilson, Bryan R. 1959. "An Analysis of Sect Development." *ASR* 24: 3–15.

———. 1966. *Religion and Secular Society*. London: Watts.

———. 1973. *Magic and the Millennium*. New York: Harper & Row.

Wilson, John. 1980. "Voluntary Associations and Civil Religion: The Case of Freemasonry." *RRR* 22: 125–36.

Wilson, John, and Darren E. Sherkat. 1994. "Returning to the Fold." *JSSR* 33: 148–61.

Wilson, John F. 1979. *Public Religion in American Culture*. Philadelphia, Penn.: Temple University Press.

Wilson, William Julius. 1996. *When Work Disappears: The World of the New Urban Poor*. New York: Knopf.

Wimberley, Ronald C. 1976. "Testing the Civil Religion Hypothesis." *SA* 37: 341–52.

———. 1979. "Continuity in the Measurement of Civil Religion." *SA* 40: 59–62.

Wimberley, Ronald C., and James A. Christenson. 1981. "Civil Religion and Other Religious Identities." *SA* 42: 91–100.

Wimberley, Ronald C., Donald A. Clelland, Thomas C. Hood, and C. M. Lipsey. 1976. "The Civil Religious Dimension: Is It There?" *SF* 54: 890–900.

Wind, James P., and James W. Lewis, eds. 1994. *American Congregations*, 2 vols. Chicago, Ill.: University of Chicago Press.

Winston, Kimberly. 1999. "The Good News on Fiction: Religious and Spiritual Themes Are Finding More Success in All Markets." *Publishers Weekly* 246 (November 8): 32–34.

———. 2000. "Religion Publishing: Sidelines Move to Center Stage. Publisher Revenues on Nonbook Items Are Now Stronger in Both Religion and General Retail Outlets." *Publishers Weekly* 247 (January 17): 28–30.

Winters, Donald E., Jr. 1985. *The Soul of the Wobblies: The I.W.W., Religion, and American Culture in the Progressive Era*. Westport, Conn.: Greenwood.

Wittberg, Patricia. 1994. *The Rise and Fall of Catholic Religious Orders*. Albany: State University of New York Press.

Woocher, Jonathan S. 1986. *Sacred Survival: The Civil Religion of American Jews*. Bloomington: Indiana University Press.

Woodberry, Robert D., and Christian S. Smith. 1998. "Fundamentalism, et al.: Conservative Protestants in America." *Annual Review of Sociology* 24: 25–56.

Wright, Chris. 1989. "Preaching to the Converted: Conversion Language and the Constitution of the TV Evangelical Community." *Sociological Review* 37: 733–60.

Wrobel, Paul. 1979. *Our Way: Family, Parish, and Neighborhood in a Polish-American Community*. Notre Dame, Ind.: University of Notre Dame Press.

Wuthnow, Robert. 1987. "The Social Significance of Religious Television." *RRR* 29: 125–34.

———. 1988. *The Restructuring of American Religion: Society and Faith Since World War II*. Princeton, N.J.: Princeton University Press.

———. 1989. *The Struggle for America's Soul: Evangelicals, Liberals and Secularism*. Grand Rapids, Mich.: Eerdmans.

———. 2005. *America and the Challenges of Religious Diversity*. Princeton, N.J.: Princeton University Press.

———. 2007. *After the Baby Boomers: How Twenty- and Thirty-Somethings Are Shaping the Future of American Religion.* Princeton, N.J.: Princeton University Press.

Wyse, Marion. 2000. "Fa Lun Gong and Religious Freedom: If 10,000 Buddhists Sat Down in Times Square without a Permit, What Would New York Do?" *Cross Currents* 50: 277–83.

Yamane, David, ed. 2007. "Symposium on the 20th Anniversary of *Habits of the Heart.*" *SoR* 68: 179–218.

Yinger, J. Milton. 1946. *Religion and the Struggle for Power.* Durham, N.C.: Duke University Press.

———. 1970. *The Scientific Study of Religion.* New York: Macmillan.

York, Michael. 1995. *The Emerging Network: A Sociology of the New Age and Neo-Pagan Movements.* Lanham, Md.: Rowman & Littlefield.

———. 2003. *Pagan Theology: Paganism as a World Religion.* New York: New York University Press.

Young, Lawrence A., ed. 1997. *Rational Choice Theory and Religion: Summary and Assessment.* New York: Routledge.

———. 1998. "Assessing and Updating the Schoenherr-Young Projections of Clergy Decline in the United States Roman Catholic Church." *SoR* 59: 7–23.

Young, Lawrence A., and Richard A. Schoenherr. 1992. "The Changing Age Distribution and Theological Attitudes of Catholic Priests Revisited." *SA* 53: 73–87.

Yuengert, Andrew. 2001. "Do Bishops Matter?: A Cross-Sectional Study of Ordinations to the U.S. Catholic Diocesan Priesthood." *RRR* 42: 294–312.

Zaleski, Peter A., and Charles E. Zech. 1992. "Determinants of Contributions to Religious Organizations: Free Riding and Other Factors." *American Journal of Economics and Sociology* 51: 459–72.

Zech, Charles E. 1994. "An Empirical Analysis of Options for Dealing with the U.S. Catholic Priest Shortage." *RRR* 35: 238–50.

———. 2000. "Generational Differences in the Determinants of Religious Giving." *RRR* 41: 545–59.

Zikmund, Barbara Brown, Adair T. Lummis, and Patricia M. Y. Chang. 1998. *Clergy Women: An Uphill Calling.* Louisville, Ky.: Westminster/John Knox.

Zimmermann, Stephanie, Joy Hart Seibert, Dwight B. Billings, and James G. Hougland, Jr. 1990. "'God's Line Is Never Busy': An Analysis of Symbolic Discourse in Two Southern Appalachian Denominations." *SA* 51: 297–306.

Zoll, Rachel. 2003. "Despite Promises, Bishops Still Fighting Lawsuits: Church Lawyers Say Institutions Are Entitled to a Vigorous Defense." *Milwaukee Journal Sentinel* (May 25): 13A.

———. 2007. "Church Payouts Now Total $2 Billion: Catholic Dioceses Surviving Despite Abuse Settlements." *South Bend (Ind.) Tribune* (July 17): A4.

Zuckerman, Phil. 1999. *Strife in the Sanctuary: Religious Schism in a Jewish Community.* Walnut Creek, Calif.: AltaMira.

Index